Evolution and the human mind

Evolution and the human mind

Modularity, language and meta-cognition

edited by

Peter Carruthers

Professor of Philosophy and Director, Hang Seng Centre for Cognitive Studies, University of Sheffield

and

Andrew Chamberlain

Senior Lecturer in Archaeology and Prehistory, University of Sheffield

Published in association with the Hang Seng Centre for Cognitive Studies, University of Sheffield

CAMBRIDGE
UNIVERSITY PRESS

PUBLISHED BY THE PRESS SYNDICATE OF THE UNIVERSITY OF CAMBRIDGE
The Pitt Building, Trumpington Street, Cambridge, United Kingdom

CAMBRIDGE UNIVERSITY PRESS
The Edinburgh Building, Cambridge CB2 2RU, UK   www.cup.cam.ac.uk
40 West 20th Street, New York, NY 10011-4211, USA   www.cup.org
10 Stamford Road, Oakleigh, Melbourne 3166, Australia
Ruiz de Alarcón 13, 28014 Madrid, Spain

First published 2000

Printed in the United Kingdom at the University Press, Cambridge

Typeface Monotype Times NR 10/12 pt   *System* QuarkXpress™   [SE]

A catalogue record for this book is available from the British Library

Library of Congress cataloguing in publication data

Evolution and the human mind: modularity, language and meta-cognition /
edited by Peter Carruthers and Andrew Chamberlain.
       p.   cm.
Includes bibliographical references and indexes.
ISBN 0 521 78331 3 (hardback) – ISBN 0 521 78908 7 (paperback)
1. Genetic psychology – Congresses.   2. Modularity (Psychology) – Congresses.
3. Metacognition – Congresses.   4. Psycholinguistics – Congresses.
I. Carruthers, Peter, 1952–   II. Chamberlain, Andrew, 1954–
BF711.E94 2000   155.7 – dc21   00-021834

ISBN 0 521 78331 3 hardback
ISBN 0 521 78908 7 paperback

for
Sir Q. W. Lee
with thanks

Contents

x   Contents

Contributors

PASCAL BOYER Dynamique du Langage, MRASH, Lyon

PETER CARRUTHERS Department of Philosophy, University of Sheffield

ANDREW CHAMBERLAIN Department of Archaeology and Prehistory, University of Sheffield

ROBIN DUNBAR School of Biological Sciences, University of Liverpool

JIM HOPKINS Department of Philosophy, King's College London

CLAIRE HUGHES MRC Child and Adolescent Psychiatry Unit, Institute of Psychiatry, London

STEVEN MITHEN Department of Archaeology, University of Reading

ADAM MORTON Department of Philosophy, University of Bristol

DOMINIC MURPHY Department of Philosophy, Caltech

GLORIA ORIGGI Dipartimento di Scienze della Comunicazione, Bologna

DAVID PAPINEAU Department of Philosophy, King's College London

ROBERT PLOMIN Social, Genetic and Developmental Psychiatry Research Centre, Institute of Psychiatry, London

RICHARD SAMUELS Department of Philosophy, University of Pennsylvania

DAN SPERBER CNRS, Paris

STEPHEN STICH Department of Philosophy, Rutgers University

THOMAS WYNN Department of Anthropology, University of Colorado

Preface

This volume is the culmination of the third project undertaken by Sheffield University's Hang Seng Centre for Cognitive Studies. (The first project resulted in *Theories of Theories of Mind*, edited by Peter Carruthers and Peter K. Smith, published by Cambridge University Press in 1996. The second project resulted in *Language and Thought: Interdisciplinary Themes*, edited by Peter Carruthers and Jill Boucher, published by Cambridge University Press in 1998.) Five interdisciplinary workshops were held over the period 1996–8, and the concluding conference was held in Stephenson Hall of Residence, University of Sheffield, in June 1998.

The intention behind the project was to bring together a select group of anthropologists, archaeologists, cognitive neuroscientists, cognitive psychologists, linguists, philosophers and primatologists to consider what light could be thrown by evolutionary considerations on the nature and origins of human cognition. Most of the participants in the project were able to meet and discuss on a regular basis over a two-year period, before a sub-set of them presented their papers at the concluding conference. By that stage the barriers between the disciplines had really begun to crumble, and almost all contributions were heavily interdisciplinary in content. Those attending judged the occasion a great success.

Good conferences do not always make good volumes, of course; and in this case the editors were presented with particular difficulties. For the total set of conference papers – excellent though most of them were – covered a range of topics far too diverse to make a coherent volume for publication. We proceeded by first narrowing down to a set of papers which we felt should certainly be published, in some venue or another, and then began to look for integrating themes. In the end, we have chosen to focus on a set of topics relating evolutionary considerations to issues connected with modularity and innateness of cognitive faculties, with the distinctively human capacity for natural language, and with the human capacity for thoughts about the mental lives of themselves and others – cognition about cognition, or 'meta-cognition'. As a result, a number of excellent papers have had to be excluded. On the other hand, we used the opportunity to commission a couple of further papers from colleagues who had attended the conference, and whose original work – closely related to the volume's topics – we had consequently come to learn of.

We would very much like to thank all those who participated in the workshop series and/or concluding conference, whose comments and contributions to discussions did much to sharpen ideas – with special thanks to all those who contributed a paper to one or another venue, but who do not have a paper in the final volume. Special thanks go to: Derek Bickerton, Michael Bishop, Paul Bloom, George Botterill, Richard Byrne, Andrew Chamberlain, Patty Cowell, Fiona Cowie, Robert Foley, Clive Gamble, Jim Hurford, Christopher Knapp, John Locke, Andrew Mayes, Bill McGrew, Colin Renfrew, Kate Robson-Brown, Jennifer Saul, Michael Siegal, Peter K. Smith and Patrice Tremoulet. Thanks also go to Ian Pitchford for help with preparing the bibliography, and to Tom Simpson for preparing the indexes. Finally, and most importantly, we should like to express our thanks to the Hang Seng Bank of Hong Kong, and especially to its Chairman (now retired) Sir Q. W. Lee, for making the whole project possible.

1 Introduction

Peter Carruthers and Andrew Chamberlain

The extension of Darwin's theory of evolution to human form, function and behaviour has always been controversial. Evolutionary explanations of the human mind, with its apparently unbounded capacities and responsiveness to environmental influences, and of human culture, with its myriad creative diversity and transcendence beyond mere functionality, have been particularly contested. As a result, evolutionary approaches in the social and cognitive sciences have gained ground slowly and haltingly. But insofar as the human body has been moulded and shaped by evolutionary pressures operating in our ancestral past, it seems likely that the biological structures and mechanisms underlying human cognition will also have been selected for; and in this sense, at least, the human mind must have an evolutionary history. What is rather more contentious is whether properties intrinsic to the mind itself were selected for in evolution. In this brief opening chapter we survey the range of stances which can be taken towards this issue, and we outline some recent developments in psychology, archaeology, anthropology, philosophy and the neurosciences which provide the background for the chapters which follow.

1 From modularity to evolutionary psychology

Ever since the cognitive revolution in psychology began, with Chomsky's devastating review (1959) of Skinner's *Verbal Behavior* (1957), the evidence has gradually been mounting in favour of the *modularity* of many mental functions and capacities – that is, in support of the view that cognition is subserved by a number of innately channelled, domain-specific systems whose operations are largely independent of, and inaccessible to, the rest of the mind. Initially the evidence only supported modularism in respect of the so-called 'input and output systems' – the information-rich sensory channels such as vision, audition, taste, touch, pain perception, and the specialised mechanism for acquiring and communicating via language. The *locus classicus* for this early form of 'peripheral systems modularism' was Fodor's *The Modularity of Mind* (1983). But evidence has since been build-

1

ing up in support of the view that many central systems too – particularly those systems charged with the generation of beliefs from perception or from other beliefs – are broadly modular in structure (Atran, 1990; Baron-Cohen, 1995; Sperber *et al.*, 1995). And while Fodor's initial characterisation of the nature of modules (as innate, fast, domain-specific, and informationally encapsulated, with proprietary inputs and shallow outputs) was highly restrictive, other theorists have since liberalised the notion (for example, dropping the requirements of shallowness and strict encapsulation) in such a way that some central conceptual systems might plausibly be thought to be modular in nature (Smith and Tsimpli, 1995; Sperber, 1996; see also Segal, 1996, for a useful review of different notions of modularity).

While modularism has generally been associated with nativism, or anti-empiricism, not every modularist has taken an evolutionary perspective. Indeed, the two most famous proponents of modularism – Chomsky and Fodor – have purposefully avoided all evolutionary theorising themselves, while often being scathing of the evolutionary explanations of others, and have been inclined to see the appearance of modules as a mere by-product of the expansion of the hominid neocortex (Chomsky, 1988; Fodor, 1998). Few would now share their position, and the contributors to this volume are united in rejecting it. For as Pinker and Bloom (1990) decisively point out, evolution by natural selection is the only form of non-cultural explanation we have of the development of organised goal-directed complexity, such as the mammalian eye manifestly has, and such as would be possessed by any of the postulated cognitive modules (see also Pinker, 1994).

It has been objected that evolutionary explanations of already-known structures come cheap, amounting to little more than just-so stories. This may well be so, if those explanations are constructed a priori, without regard to other relevant evidence. But in fact a good explanation needs to be constrained by what is known, or can reasonably be inferred, about the environments in which the structures first appeared, and the selective pressures operating within them. Here the would-be evolutionary explainer needs to look to the evidence provided by archaeology, palaeontology and comparative biology. The task of providing evolutionary explanations of cognitive structures, in particular, is inherently interdisciplinary, requiring input from each of these disciplines, as well as from cognitive psychology and neuroscience.

Not only are evolutionary explanations of cognitive structures quite legitimate (and the good ones not especially cheap), but also in our view evolutionary thinking can also prove fruitful for psychology itself. For by thinking hard about the adaptive problems which our ancestors probably faced, we can generate novel, testable hypotheses concerning the cognitive adaptations which we may possess. Thus Cosmides and Tooby (1992) argue, for example, that since our hominid ancestors very probably engaged in reciprocal social exchanges of various sorts, which would have been crucial both for reproduction and for survival, they are likely therefore to have possessed an evolved adaptive mechanism for rationally negotiating such exchanges – for calculating the cost-benefit structure of an exchange, for keeping track of who owes what to whom, and for detecting cheaters and free-riders. Cosmides and Tooby then set out to test this hypothesis by seeing whether people reason better in tasks which have a cost-benefit structure than they do in structurally identical tasks which lack such a structure – with dramatically confirmed results.

The intellectual movement now known as 'evolutionary psychology' goes even further than this again, in postulating that the mind contains a whole suite of modular adaptations (Barkow *et al.*, 1992; Pinker, 1997b). This is the *Swiss-army knife model* of cognition (to be contrasted with the empiricist model of the mind as a large general-purpose computer). According to this model, the mind consists (more or less exclusively) of a whole host of modular adaptations, selected for at different points in our evolutionary ancestry, but maintained to the present day either through inertia or through continued stabilising selection. This view is said to have biological plausibility on its side, since in general natural selection is claimed to operate by bolting-on specialist adaptations to existing structures in response to specific adaptive pressures (Cosmides and Tooby, 1987). Not all the contributors to the present volume endorse this model, by any means. But it undoubtedly provides a useful foil to both empiricism (or the big general-purpose computer model), on the one hand, and to the anti-evolutionary modularism of Fodor (1983, 1998) on the other.

An important distinction can be made between contemporary evolutionary psychology and the earlier intellectual movement known as 'socio-biology' (Alexander, 1974; Wilson, 1975, 1978). Socio-biology and its modern linear descendant, behavioural ecology, emphasise the adaptive function of behaviour, and view behavioural variability as demonstrating that organisms (as individuals or as typical members of a species) possess a flexible repertoire of optimised responses to varying environmental conditions (Irons, 1979). Evolutionary psychology, by way of contrast, eschews arguments about the functionality of behaviour *per se*, and focuses instead on cognitive *mechanisms* – specifically systems for generating beliefs and goals. What behaviours – if any – then result may be quite variable, since they will depend upon what other beliefs and desires the agents in question possess. Although it is likely that cognitive mechanisms will only have been selected for in so far as they reliably generate behaviour that influences fitness (Borgerhoff Mulder, 1991), evolutionary psychology places this

selective environment in the distant past, thus deflecting the naive accusa-
tion of 'environmental determinism' that has frequently been levelled at
socio-biology. On one way of picturing the matter, the evolved mechanisms
postulated by evolutionary psychologists generate many of our beliefs and
desires for us; what we then *do* in the light of our beliefs and desires will
depend upon the operations of our practical reason, social adeptness and
individual preferences and inclinations – and these can be as non-determin-
istic as you please.

2   Cognitive archaeology and evolutionary anthropology

Much of the research effort in evolutionary psychology has focused on features of the mind that are more or less unique to humans (e.g. language,
consciousness of self and others, aesthetic preferences and psychopathology, to name but four examples). Rudimentary precursors of these
cognitive domains and faculties exist in great apes and some other primates,
but in its salient properties the human mind is really rather different from
the minds of non-human animals. This causes some problems for an evolutionary theory of the mind: the uniqueness of the human mind implies that
the comparative method – in this case, comparing human mental faculties
with those of non-human animals – may not be a particularly fruitful
source of insight, and correspondingly a premium is placed on any evidence
which can be obtained from the palaeontological and archaeological
records that relate more directly to human evolutionary history.

If fossilised hominid brains could be found that preserved details of
neuronal structures, or if there was durable and unequivocal material evidence for hominid beliefs and intentions, then palaeoneurology and palaeolithic archaeology would be well placed to document the evolutionary
history of the mind. But unfortunately the quality of the fossil and
archaeological evidence falls well short of this ideal. From the study of
hominid cranial endocasts – replicas of brains derived from the negative
relief of the internal surface of the skull – the amount and rate of brain size
increase in human evolution can be determined (this provides, *inter alia*, the
empirical evidence for Dunbar's hypothesis of increased group size in early
Homo; Dunbar, 1993). But the evidence for changes in neural structure and
cortical organisation is much less clear, as exemplified by the debate
between Holloway (1983a) and Falk (1985, 1989) on the size of the visual
cortex in *Australopithecus*, and the uncertainty over the identification of
language centres on the endocasts of early *Homo* (Holloway, 1983b;
Tobias, 1987). Given that important domains such as consciousness are
now thought to involve a widely distributed neural substrate (Tononi and
Edelman, 1998), there is likely to be little prospect of inferring the details of

hominid cognition from the shapes of the bulges and indentations observable on hominid brain endocasts.

Archaeology's intellectual roots are very firmly anchored in the social sciences, and despite well-publicised appeals for the establishment of a research programme in cognitive archaeology (e.g. Renfrew, 1982) many archaeologists remain unwilling to relinquish the primacy of social factors in their explanations of past material culture and human subsistence behaviour. Social archaeologists (such as Hodder) see individual decision making and agency as inextricably enmeshed in social structures and sociocultural relations that are historically contingent and culturally specific:

There are few if any aspects of cognition which do not partly depend on social rules and goals – on the social context. Thus an adequate approach to cognition must also consider social meanings, social structures, relations of power and domination. (Hodder, 1993, 256)

Others (such as Clark) have criticised the aims of cognitive archaeology on the operational grounds that individuals and their actions are not traceable in the archaeological record:

I submit that, since the actions of individuals are forever likely to be beyond the resolution of the Palaeolithic archaeological record, we are compelled to adopt the group as the analytical unit if we ever hope to submit our ideas about the human past to any kind of an empirical test. (Clark, 1992, 107)

This reluctance to concede that individuals can be extracted from their social context, together with a continuing uncritical reliance on group selection as a mechanism for explaining past cultural change (cf. Mithen, 1993), has contributed to the tardy and equivocal reception of cognitive approaches in archaeology, and it is only in the last decade that serious and sustained attempts have been made to integrate archaeological theory and data into accounts of human cognitive evolution (Donald, 1991; Renfrew and Zubrow, 1994; Mithen, 1996b).

While it is undeniable that palaeopsychology will continue to be a difficult and challenging field of study, particular categories of archaeological evidence have the potential to illuminate aspects of human cognitive evolution. Wynn (this volume, chapter 6) points out that a more or less continuous sequence of evolutionary development in geometric and technological competence can be reconstructed from the archaeological record of stone tool manufacture. Decisions that were executed in the procurement of raw materials and in the *chaîne opératoire* – or sequence of flake removals whereby an unmodified core is converted into a finished artefact – can also reveal the extent to which the behaviour involved in stone tool manufacture was opportunistic or purposive (Mithen, this volume, chapter 9). The caveats, of course, are numerous: only a minimum level of competence may be revealed in stone artefacts, and archaeologists are aware that there is no correlation between technological sophistication and cognitive ability among the great diversity of ethnographically documented modern human cultures.

Symbols are central to human thought and language, and the emergence of material evidence for symbolic behaviour at the beginning of the Upper Palaeolithic, some 35,000 years ago, has been linked to the evolution of a fully modern cognitive capacity (Lindly and Clark, 1990). Together with the appearance of representational and decorative art, the introduction of burial rituals and the accelerated diversification of technology, this complex of innovations constitutes the 'cultural explosion' at the Middle–Upper Palaeolithic transition. Many archaeologists believe that the emergence of fully-modern language correlates with the Upper Palaeolithic cultural revolution, but this proposal is contradicted by palaeontological arguments which place the origins of language considerably earlier in human evolution.

The concept of an Upper Palaeolithic 'cultural explosion' has itself been challenged on the grounds that it is only in western Europe that a clear-cut contrast is apparent between the behaviour of archaic Neanderthals and modern Cro-Magnon humans, and even in Europe some of the late Neanderthals are associated with an Upper Palaeolithic style of technology (Hublin *et al.*, 1996). Elsewhere in the world patterns of modern human behaviour seem to emerge either contemporaneously or earlier than in Europe (Bahn, 1991), and in a more gradual fashion (Harrold, 1992), indicating that the abrupt behavioural transition in Europe at the beginning of the Upper Palaeolithic may have been atypical and may not necessarily have coincided with a sudden advance in cognitive capacity.

Anthropology, too, is rooted in the social sciences, and shares the same background conception of the mind as socially and linguistically determined. Indeed, anthropologists have traditionally delighted in attesting to the almost-infinite diversity of human belief-systems, social practices and behaviours, which seemed to reinforce their picture of the mind as a social–linguistic construct. But in recent decades a number of anthropologists have advocated Darwinian explanations of human culture and thought, with their approaches falling broadly into two movements. The first, which has been advanced under the banner of evolutionary culture theory (Boyd and Richerson, 1985; Durham, 1991, 1992; see O'Brien, 1996, for applications to archaeology) seeks to explain the observed variation in human cultural systems through an explicit model of transmission with selective retention, in a direct analogy with the role of natural selection in biological evolution. Although the approach is clearly distinguished from socio-biology in not explicitly and directly linking human behaviour to *genetic* fitness, evolutionary culture theory remains problematic on several counts, including disagreements about the nature of the cultural elements transmitted, and uncertainties over the roles of purposeful versus random selection and the relative contributions of selection acting on groups versus the effects of selective pressures on individuals.

The second – and in our view more successful – approach abandons direct evolutionary explanations of specific cultural repertoires and behaviours, and seeks instead to discover the cognitive universals which underpin the diversity of human thought and action (e.g. Atran, 1990, 1998; Brown, 1991; Boyer, 1994b; Sperber, 1996). By combining psychological and anthropological data, and through broad cross-cultural comparisons incorporating studies of both modern and traditional cultures, the structural elements of a range of different domains of naive- or folk-knowledge have been elucidated. Insofar as these cognitive universals must have been inherited from our species' common ancestor, they are likely to have evolved through natural (as opposed to cultural) selection and are presumably components of an adaptive cognitive response to features of Pleistocene environments and Palaeolithic social organisation.

3   Developments in philosophy

The recent developments in philosophy which are most relevant to the current project are of a rather different sort from those in psychology, archaeology and anthropology – *domain-general* as opposed to *domain-specific*, as you might say. It is true that the thought of some philosophers has taken a directly evolutionary turn, specifically as regards the proper explication of intentional content or meaning, where there is now a flourishing tradition of *teleosemantics* (Millikan, 1984, 1989; Papineau, 1987, 1993). But of more relevance to the topics discussed in the current volume is an increasing willingness on the part of some philosophers to engage directly in interdisciplinary work, across a variety of fields. While some philosophers continue to guard jealously what they consider to be the proprietary domain of philosophy – namely conceptual analysis and a priori argument – many others have thought that philosophers can also address substantive questions, in science and elsewhere. In part this trend may be influenced by Quine (1951), who denies that there is any sharp distinction between philosophy and science – rather, there is simply the web of our beliefs, within which certain assumptions may be more or less deeply embedded. But more importantly, it may stem from a realisation that there is nothing to *prevent* philosophers from engaging in substantive enquiries, and that in some respects they are especially well placed to contribute to debates of an interdisciplinary sort.

Philosophers have traditionally concerned themselves with the *big* questions, or with the questions of utmost generality – for example, 'Must every event have a cause?', 'Must the world have a beginning?', 'What distinguishes mind from matter?', 'What is life?', and so on. (Indeed, when seen from a historical perspective, the twentieth-century concentration on questions of a priori conceptual analysis seems like a statistical blip.) Many of these questions now properly fall within the domain of some science or other, of course – thus the question, 'What is life?' is now asked (and answered successfully) within scientific biology. But there remains plenty of scope for philosophers to concern themselves with questions of the same highly general sort, especially ones which cross the boundaries of scientific investigation. Moreover, the traditional philosophical skills of distinguishing carefully between different questions, or different variants of a theory, and of teasing out the implications of theories proposed in a given area, or uncovering the implicit assumptions of the theory proposers, are just what interdisciplinary investigation requires. (We do not claim that philosophy is *uniquely* well placed to contribute to interdisciplinary debates, of course, only that it is no accident that contributions made by philosophers can often prove fruitful.)

4 A guide through the volume

All of these developments – the build-up of evidence for modularity in psychology and neuroscience; an increasing willingness to seek evolutionary explanations of cognitive abilities; the advent of evolutionary psychology as an intellectual movement; an increasing willingness amongst archaeologists to draw inferences about hominid cognition from their data; the beginning of a search for cognitive universals by anthropologists; and a willingness amongst philosophers to engage in interdisciplinary investigation of a substantive sort – serve to set the background for the project of this book. In this section we shall briskly guide the reader through the chapters which follow, drawing attention to a variety of recurring themes and cross-connections.

The first five substantive chapters of the book (2 to 6) focus in different ways on the thesis of mental modularity and its applications. Samuels (chapter 2) is concerned to distinguish two different versions of modularity thesis, and to defend both against anti-nativist attacks. He distinguishes *computational* from *intentional* modularity. According to the first, the mind contains many innately-channelled discrete domain-specific computational mechanisms (this is the 'Swiss-army knife model'); according to the second (which Samuels calls the 'Chomskian model' of cognition) the mind contains innate domain-specific bodies of specialised knowledge which are accessed and processed centrally by general-purpose, non-modular, cognitive mechanisms. Although almost all evolutionary psychologists commit themselves to the computational variety, Samuels argues that the evidence does not currently favour it over the Chomskian model. He then takes up the challenge to the nativistic element in either form of modularity mounted by Elman *et al.* (1996), showing that their main arguments make unwarranted assumptions.

One major tenet of evolutionary psychology is that mental modules are adaptations, each of which evolved in response to a particular problem posed by the environment of evolutionary adaptation. In contrast to domain-general accounts of cognitive ability, the modular model does not posit a common underlying genetic basis to abilities in different domains. Hughes and Plomin (chapter 3) present dramatic results from a study of theory of mind and verbal ability in pairs of normal three-year-old twins. Their data show, *inter alia*, that most of the variance in theory-of-mind abilities at age three is genetic, and that most of the genes in question are independent of genetic variance in verbal IQ, supporting the case for an independent origin for these two modules.

The next two chapters (4 and 5) explore the implications of evolutionary psychology and mental modularity for other disciplines, hence providing a sort of back-handed defence by demonstrating the *fruitfulness* of the approach. While much of the support for the modularity of mind stems from studies of cognitive dysfunction in individuals who have been diagnosed as suffering from mental disorders, the current standard for the diagnostic classification of mental disorders is structured on pre-evolutionary principles, as Murphy and Stich point out (chapter 4). Murphy and Stich show how a computational systems approach to modular structure permits mental disorders to be divided into distinct categories, according to whether the deficits are module-internal, or affecting input to other normally-functioning modules, or indeed whether a module is functioning correctly but the current environment has changed from the ancestral one in which the module's function was optimised.

Boyer (chapter 5) tackles the thorny issue of the appearance and dissemination of religious concepts. Although there are plenty of adaptive explanations for the existence of religious ideologies in general, the structure and content of religious beliefs are traditionally regarded as being unbounded and idiosyncratic. Boyer demonstrates that religious concepts are strongly constrained by the structure and logic of intuitive ontology, where this ontology is delivered by innately-channelled modular systems for folk-psychology, folk-physics, naive-biology and the domain of artefacts. He shows how ideas which violate the principles of some of these intuitive domains (such as an artefact which listens to prayers) but which nevertheless allow us to access the rich inferential principles of the under-lying knowledge base, are much more readily remembered. It is then easy to see that this would give rise to cross-cultural regularities in the kinds of concepts which are culturally stable and easily propagated, of just the sort that anthropologists observe.

Wynn (chapter 6) – like Papineau (chapter 8) – is concerned to defend a form of non-domain-specific, or general-process, cognition in face of a threatened hegemony of domain-specific modules (the 'Swiss-army knife model' taken to extremes). He uses the property of symmetry in stone tool artefacts as an index of the evolving perceptual and cognitive abilities of pre-modern species of hominid. The symmetry manifest in the artefacts increases in regularity and complexity over time, with essentially modern spatial abilities appearing by 300,000 years ago. Wynn argues that the sophisticated symmetries of these stone tool artefacts demonstrate the presence in these hominids of a central system – or some sort of general processor – which deploys and wields a modular visuo-spatial capacity, rather than a visuo-spatial system which is wholly domain specific.

The remaining essays in the book are all concerned, in one way or another and to varying degrees, with the questions of the evolution of language and of 'theory of mind' (or meta-cognition); and with the questions of the contributions made by these presumably modular faculties to the evolution of other cognitive capacities, and of their involvement in them. Origgi and Sperber (chapter 7) address head-on the question of the evolutionary origins of language. They use some of the conceptual framework provided by Millikan (1984) – in particular her distinction between *direct* and *derived* proper functions – to articulate a certain view of the relations between biological and cultural evolution of language. But they are at pains to dissociate themselves from her 'code conception' of language meaning. In the sort of post-Gricean, relevance-theoretic approach which Origgi and Sperber defend, the question of the evolution of language becomes intimately connected with the evolution of capacities for higher-order thought.

The next three chapters (8 to 10) address the evolution of the human capacity for rational and/or imaginative thought. Papineau (chapter 8) is concerned to explain the evolution of epistemic rationality. He aims to show how knowledge and the systematic pursuit of knowledge (of the sort undertaken by science) are possible, in light of the psychological evidence of widespread epistemic irrationality. There are two main elements in his account: the taking of *truth* as a goal (with reliable belief-formation as the means), and the use of means-ends reasoning in pursuit of that goal. The first is made possible by hominid theory-of-mind capacities, which provide us with concepts of truth and falsehood (perhaps supplemented by an innate desire for knowledge). The second is said to originate (perhaps) from an evolved, non-modular, capacity for forward planning.

Mithen (chapter 9) discusses the puzzle of the 'cultural explosion' which took place more or less simultaneously amongst humans dispersed around the globe between 60,000 and 30,000 years ago. The puzzle arises because it is now believed that fully modern humans, with a capacity for language, had existed from much earlier – probably from 120,000 years ago, and at least from 100,000 years ago; and that humans then immediately began to disperse and colonise different global regions. Mithen argues that what might have played the main role in the later explosion of creativity and cultural innovation were accretions of material culture, which could serve to externalise certain mental operations and mental powers, somewhat as we use pencil-and-paper calculations and written records today.

Morton (chapter 10) explores how strategic thinking can emerge from competitive and/or co-operative interactions between intelligent interactors. He uses a variety of game-theoretic models and arguments to examine the conditions under which strategic thinking would emerge in evolution, and – like Dunbar (chapter 11) – he draws implications concerning expected group size amongst apes and hominids. Morton argues that different modal sizes of human groups are adaptive for solving different kinds of strategic problem.

Dunbar (chapter 11) examines the anthropological evidence bearing on the origins and adaptive purpose of human theory of mind. In previous work he has established a correlation between brain size and normal group size in monkeys and apes (including human beings), arguing that larger group sizes need to be supported by increasingly sophisticated theory-of-mind abilities (e.g. Dunbar, 1993). In the present chapter he takes up the question of *direction of causality* – did theory of mind develop because of evolutionary pressure towards larger group sizes? Or was there some adaptive pressure for increased theory-of-mind abilities which facilitated larger group sizes as a by-product? He defends the former alternative, and tentatively puts forward the hypothesis that the pressure towards increased group size in hominids was the need to defend crucial resources such as water holes.

In the final two chapters (12 and 13) Carruthers and Hopkins take an evolutionary perspective on the nature of human consciousness. Carruthers (chapter 12) reviews alternative explanations of subjective – or 'phenomenal' – consciousness, and presents the case for this emerging as a by-product of the emergence of the theory-of-mind module. More specifically, he uses evolutionary considerations to adjudicate between four different forms of 'higher-order' theory of phenomenal-consciousness, according to all of which it is the mind's capacity to represent its own states and operations which gives rise to phenomenally conscious states. The theories in question are: higher-order experience, or 'inner sense' models; actualist higher-order thought theory; dispositionalist higher-order thought theory; and higher-order linguistic description theory. The third of these is argued to be significantly superior to any of the others.

Hopkins (chapter 13) pursues a similar line of argument in showing that introspection does not provide direct (i.e. non-representational) perceptual access to states and processes of the mind. Rather, evolution has led to the internal states of the mind being represented metaphorically, using analogous reasoning based on mechanisms used to attribute internal causes when making sense of events in the physical world. Hopkins shows how the metaphor of the mind as 'internal' gives rise to much that we find most paradoxical about the relations between mind and body.

Conclusion

These are heady times for the understanding of the human mind. Much excellent and innovative work is being done within the particular disciplines of anthropology, archaeology, cognitive neuroscience, cognitive psychology, evolutionary psychology, linguistics, philosophy and primatology. But we believe that it is important, now, that there should be an increased degree of cross-talk between them, of the sort partially represented in this volume. And one crucial peg on which such talk needs to be hung is the evolution of human cognitive mechanisms and faculties. The essays in this book contribute to and advance many specific debates. But the main message is implicit (hereby made explicit): it is that the understanding of the human mind increasingly needs interdisciplinary awareness and collaboration.

The authors would like to thank all those who participated in the 'Evolution and the human mind' Hang Seng Centre workshops and conference, for increasing our understanding of these issues, and also Robin Dunbar for his comments on an earlier draft.

2   Massively modular minds: evolutionary psychology and cognitive architecture

Richard Samuels

In recent years evolutionary psychologists have defended a massively modular conception of cognitive architecture which views the mind as composed largely (or perhaps even entirely) of innate, special-purpose computational mechanisms or 'modules'. This chapter has a pair of aims. First, I aim to dispel much of the confusion that surrounds discussions of evolutionary psychology by clarifying the massive modularity hypothesis (MMH) and contrasting it with other accounts of our cognitive architecture. Second, I aim to evaluate the plausibility of the MMH in light of the currently available arguments and evidence. Though the case in support of massive modularity fails to discriminate between MMH and other related accounts of cognition, I argue that it constitutes a plausible hypothesis that deserves to be taken very seriously. Moreover, I argue that the case *against* massive modularity is weak.

1   Introduction

What are the elements from which the human mind is composed? What structures make up our *cognitive architecture*? One of the most recent and intriguing answers to these questions comes from the newly emerging inter-disciplinary field of evolutionary psychology. Evolutionary psychologists defend a *massively modular* conception of mental architecture which views the mind – including those parts responsible for such 'central processes' as belief revision and reasoning – as composed largely or perhaps even entirely of innate, special-purpose computational mechanisms or 'modules' that have been shaped by natural selection to handle the sorts of recurrent information-processing problems that confronted our hunter-gatherer forebears (Cosmides and Tooby, 1992; Sperber, 1994a; Samuels, 1998a).

Over the past few years, evolutionary psychology and the massively modular conception of cognition that it defends has been the focus of heated debate in cognitive science and has inspired the production of numerous books, articles and edited volumes. Indeed, the dispute has even spilled onto the pages of the non-specialist press, where such prominent intellectual figures as Stephen Jay Gould, Stephen Pinker, Daniel Dennett and Jerry Fodor have vigorously debated the merits of evolutionary psychological accounts of cognition (Dennett, 1997; Gould, 1997; Pinker, 1997a; Fodor, 1998). Nevertheless, it remains unclear what exactly the evolutionary psychologist's *massive modularity hypothesis* (MMH) amounts to, and whether or not it ought to be taken seriously as an account of our cognitive architecture.

This chapter has two aims. First, I aim to dispel much of the confusion that surrounds discussions of evolutionary psychology by clarifying the massively modular account of cognition that it defends. Towards this end, in section 2 I provide a brief overview of the central commitments of evolutionary psychology and distinguish between two importantly different notions of a module: *computational modules*, which are a species of *computational mechanism*; and what I call *Chomskian modules*, which are domain-specific bodies of *mental representations*. Further, I develop a characterisation of the version of MMH endorsed by evolutionary psychologists which maintains that the human mind is largely or perhaps even entirely composed of a species of computational module, which I call *Darwinian modules*. Of course, merely outlining these general evolutionary-psychological commitments ignores a range of important issues about how one can and should develop the massively modular conception of cognition. Consequently, in section 3 I explore some of the more important issues that arise when one attempts to provide a detailed articulation of massive modularity.

The second central aim of this chapter is to evaluate the plausibility of the evolutionary psychologists' version of MMH in light of the currently available arguments and evidence. In section 4, I focus on what I take to be the main general arguments *for* massive modularity – two highly influential arguments from the work of Cosmides and Tooby. I show that while these arguments may provide support for *some* form of modularity – views that posit *either* computational (Darwinian) modules *or* Chomskian modules – they do not provide us with reason to adopt the evolutionary psychologists' MMH with its commitment to the existence of *Darwinian* modules. In section 5, I then consider some of the experimental evidence for 'central systems' that are Darwinian modules and highlight the problems we confront in trying to provide empirical support for the existence of such entities. I argue that while the empirical evidence for Darwinian modular central systems is hardly overwhelming, it does provide us with a prima-facie warrant for taking the claim that there are modular central systems – whether Darwinian or Chomskian modules – very seriously indeed as a candidate hypothesis about our cognitive architecture.

Finally, in section 6 I discuss the case against massive modularity. I start by showing that most of the arguments levelled against massive modularity fail to even address – let alone undermine – the view endorsed by evolutionary psychologists. Second, I consider a recent and highly influential argument from experimental neuroscience which purports to show that the human mind contains little, if any, innate domain-specific structure (Quartz and Sejnowski, 1994; Elman *et al.*, 1996). If sound, this *neurobiological argument* would constitute a serious objection to the evolutionary psychologists' MMH, since evolutionary psychologists think of Darwinian modules as innate, domain-specific structures. Moreover, it would also undermine views that are committed to the existence of Chomskian modules – bodies of innate, domain-specific representations. I argue, however, that this neurobiological argument is deeply unsatisfactory and, hence, need not be of concern to advocates of innate, domain-specific cognitive structure. My conclusion is, therefore, that although the case in support of massive modularity does not discriminate between computational (or Darwinian) and Chomskian forms of modularity, the case against modularity doesn't work for either form.

2   The central tenets of evolutionary psychology

2.1   Four central tenets

Though the interdisciplinary field of evolutionary psychology is too new to have developed any precise and widely agreed upon body of doctrine, there are four basic theses that are clearly central (Samuels, 1998a). The first is that the human mind is an information processing device that can be described in computational terms as 'a computer made out of organic compounds rather than silicon chips' (Barkow *et al.*, 1992, p. 7). In expressing this view, evolutionary psychologists clearly see themselves as adopting the *computationalism* that is prevalent in much of cognitive science (*ibid.*).

The second central claim of evolutionary psychology is that, contrary to what has been the dominant view in psychology for most of the twentieth century, much of the structure of the human mind is innate. Evolutionary psychologists thus reject the familiar empiricist proposal that the innate structure of the human mind consists of little more than a general-purpose learning mechanism in favour of the *nativism* associated with Chomsky and his followers (Pinker, 1997b).

The third fundamental thesis which evolutionary psychologists endorse is the *adaptationist* claim that our cognitive architecture is largely the product of natural selection. On this view, our minds are composed of *adaptations* that were 'invented by natural selection during the species' evolutionary history to produce adaptive ends in the species' natural environment' (Tooby and Cosmides, 1995, p. xiii). Evolutionary psychologists thus maintain that our minds were designed by natural selection in order to solve *adaptive problems*: 'evolutionary recurrent problem[s] whose solution promoted reproduction, however long or indirect the chain by which it did so' (Cosmides and Tooby, 1994, p. 87). Thus not only do evolutionary psychologists commit themselves to the claim that much of our cognitive architecture is innately specified, they also commit themselves to a theory about how it came to be innate – namely via natural selection.

The final central tenet of evolutionary psychology is the *massive modularity hypothesis* (Sperber, 1994a; Samuels, 1998a). Very roughly, this is the thesis that the human mind is largely, or perhaps even entirely, composed of highly specialised cognitive systems or *modules*. As stated, however, this claim is exceedingly vague and clearly more needs to be said in order to appreciate precisely how evolutionary psychologists construe the proposal. Towards this end, in 2.2 I discuss some of the ways in which the term 'module' is deployed in cognitive science and explain how evolutionary psychologists tend to understand this notion. In 2.3 I elaborate on the MMH endorsed by evolutionary psychologists and highlight the way in which it differs from other familiar modular accounts of cognition.

2.2   What is a cognitive module?

The term 'module' has gained considerable currency in contemporary cognitive science. When using this term, cognitive scientists are almost invariably referring to mental structures that can be invoked in order to explain various cognitive capacities. Moreover, it is ordinarily assumed that modules are *domain specific* (or functionally specific) as opposed to domain general.[1] But there are also important differences in the ways in which different theorists use the term.[2] And one of the most significant of these differences concerns the fact that it tends to be used to refer to two fundamentally different sorts of mental structure. Sometimes 'module' is used to refer to systems of *mental representations*. On other occasions, however, it is used to talk about *computational mechanisms*. I call modules of the first

---

[1] To say that a cognitive structure is domain-specific means (roughly) that it is dedicated to solving a restricted class of problems in a restricted domain. For instance, the claim that there is a domain-specific cognitive structure for vision implies that there are mental structures which are brought into play in the domain of visual processing and are not recruited in dealing with other cognitive tasks. By contrast, a cognitive structure that is *domain-general* is one that can be brought into play in a wide range of different domains.

[2] The notions of modularity discussed in this section by no means exhaust the ways in which the term 'module' is used in contemporary cognitive science. For a more comprehensive review see Segal (1996).

sort *Chomskian modules* and modules of the second sort *computational modules*.

2.2.1   *Chomskian modules* A Chomskian module, to a first approximation, is a domain-specific body of mentally represented knowledge or information that accounts for a cognitive capacity. As the name suggests, the notion of a Chomskian module can be traced to Chomsky's work in linguistics – in particular, to the claim that our linguistic competence consists in the possession of an internally represented grammar of our natural language (Chomsky, 1988). This grammar is a paradigm example of what I mean when speaking of Chomskian modules. But, of course, Chomsky is not the only theorist who posits the existence of what I'm calling Chomskian modules. Many developmental psychologists, for example, have argued that young children have domain-specific *theories* – systems of mentally represented principles – for such domains as physics, biology and mathematics (Carey and Spelke, 1994; Gopnik and Meltzoff, 1997).[3] As I use the term, these structures are also Chomskian modules.

There are many problems with trying to characterise the notion of a Chomskian module in more precise terms. One issue – though perhaps largely terminological in character – concerns whether or not we should use the term 'Chomskian module' to refer only to *truth-evaluable* systems of mental representations – i.e. systems for which it makes sense to ask of the representations whether they are true or false (Stich and Ravenscroft, 1996). Systems of representations need not be, of course, truth evaluable. Consider, for example, the set of rules contained in a recipe for baking a cake. Moreover, it may well be the case that human beings possess non-truth-evaluable, *mental* representations – e.g. for how to play chess, how to do deductive reasoning, or how to detect cheaters in social exchange settings. Nevertheless, the central examples of the representational structures which I want to call Chomskian modules do appear to be truth-evaluable. Thus, for example, as Fodor (1983) observes, 'when Chomsky says that there is an innately specified "language organ" what he means is primarily that there are truths (about the structure of possible first languages) that humans innately grasp' (Fodor, 1983, p. 7). Similarly, the theories posited by developmental psychologists, such as Carey and Spelke, appear to be truth-evaluable representational structures – bodies of truth-evaluable claims about, for example, physical, biological and mathematical entities

---

[3] It is worth noting, however, that in developmental psychology domain-specific theories are almost invariably contrasted with modules rather than viewed as a kind of module (see, for example, Gopnik and Meltzoff, 1997, chapter 1). This is because developmentalists tend to use the term 'module' in order to refer to computational mechanisms – i.e. computational modules.

(Carey and Spelke, 1994). Consequently, for present purposes, I assume that Chomskian modules are systems of truth-evaluable representations.

A second problem with characterising the notion of a Chomskian module is that, clearly, we do not want to treat just any domain-specific collection of (truth-evaluable) mental representations as a Chomskian module, since this would render the notion theoretically uninteresting. We do not want, for example, to treat a child's beliefs about toy dinosaurs as a module. Consequently, it is necessary to impose additional constraints in order to develop a useful notion of a Chomskian module. Two commonly invoked constraints are (i) innateness and (ii) restrictions on information flow. So, for example, according to Chomsky, Universal Grammar is an innate system of mental representations, and most of the information that is contained in the Universal Grammar is not accessible to consciousness. Similar constraints are imposed by Carey, Spelke and other developmental psychologists when speaking of innate theories for such domains as physics and biology. (See Segal, 1996, for an elaboration of these points.) I don't propose to pursue the issue of constraints any further, however, since as will soon become clear, when evolutionary psychologists speak of modules, they are usually concerned with a rather different cognitive structure – a *computational* module. For present purposes, then, I adopt a rough characterisation of Chomskian modules as domain-specific systems of truth-evaluable mental representations that are innate and/or subject to informational restrictions.

2.2.2   *Computational modules* Computational modules are a species of computational device. As a first pass, we can characterise them as domain-specific computational devices. A number of points of elaboration and clarification are in order, however. First, computational modules are ordinarily assumed to be *classical* computers – symbol (or representation) manipulating devices which receive representations as inputs and manipulate them according to formally specifiable rules in order to generate representations (or actions) as outputs (Pylyshyn, 1984; Segal, 1996). Classical computers of this sort contrast sharply with certain sorts of connectionist computational systems which cannot plausibly be viewed as symbol manipulating devices.

Second, it is ordinarily assumed that computational modules are dedicated to solving problems in a specific domain because they are only capable of carrying out computations on a restricted range of inputs, namely representations of the properties and objects found in a particular domain (Fodor, 1983, p. 103). So, for instance, if phonology constitutes a domain, then a phonology computational module will only provide analyses of inputs which are about phonological objects and properties.

Similarly, if arithmetic is a domain, then an arithmetic computational module will only provide solutions to arithmetical problems.

Third, computational modules are usually assumed to be relatively autonomous components of the mind. Though they receive input from, and send output to, other cognitive processes or structures, they perform their own internal information processing unperturbed by external systems. For example, David Marr claims that the various computational modules on which parts of the visual process are implemented 'are as nearly independent of each other as the overall task allows' (Marr, 1982b, p. 102).

Fourth, I want to emphasise the fact that computational modules are a very different kind of mental structure from Chomskian modules. Chomskian modules are *systems of representations*. In a sense, they are 'inert'. They only eventuate in behaviour when manipulated by various cognitive mechanisms. By contrast, computational modules are processing devices – mechanisms that *manipulate* representations. Computational modules and Chomskian modules are thus importantly different with respect to the functional roles that they play in our cognitive economy.[4] However, computational modules can co-exist with Chomskian modules. Indeed, it may be that Chomskian modules, being bodies of information, are often manipulated by computational modules. Thus, for instance, a parser might be conceived of as a computational module that deploys the contents of a Chomskian module devoted to linguistic information in order to generate syntactic and semantic representations of physical sentence-forms (Segal, 1996, p. 144).

But it is also important to note that the existence of Chomskian modules does *not* entail the existence of computational modules. This is because it is entirely possible for a mind to contain Chomskian modules while not containing any computational modules. For example, while humans may possess domain-specific systems of knowledge for physics or geometry, it does not follow that we possess domain-specific computational mechanisms for processing information about physical objects or geometrical properties. Rather it may be that such domain-specific knowledge is only utilised by *domain-general,* and hence non-modular, computational mechanisms. Indeed, such a view is suggested by the work of a number of prominent cognitive scientists, including Gopnik and Meltzoff (1997) and Fodor (1983). In section 3, we'll consider this possibility in more detail.

A final point worth making is that the notion of a computational module has been elaborated in a variety of different ways in the cognitive science literature. Most notably, Fodor (1983) developed a conception of modules as

---

[4] Another important difference between Chomskian and computational modules, as I am using these terms, is that the former are truth evaluable while the latter, *qua* mechanisms, are not.

domain-specific, computational mechanisms that are also (1) information-ally encapsulated, (2) mandatory, (3) fast, (4) shallow, (5) neurally localised, (6) susceptible to characteristic breakdown, and (7) largely inaccessible to other processes. Although the full-fledged Fodorian notion of a module has been highly influential in cognitive science (Garfield, 1987), evolution-ary psychologists have not typically adopted it. For example, in his recent book *Mindblindness*, Simon Baron-Cohen explicitly denies that the modules involved in his theory of 'mind-reading' need to be information-ally encapsulated or have shallow outputs (Baron-Cohen, 1994, p. 515).

2.2.3   *Darwinian modules* What, then, do evolutionary psychologists typically mean by the term 'module'? The answer, unfortunately, is far from clear, since evolutionary psychologists don't attempt to provide any precise characterisation of modularity and rarely bother to distinguish between the various notions that we have set out in this section. Nevertheless, from what they do say, I think it is possible to piece together an account of what I propose to call a *Darwinian module*. The resulting notion of 'module' is heavily informed by the core evolutionary-psychological commitments out-lined in section 2.1 and can be viewed as a sort of prototype of the evolu-tionary psychologists' notion of modularity. Darwinian modules have a cluster of features, and when evolutionary psychologists talk about modules, they generally have in mind something that has most or all of the following three features.

First, in accordance with their computationalism, evolutionary psycholo-gists characterise modules as domain-specific computational mechanisms – 'functionally dedicated computers (often called modules)' (Tooby and Cosmides, 1995, p. xiii). Thus, Darwinian modules are not Chomskian modules but rather a species of *computational* module. However, evolution-ary psychologists also assume that many Darwinian modules utilise domain-specific systems of knowledge (i.e. Chomskian modules) when doing computations or solving problems, and that in some cases this domain-specific knowledge is accessible only to a single Darwinian module. The 'theory-of-mind' module posited by a number of recent theorists may provide an example (Leslie, 1994; Baron-Cohen, 1995). This module is typ-ically assumed to employ innate, domain-specific knowledge about psycho-logical states when predicting the behaviour of agents, and much of that information may not be available to other systems in the mind. Second, in keeping with their nativism, evolutionary psychologists tend to think of Darwinian modules as *innate* cognitive structures whose characteristic properties are largely determined by genetic factors. Finally, in accord with their adaptationism, they maintain that many or perhaps even all Darwinian modules are the products of natural selection. They are, according to Tooby and Cosmides, 'kinds invented by natural selection during the species' evolutionary history to produce adaptive ends in the species' natural environment' (Tooby and Cosmides, 1995, p. xiii; see also Cosmides and Tooby, 1992).

2.3   The Massive Modularity Hypothesis

As I mentioned in section 2.1, the MMH is roughly the claim that the human mind is largely or perhaps even entirely composed of modules. Given our discussion in section 2.2, however, we are now in a position to see that there are a number of different versions of the MMH which vary with respect to *what kinds* of modules they posit. So, for example, one version of the MMH (which we'll return to in section 3), maintains that the human mind is largely or perhaps even entirely composed of *Chomskian modules* but few, if any, computational modules. We might call this the *Chomskian MMH*. But this, of course, is not the version of MMH which evolutionary psychologists endorse. Rather they maintain that the human mind is largely or entirely composed of *Darwinian* modules – computational mechanisms which satisfy the conditions described in section 2.2.3.

But we can go further in articulating the evolutionary psychological version of MMH by characterising it as the conjunction of two claims. The first of these claims is that the human mind contains *a large number* of Darwinian modules. Thus, Tooby and Cosmides (1995) claim that, on their view, 'our cognitive architecture resembles a confederation of hundreds or thousands' of modules (Tooby and Cosmides, 1995, p. xiii). So, according to this version of MMH, it is not merely the case that the human mind is largely composed of Darwinian modules; it is also the case that there are *lots* of modules from which the human mind is composed.

The second central claim made by the evolutionary psychologists' version of MMH is that, contrary to what has been argued by Fodor (1983) and others, the modular structure of the mind is not restricted to input systems (those responsible for perception and language processing) and output systems (those responsible for producing actions). Evolutionary psychologists accept the Fodorian thesis that such *peripheral* systems are modular in character. But *pace* Fodor, they maintain that many or perhaps even all so-called *central capacities,* such as reasoning, belief fixation and planning, can also 'be divided into domain-specific modules' (Jackendoff, 1992, p. 70). So, for example, it has been suggested by evolutionary psychologists that there are modular, computational mechanisms for such central processes as 'theory of mind' inference (Leslie, 1994; Baron-Cohen, 1995) social reasoning (Cosmides and Tooby, 1992), biological categorisation (Pinker, 1994) and probabilistic inference (Gigerenzer, 1994, 1996).

To sum up, according to evolutionary psychologists, the human mind – including those parts responsible for 'central processes' – contains a large number of Darwinian modules; (prototypically) innate, naturally selected, domain-specific computational mechanisms which may have access (perhaps even unique access) to a domain-specific system of knowledge of the sort that I've been calling a Chomskian module. From here on, unless specified otherwise, I reserve the expressions 'massive modularity' and 'MMH' in order to refer to this view. Moreover, since we are concerned primarily with the plausibility of *massive* modularity and not modularity *tout court*, in what follows I assume for the sake of argument that we possess at least some peripheral modules – e.g. for language or visual processing.

3   Varieties of massive modularity

The MMH endorsed by evolutionary psychologists provides us with an abstract proposal about the structure of the human mind. But it should be clear that there are numerous distinct ways in which the details of the view might be spelled out. In this section I propose briefly to survey some of the more important issues that emerge when one tries to articulate a worked-out version of massive modularity. In 3.1 I discuss different answers to the question of how modules are neurally implemented. In 3.2 I consider the relationship between modules and the adaptive problems they help solve. Then in 3.3 I focus on issues about the flow of information and control within a massively modular architecture. Finally, in 3.4 I discuss the distinction between two versions of MMH – strong and weak MMH – which provide different answers to the question of precisely how modular the human mind is.

3.1   The neural implementation of Darwinian modules

While evolutionary psychologists assume that Darwinian modules are in some way implemented in neural structures, the notion of a Darwinian module clearly implies no *specific* story about how such cognitive structures are implemented. One obvious possibility is that modules can be neatly mapped onto discrete, spatially localised pieces of neural tissue (Fodor, 1983). For example, as Dehaene and Cohen (1995) suggest, it may be that the cognitive mechanism responsible for producing representations of arithmetic properties is located at a particular position in the right inferior parietal cortex. According to this story, then, each Darwinian module is implemented by a physiologically discrete neural structure or *neural module* (Churchland and Sejnowski, 1992, p. 318).

But contrary to what many neuroscientists appear to suppose (Quartz and Sejnowski, 1994), this is *not* the only way in which Darwinian modules might be neurally implemented. Another possibility is that at least some Darwinian modules are instead subserved by complex, widely distributed brain structures. Thus, for example, in a discussion of the modularity of 'theory of mind' Segal suggests that it is at least a priori possible that distributed, global characteristics of the brain realise modules (Segal, 1996, pp. 145–6). And if this is correct, then the existence of Darwinian modules does *not* imply the existence of *neural* modules. This fact has implications for what neurobiological data can tell us about the extent to which the human mind is and is not modular in structure (Scholl, 1997). Specifically, it blocks the inference from the claim that there is no *neural* module for a particular task T to the conclusion that there is no *Darwinian* module for T. For instance, even if it were to turn out that no specific neural module subserved a theory of mind mechanism, it would not follow that humans possess no Darwinian module for theory of mind.

3.2 Modules and adaptive function

Another important issue about Darwinian modules concerns the relationship between natural selection, modules and the adaptive problems that they are designed to solve. Evolutionary psychologists maintain, of course, that modules were designed by natural selection in order to solve adaptive problems (Cosmides and Tooby, 1994). But even if one endorses this position, there still remain a number of different relationships that might obtain.

One conception of this relationship that is implicit in a considerable amount of research in evolutionary psychology is what Knapp *et al.* (1998) call the '*elegant machines*' conception of modularity. This view consists of two claims. First, it maintains that the relationship between adaptive problems and the modules that contribute to their solution will be a straightforward one – in particular, that there will be a functionally dedicated module corresponding to each adaptive problem that our minds solve. Stephen Pinker appears to endorse this claim when suggesting that natural selection would have designed 'our modular, multiformat minds' so that 'each module should do *one* thing well' – namely solve a specific *adaptive* problem (Pinker, 1997b, p. 91, emphasis added). Second, according to the 'elegant machines' view, not only is each Darwinian module dedicated to solving one particular adaptive problem, but it does so in a particularly *elegant* fashion – in the manner that a competent, rational designer would solve the problem. This point is also suggested by Pinker's discussion of modularity. According to Pinker, each module solves an adaptive problem in the manner in which a program designed by a first-rate computer scientist would. Thus he suggests that modules use subroutines, 'hide something' from the system as a whole, localise inputs and outputs in subroutines, and use data representations that make the program simple (*ibid.*). According to the 'elegant machines' view, then, the mind is composed of a multitude of elegant machines: discrete, functional mechanisms that are dedicated to a particular adaptive task and whose internal structure bears the stamp of a rational designer (Tooby and Cosmides, 1995, p. xiv).

An important feature of the 'elegant machines' conception of modularity is the manner in which it meshes with one of the central methodological commitments of evolutionary psychology – the claim that *evolutionary analysis* can play a crucial role in the study of human cognition (Samuels *et al.*, 1999). In brief, evolutionary analysis is a strategy for generating hypotheses about the structure of the human mind by analysing the adaptive problems whose successful solution would have contributed to reproductive success in the environment in which our evolutionary ancestors lived – the so-called *environment of evolutionary adaptation* or *EEA*. Evolutionary psychologists suggest that once such a problem has been identified and characterised, we should explore the hypothesis that the human mind contains modules that would have done a good job at solving that problem in the EEA. In short, evolutionary analysis 'allows one to pinpoint the important, long-enduring adaptive problems for which human beings are most likely to have cognitive adaptive specialisations' (Cosmides and Tooby, 1994, p. 94).

Now if the 'elegant machines' conception of modularity is correct, then evolutionary analysis is a very attractive research strategy. For once we identify an adaptive problem that requires a cognitive solution, we thereby have reason to think that there is a Darwinian module that is dedicated to addressing that problem. Moreover, we also have reason to think that reflection upon the principles guiding the contemporary design of information-processing systems will provide us with insight into the structure of the module. By contrast, a proponent of MMH who rejects the 'elegant machines' view is no longer in a position to make these assumptions. For example, the discovery that social reasoning is an adaptive problem would not provide us reason to take seriously the hypothesis that we possess a module that is dedicated to social reasoning. Nor, for that matter, would we be in a position to assume that reflection on the principles of rational design would provide us with insight into the internal structure of cognitive mechanisms. In short, even if one endorses MMH, evolutionary analysis starts to look much less attractive as a research strategy if we reject the central tenets of the 'elegant machines' view (Knapp *et al.*, 1998).

But are there any good reasons to reject these central tenets? Though this is not the place to discuss this question in detail, it is worth pointing out that there are prima-facie grounds for questioning the 'elegant machines' conception of modularity. First, it is not implausible to question the assumption that every Darwinian module is dedicated to the solution of a *single* adaptive problem. One reason for this is that it is far from obvious that modules cannot contribute to the solution of two or more adaptive problems. After all, multiplicity of function certainly appears to occur in the case of non-cognitive traits (Mayr, 1982). To use a well worn example, bird feathers contribute both to thermo-regulation and to the facilitation of flight. And if this is so, one may reasonably wonder why multiplicity of function should not also be a feature of cognitive modules. Second, it is far from obvious that a proponent of MMH should assume that the internal structure of modules will operate according to rational design principles. Instead it may be that modules are *kludges* of one kind or another – systems that from an a-historical, design-orientated viewpoint look messy and inefficient (Clark, 1989, p. 69). Thus, for example, some modules might not 'localise inputs and outputs in subroutines' or 'use data representations that make the program simple' or obey any of the other design principles that Pinker suggests that they should. One reason this might occur is because Mother Nature needs to deal with *pre-existing conditions*. Designing new features into a system that is already in place means that the designer must not only come up with a mechanism that solves the particular problem but also must do so in a manner that does not clash with pre-existing systems (Knapp *et al.*, 1998). Mother Nature faces this constraint with a vengeance, since she designs new mechanisms into ancient structures that have been repeatedly updated and modified over many millennia. As a result, the structure of the human mind and the modules from which it is composed may be far more baroque than any system a rational human engineer would ever produce.

3.3   Connections: the flow of information and control between modules

A third concern that arises when one attempts to provide a detailed articulation of MMH regards the *interconnections* between different modules. Broadly speaking, we might distinguish between two types of such concerns: issues about the flow of *information* and issues about the flow of *control*.

Information flow. Massively modular cognitive architectures are, of course, composed of large numbers of functionally specialised subsystems. But these mechanisms do not exist in splendid informational isolation – they communicate in various ways. One central issue concerns the *extent* to which each mechanism is able to communicate with the others. At one extreme, we can imagine that each module is only connected to an extremely restricted number of other mechanisms – that the *informational channels* connecting modules are *sparse*. By and large, it is this view that has dominated modular approaches to cognition. Thus, for example, the visual processing modules that Marr posits only receive information from a highly restricted range of sources (Marr, 1982b). Indeed Jerry Fodor has suggested that *the* central feature of cognitive modules is that they are *informationally encapsulated* – that they have access to less than all the information available to the system as a whole – and hence only have a restricted range of connections to other cognitive mechanisms (Fodor, 1983). But in spite of this preference among modularity theorists for sparse models of intermodular connectivity, we can also imagine massively modular systems in which informational channels are exceedingly *dense*. Indeed, we can imagine that each module is connected to every other module – that everything is connected – so that any item of information that is accessible to any module is accessible to *every* module. Of course, this conception of information flow is one that many modularity theorists would not be inclined to accept. Indeed it is precisely this characterisation of information flow that is precluded by the Fodorian proposal that modules are informationally encapsulated. Nevertheless, evolutionary psychologists do not assume that Darwinian modules are encapsulated (see section 2.3). In which case, there is presumably no reason to suppose that they rule out a priori the possibility that our cognitive architecture might approximate such a highly interconnected system to some interesting degree.

Control flow. In addition to specifying the flow of information, a well-articulated version of MMH must also describe the flow of *control* – i.e. the *control structures* that govern the behaviour of the system as a whole. There are extremely wide ranges of ways to organise the flow of control within a massively modular system. But for the moment let me mention just three alternatives. One possibility – though surely one that most modularity theorists would be unhappy to countenance – is that there is some 'central executive' that is responsible for allocating problems to specialised modules. On this view, modular central systems are under the control of a general-purpose overseer that makes the decision about which module gets to address which problem. So, for example, it is a central executive that determines whether a problem is addressed by the theory-of-mind module or by the cheater detection mechanism, and so on.

A second possibility is that while there exists no central executive, there are nevertheless various *allocation mechanisms* – computational mechanisms that determine which of the many cognitive modules get called on to deal with a given problem (Samuels *et al.*, 1999). So, for example, one such mechanism might determine whether a given problem is dealt with by a module for reasoning about frequencies or by some other module that employs various heuristics for reasoning under conditions of uncertainty – e.g. availability and representativeness heuristics (Kahneman and Tversky, 1972; Samuels *et al.*, 1999). Such a massively modular system thus treats the problem of allocating control as a computational problem, albeit one that is solved by a distributed system of mechanisms as opposed to one central executive.

A third possibility is that the problem of control within a massively modular mind does not have a computational solution – that is, it is not solved by a computational mechanism at all. Instead the flow of control within the system might be *hard wired*. So, for example, it might be the case that modules are connected up in such a way that information is passed through the system, and the first module that is able to compute a solution to the input deals with the problem. Notice that within such a system there is no computational device that is dedicated to allocating problems. Allocation, on this view, is not subserved by any specific computational device but results from the way in which the entire cognitive system is structured.

3.4   Composition: strong versus weak massive modularity

The final difference between versions of MMH that I will discuss is a crucial distinction between two views about the extent to which the human mind is massively modular. According to MMH, the mind – including those parts that subserve central processes – is largely or even entirely composed of Darwinian modules. But this way of formulating the proposal accommodates two different positions which I call *strong* and *weak* massive modularity. According to strong MMH, *all* cognitive mechanisms are Darwinian modules. Such a view would be undermined if we were to discover that *any* cognitive mechanism was non-modular in character. By contrast, weak MMH maintains only that the human mind – including those parts responsible for central processing – is *largely* modular in structure. In contrast to strong MMH, such a view is clearly compatible with the claim that there are some non-modular mechanisms. So, for example, the proponent of weak MMH is able to posit the existence of some domain-general, hence non-modular, devices for reasoning and learning.

Which version of MMH do evolutionary psychologists endorse? It is not entirely clear. But I suspect that while *some* maintain that strong MMH *might* be true, evolutionary psychologists only intend to *commit* themselves to the weaker thesis. One reason for making this claim is that some evolutionary psychologists explicitly *reject* strong MMH. Cummins (1996), for example, maintains that we have excellent reason to posit the existence of some general-purpose central processors. A second reason is that virtually all formulations of MMH in the evolutionary psychological literature express a commitment only to the weak thesis. Having said that, some prominent evolutionary psychologists occasionally *appear* to endorse the strong thesis. For example, Cosmides and Tooby have said of natural selection that 'it is unlikely that a process with these properties would design central systems that are general purpose and content-free' (Cosmides and Tooby, 1994, p. 60). Since they clearly think that cognitive mechanisms are the products of selection, one natural reading of this quotation would commit them to (the probable truth of) strong MMH. But it isn't clear that this is what Cosmides and Tooby really want to maintain. This is because in their more careful moments, when they more explicitly formulate their account of cognitive architecture, they are inclined only to endorse the weaker version of massive modularity – that 'although some mechanisms in the cognitive architecture may be domain-general' these must have been 'embedded in a constellation of specialised mechanisms' (Cosmides and Tooby, 1994, p. 94). In short, while Cosmides and Tooby leave open the *possibility* that strong MMH is true, they only *commit* themselves to the weaker thesis.

One final reason for not attributing strong MMH to evolutionary psychologists is that principles of charity would suggest that we shouldn't saddle them with this commitment. Specifically, in the absence of widespread explicit claims to the contrary, we should only attribute to them the weaker version of massive modularity because the strong thesis is implausible. When saying this, I do not intend to imply that we currently possess *decisive* reason to reject strong MMH. Indeed I doubt that any such argument exists. Rather I maintain only that given the current state of our knowledge, it is not a particularly *plausible* view to adopt and that evolutionary psychologists are surely aware of this. One problem with strong MMH is that there are a number of cognitive phenomena that are hard to accommodate within an entirely modular account of cognition. For example, human beings seem capable of reasoning about an indefinitely wide range of contents and integrating evidence from an indefinitely wide range of domains in order to evaluate the truth and plausibility of different hypotheses (Fodor, 1983). And while it is surely too early to conclude that such phenomena *cannot* be accommodated within a strongly modular account of cognition, it is at present hard to see how an *entirely* modular mind would be able to manifest such capacities (though see Sperber, 1994a, for an interesting attempt to sketch an answer to this problem).

A second problem with strong MMH is that, in many areas of psychology, the only extant theories are ones that presuppose the existence of at least some domain-general cognitive mechanisms. For instance, all extant theories of analogical reasoning appear to presuppose the existence of domain-general cognitive mechanisms (Gentner, 1989; Holyoak and Thagard, 1995). Moreover, even when we turn to paradigmatic examples of *modular* explanations of cognitive phenomena, many of them presuppose at least some interestingly domain-general machinery. So, for example, though Alan Leslie's work on 'theory of mind' is frequently cited as a paradigmatic example of a modular approach to cognition, he in fact posits mechanisms that are interestingly domain-general in character. Specifically, he postulates a domain-inspecific 'selection processor' – a mechanism that operates across domains in order to perform the 'executive' function of 'inhibiting a pre-potent inferential response and selecting the relevant substitute premise' (Leslie, 1994, p. 229). Now, of course, it *may* be that these explanations will be supplanted by alternative and better explanations that only posit modular cognitive devices. But at this point in time, this is surely not to be considered a probable outcome.

To sum up, while some evolutionary psychologists think that strong MMH *might* be true, evolutionary psychology is only committed to the weaker thesis. Moreover, I claim that given the current state of our knowledge, this is the more plausible of the two positions to adopt. In view of this, for the remainder of the chapter I will be concerned primarily with the weak MMH.

4   Theoretical arguments for massive modularity

Is the (weak) MMH correct? Is the human mind largely composed of Darwinian modules? This question is fast becoming one of the central issues of contemporary cognitive science. In this section, I discuss what I take to be the main theoretical arguments that evolutionary psychologists have developed in support of massive modularity: two arguments proposed by Cosmides and Tooby that I call *the optimality argument* and *the solvability argument* (Samuels, 1998a).[5] I show that although these arguments may well provide support for *some* modular view of cognition – one which posits computational (Darwinian) or Chomskian modules – they do not provide us with reason to adopt the version of MMH defended by evolutionary psychologists. And this is because they fail to discriminate between the evolutionary psychologists' MMH and what I earlier called Chomskian MMH – the claim that cognition is largely subserved by non-modular computational mechanisms which have access to domain-specific bodies of mentally represented information.

[5] For further arguments for MMH see Tooby and Cosmides (1992) and Sperber (1994a).

4.1   *The optimality argument*

Cosmides and Tooby's optimality argument purports to show that once we appreciate both the way in which natural selection operates and the specific adaptive problems that human beings faced in the Pleistocene, we will see that there are good reasons for thinking that the mind contains a large number of distinct modular mechanisms. In developing the argument, they first attempt to justify the claim that when it comes to solving adaptive problems, selection pressures can be expected to produce highly specialised cognitive mechanisms – i.e. modules. According to Cosmides and Tooby, 'different adaptive problems often require different solutions'; and while a specialised mechanism can be fast, reliable and efficient because it is dedicated to solving a specific adaptive problem, a general mechanism that solves many adaptive problems with competing task demands will only attain generality at the expense of sacrificing these virtues. Consequently:

(1) As a rule, when two adaptive problems have solutions that are incompatible or simply different, a single solution will be inferior to two specialised solutions. (Cosmides and Tooby, 1994, p. 89)

Notice that (1) is not specifically about cognitive mechanisms but about solutions to adaptive problems in general. Nevertheless, according to Cosmides and Tooby, what applies generally to solutions to adaptive problems also applies to the specific case of *cognitive* mechanisms. Consequently, they maintain that we should expect domain-specific cognitive mechanisms to be superior to domain-general systems as solutions to adaptive problems. Moreover, since natural selection can be expected to favour superior solutions to adaptive problems over inferior ones, Cosmides and Tooby conclude that when it comes to solving adaptive problems:

(2) . . . domain-specific cognitive mechanisms . . . can be expected to systematically outperform (and hence preclude or replace) more general mechanisms (p. 89)

But this alone is not sufficient to provide us with good reason to accept the claim that the mind contains a *large number* of modules. It must also be the case that our ancestors were confronted by a large number of adaptive problems that could be solved only by *cognitive* mechanisms. Accordingly, Cosmides and Tooby insist that:

(3) Simply to survive and reproduce, our Pleistocene ancestors had to be good at solving an enormously broad array of adaptive problems – problems that would defeat any modern artificial intelligence system. A small sampling include foraging for food, navigating, selecting a mate, parenting, engaging in social exchange, dealing with aggressive threat, avoiding predators, avoiding pathogenic contamination, avoiding naturally occurring plant toxins, avoiding incest and so on. (p. 90)

Yet if this is true and if it is also true that when it comes to solving adaptive problems, domain-specific cognitive mechanisms can be expected to preclude or replace more general ones, then it would seem to follow that:

(4) The human mind can be expected to include a large number of distinct, domain-specific mechanisms.

And this is just what the Massive Modularity Hypothesis requires.

Of course, the optimality argument is not supposed to be a deductive proof that the mind is massively modular. Rather, it is only supposed to provide, at most, plausible grounds to expect the mind to contain many modules. Nonetheless, if the conclusion of the argument is interpreted as claiming that the mind contains lots of *Darwinian* modules, then I suspect that the argument claims more than it is entitled to. One obvious objection that is frequently levelled against this sort of argument is that the optimality principle on which it depends – the principle that evolution produces optimal designs[6] – is either generally implausible (Kitcher, 1985; Stich, 1990a; Sober, 1993) or, at least, implausible when applied to psychological traits (Fodor, 1996). But even if we grant this optimality assumption and accept that natural selection has contrived to provide the human mind with many specialised solutions to adaptive problems, it still does not follow that these specialised solutions will be prototypical *Darwinian* modules. Rather than containing a large number of specialised computational devices, it might instead be the case that the mind contains lots of innate, domain-specific items of knowledge, and that these are employed in order to solve various adaptive problems. Thus, rather than exploiting Darwinian modules, our minds might contain many innate *Chomskian* modules. Moreover, as mentioned in section 2.2.2, it may be the case that these Chomskian modules are only deployed by domain-general – or general-purpose – cognitive mechanisms. In which case, though the argument might support *some* form of modularity, it does not show that we should adopt the MMH defended by evolutionary psychologists.

One way to develop this point is to focus on the fact that premise (1) of the argument is ambiguous. On one reading, the term 'solution' is read in a liberal fashion so that it refers literally to any kind of solution to an adaptive problem whatsoever. A solution in this sense need not be a cognitive *mechanism*. Rather, it might be something else, such as a body of knowledge – a Chomskian module. On the second reading, however, 'solution' is given a more restrictive reading. According to this reading, when Cosmides and Tooby speak of solutions to adaptive problems, they really

---

[6] Of course, this does *not* mean that the fittest of all possible (or imaginable) traits will evolve. Rather it means that the fittest of the traits *actually present in the reproductive population* will evolve (Sober, 1993, p. 120).

mean *mechanisms* for solving adaptive problems. In other words, premise (1) ought to be read as:

(1*) As a rule, when two adaptive problems have solutions that are incompatible or simply different, a single *mechanism* for solving both problems will be inferior to two specialised *mechanisms*.

It should be clear that if we adopt the first reading, then premise (1) provides us with no reason to prefer the sorts of domain-specific cognitive mechanisms posited by evolutionary psychologists to domain-specific bodies of knowledge. Under the first reading, if we grant that (1) is true, all that follows is that we should expect natural selection to have contrived to provide the human mind with specialised solutions to adaptive problems. But it does not follow from this that these solutions will be specialised, *computational mechanisms*. Instead, it may be the case that the mind contains domain-specific bodies of information, and these are employed in order to solve various adaptive problems. Thus rather than exploiting Darwinian modules, our minds might instead contain Chomskian modules. And, as we have already noted, it is perfectly consistent with this claim that the information is utilised only by *domain-general* and, hence, non-modular computational mechanisms.

But perhaps premise (1) is intended to be read as (1*). Even so, it is far from clear that we now have reason to prefer the view that there are lots of Darwinian modules to the view that we possess many Chomskian modules that are deployed by general-purpose computational mechanisms. For while *some* general-purpose mechanisms may typically perform less well than more specialised ones, the sorts of mechanisms that have access to lots of specialised information don't seem to be general-purpose mechanisms of this kind. When developing the claim that general-purpose mechanisms are inferior to more specialised ones, Cosmides and Tooby focus on mechanisms that make no specific provision for the different kinds of problems that they confront. Here is how Cosmides and Tooby characterise such mechanisms:

At the limit of perfect generality, a problem solving system can know nothing except that which is always true of every situation in any conceivable universe and, therefore, can apply no techniques except those that are applicable to all imaginable situations. In short, it has abandoned virtually anything that could lead to a solution. (Tooby and Cosmides, 1992, p. 104)

Thus the mechanisms discussed by Cosmides and Tooby are general purpose in the sense that they treat all problems in an undifferentiated fashion. Let us call this the *problematic sense* of 'general-purpose mechanism'.

Now if *this* is what Cosmides and Tooby mean by 'general-purpose mechanism', then I concede that, in most cases, we would expect specialised mechanisms to outperform more general ones. But domain-general mechanisms that have access to Chomskian modules are not general purpose in the above problematic sense. Such mechanisms need not treat all problems in the same way. Rather, they can treat different problems in different ways by virtue of using different bodies of specialised knowledge. Thus, far from abandoning all specialised knowledge that will aid in the solution of adaptive problems, such domain-general cognitive mechanisms utilise large amounts of domain-specific knowledge. They are, therefore, not general purpose in the above problematic sense. But if this is so, then what reason do we have for thinking that domain-specific cognitive mechanisms (e.g. Darwinian modules) will outperform domain-general mechanisms that have access to Chomskian modules? To my knowledge, Cosmides and Tooby do not address this question. Nor is it clear why they make the claim. Indeed, in the absence of an argument it is surely very implausible to claim that Darwinian modules will outperform such domain-general mechanisms. And, at present, it is far from clear that anyone knows how such an argument would go.

4.2 The solvability argument

Let us now turn our attention to the solvability argument for MMH. According to Cosmides and Tooby, this argument is supposed to show that:

... it is in principle impossible for a human psychology that contained nothing but domain-general mechanisms to have evolved, because such a system cannot consistently behave adaptively. (Cosmides and Tooby, 1994, p. 90)

Instead they maintain that only a system that contains 'a constellation of specialised mechanisms' could have evolved (p. 94). In arguing for this claim, Cosmides and Tooby start by suggesting the following condition of adequacy on any hypothesis about our cognitive architecture:

The Minimal Solvability Constraint (MSC): A proposed hypothesis about the design of our cognitive architecture is adequate only if it is possible, in principle, for the design to 'produce minimally adaptive behaviour in ancestral environments' (p. 91)

According to this constraint, any proposed architecture must, in principle, be able to 'solve all of the problems that were necessary to survival and reproduction in the Pleistocene' (p. 91). The justification is straightforward: human beings have survived until today and we would not have done so unless we were able to produce those behaviours that were necessary for survival and reproduction in our ancestral environment.

Clearly, MSC provides a basis for testing competing proposals about the architecture of the human mind, since if it can be shown that a proposed design cannot satisfy MSC, then it follows that the mind does not have that design. The question that arises is this: Are there any reasons for thinking that *only* a massively modular architecture could satisfy MSC? According to Cosmides and Tooby there are at least three such reasons.

1. Some information that is crucial for adaptive behaviour cannot be learned from perceptual information alone. According to Cosmides and Tooby, domain-general systems possess no innate, domain-specific information but are instead 'limited to knowing what can be validly derived by general processes from perceptual information' (p. 92). But they urge that certain kinds of knowledge which are crucial to producing adaptive behaviour (e.g. knowledge of Hamilton's kin selection equation) cannot be learned in this way because 'they depend on statistical relationships . . . that emerge only over many generations' (p. 91).

2. What counts as fit behaviour differs from domain to domain. In order to satisfy MSC one must avoid making the kinds of errors that prevent one from reproducing. And presumably this requires that either one possesses innate knowledge of how to behave in different contexts or else possesses the capacity to learn how to act in different contexts. Clearly, Cosmides and Tooby think that domain-general mechanisms cannot possess innate knowledge of this sort. Moreover, they argue that a domain-general system could not *learn* to behave in the appropriate fashion. It is not entirely clear what their argument for this claim is. But the rough idea appears to be that in order to learn how to avoid making errors that result in maladaptive behaviour, one must possess some *standard of error* that correlates with fitness. Cosmides and Tooby appear to assume that a domain-general system could possess such a standard *only if* it were a domain-general standard. But they also maintain that, as a matter of fact, there is no domain-general criterion of success or failure that correlates with fitness. Rather what counts as an error differs from domain to domain. So, for example, 'in the sexual domain, error = sex with kin. In the helping domain, error = not helping kin given the appropriate envelope of circumstances. In co-operative exchanges, error = being cheated' and so on (Cosmides and Tooby, 1994, p. 91). Thus Cosmides and Tooby claim that domain-general – hence non-modular – mechanisms couldn't learn to behave in a minimally adaptive fashion.

3. A domain-general cognitive system would be paralysed by combinatorial explosion. According to Cosmides and Tooby, domain-general cognitive mechanisms lack 'any content, either in the form of domain-specific knowledge or domain-specific procedures that can guide it towards the solution of an adaptive problem' and as a result 'must evaluate all alternatives it can define' (p. 94). But if true, this poses an obvious problem for any domain-general mechanism. Given the complexity of biological problems and given the fact that 'alternatives increase exponentially as the problem complexity increases' (p. 94), 'a mechanism that contains no domain-specific rules of relevance, procedural knowledge, or privileged hypotheses could not solve the problem in the amount of time the organism has to solve it' (p. 94).

Thus, according to Cosmides and Tooby, an organism that possessed only domain-general cognitive mechanisms would fail to be minimally adaptive – and, hence, to satisfy the Minimal Solvability Constraint (MSC) – simply because it would be unable to perform in real-time many of the tasks that are essential to its survival. They therefore conclude that:

> Although some mechanisms in the cognitive architecture may be domain-general, these could not have produced fit behaviour under Pleistocene conditions (and therefore could not have been selected for) unless they were embedded in a constellation of specialised mechanisms. (p. 94)

And this is, of course, precisely what the Massive Modularity Hypothesis requires.

The solvability argument fails to provide strong grounds for adopting the version of MMH defended by evolutionary psychologists. Suppose, for the sake of argument, that it shows that the human mind must possess domain-specific structures in order to satisfy MSC. Perhaps this is all the argument is supposed to show. Nonetheless, if it is supposed to show that the mind is largely composed of *Darwinian modules*, then it claims more than it is entitled to. This is because, once again, it does not provide us with reason to prefer the evolutionary psychologists' MMH over the alternative hypothesis that the mind contains lots of bodies of domain-specific information (Chomskian modules) that are deployed by domain-general, hence non-modular, computational mechanisms. In order to see this we must first distinguish two different notions of 'domain-general computational mechanism' that appear to be conflated in Cosmides and Tooby's argument:

(i) A domain-general computational mechanism is one that is not domain-specific – i.e. one that is not dedicated to solving problems in a specific cognitive domain.

(ii) A domain-general computational mechanism is one that is not domain-specific *and does not have access to any innate, domain-specific knowledge.*

A mind that contained only mechanisms that were domain-general in sense (ii) would contain no innate, domain-specific information whatsoever. It would be a *tabula rasa*. By contrast, a mind that contained only mechanisms that were domain-general in sense (i) – and so contained no Darwinian modules – might be anything but a blank slate. Indeed such a mind could contain huge amounts of innate, domain-specific information.

As we have already seen, a mechanism can be domain-general in this sense and still have access to domain-specific information.

Let us assume for the sake of argument that the solvability argument shows that the human mind is not a *tabula rasa*. Even so, if the argument is supposed to show that the human mind contains Darwinian modules, then it fails to achieve this goal. This is clear once the above two notions of 'domain-general mechanism' are disentangled. First, consider the claim that definitions of error are domain-dependent. The problem that this is alleged to pose for domain-general systems is that they are unable to acquire knowledge of what the various standards of error are. Yet, on the face of it, it seems that a computational mechanism that is domain-general [in sense (i)] can possess innate knowledge of these various standards of error, in which case, it does not face the problem of trying to learn these standards. Thus, the present consideration fails to provide us any reason to think that the mind must possess domain-specific computational mechanisms – for example Darwinian modules. Second, consider the claim that certain relations that are essential to the regulation of adaptive behaviour are unlearnable during a single lifetime. Even if this is true, it does not follow that there are domain-specific *computational mechanisms*. A computational mechanism that is domain-general in sense (i) can have access to innate information about such regularities. So, for instance, a domain-general mechanism could have access to innate knowledge of Hamilton's equation. But if this is so, then once more we have no reason to infer that humans possess Darwinian modules.

Finally, consider Cosmides and Tooby's claim that domain-general computational mechanisms are subject to combinatorial explosion. The reason such mechanisms are supposed to face this problem is that they possess no domain-specific knowledge that can help them reduce the number of possibilities that need to be considered when solving a problem. But, yet again, it seems that there is no reason to think that domain-general mechanisms [in sense (i)] cannot possess innate, domain-specific knowledge that helps constrain the search space for a given problem. Thus it is implausible to claim that the threat of combinatorial explosion provides us with reason to think that the mind contains Darwinian modules.

In summary, the general arguments developed by Cosmides and Tooby fail to show that we should endorse the MMH defended by evolutionary psychologists. Even if we accept the optimality assumption – that natural selection tends to produce optimal designs – the arguments still fail to show that we have reason to prefer MMH – the view that our minds are composed of lots of *Darwinian* modules – over the competing claim that our minds are composed of domain-general cognitive mechanisms with access to specialised bodies of knowledge – i.e. *Chomskian* modularity. Of course, given that Chomskian modules are a species of module, the suggestion is that, once we adopt some suitable version of the optimality assumption, Cosmides and Tooby's arguments do support *some* form of modularity. It's just that they do not support the MMH. And this is a useful point to recognise, for it tells us that the space of candidate theories about the architecture of the human mind is larger than one might think from reading the work of evolutionary psychologists. Theorists like Cosmides and Tooby raise the sorts of evolutionary considerations discussed in this section in order to constrain the class of acceptable theories of cognitive architecture. Moreover, they appear to think that such considerations leave MMH as the only plausible candidate. What our discussion suggests is that this is incorrect. Though the MMH defended by evolutionary psychologists is one kind of theory that satisfies these general evolutionary constraints, it is not the only one. Theories that posit domain-general mechanisms with access to Chomskian modules also satisfy Cosmides and Tooby's evolutionary requirements.

5   The experimental case for massive modularity

We have now considered the main, general arguments for positing lots of Darwinian modules and found them wanting. But what of the empirical evidence? While a systematic review would be beyond the scope of this essay, it is important to have some feel for the current state of the evidence for the existence of Darwinian modules. In this section I present a brief sketch of the sorts of data that have been invoked in support of modularity and highlight some of the problems these confront. In particular, I highlight the fact that the kinds of experimental data that are most commonly invoked in support of modularity fail to distinguish between views that posit Darwinian modules and theories that posit general-purpose mechanisms with access to Chomskian modules. (For a comprehensive and readable introduction to the experimental data for MMH, see Pinker, 1997b.)

While there is a fair amount of evidence for modularity in the literature, it is widely agreed that the best available empirical evidence concerns peripheral as opposed to central systems. For instance, there is considerable evidence for the existence of computational modules for language and vision which are paradigmatic cases of Fodorian input systems (Garfield, 1987). But *why* is there so little experimental evidence for the existence of computational modules for 'central capacities'? In particular, why is there so little evidence that would enable us to distinguish claims about Darwinian modules and Chomskian modules in central cognition? Part of the answer is that, until relatively recently, people simply hadn't looked too carefully. And part of the reason why they hadn't looked was that few theorists had taken seriously the claim that there are Darwinian modules for central processes. This, however, is not the only reason. A second reason is that it's *very hard* to find data in favour of one and against the other. In order to illustrate this point, consider a claim that I have alluded to on a number of occasions in this chapter – the thesis that we possess a 'Theory of Mind' (ToM) module that is dedicated to reasoning about the mental states and behaviour of people (Baron-Cohen, 1995).

ToM constitutes perhaps the most well-developed experimental case for a computational or Darwinian module that is not peripheral in character. Nonetheless, it is far from clear that the available data provide us with reason to prefer the claim that there is a ToM computational module over the competing claim that there is a domain-specific body of ToM *knowledge*. The main source of experimental evidence for a ToM computational module comes from dissociative studies: studies which demonstrate that, in one group of subjects, ToM capacities are selectively impaired, while in another group they are selectively spared. Perhaps the most well-known of these dissociative studies are those which concern 'standard' false-belief tasks.[7] Numerous studies have been conducted in order to determine who can and cannot pass these tasks.[8] For our present purposes, one particularly relevant case concerns two groups of psychopathological subjects: autistics and people with Williams syndrome. Many studies show that adolescents and adults with autism, even with IQs within the normal range, have considerable difficulty passing false-belief tasks – tasks that are routinely passed by normal four-year-old subjects (Leslie and Frith, 1988). By contrast, in spite of having wide ranges of cognitive impairment (e.g. in number and spatial cognition) and low IQs (full IQ in the 50's–60's), Williams subjects routinely pass the standard false-belief tasks.

The above sort of data is often taken to provide strong evidence for the existence of a computational module for ToM. After all, one obvious explanation of the fact that autistics fail the false-belief task while people with Williams syndrome do not is that there is a ToM computational module that is selectively impaired in the case of autistics but selectively spared in Williams subjects. It should be clear, however, that one can mimic

---

[7] False-belief tasks are intended to evaluate whether or not experimental subjects understand when someone might hold a false belief. One 'standard' version of the task – sometimes called the 'Sally-Ann Task' – involves watching Sally put a marble in one place (location A) and later, while Sally is away, Ann putting the marble elsewhere (location B). The subject is then asked, 'Where will Sally look for her marble?' In order to answer this question correctly, the subject needs to appreciate that, since Sally was absent when her marble was moved from A to B, she will have the false belief that it is at A (Baron-Cohen, 1995, p. 70).

[8] For example, numerous studies have been conducted which establish that normal (i.e. unimpaired) three-year-olds typically do not pass this task whereas normal four-year-olds do (e.g. Wimmer and Perner, 1983; Perner *et al.*, 1987).

this explanatory strategy by invoking the claim that there is a specialised body of knowledge for ToM. According to this explanation, autistics fail the false-belief task because their specialised body of ToM *knowledge* is impaired whereas Williams subjects solve the false-belief task because their ToM knowledge is intact. It would appear, then, that although it is very plausible to explain the above dissociative data by positing some kind of modular cognitive structure, it does not provide us with reason to favour the computational module account of ToM over the Chomskian module alternative. (See Samuels, 1998a, for a more sustained defence of this conclusion.) In short, the evidence fails to distinguish between computational and Chomskian modularity about theory of mind.

Similar problems arise in other domains of cognition. Consider, for example, recent work on social reasoning. Here the main source of data comes not from studies on pathological populations but from experiments on normal subjects. What the available data suggest is that people reason differently in tasks that appear to be identical with respect to their formal characteristics and differ only with respect to their semantic contents. So, for example, numerous studies indicate that responses to various versions of Peter Wason's famous selection task are highly sensitive to whether or not the particular problem concerns social exchange relations (Cheng and Holyoak, 1985; Cosmides and Tooby, 1992). Although how such *content effects* ought to be explained remains an area of active research, there has been a growing consensus among researchers that human beings possess domain-specific cognitive structures for reasoning about social exchanges (Cheng and Holyoak, 1985; Cosmides, 1989; Cosmides and Tooby, 1992). But among those theorists who form this consensus it still remains a point of considerable dispute whether or not these specialised cognitive structures take the form of computational modules (e.g. Darwinian modules) or bodies of information (Chomskian modules) that are deployed by a domain-general cognitive mechanism. Thus, for example, Cosmides, Tooby and other evolutionary psychologists have proposed that we possess one or more Darwinian modules designed to deal with social exchanges (Cosmides and Tooby, 1992; Gigerenzer and Hug, 1992; Pinker, 1997b). By contrast, Cheng, Holyoak and their colleagues have proposed that we possess *pragmatic reasoning schemas* – domain-specific sets of rules that are deployed by general-purpose reasoning mechanisms in order to reason about social exchange relations (Cheng and Holyoak, 1985, 1989; Cheng *et al.*, 1986). Once again, although it seems plausible to posit some kind of modular structure in order to explain the experimental data, the available evidence doesn't seem to distinguish between computational modular stories of the sort advocated by evolutionary psychologists and theories that posit Chomskian modules that are only utilised by domain-general computational mechanisms.

To summarise, it seems plausible to explain phenomena such as those outlined above by positing some form of modular cognitive structure – whether computational (Darwinian) or Chomskian in character. But the task of providing experimental data that distinguish, for central processes, between explanations that posit computational modules and those that posit only domain-general mechanisms with access to Chomskian modules, is an extremely difficult one that is yet to be satisfactorily resolved. I do not wish to suggest, however, that the absence of such data implies that we ought not to take the evolutionary psychologists' MMH seriously. On the contrary, there are accounts of various central processes – including theory-of-mind inference and social exchange reasoning – which posit Darwinian modules and accommodate all the available experimental data. In which case, we should surely take such theories and the massively modular view which they support very seriously indeed *unless* we have independent reason to reject these proposals. But do we possess any such reasons? In the final section of this chapter I propose to consider briefly some of the more prominent arguments that have been levelled against MMH.

6   The case against massive modularity

An initial point worth making about the objections to MMH is that, even if sound, virtually all of them only provide us with reason to reject strong and *not* weak MMH. But, as I argued in section 3.4, evolutionary psychologists only commit themselves to the weaker thesis. In which case, the vast majority of the objections to massive modularity pose no threat whatsoever to the view that evolutionary psychologists, in fact, endorse.

Consider, for example, Fodor's (1983) argument that we require domain-general, and hence non-modular, cognitive mechanisms in order to integrate perceptual information from different sensory modalities. According to Fodor:

The representations that input systems deliver have to interface somewhere and the computational mechanisms that effect the interface must ipso facto have access to information from more than one cognitive domain. (Fodor, 1983, p. 102)

As Fodor notes, this argument (at most) shows that 'even if input systems are domain-specific, there must be some cognitive mechanisms that are not' (Fodor, 1983, p. 101). But this conclusion is clearly consistent with weak MMH. After all, even if we possess *some* central systems that are domain general and hence non-modular, it clearly does not follow that we don't possess lots of other central systems that *are* modular. In short, Fodor's argument is, at best, an objection to strong MMH and not to the version of massive modularity that evolutionary psychologists endorse.

Similar points apply to virtually all the currently available arguments against MMH, including those developed in Fodor (1983), Anderson (1992), Karmiloff-Smith (1992), and Mithen (1996b). But since we are primarily concerned with the version of massive modularity that evolutionary psychologists are committed to – i.e. weak MMH – I won't discuss these objections here. Instead I propose to focus on a recent and highly influential challenge from experimental neuroscience. This *neurobiological argument* purports to show that we have excellent grounds for thinking that the human mind contains little if any innate, domain-specific structure (Quartz and Sejnowski 1994, 1996; Elman *et al.* 1996).[9] If sound, this argument would clearly pose a serious challenge to the evolutionary psychologists' MMH, since Darwinian modules are supposed to be both innate and domain specific. Moreover, it would also pose a serious challenge to *Chomskian modular* views, such as those defended by Carey, Chomsky, Gopnik and Spelke, which posit innate, domain-specific systems of mental representations. So, if sound, the neurobiological argument would pose a serious problem for all of the modular accounts of cognition considered in this chapter.

According to the neurobiological argument 'evidence has been mounting against the notion of innate domain-specific microcircuitry as a viable account of cortical development' (Elman *et al.*, p. 26). The evidence in question comes from a variety of studies on cortical plasticity:

In a number of recent studies with vertebrate animals, investigators have changed the nature of the input received by a specific area of cortex, either by transplanting plugs of foetal cortex from one area to another (e.g. somatosensory to visual or vice versa, O'Leary, 1993; O'Leary and Stanfield, 1989), by radically altering the nature of the input by deforming the sensory surface (Friedlander, Martin and Wassenhove-McCarthy, 1991; Killackey *et al.*, 1994) or by redirecting inputs from their intended target to an unexpected area (e.g. redirecting visual inputs to auditory cortex (Frost, 1982, 1990; Pallas and Sur, 1993)). (Elman *et al.*, p. 26)

Though there is much that could be said about these studies, the key point for our current purposes is that proponents of the neurobiological argument maintain that the outcome of these studies pose a serious problem for nativism about domain-specific cognitive structure. According to these theorists, if we possess such innate, domain-specific structures, then the

---

[9] Although Quartz and Sejnowski explicitly formulate the neurobiological argument as an objection to modular accounts of cognition, Elman *et al.* present their version of the argument as a criticism of representational nativism (RN) – the claim that we possess innately specified, domain-specific representations. In what follows, I will be primarily concerned with the argument as a criticism of massively modular accounts of cognition. This is warranted because, as Quartz and Sejnowski clearly recognise, if the evidence invoked by the neurobiological argument is sufficient to undermine RN, then it also provides us with reason to reject the existence of innate *modules*.

cognitively salient properties of foetal cortical tissue – e.g. what the pieces of tissue represent or what functions they compute – would not be significantly altered by the above kinds of experimental manipulations. But this is not what occurs:

> Surprisingly, under these aberrant conditions, the foetal cortex takes on neuro-anatomical and physiological properties that are appropriate for the information received ('When in Rome, do as the Romans do . . .'), and quite different from the properties that would have emerged if the default inputs for that region had occurred. (Elman *et al.*, 1996, pp. 26–7)[10]

On the basis of this result, Elman *et al.* (1996) conclude that 'the cortex appears to be an organ of *plasticity*' – an organ whose representational properties are highly flexible in response to environmental change (p. 315). And from this they infer that 'right now the case for innate representations does not look very good' (pp. 26–7). Similarly, Quartz and Sejnowski conclude on the basis of the same evidence that 'from a neurobiological perspective, the nativist position and the related modularity thesis are highly implausible' (Quartz and Sejnowski, 1994, p. 726).

As already noted, if the neurobiological argument is sound, then the implications are profound. Not only would it succeed in undermining MMH, but it would also require the wholesale rejection of a range of widely accepted theories in cognitive science that posit innate representations or domain-specific mechanisms, including theories that posit the existence of innate, Chomskian modules. Fortunately, the argument is *not* sound. Indeed it is subject to a large number of serious objections. I have developed these objections elsewhere in considerable detail (Samuels, 1998b). But let me briefly summarise two central criticisms.

The first objection is that the neurobiological argument depends upon the following implausible principle:

Principle of Invariance: The innately specified (representational and/or cognitive) properties of a piece of cortical tissue T are invariant under alterations in T's location within the brain and alternations in the afferent inputs to T.[11]

---

[10] For instance, in a series of experiments, Dennis O'Leary and his colleagues successfully transplanted pieces of foetal cortical tissue from one region of the new-born rodent cortex (e.g. the visual cortex) to another (e.g. the somatosensory region) (Stanfield and O'Leary, 1985; O'Leary and Stanfield, 1989). What they discovered is that the transplanted tissue takes on the structural and functional properties of its new location as opposed to maintaining the structure–function of its developmental origins and that these structural and functional properties are determined, in part, by the character of the sensory inputs that the transplanted tissue receives.

[11] Obviously, this principle needs to be hedged in various ways in order to be rendered (even superficially) plausible. Therefore, for example, presumably no one insists that cortical tissue must hold onto its innate properties even when it is severely damaged by experimental manipulation. Therefore, we ought to add the following caveat to the above principle: '. . . unless seriously damaged'. Since my criticisms do not turn on the precise formulation of the principle, however, I will not bother to provide one.

The rough idea is that if a property of a piece of neural tissue – e.g. representing the colour *red* – is innate, then the tissue ought to be inflexible or unplastic with respect to that property. Specifically, experiments which involve transplanting the tissue from one brain region to another, or which involve changing the afferent inputs to the tissue, ought not to affect whether or not the tissue possesses the innately specified property. Though the above principle is never explicitly stated by proponents of the neurobiological argument, it should be clear that the argument has no chance of working unless we make such an assumption. After all, if the innately specified properties of neural tissue need not conform to the Principle of Invariance, then the fact that the properties of neural tissue alter as a result of experimental manipulation would not count against nativist claims about the existence of domain-specific cognitive structure.

But how plausible is this principle? The answer, I maintain, is that it is not very plausible at all. If it were plausible, then presumably nativists about non-cortical features of the body ought to be committed to analogous principles. For the nativist about domain-specific cognitive structure surely does not want to claim that innate representations or modules are somehow *more* innate than skin, hearts, teeth and the like. But it would presumably be singularly implausible to conclude that a certain group of cells C (in a normally developing organism) is not innately specified to become, say, teeth, on the grounds that if C were transplanted to a different location in the organism early enough in development, then it would develop into (say) part of the belly region.[12] In other words, the claim that C is innately specified to develop into teeth (or hearts or skin, etc.) does not entail that C is subject to a principle of invariance. But if claims about the innate specification of non-cortical tissue do not entail that the tissue is subject to a principle of invariance, then why should the nativist about cognitive structure be committed to such a principle? As far as I can see, there is no reason.

But let us suppose for the sake of argument that the innately specified properties of neural tissue must satisfy the Principle of Invariance. Would the experiments cited by Elman *et al.* now show that nativists about domain-specific cognitive structure are wrong? The answer, I maintain, is 'No'. And this is because the neurobiological argument crucially misidentifies the position that contemporary proponents of nativism about cognitive structure – including evolutionary psychologists – wish to defend. As a result, even if we assume that the argument undermines *some* version of nativism, it is clear that it fails to undermine the thesis that actual

---

[12] For classic experiments of this kind see Spemann (1938). See Muller (1997) and Gilbert (1994) for other examples of transplant studies in developmental biology.

nativists wish to endorse. In order to make this point, let me start by distinguishing between two versions of nativism: what I call *tissue nativism* and *organism nativism.* Tissue nativism is a thesis about the innately specified properties of pieces of cortical tissue. According to tissue nativism, there are cognitively salient properties – in particular, representational properties or domain-specific computational properties – that specific pieces of cortical tissue are innately specified to possess. To express the point in a slightly different way, according to tissue nativism, specific pieces of cortical tissue are innately specified to encode certain representations or to compute particular domain-specific functions. So, for example, it might be innately specified that a specific cluster of neurons in the orbitofrontal cortex encodes the representation BELIEF or is dedicated to determining the mental states of a person on the basis of their observable behaviour.

In contrast to tissue nativism, organism nativism is a thesis about *whole organisms* and the cognitive structures that they possess. According to organism nativism, it is innately specified that organisms possess certain domain-specific cognitive structures. What it claims is that people – or more generally organisms – possess innately specified domain-specific cognitive mechanisms and/or innately specified mental representations that encode for various forms of domain-specific knowledge. So, for example, it might be innately specified that human beings possess such mental representations as BELIEF and ONE and/or possess innately specified cognitive mechanisms for reasoning about mental states and numbers.

With the above distinction in hand, let's consider the question of what *can* be inferred from the conjunction of the Principle of Invariance and the experimental data on cortical plasticity mentioned above. Suppose, for the sake of argument, that the Principle of Invariance is true and that the experimental data provide support for the idea that the human cortex is an 'organ of plasticity': specifically, that all the domain-specific cognitive – i.e. representational and computational – properties of any piece of cortical tissue can be altered as a result of experimental manipulations. Then we may infer the following:

(~TN) It is not innately specified that any particular piece of neural tissue has any specific domain-specific cognitive property P.

Now, if this is true, then it follows that tissue nativism is false. After all, tissue nativism claims that it *is* innately specified that specific pieces of cortical tissue code for certain domain-specific cognitive properties. So, if (contrary to fact) we accept both the Principle of Invariance and the thesis that the cortex is highly plastic, then we appear to have good reason to reject tissue nativism.

This conclusion, however, is unlikely to worry nativists. This is because it is clear that the version of nativism endorsed by contemporary theorists – such as Chomsky, Fodor, Leslie, Gopnik, Spelke and Carey – is *organism nativism* and *not* tissue nativism. That is, contemporary theorists who defend nativism about domain-specific cognitive structure are concerned with claims about what innate cognitive structures *people* (and other organisms) possess and *not* claims about the properties of specific pieces of neural tissue. So, for example, Carey and Spelke (1994) argue that 'human reasoning is guided by a collection of innate domain-specific systems of knowledge' where 'each system is characterised by a set of core principles that define the entities covered by the domain' (Carey and Spelke, 1994, p. 169).[13] Notice, however, that this is a claim about organisms – specifically, human beings – and not a claim about the innate properties of specific pieces of cortical tissue. By contrast, (~TN) expresses a claim about the properties of *neural tissue*. It expresses a fact (if indeed it is a fact) about our neurobiology: a neural level claim and not a psychological one. And clearly we cannot directly infer from (~TN) that organism nativism is false – that organisms possess no innately specified *mental representations* or *cognitive modules*.[14] The neurobiological argument thus fails to undermine the claim that we possess either innate Chomskian modules or Darwinian modules.

7   Conclusion

We started by contrasting between computational modules and Chomskian modules and noting that evolutionary psychologists commit themselves to MMH – the hypothesis that our cognitive architecture is largely composed of Darwinian modules – that is, naturally selected, innate, domain-specific, computational mechanisms. We then explored a range of ways in which this general architectural claim might be developed. Next, we saw that the main evolutionary-psychological arguments for this general thesis fail to provide us with any reason to prefer the version of MMH endorsed by evolutionary psychologists over a competing view, according to which our minds are composed primarily of domain-general mechanisms with access to Chomskian modules. We also saw that while the currently available experimental evidence does not distinguish between these two hypotheses, it nonetheless gives us some reason to take MMH

---

[13] Similar claims abound in the developmental literature. See, for example, Spelke (1994), Leslie (1994) and Gopnik and Meltzoff (1997).

[14] One might think that the falsity of organism nativism *does* follow from the falsity of tissue nativism *plus* additional assumptions about the relationship between neural structures (states or processes) and the mental structures (states or processes) of organisms. For a response to this suggestion see Samuels (1998b).

very seriously indeed. Finally, we saw that the main objections to massive modularity fail to provide us with good reason to reject the conception of cognitive architecture endorsed by evolutionary psychologists.

These are busy and exciting times for those studying the architecture of the human mind, and there is obviously much that remains to be discovered. Though I do not know, and am not inclined to venture a judgement – even a tentative one – on which view will ultimately prove most promising, I do believe that we can safely conclude that massively modular conceptions of cognition deserve to be taken very seriously.

I would like to thank Peter Carruthers, Andrew Chamberlain and two anonymous referees at Cambridge University Press for helpful comments on an earlier draft of this chapter.

3   Individual differences in early understanding of mind: genes, non-shared environment and modularity

Claire Hughes and Robert Plomin

This chapter will focus on the origins of individual differences in young children's understanding of mind. While several recent studies have documented the importance of individual differences in understanding mind for children's social development, these studies have been purely phenotypic. The study presented in this chapter is the first to adopt a genetically sensitive design in order to explore both genetic and environmental influences on theory-of-mind performance. The findings suggest a strong genetic influence upon individual differences in theory of mind, and also highlight the importance of 'non-shared' environmental influences. The implications of these findings for the modularity of mind-reading are discussed.

1   Overview

Recent research into children's development of a 'theory of mind' has highlighted the importance of individual differences in this domain for children's early social relationships. For example, differences in young children's understanding of mind are strongly linked with differences in their shared pretence (Astington and Jenkins, 1995; Hughes and Dunn, 1997; Taylor and Carlson, 1997; Youngblade and Dunn, 1995), communication (Dunn and Cutting, 1999; Hughes and Dunn, 1998; Slomkowski and Dunn, 1996), as well as self-judgements and sensitivity to criticism (Dunn, 1995). Given that individual differences in understanding mind appear pivotal to young children's ability to adapt to their social worlds, an important new question for research is: how should these individual differences be explained?

Ultimately, all individual differences are explained by either genetic or environmental factors (or their interaction). These influences can be explored using genetically sensitive designs, such as twin or adoption studies. In this chapter we present findings from the first study to examine theory-of-mind performance in young twins. It is hoped that this novel approach will provide unique insights into the causes of individual differences in young children's understanding of mind. There are three reasons

for this. First, existing evidence for genetic influence on mental-state awareness rests heavily on findings from atypical populations, such as individuals
with autism or Turner's syndrome. Extrapolating from pathology to
normal individual variation may well be unwarranted, and so direct assessment of genetic influences upon theory-of-mind performance in typically
developing children is needed. Second, environmental influences on
mental-state awareness often overlap with genetic influences. Since environmental and genetic effects cannot be teased apart without a genetically sensitive design, current accounts that are based on a purely phenotypic
approach may be misleading. Third, genetically sensitive designs enable an
important refinement in the concept of environmental influences, since they
provide a means of distinguishing between 'shared' and 'non-shared'
environmental influences (i.e. environmental factors that have either a
common or a differential impact upon siblings). These three points are considered in turn, then the main findings from the twin study are summarised
and their implications for the current debate as to the 'modularity' of mind-
reading are discussed.

1.1   Genetic influences on mental-state awareness

The strongest evidence in favour of genetic influences on mental-state
awareness is that individuals with autism perform very poorly on simple
false-belief tasks (Baron-Cohen *et al.*, 1985; Frith, 1989). Autism is a rare
and very severe developmental disorder that has its onset in the first years of
life and is defined by a triad of impairments: (i) profound lack of social
relatedness; (ii) marked language delay and impaired communicative skills;
and (iii) absence of imaginative activity, coupled with repetitive ritualistic
behaviour and insistence on sameness. First described by Leo Kanner
(1943), for more than twenty years autism was mistakenly thought to be
caused by a cold family environment. However, a landmark twin study
showed that the incidence of autism is strongly influenced by genetic
factors (Folstein and Rutter, 1977). Numerous other investigations have
since confirmed that autism is a highly heritable disorder (see Bailey *et al.*,
1998, for a recent review). In addition, three recent studies have demonstrated that poor social interactions in individuals with autism are
significantly associated with problems on standard false-belief tasks
(Fombonne *et al.*, 1994; Frith *et al.*, 1994; Hughes *et al.*, 1997). These
findings suggest that the simple mentalising skills that are so important for
effective social interaction may be influenced by genetic factors. This
conclusion is supported by new evidence from a different atypical population, children with Turner's syndrome. Specifically, Skuse *et al.* (1997) have
reported that females with Turner's syndrome who retain the paternal X

chromosome achieve better cognition and social adjustment scores than those with the maternal X chromosome. On the strength of this finding, these authors have suggested that there is an imprinted genetic locus for social cognition.

An important caveat should be made at this point, and that is that atypical populations may fail false-belief tasks or show poor social adjustment for very different reasons from young normal children. As a result, extrapolations from pathology to normal individual differences should be treated with caution. However, work with typically developing children suggests another source of evidence for genetic influences on mind-reading skills, namely the strong association between verbal ability and false-belief comprehension (Happé, 1995; Jenkins and Astington, 1996). Since verbal ability is known to be highly heritable (Plomin et al., 1994; Reznick et al., 1997), a simple explanation of the link between language and theory of mind is that common genes influence both domains. Note, however, that it is equally possible that verbal ability and false-belief comprehension are associated primarily because individual differences in each domain depend upon similar environmental influences (e.g. caregiver's interactional style – Meins, 1997). These rival hypotheses can be tested directly in a genetically sensitive design such as the present twin study.

1.2   Environmental influences on mental-state awareness

Evidence for environmental effects on individual differences in mental-state awareness comes from two separate bodies of research. First, studies of typically developing children indicate accelerated development in false-belief comprehension among children from larger families (Perner et al., 1994; Lewis et al., 1996; Ruffman et al., 1998). Second, recent research involving congenitally deaf children shows that only late-signing children display any significant delay in their acquisition of a theory of mind (Peterson and Siegal, 1997). Taken together, these findings suggest that children's social environments act as an important informational source for the acquisition of a concept of mind. As a result, children from socially enriched family environments are likely to acquire an awareness of mental states at a faster pace than others.

Findings from other studies are consistent with the environmental influence proposed above. For example, accelerated theory-of-mind development has been reported for: (i) children from families who show high levels of talk about feelings (Dunn, Brown and Beardsall, 1991); (ii) children showing a secure pattern of attachment to the primary caregiver (Fonagy et al., 1997; Meins, 1997): and (iii) children who as toddlers enjoyed co-operative interactions with siblings (Brown, Donelan-McCall and Dunn, 1996). However, these correlations do not provide a basis for drawing conclusions about the direction of causality. In other words, frequent talk about feelings, secure attachment and co-operative sibling relations may each be a consequence rather than a cause of individual differences in early mental-state awareness.

In addition, as noted earlier, environmental and genetic influences frequently overlap and interact with each other. How might this be? One explanation stems from recent studies that have shown that even very young infants are capable of tracking intentions (Gergely *et al.*, 1995; Plomin, Fulker *et al.*, 1997). This ability is demonstrated by early gaze-following and shared attention gestures, behaviours that research into early temperament suggests are at least partially determined by genetic factors (Plomin, Fulker *et al.*, 1997). Individual differences in these infant behaviours evoke different responses from caregivers and siblings, creating differences in the environments experienced by each infant. In other words, it is likely that the above associations reflect an active interplay between genetic and environmental influences. (Behavioural geneticists call this interplay 'evocative G–E correlation'.)

Another account of the overlap between genetic and environmental factors hinges on the association between false-belief comprehension and parental educational and occupational status (Cutting and Dunn, 1999). This is because most caregivers provide not only their child's environment, but also their child's genes. This strong covariance between environmental and genetic influences (termed 'passive G–E correlation' in the language of behavioural genetics) provides another example of how an apparently environmental effect may in fact be driven by genetic factors. Establishing the magnitude of genetic and environmental influences upon early understanding of mind is therefore a vital first step towards elucidating the dynamic interaction between children and their environment in the development of social understanding.

In fact, behavioural genetic data provide some of the best available evidence for the importance of environmental influence. This is because heritabilities are seldom greater than 50%, indicating that environmental factors often account for at least half of the variance in a given trait. Moreover, genetically sensitive designs can begin to disentangle the developmental interplay between nature and nurture. For instance, behavioural genetic studies have shown that the heritability of cognitive skills shows significant developmental change (Plomin and Daniels, 1987; Hetherington *et al.*, 1994; Plomin, 1995). For example, in a large-scale twenty-year, longitudinal parent-offspring adoption study, it has been reported (Plomin, Fulker *et al.*, 1997) that adopted children resembled their adoptive parents in early childhood but not at all in middle childhood or adolescence. This finding suggests that the genes that affect cognitive abilities in adulthood do not all come into play until quite late in development. In other words, although one might intuitively expect environmental influences to have a cumulative effect across the life span, the reverse appears to be true: environmental factors have their greatest influence in early childhood. Since children's social understanding shows rapid improvement in the pre-school years, individual differences in this domain may well show significant environmental influence. Moreover, behavioural genetic designs provide clues for identifying specific environmental factors since they enable one to distinguish between two contrasting types of environmental influence (see below).

1.3   Shared versus non-shared environment

We hope it is clear from the above section that a genetically sensitive design is needed to determine the extent to which environmental factors influence individual differences in early mental-state awareness. However, our third argument goes beyond this point. Specifically, behavioural genetic studies have also led to a radical shift in how environmental influences are conceptualised. Previous research into environmental influences on children's understanding of mind has focused on 'shared' environmental factors that have similar influences on siblings within the same family (e.g. parental income and education). However, numerous independent studies have shown remarkable differences between siblings: in their close relationships, their personality, their psychopathology and their cognitive ability (Dunn and Plomin, 1990; Dunn and McGuire, 1994). These differences often extend far beyond what would be predicted from the genetic relatedness of siblings.

That is, environmental influences often serve to make siblings *different* from each other. Recent research interest has therefore shifted away from shared environmental factors to document the 'non-shared' environmental factors that have a differential impact upon siblings (Plomin and Daniels, 1987; Hetherington *et al.*, 1994; Plomin, 1995). Examples include between-sibling contrasts in parent-child relationships, effects of birth order and child-specific life-events such as illnesses. To our knowledge, the study reported in this chapter (and presented more fully in Hughes and Cutting, 1999) is the first to compare false-belief comprehension in siblings, and therefore the first to consider both shared and non-shared environmental influences on children's early understanding of mind.

1.4   The twin design

The twin design is elegantly simple and hinges upon the fact that monozygotic (MZ) twin-pairs are genetically identical, but dizygotic (DZ) twin-pairs have on average only half their genes in common. Doubling the difference between MZ and DZ within-pair correlations therefore provides an estimate of a trait's 'heritability' (i.e. the proportion of trait variance attributable to genetic influences). Similarly, subtracting heritability from the MZ correlation provides a rough estimate of how much trait variance reflects shared environmental influences (since, by definition, shared genes and shared environment together fully account for the similarity between siblings). In addition, since MZ twins are genetically identical, any difference between MZ twin pairs can be attributed to the effects of non-shared environment. Each of these estimates can be tested more rigorously by structural equation model-fitting approaches. Indeed, the twin design has been robustly defended as 'the perfect natural experiment' (Martin *et al.*, 1997) in which to assess the bottom line of transmissible genetic effects on behaviour, regardless of the number of genes involved, the complexity of their interactions or the influence of non-genetic factors.

Twin comparisons do have some limitations, however. Some problems inflate heritability estimates, most notably the possibility that MZ twins share more similar postnatal environments than DZ twins. However, it appears that this is not usually a cause of MZ twins' greater phenotypic similarity but rather a *consequence* of their genetic identity (Reznick *et al.*, 1997). Other problems are conservative from a genetic perspective. For example, disorders arising from atypical gestation may produce differences between MZ twins (Phillips, 1993), and assortative mating may inflate DZ correlations for cognitive ability (Vandenberg, 1972); both phenomena reduce heritability estimates. Despite such difficulties, however, the twin method yields similar results for cognitive abilities to the other major design, the adoption method, which carries quite different assumptions (Plomin, DeFries *et al.*, 1997a).

2   The TRACKS twin study

2.1   The children

The sample for this study came from the TRACKS Twin Study of 250 same-sex three-year old twins recruited via hospital birth records and regional twin clubs in several metropolitan and rural areas in England. The sample included 238 children (58% female) with complete false-belief performance data. Most of the families were Caucasian (93%), but the sample was diverse in terms of socio-economic circumstances, with approximately one-third from working class families (Office of Population Censuses and Surveys, 1991). Each family was seen twice; once in a laboratory 'playroom' and once at home (with a mean interval of three weeks between visits). Across both visits, a battery of theory-of-mind tasks (detailed below) was administered to each child individually, together with two verbal subtests (vocabulary and comprehension) from the Stanford Binet Intelligence Scales (Thorndike *et al.*, 1986). The group mean age at test was 44 months ($SD = 25$ days). The sample included 61 MZ twin-pairs and 58 DZ twin-pairs. Zygosity was determined using a parent questionnaire (adapted for British samples – Goldsmith, 1991) that includes descriptions of the physical similarity of the twins. This method of determining zygosity has been shown to be highly reliable compared to blood testing procedures (Plomin *et al.*, 1991). In addition, the zygosity of 5% of the twins was checked using DNA from cheek cells (all tests confirmed the questionnaire results).

2.2   Experimental tasks

The theory-of-mind task battery included eight false-belief puppet stories (see Figure 1) and two deception tasks. Two of the puppet stories involved an unexpected identity, and children were asked to (i) attribute a false belief to the puppet and (ii) recall their own previous false belief. Two other stories involved either a nice or nasty surprise; here, children were asked to attribute a false belief, and if successful, to predict (and justify) how the puppet felt before discovering the surprise (happy or sad). The remaining four stories involved an unexpected location: in two stories, the contents of a prototypical container (e.g. an eggbox) were revealed to be in a different, unmarked box; in two other stories a puppet moved an object (e.g. a ball) while another puppet was 'off-stage'. In these stories, children were asked either to predict where the puppet with the false belief would search for the object, or to explain why the puppet searched in the mistaken location. If a spontaneous belief-based answer was not forthcoming in the explanation tasks, the prompt, 'What does (puppet) think?' was given. Children passed each test-question only if they also correctly answered control questions designed to check their understanding and recall of the story. Children scored 1 point for each correct response to a maximum of 14 test questions, with a bonus point for spontaneous correct responses on the two explanation questions.

The first deception task involved non-verbal and verbal co-operation and deception (Sodian and Frith, 1992). To win prizes, children had to help a nice puppet (by opening a lockable box, or by telling the puppet the box was open) and deceive a mean puppet (by locking the box or by telling the puppet a lie – that the box was locked). Children scored 2 points for success on all 4 test trials, 1 point if they succeeded in the non-verbal trials only, and 0 points for any other pattern of performance. In the second deception task the child had to guess in which hand the researcher had hidden a coin. After 3 trials, the child was invited to hide the coin in the same way for 3 test trials.

Fig. 3.1 *The 'Sally-Ann' task, illustrating the basic plot of a typical false-belief task*: 1. Sally and Ann in the playroom. 2. Sally places the ball in the basket. 3. Sally leaves the room. 4. Ann moves the ball to the box. 5. Sally returns. Test question: 'Where will Sally look for the ball?' or 'Why is Sally looking in the basket?' (By kind permission of the artist, Axel Scheffler. Reprinted from Frith 1989.)

Children scored 1 point if they successfully hid the coin on one trial, and 2 points if they were successful on at least 2 trials.

2.3   Initial descriptive findings

Together, the tasks provided children with a maximum of 20 points. Task inter-correlations were high (Cronbach's alpha = 0.83). In calculating each child's aggregate score, tasks in which the child failed any control question were excluded, to ensure that success or failure could not be attributed to differences in children's story comprehension or recall. Across the tasks, a total of 11 control questions were asked; over 70% of the sample (167 children) responded correctly to all 11 questions, and only 8% of the sample (20 children) failed 3 or more control questions. Children with missing data on a particular task were also excluded from that task. These missing data were random and infrequent; only 24 out of 238 children were missing any task at all. The theory-of-mind score was calculated by pro-rating children's mean total score, to give an equivalent score out of 20. The group showed wide individual variation in performance (range of scores = 0–19, $M = 7.8$, $SD = 4.5$), and a normal distribution of verbal IQ scores ($M = 107.8$, $SD = 12.7$). The mean verbal IQ score was slightly higher than the population mean, but consistent with the general rise since the last standardisation (Flynn, 1987). Theory-of-mind and verbal IQ scores correlated significantly (r (230) = 0.43, $p < .001$). There were no gender differences in either measure.

2.4   Genetic and environmental influences on theory of mind and verbal ability

Monozygotic (genetically identical) twins showed significantly greater similarity than dizygotic (fraternal) twins in their scores for both theory-of-mind performance and verbal ability (see Figure 3.2a). This contrast indicates significant genetic influence on both domains. As in other studies, shared environmental influence on verbal ability is indicated as well by the relatively high correlation for DZ twins. However, the twin correlations suggest no shared environmental influence for theory-of-mind performance.

Individual scores for theory of mind and verbal ability were then entered into a standard maximum likelihood model-fitting analysis for twin data (Neale and Cardon, 1992), which confirmed conclusions gleaned from the twin correlations (see Figure 3.2a). The results of this analysis (and of subsequent bivariate modelling) are presented in full elsewhere (Hughes and Cutting, 1999), and so here we shall simply summarise the three main findings from these analyses:

A

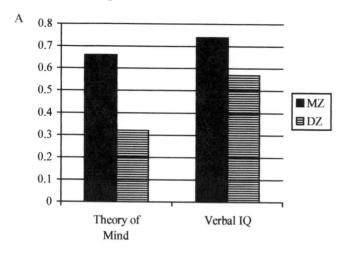

B

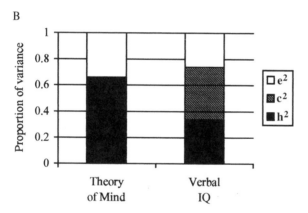

Fig. 3.2 A. Intraclass correlations for identical (MZ) and fraternal twins (DZ), for theory of mind and verbal IQ.
B. Estimates of heritability (h^2), shared environmental variance (c^2), and non-shared environmental variance (e^2), for theory of mind and verbal IQ (based on twin-correlations).

1) Genetic factors accounted for two-thirds of the variance in theory-of-mind scores, and child-specific environmental factors accounted for all the remaining variance (see Figure 3.2b).

2) Most of the genetic influence on theory-of-mind performance was independent of genetic influence on verbal IQ (only a third of the genetic effect on theory-of-mind scores was shared with genetic influence on verbal ability).

3) However, the genetic influences common to both theory of mind and

verbal ability accounted for just over half (53%) of the significant pheno-typic correlation between these domains.

3   Discussion

3.1   *Genes and non-shared environments underlie individual differences in mental-state awareness*

What conclusions can be drawn from the above results? Most importantly, the findings of this study suggest that individual differences in children's understanding of mind are strongly influenced by genetic factors. This may seem surprising, given that most research to date has highlighted the impor-tance of environmental influences on individual differences in early mental-state awareness. However, the finding of strong genetic influences on early mental-state awareness does provide an important bridge between work with typical and atypical populations. Recall that evidence from both indi-viduals with autism and children with Turner's syndrome suggests significant genetic effects on social cognition. The present findings provide a direct demonstration that even *normal* variation in children's under-standing of mind is heavily influenced by genetic factors.

A second conclusion is that future research into environmental influe-nces on individual differences in early mental-state awareness should focus on factors that are likely to have a differential impact on children within the same family. Unlike shared environmental factors (that had only a negligi-ble influence on theory-of-mind scores), non-shared environmental factors of this kind accounted for one-third of the variance in children's theory-of-mind performance.

What factors might make environmental influences child-specific? In other studies, two obvious examples are differences between siblings in age and gender. With regard to age, a recent meta-analysis suggests that it is only *older* siblings that confer an advantage for children's false-belief comprehension: that is, the facilitatory effect of siblings is differentially experienced by younger siblings (Ruffman et al., 1998). In other words, the same factor (sibship size) can have a differential impact on two children in the same family. With regard to gender, it has recently been reported that although boys and girls perform equally well on standard false-belief tasks, girls show more frequent and more developed mental-state talk than boys in their dyadic interactions with friends (Hughes and Dunn, 1998). Once again, the same factor (time spent interacting with a sibling) appears to have quite different influences on children within the same family.

So two plausible sources of non-shared environmental effects are age and gender differences. However, the non-shared environmental effects observed in the present study cannot reflect differences in either age or gender since the sample consisted of pairs of same-sex twins. Yet differential sibling experiences may be especially salient for developments in understanding of mind, since they provide children with powerful evidence of the subjective nature of people's thoughts and feelings. Conversely, individual differences in young children's understanding of mind may magnify the importance of differential sibling experiences, since the impact of a particular event is likely to depend upon how that event is *perceived* by the child. In addition, the understanding that beliefs can be mistaken enables children to become much more sophisticated social partners, and this transformation may in turn exert a powerful influence upon the behaviour of close others, facilitating further developments in the child's understanding of mind. Taken together, these two proposals illustrate an important point. Far from being determinative, genetic effects are probabilistic and operate in concert with environmental influences. In interpreting the results of this study, this type of interplay between genetic and environmental factors should be kept in mind.

The third set of conclusions that arise from the results of the twin study concerns the relation between verbal ability and theory of mind. Consistent with previous findings, individual differences in children's understanding of mind and verbal ability were positively correlated. However, this association has been interpreted in contrasting ways by different researchers. For some, language is a necessary prerequisite for mental-state awareness, either because grammatical structures such as complementation are needed for meta-representation (de Villiers and Pyers, 1997), or because narrative ability is considered a precursor for understanding false belief (Lewis *et al.*, 1994), or because language is the medium through which children acquire a folk-concept of mind (Astington, 1996; Siegal, 1996). For others, the association between false-belief comprehension and verbal ability arises because language acquisition itself depends upon a sensitivity to speakers' intentions; this sensitivity may be an innate characteristic of the infant (Bretherton and Beeghly, 1982; Happé, 1995), or may be shaped by environmental influences, such as the 'mind-mindedness' of the caregiver's interactional style (Meins, 1997). Note that these accounts differ not only in the assumed direction of influence, but also in the relative importance of environmental versus genetic influences on the association between language and theory of mind.

In fact, the results of the twin study reported here demonstrate that about half of the phenotypic correlation between verbal ability and theory of mind is attributable to shared environmental influences, and about half to common genes. Accounts of the association between verbal ability and theory of mind that focus exclusively on either nature or nurture must therefore miss at least half of the story. Note also that although only a third of the genetic effects on theory of mind were implicated in verbal ability, these accounted for half of the phenotypic correlation between these domains. This result mirrors recent findings of general influences of genes in developmental psychopathology. For example, genetic influences on childhood depression appear to show substantial overlap with genetic influences on anxiety (Eley and Stevenson, 1999). As a result, co-morbidities between these disorders (previously assumed to reflect common environmental risk factors) are now thought to result from common genetic factors, with specific environmental stressors influencing the exact nature of the disorder (Eley, 1997). A similar account may be appropriate for our understanding of the positive association between verbal ability and theory of mind. Links between these domains probably stem from common genes and shared environment, whilst dissociations reflect significant non-shared environmental factors, as well as specific genetic influences.

3.2   Genetic and environmental influences on the 'modularity' of mind-reading

A final question for this chapter concerns the implications of the twin results for the issue of 'modularity' in mind-reading. The concept of modularity has an extremely long history reaching back into classical antiquity, but it was popularised by nineteenth-century phrenologists. Later neuropsychological studies highlighted the plasticity of the brain (e.g. Lennenberg, 1967), and so the simple mapping between function and brain location proposed by these early modularists fell into disfavour. However, recent advances in neuropsychology and neuroimaging have set the path for more refined accounts of modularity, and these accounts have gained rapid ground in current cognitive neuropsychology.

Theoretically, a seminal influence upon the new generation of research into modular processes is Marr's (1982a) classic study of 3D-visual perception. Marr argued that it would make evolutionary sense if cognitive processes were composed of mutually independent components, in order that small improvements could be made in one part of the cognitive system without affecting the remaining parts. This simple idea was developed further by Fodor (1983) in his elaboration of the defining characteristics of a cognitive module. According to Fodor, the most important of these are that cognitive modules show mandatory processing, are innately defined, function independently from each other and accept only specific types of input. Each of these characteristics has been questioned by various cognitive neuropsychologists, so that the concept of modularity is now much broader than in Fodor's original definition.

From the viewpoint of this chapter, the most salient challenge concerns the question of whether cognitive modules are necessarily innate. In defence of the strong Fodorian view of 'modular beginnings', Frith and Happé

(1998) have recently argued that early mental-state awareness depends upon an innately specified dedicated cognitive mechanism. According to this model, genes influencing early mental-state awareness are expected to be largely independent from genes affecting other cognitive abilities. That is, mental-state awareness is held to display *genetic modularity*.

In contrast, Karmiloff-Smith (1992; 1998) has proposed that its development involves a process of gradual modularisation, so that modules could become established and emerge over time. From this perspective, functionally distinct modules may share common genetic influences. Multivariate twin studies allow one to examine the extent to which different traits are influenced by the same genes (i.e. their 'genetic correlation'). In fact, numerous behavioural genetic investigations have shown that quite disparate cognitive abilities show common genetic influences, such that the differentiation of cognitive systems appears to be driven primarily by environmental factors (see Petrill, 1997, for a review). In this chapter we shall call this account the *environmental modularity* hypothesis.

Common genetic influences are also predicted from the *domain-general* accounts of the processes underlying the development of mental-state awareness proposed by researchers such as Frith and Happé (1998). According to this domain-general view (and unlike the predictions from the emergent modularity model) strong phenotypic correlations are also expected between mental-state awareness and other cognitive abilities. Genetically sensitive designs such as a twin study enable one to examine associations at both genetic and phenotypic levels, and so offer a unique opportunity for evaluating competing hypotheses concerning the modularity (or otherwise) of mind-reading.

That is, identifying unique genetic influences upon children's false-belief comprehension would support the view that 'mind-reading' is underpinned by an innately determined dedicated cognitive system. Conversely, if individual differences in children's understanding of mind and verbal ability overlap significantly, then both the domain-general and gradual modularisation views of mental-state awareness would be strengthened. The relative merits of these accounts can then be compared by examining phenotypic associations between false-belief performance and verbal ability.

What implications do the results of the present twin study carry for competing accounts of the modularity of mind-reading? The first point to be made concerns the importance of distinguishing functional modularity from specificity in genetic and environmental influences, since conclusions about dissociations between cognitive domains are fundamentally different from conclusions about the underlying processes. Second, both genetic and environmental factors appear to contribute to dissociations between theory of mind and verbal ability. Looking first at genetic factors, one striking finding was that most of the genetic influences on theory of mind were independent of genetic influences on verbal ability. This independence is consistent with the predictions from the Fodorian 'modular beginnings' account proposed by Frith and Happé (1998). However, as they stand the findings from this study cannot be used to argue for *unique* genetic influences on theory of mind, since many other cognitive characteristics known to show strong associations with false-belief performance (e.g. executive functions such as inhibitory control, working memory and embedded rule-reasoning) were not considered. Moreover, findings from other studies suggest that, as a rule, genetic factors have domain-general influences (see Petrill, 1997). The genetic independence reported here is therefore rather surprising. Investigations that examine the overlap in genetic variance in theory-of-mind performance and in each of these other cognitive abilities are needed before strong conclusions as to the genetic modularity of mind-reading can be drawn.

Turning to environmental influences on modularity, the twin results reported in this chapter highlight the importance of distinguishing between environmental factors that operate uniformly within a family from those that have a differential effect on individual family members, since it is the non-shared, individually experienced environment that appears to play a key role in modularity in cognitive functioning. Recall that non-shared environmental factors accounted for one-third of the variance in theory-of-mind scores, but did not contribute at all to the association between theory of mind and verbal ability. That is, consistent with the alternative model of 'emergent modularity', the child's specific experiences of his or her environment have a differential impact upon functionally distinct cognitive systems and so contribute to the gradual modularisation of cognitive processes.

To conclude, the results of this study suggest major genetic influences on the development of young children's understanding of mind. The findings also indicate an important role for children's unique or non-shared environmental experiences in their theory-of-mind development. Genetic influences on theory of mind appear to be largely independent from genetic influences on verbal IQ, despite the phenotypic correlation between these domains. Taken together, these results suggest that, whilst our genes do not determine our ability to understand and interact with other people, they play a strong role in the development of social understanding, and, via this, may ultimately exert a long-term and pervasive influence on many aspects of our social lives.

In addition to the two authors, the TRACKS team includes: Dr Alex Cutting, Dr Kirby Deater-Deckard, Dr Thomas O'Connor, Dr Stephen Petrill, and Dr Alison Pike. We would also like to thank all the parents and twins who participated in TRACKS.

4   Darwin in the madhouse: evolutionary
     psychology and the classification of mental
     disorders

Dominic Murphy and Stephen Stich

In recent years there has been a ground swell of interest in the application of
evolutionary theory to issues in psychopathology (Nesse and Williams,
1995; Stevens and Price, 1996; McGuire and Troisi, 1998). Much of this
work has been aimed at finding adaptationist explanations for a variety of
mental disorders ranging from phobias to depression to schizophrenia.
There has, however, been relatively little discussion of the implications that
the theories proposed by evolutionary psychologists might have for the
classification of mental disorders. This is the theme we propose to explore.
We'll begin, in section 1, by providing a brief overview of the account of the
mind advanced by evolutionary psychologists. In section 2 we'll explain
why issues of taxonomy are important and why the dominant approach to
the classification of mental disorders is radically and alarmingly unsatisfactory. We will also indicate why we think an alternative approach, based on
theories in evolutionary psychology, is particularly promising. In section 3
we'll try to illustrate some of the virtues of the evolutionary-psychological
approach to classification. The discussion in section 3 will highlight a quite
fundamental distinction between those disorders that arise from the
malfunction of a component of the mind and those that can be traced to
the fact that our minds must now function in environments that are very
different from the environments in which they evolved. This mismatch
between the current and ancestral environments can, we maintain, give rise
to serious mental disorders despite the fact that, in one important sense,
there is nothing at all wrong with the people suffering the disorder. Their
minds are functioning exactly as Mother Nature intended them to. In
section 4, we'll give a brief overview of some of the ways in which the sorts
of malfunctions catalogued in section 3 might arise, and sketch two rather
different strategies for incorporating this etiological information in a
system for classifying mental disorders. Finally, in section 5, we will explain
why an evolutionary approach may lead to a quite radical revision in the
classification of certain conditions. From an evolutionary perspective, we
will argue, some of the disorders recognised in standard manuals like
DSM-IV (American Psychiatric Association, 1994) may turn out not to be

disorders at all. The people who have these conditions don't *have* problems; they just *cause* problems!

1 The evolutionary psychology model of the mind

The model of the mind advanced by evolutionary psychology is built around two central theses which we'll call the *Massive Modularity Hypothesis* and the *Adaptation Hypothesis*. The Massive Modularity Hypothesis maintains that the mind contains a large number of distinct though interconnected information-processing systems – often called 'modules' or 'mental organs'. These modules can be thought of as special-purpose or domain-specific computational mechanisms. Often a module will have proprietary access to a body of information that is useful in dealing with its domain. The information is 'proprietary' in the sense that other modules and non-modular mental mechanisms have no direct access to it.[1] Like other organs, modules are assumed to be innate and (with the possible exception of a few gender-specific modules) they are present in all normal members of the species. Some evolutionary psychologists also assume that there is little or no heritable inter-personal variation in properly functioning mental modules and thus that a given type of module will be much the same in all normal people.[2] Paul Griffiths has dubbed this 'the doctrine of the monomorphic mind'. Both Griffiths and David Sloan Wilson have argued, in our opinion quite persuasively, that this doctrine is very implausible (Wilson, 1994; Griffiths, 1997, sec. 5.5; the point goes back to David Hull, 1989). So, along with Wilson and Griffiths, we will assume that there may be a fair amount of heritable variation in the modules found in the normal population. That assumption will play an important role in section 6, where we argue that some of the conditions that have been classified as mental disorders are not disorders at all.

Since the appearance, in 1983, of Jerry Fodor's enormously influential book, *The Modularity of Mind*, the term 'module' has become ubiquitous in the cognitive sciences. But the sorts of modules posited by the Massive Modularity Hypothesis differ from Fodorian modules in two crucial respects. First, Fodor sets out a substantial list of features that are characteristic of modules, and to count as a Fodorian module a mental

[1] For a much more detailed discussion of the Massive Modularity Hypothesis see Samuels (1998a and this volume).
[2] Tooby and Cosmides, who are among the leading advocates of evolutionary psychology, defend this 'psychic unity of mankind' in numerous places including their 1990a, 1990b and 1992.

mechanism must have most or all of these features to a significant degree. For Fodor, modules are:
    i. informationally encapsulated
    ii. mandatory
    iii. fast
    iv. shallow
    v. neurally localised
    vi. susceptible to characteristic breakdown
    vii. largely inaccessible to other processes.
The notion of a module invoked in the Massive Modularity Hypothesis is much broader and less demanding. Evolutionary psychologists count as a module any domain-specific computational device that exhibits (i) and (vii), and occasionally even these restrictions are not imposed. The second important way in which Fodorian modules differ from the sorts of modules envisioned by the Massive Modularity Hypothesis is that, for Fodor, modules only subserve 'peripheral' mental processes – those responsible for perception, language processing and the production of bodily movements. Evolutionary psychologists, by contrast, expect to find modules subserving a wide range of other, more 'central' cognitive and emotional processes.

The Adaptation Hypothesis, the second central theme in evolutionary psychology, claims that mental modules are *adaptations* – they were, as Tooby and Cosmides have put it, 'invented by natural selection during the species' evolutionary history to produce adaptive ends in the species' natural environment' (Tooby and Cosmides, 1995, p. xiii). To serve as a reminder of the fact that the modules posited by evolutionary psychology are adaptations, and to distinguish them from Fodorian modules, we will sometimes call them *Darwinian modules*.

The picture of the mind that emerges from the conjunction of the Massive Modularity Hypothesis and the Adaptation Hypothesis is nicely captured by Tooby and Cosmides in the following passage:

[O]ur cognitive architecture resembles a confederation of hundreds or thousands of functionally dedicated computers (often called modules) designed to solve adaptive problems endemic to our hunter-gatherer ancestors. Each of these devices has its own agenda and imposes its own exotic organisation on different fragments of the world. There are specialised systems for grammar induction, for face recognition, for dead reckoning, for construing objects and for recognising emotions from the face. There are mechanisms to detect animacy, eye direction, and cheating. There is a 'theory of mind' module . . . . a variety of social inference-modules . . . . and a multitude of other elegant machines. (Tooby and Cosmides, 1995, p. xiv)

There are two points that we would add to this colourful account. First, these functionally dedicated computers are linked together in complex networks. The output of one module will often serve as the input (or part of the input) for one or more modules that are 'downstream.' Second, there is

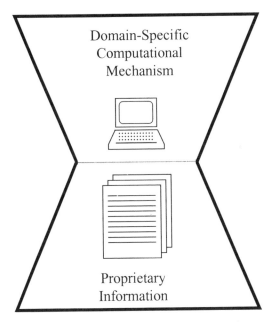

Fig. 4.1 Darwinian modules are adaptations that can be thought of as special purpose or domain-specific computational devices which often have proprietary access to a body of information that is useful in dealing with their domain.

no reason to suppose that *all* of the mechanisms to be found in the mind are plausibly viewed as modular. In addition to the swarm of modules, the evolutionary psychology model of the mind can accommodate computational devices that are not domain specific, stores of information that are not proprietary, and a variety of other sorts of mechanisms. Figure 4.2 is a sketch of the sort of mental architecture posited by evolutionary psychology. Figure 4.3 is a close-up of part of the system portrayed in Figure 4.2.

2   The taxonomy crisis: what's wrong with the DSM approach, and why taxonomy matters

In 1964, Carl Hempel thought it very likely 'that classifications of mental disorders will increasingly reflect theoretical considerations' (1964, p. 150). Hempel was a first-class philosopher but an unreliable prophet; the last thirty years have seen the old psychoanalytically based paradigm replaced by an approach to classification which aims to be 'operationalised', 'a-theoretical' and 'purely descriptive'.[3] Among the most notable products of this

---

[3] McCarthy and Gerring (1994) is a good brief history.

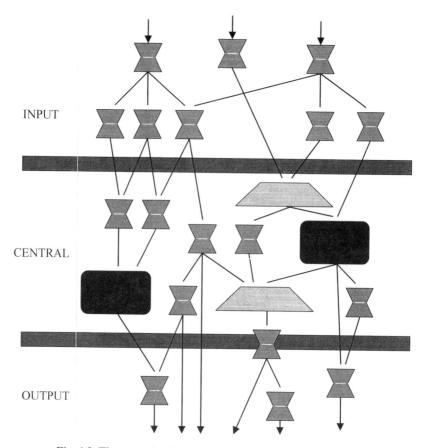

Fig. 4.2 The mental architecture posited by evolutionary psychology includes networks of Darwinian modules subserving central cognitive and emotive processes as well as peripheral processes.

approach are DSM-III and its successors DSM-IIIR and DSM-IV (American Psychiatric Association, 1980, 1987, 1994). DSM categories are typically specified by providing a list of sufficient conditions (often disjunctive and with an occasional necessary condition thrown in) stated almost exclusively in the language of 'clinical phenomenology' which draws heavily on folk psychological concepts and proto-scientific clinical concepts (like self-esteem, delusion, anxiety and depressed mood). The classification systems set out in DSM-III and its successors play a central role in guiding research and clinical practice in the United States and, to a lesser extent, in other countries as well. Moreover, as Poland *et al.* note (1994, p. 235), 'DSM categories play pivotal roles in financing mental health care, maintaining hospital and clinical records, administering research funds, and

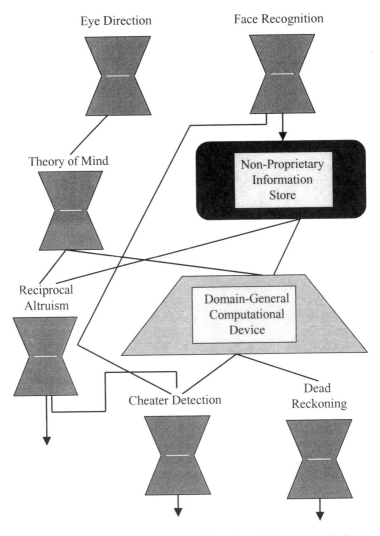

Fig. 4.3 In addition to Darwinian modules, the evolutionary psychology
model of the mind can accommodate computational mechanisms that are
not domain specific and stores of information that are not proprietary.

organising educational materials . . . concerned with psychopathology.'
Poland and his colleagues go on to claim – and we agree – that the DSM
approach 'is deeply flawed and not doing the work it should be doing' and
that as a result, the current situation regarding the classification of mental
disorders 'involves a crisis' (p. 255).

According to Poland *et al.*, a classification scheme in psychopathology has two primary purposes. It should enhance the effectiveness of clinical activity, and it should facilitate scientific research concerned with psycho-pathology and its treatment. The DSM approach, they argue, does neither. Though Poland and his colleagues offer a number of reasons for their deeply sceptical and rather disquieting conclusion, we think that one of these is central. The DSM approach is alleged to be a-theoretical, thus allowing clinicians from different theoretical backgrounds to agree on a diagnosis. But in fact the DSM approach is far from a-theoretical. Rather, it embraces the highly problematic theory that there exist, in the domain of psychopathology, a substantial number of what Poland *et al.* call 'syndromes with unity'. These are clusters of associated attributes, character-ised in the folk psychological and proto-scientific language of clinical phenomenology

that exhibit such dynamic characteristics as typical course, outcome and responsiveness to treatment, and that are related to underlying pathological condi-tions and etiological factors of development (e.g. genetic and environmental factors). . . . [T]he operationally defined categories within the DSM system are sup-posed to be *natural kinds* with a characteristic causal structure (i.e. a core pathol-ogy) that underwrites the various lawful regularities characteristic of the disorder (e.g. association of criterial features, dynamic properties of the syndrome). (Poland *et al.*, p. 241)[4]

The problem with all of this is very simple: the theory is false. Though there may be a few syndromes with unity in psychopathology, it is unlikely that there are very many. One reason for this is the all but exclusive reliance on the concepts and categories of clinical phenomenology to characterise syn-dromes. These concepts are notoriously vague, imprecise and unquantified. Moreover, since highly subjective judgements about their application to a particular case must typically be made in emotionally charged settings in which hidden agendas abound, these judgements are often biased. By limit-ing the data gathered in diagnosis to the salient and easily identifiable signs and symptoms of clinical phenomenology, the DSM scheme fails to attend to a wide range of other data about mental functioning that can be gathered by psychometric techniques and by methods used in cognitive science and neuroscience.

   Another, closely related, reason to think that there are relatively few psychopathological syndromes with unity is the fact that the DSM

---

[4] Some advocates of the DSM approach would grant that many currently recognised DSM classifications fail to pick out natural kinds, though they expect that with more research, based on existing assumptions, operationally defined DSM-style diagnoses will converge on natural kinds. The basic 'syndromes with unity' theory is assumed to be correct and in need of more empirical elaboration, rather than conceptual overhaul. See, for example, Goodwin and Guze (1995).

approach to classification is not guided by any theory about the structure and functioning of normal minds and makes no attempt to uncover and use facts about the underlying psychological, biological and environmental mechanisms and processes that give rise to symptoms. Imagine for a moment trying to construct a classification system for malfunctions in some complex and well-engineered artefact which is built from numerous carefully designed components – a television set, perhaps, or a computer network. Imagine further that the classification system must be based entirely on clusters of user-salient symptoms, without any inkling of how the mechanism was designed to operate and without any theory about its component parts and their functions. The result, almost certainly, would be a set of categories that are *massively heterogeneous* from the point of view of someone who understands how the system works. It would classify together problems which are caused by totally different underlying mechanisms or processes and which require totally different remedies. It would also fail to classify together problems with the same underlying cause (and requiring the same remedy) if they manifest themselves in different ways under slightly different conditions. This, near enough, is just what we should expect in a DSM-style classification of mental disorders. For surely the mind, too, is a complex and well-engineered system in which many well-designed components interact.[5] Thus, as Poland and his colleagues conclude:

It appears *unlikely* that the domain of psychopathology is best conceived of in terms of syndromes with unity or that natural kinds will be discovered at the level of clinical phenomenology. There is simply no reason to suppose that the features of clinical phenomenology that catch our attention and are the source of great human distress are also features upon which a science of psychopathology should directly focus when searching for regularities and natural kinds. Human interests and saliencies tend to carve out an unnatural domain from the point of view of nomological structure. Hence the relations between the scientific understanding of psychopathology and clinical responsiveness to it may be less direct than is commonly supposed. In insisting that classification be exclusively focused on clinical phenomenology, DSM not only undermines productive research but also undermines the development of effective relations between clinical practice and scientific understanding. (Poland *et al.*, p. 254)

[5] This heterogeneity in DSM classifications is magnified by the fact that actual DSM categories often group together very different symptom profiles as manifestations of the same disorder. Thus, for example, according to the DSM criteria, one can qualify as having a Major Depressive Episode even though one does not experience a depressed mood, provided that one does exhibit a markedly diminished interest in daily activities (DSM-IV, p. 327). And by one reckoning, there are fifty-six different ways to satisfy the criteria for Borderline Personality Disorder! (Clarkin *et al.*, 1983.) As one might expect, these heterogeneous categories are poor predictors of the patients' future trajectory or of their response to treatment, and thus the vast majority of DSM categories remain 'unvalidated'.

The remedy that Poland *et al.* propose is one that we strongly endorse. There is a need for a new approach to the classification of mental disorders that is 'based on a more intimate relationship with basic science than is DSM' (p. 255). In trying to construct this new taxonomy, a natural first step is to ask: *which science or sciences are the appropriate ones?* We don't think there is any single right answer to this question. Many sciences can contribute to the construction of a taxonomy that will serve the needs of clinical practice and scientific research into the causes and treatments of mental disorders. But it is our contention that evolutionary psychology has a natural and quite central role to play in this scientifically based reconstruction of the classification system for mental disorders. Evolutionary psychology, as we have seen, seeks to explain how the mind works by characterising the many computational mechanisms from which it is constructed and attempting to discover the function for which these mechanisms were designed. That sort of account of the mind and its working looks to be just what is needed if we are to take seriously the analogy with a malfunctioning well-engineered artefact. Of course evolutionary psychology is not alone in viewing the mind as made up of lots of components that were designed by natural selection. Neuroscience, at various levels of analysis from the molecular to the computational, takes much the same view. And while we certainly don't want to deny that these sciences will be of enormous importance in working toward a new taxonomy, it is our prediction that, in the short run at least, classifications based on evolutionary psychological theories will be particularly useful for clinicians, since they will be at a level of analysis that meshes comfortably with current clinical practice.

Our goal in the remainder of this chapter is to make this prediction plausible. To do this we propose to explore some of the problems that might befall a mind that is structured in the way sketched in section 1 and that contains some of the mechanisms posited by evolutionary psychologists. In many cases, as we shall see, those problems offer plausible explanations for the sorts of troubling symptoms that manuals like DSM-III and its successors take to indicate the presence of a mental disorder. However, it will often be the case that the classification suggested by evolutionary psychological theories recognises several distinct disorders where current diagnostic manuals see only one. Thus there is reason to hope that a classification system that takes account of theories in evolutionary psychology will begin to reduce the massive heterogeneity that plagues DSM-style classifications. Another virtue of taxonomising disorders along the lines suggested by evolutionary psychology is that it pulls apart two very different sorts of disorders: those in which components of the mind are malfunctioning and those attributable to a mismatch between the environment in which we live and the environment in which we were designed to live. A third virtue of the evolutionary-psychological approach is that it provides a clear theoretical framework in which we can ask one of the most vexing questions that the study of psychopathology must face: what conditions count as disorders at all?[6]

Before setting out our taxonomic proposals we should stress that evolutionary psychology is still very much in its infancy, and the theories about mental mechanisms that we will invoke are all both speculative and controversial. We don't pretend to be offering a set of diagnostic categories that mental health professionals might use in preference to those in DSM-IV. Rather, our aim is to begin to explore the ways in which evolutionary psychology can contribute to the elaboration of a taxonomy of the sort that Poland *et al.* advocate – one that is 'based on a more intimate relationship with basic science.'

3   A taxonomy of disordered minds

The range of symptoms recognised by modern diagnoses is very broad. To begin with there are cognitive symptoms with highly salient phenomenologies, such as delusions and unwelcome or obsessive thoughts. There are also feelings of 'thought disorder', in which patients report thinking someone else's thoughts or having their own thoughts controlled by another. Other cognitive symptoms include such incapacities as the amnesias, agnosias and aphasias. Then we have behavioural problems, including voluntary patterns of antisocial action and involuntary problems such as drug dependence, motor retardation, sleep disorders and disruptions to the autonomic nervous system like irregular heartbeat. There are also more intuitively qualitative symptoms; some of these are relatively prolonged, such as low affect ('feeling blue'), and others are transitory, such as dizziness, nausea and feelings of anxiety. So there are a great many kinds of symptoms to explain. The exciting thing about evolutionary psychology is the theoretically motivated range of explanatory resources it brings to bear on all this diverse symptomatology.

---

[6] For reasons that we'll set out in section 6, we are inclined to think that this is best understood as a *pair* of questions: namely, (i) What conditions count as *mental disorders*? and (ii) What conditions count as *problems that may beset an evolved mind (or 'E-M problems' as we'll sometimes say)*? The category of mental disorders, we'll argue, is a subset of the category of E-M problems. The taxonomy that we are about to sketch, in section 4, should be read as an account of the broader category – the category of E-M problems, though for ease of exposition we propose not to emphasise the distinction until section 6.

The evolutionary perspective enables us to make a number of important distinctions among problems that may lead to symptoms of mental disorder. The most theoretically interesting and novel of these is the distinction between problems which are internal to the person and problems which lie in the environment surrounding the person. This marks the first major break in our taxonomy.

Problems which are internal to the person are what we commonly think of when we envisage mental disorders. The official orthodoxy, enshrined in DSM-IV, views mental illness as Janus-faced, with socially disvalued or disabling symptoms being produced by an underlying *malfunction*. (The extent to which this conception is honoured in the discussion of particular disorders is another matter – Wakefield, 1997.) However, it is important to recall that the evolutionary perspective on the mind stresses that our psychological mechanisms originated in a past environment, and although those mechanisms may have been adaptive in that past environment, it is entirely possible that the environment has changed enough to render aspects of our cognitive architecture undesirable or obsolete in the modern world. We will discuss this in more detail below. To begin with, though, we'll focus on cases of disorders which are internal to the person.

3.1   Disorders within the person

As we've seen, the evolutionary-psychology model recognises several different sorts of mental structures – modules, stores of non-proprietary information, computational devices that are not domain specific, and pathways along which information can flow from one mechanism to another – and since all of these can break down in various ways, the model will admit of a number of different sorts of disorders. However, since Darwinian modules are the most prominent structures in the evolutionary-psychology model it is natural to begin our taxonomy of disordered minds with them. The most obvious sort of difficulty that can beset a mind like the one depicted in Figures 4.2 and 4.3 is that one of the modules can behave problematically, producing output which directly or indirectly leads to the symptoms on which diagnoses of mental disorder depend.

There are two very different reasons why a Darwinian module may produce such symptoms, and this distinction generates a first major divide in within-person cases. Sometimes when a Darwinian module generates problematic output the trouble is *internal* to the module – its special-purpose computer is malfunctioning or its proprietary store of information is not what it should be (or both). In other cases the problem will be *external* to the module. In these cases something has gone amiss earlier on in the causal network and 'upstream' in the flow of information, with the result that the module which is producing problematic output is being given *problematic input*. In the colourful language of computer programmers, 'garbage in, garbage out'.

3.1.1   Disorders resulting from module-internal problems: some examples

Perhaps the best known example of a disorder which has been much studied as a case of modular breakdown is autism (Baron-Cohen *et al.*, 1985; Leslie, 1987, 1991; Frith, 1989; Leslie and Thaiss, 1992; Baron-Cohen, 1995). Recent work has suggested that autism is best explained as a breakdown in the module or system of modules that handle 'theory-of-mind', the capacity of all normal adults to attribute intentional states like beliefs and desires to other people and to explain their behaviour in terms of the causal powers of beliefs and desires. One widely used test of whether a person has a normal adult theory-of-mind module is the ability to pass the false-belief task, at which autistic children are spectacular failures.[7] They do worse at the false-belief task than do children with Down's Syndrome, even though in general their grasp of causal cognition exceeds the latter's (Baron-Cohen *et al.*, 1986). Some people diagnosed with Asperger's Syndrome – high functioning autistic people whose IQs are normal or higher – have offered quite moving accounts of their puzzlement when they realised how much more normal people seemed to know about what others were thinking in social situations. One example, made famous by Oliver Sacks, is Temple Grandin's comment that her social experience in adolescence was like being 'an anthropologist on Mars' (Grandin and Scariano, 1986; Frith, 1989; Sacks, 1995).

A similar explanation in terms of a broken module occurs in Blair's discussion of psychopathy. Three core features in the characterisation of psychopathy are (i) early onset of extremely aggressive behaviour; (ii) absence of remorse or guilt; and (iii) callousness and a lack of empathy. Blair (1995) explains psychopathic behaviour as due to the absence or malfunctioning of a module which he calls the *violence inhibition mechanism* (VIM). The central idea was borrowed from ethology, where research had long suggested the existence of a mechanism which ended fights in response to a display of submission. A well-known example is the canine tendency to

---

[7] False-belief tasks are intended to evaluate whether or not experimental subjects understand when someone might hold a false belief. One standard version of the task – sometimes called the 'Sally-Ann Task'– involves watching Sally put a piece of chocolate in one place (location A) and later, while Sally is away, Ann moving the chocolate elsewhere (location B). The subject is then asked 'Where will Sally look for her chocolate?' In order to answer this question correctly, the subject needs to appreciate that, since Sally was absent when her chocolate was moved from A to B, she will have the false belief that it is at A (Baron-Cohen, 1995, p. 70).

bare the throat when attacked by a stronger conspecific. The assailant then ceases the attack, rather than taking advantage of the opportunity to press it home. Blair hypothesises that a similar mechanism exists in humans, activated by the perception of distress in others. When the VIM is activated it causes a withdrawal response which people experience as aversive. Following Mandler, Blair suggests that this aversive experience is one of the building blocks for such moral emotions as guilt and remorse.

On Blair's account, the VIM acquires new triggers via classical conditioning. Since engaging in aggressive activity will often lead the victim to exhibit distress cues, aggressive activity becomes a conditioned stimulus for the aversive response. Distress cues are also typically paired with the construction of a mental representation of the victim's suffering, and as a result these thoughts also become triggers for the VIM. This linkage, Blair maintains, is a crucial step in the development of empathy. Since psychopaths do not have a properly functioning VIM, they do not experience the effects of their violence on others as aversive, and this explains why psychopathy is associated with an increase in violent tendencies at an early age. Their deficit does not lead psychopaths to become aggressive, but when they do, they are much less inclined to stop. Blair's model also explains why psychopaths fail to develop the moral emotions and fail to experience any empathic response to the suffering of others. The most intriguing part of Blair's theory is his argument that people lacking a properly functioning VIM would not be able to recognise the distinction between moral transgressions which cause other people to suffer and other social transgressions which do not. This prediction was confirmed in a study comparing the moral cognition of psychopathic murderers with the moral cognition of murderers who were not diagnosed as psychopaths.

Since the publication of Robert Trivers' seminal paper on reciprocal altruism (Trivers, 1971), the capacity to engage in reciprocal exchanges has played an important role in the thinking of socio-biologists and evolutionary psychologists. More recently a number of theorists, including Cosmides, Tooby and Gigerenzer, have argued that this capacity is subserved by a module or a cluster of modules designed to compute what is and is not required in reciprocal exchange arrangements and to detect 'cheaters' who fail to reciprocate (Cosmides, 1989; Cosmides and Tooby, 1992; Gigerenzer and Hug, 1992). If the module that computes what is required in reciprocal altruism malfunctions, the likely result will be that the module's owner will systematically misunderstand what is expected in co-operative behaviour and reciprocal exchanges. Such a person might regularly over-estimate the value or importance of his own contribution in a reciprocal relationship and/or regularly under-estimate the value or importance of the other party's contribution.[8] From the point of view of the person with a malfunctioning reciprocal altruism module (though not from the point of view of those he interacts with), he would be regularly exploited or cheated in social exchanges, and this might well lead him to avoid social interaction and to be in a depressed mood for extended periods.

In an important series of publications, McGuire and his colleagues have argued that this sort of malfunction may be a central factor in many individuals who fit the DSM criteria for dysthymia, which is an affective disorder characterised by persistent depressed mood for over two years, but without major depressive or manic episodes. In one study, McGuire and his colleagues found that dysthymic patients had a notable deficit in their ability to achieve social goals and carry out simple social tasks. They tended to blame others for their dissatisfactions, rather than considering their own behaviour (as did a matched control group.) Dysthymic patients were also less likely than controls to interact socially with others. Perhaps the most striking finding of the study was that dysthymic subjects 'believed that they helped others *significantly more* than they were helped by others. Thus, by their own reckoning, they were co-operators.' However, 'a detailed analysis of their social interactions, which involved collecting data from siblings or friends, strongly suggested otherwise'. Subjects with dysthymic disorder 'not only tended to exaggerate their helpfulness to others, but they also downplayed the value of others' help . . . In addition, they were sceptical of others' intentions to help as well as to reciprocate helping that [they] might provide. For the majority of [dysthymic subjects], these views began *prior* to adolescence . . .' (p. 317).

A defective module (or 'algorithm') for computing what is expected or required in reciprocal relations is not the only sort of defect that might lead dysthymic persons to exaggerate their own helpfulness and downplay the helpfulness of others. Though the basic principles of reciprocal exchange may be universal, the value of specific acts varies enormously from culture to culture. In one culture giving your neighbour a hot tip on a stock counts as a valuable favour, while paying a shaman to chant secret prayers for his child who is down with the flu does not. In other cultures this pattern is reversed. A person who had failed to master the local culture's value system might well end up thinking that he helped others vastly more than they helped him. It is plausible that information about the value that one's culture assigns to various actions is not proprietary to any given module,

---

[8] Of course, the mere fact that the reciprocal altruism module malfunctions does not entail that a person will over-value his own contribution and under-value the other party's. Various other patterns are possible. And if the first pattern is typical, some further explanation is needed for this fact.

but is stored in a location to which many mental mechanisms have access. If that is right, then dysthymia may be a heterogeneous category since the tendency of dysthymic people to misunderstand reciprocity relationships might have two quite different causes. This suggests an intriguing hypothesis. Suppose that some people diagnosed as dysthymic have defective reciprocal altruism modules, while others have normal modules and have simply failed to master the prevailing principles of social value. If so, it might well be the case that this latter group, but not the former, could be treated effectively by a regimen of cognitive psychotherapy that sought to inculcate the social codes they have failed to internalise.

In the preceding cases we have focused on modules for whose existence we have some independent empirical or theoretical support. Some of the symptoms that characterise the disorders we've considered are those we would expect when these modules malfunction. Indeed, in the case of autism the clinical data have been taken to provide important additional support for the hypothesis that a theory-of-mind module exists. Especially noteworthy in this connection is the double-dissociation evidence provided by studies of Williams' Syndrome patients (Karmiloff-Smith *et al.*, 1995; Bellugi *et al.*, 1997). For the reasons set out in section 3, it is probably unwise to expect the fit between hypothetical mechanisms and currently recognised symptomatologies to be too exact. In some cases – autism is one – the hypothesised modular deficit does not generate all the symptoms which current clinical thinking takes to characterise the disorder. In these cases there are at least the following two possibilities when it comes to mapping the diagnosis onto the architecture. In many cases the full suite of recognised symptoms is not necessary for the diagnosis at all – a subset of the recognised symptoms will do. When it comes to relating the current diagnosis to our mental architecture, we can isolate a broken module which might explain a subset of the symptomatology which is sufficient for diagnosis. Further clusters of symptoms could be due to other causes. In such cases it is possible that what we are dealing with is actually several disorders, represented by the different sets of symptoms which are currently thought to be variant forms of one disorder. This is the first possibility we have in mind. These different conditions might co-occur due to a common cause which disrupts several mechanisms. The second possibility is that this co-occurrence is more coincidental, and that the different disorders sometimes just happen to occur together. Since the DSM categories are not validated, it probably happens quite often that DSM picks out symptom clusters that are not in fact all that reliably linked with one another. It is even possible that the cause of some of the unexplained symptoms may not be a disorder at all. They may, for example, just represent the stress of being in treatment for a different condition, or be responses to what are termed 'problems in living.' Evolutionary psychology offers a model of the mind which allows us to disentangle one set of symptoms from the wider collection and recognise it as a distinct condition.

Though the modules that have played a role in our discussion thus far are ones which we have non-clinical reasons for recognising, there have been cases, especially in the neuropsychological literature, in which the discovery of particular deficits has led investigators to argue for the presence of specialised systems or modules in the mental architecture. For example, dorsal simultanagnosics can recognise the spatial relations among parts of an object but are unable to compute the spatial relations between objects. This suggests that there are separate systems underlying these two forms of spatial perception (Farah, 1990). It is noteworthy that in this case the symptoms that led to a hypothesis about the underlying mechanism are not among the standard items of clinical phenomenology that loom so large in DSM-III and its successors. Indeed, for a variety of historical and practical reasons, the agnosias, amnesias and aphasias are not even in DSM-IV as conditions, although some of their characteristic symptoms are.

3.1.2   Disorders resulting from upstream problems in the cognitive system

As we noted earlier, when a module behaves problematically, there can be two very different sorts of reasons. In some cases, the module itself is to blame. In other cases, the trouble is further upstream. Many modules receive input from other modules, so it will often be the case that if an upstream module is malfunctioning, one or more of the modules to which it is supposed to provide information will also produce output that yields symptoms of mental disorder. If the broken upstream module provides information to several separate downstream systems, an upstream problem can result in several quite different clusters of symptoms (see Figure 4.4). The possibility that a single malfunctioning module may cause several other modules to produce problematic outputs may provide a partial explanation for the very high rate of comorbidity that is found in psychiatric patients. A lot of people have more than one disorder at the same time. The National Comorbidity Survey concluded that 'more than half of all lifetime disorders occurred in the 14% of the population who had a history of three or more comorbid disorders' (Kessler et al., 1994).[9]

Our picture does not mandate that if one module feeds information to another it must always be the case that the second will produce problematic

---

[9] It is worth stressing that this is only one sort of explanation for comorbidity, even at the architectural level. For example, if there are domain-general systems, then if these systems are damaged we might get a general reduction of functioning which causes problems in several areas.

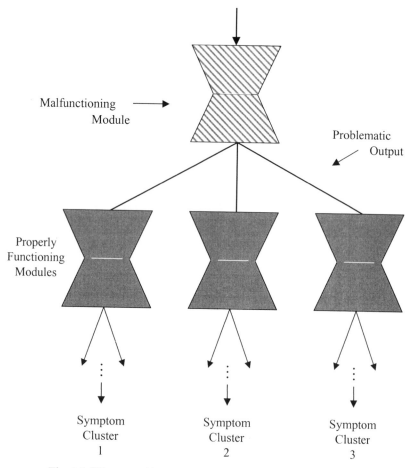

Fig. 4.4 When a malfunctioning module provides information to several separate downstream systems, the upstream problem can result in several quite distinct clusters of symptoms.

output as a result of a breakdown in the first. There are typically several ways in which a single module can malfunction, and each of these is a matter of degree. So it may happen that a malfunction upstream produces problems in a second module in some people, while in other people it does not. All of this can be iterated for modules which are further downstream. The result is that the profile for a specific patient is likely to be quite complex.

This suggests a way of classifying mental disorders which are internal to the subject. The idea would be that such disorders are to be identified with a chain or network of modules each of which is producing problematic outputs. Those outputs in turn are responsible for a suite of symptoms that is characteristic of the disorder. The canonical specification of a disorder would also include, for each module in the network, an indication of whether it is itself broken or whether it is receiving tainted input from elsewhere in the network. This cuts things up rather finely, but it does allow for some important theoretical distinctions. Suppose that two modules are each delivering problematic outputs, but only the first is actually malfunctioning. The second is producing problematic output because it is downstream from the first and is being provided with problematic input. In this case the solution to the problem lies in repairing the upstream module that is the source of the trouble. However, if both modules are malfunctioning then both will have to be repaired if the disorder is to be dealt with. Merely noting that in each case the two modules form the network underlying the disorder is insufficient to direct therapeutic interventions (Figure 4.5).

An example of a disorder which may be caused by problems upstream in the flow of information is the Capgras Delusion. Patients with Capgras believe that someone close to them – typically a spouse – has been replaced by an exact replica. Recent work suggests that part of the explanation for the delusion is that the face recognition system appears to have the structure of an and-gate; it requires two sorts of input. The first sort is the input which is absent in prosopagnosics, who are unable to recognise the faces of close relatives, or even their own face in a mirror. It has been suggested that the mechanism which produces this input is either a template-matching system or a constraint-satisfaction network (Farah, 1990). However, it appears that there is also an affective response needed to underwrite face recognition, a neural pathway that gives the face you see its emotional significance. Only if both these sorts of inputs feed into the face recognition gate does full recognition take place. Several authors have suggested that it is the system subserving this affective response that is disrupted in Capgras patients. As a result, these patients have an experience analogous to seeing an identical twin of one's best beloved. The visual match is there but not the emotional response.

This cannot be the whole story, however. Most of us would think that the trouble lay within ourselves if we started having such an experience. It appears that in Capgras the facial recognition system, getting only one sort of appropriate information, sends this on to more central systems which are also in trouble. Stone and Young (1997) argue that in addition to their agnosia, Capgras' patients have a belief system which is too heavily weighted towards observational beliefs at the expense of background knowledge. Another possibility is that normal subjects have a mechanism which sets an upper boundary on the weirdness of permissible beliefs, and

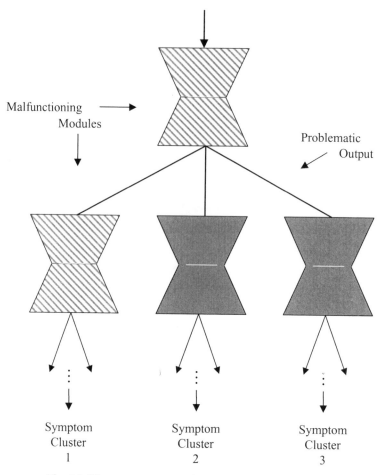

Fig. 4.5 The same symptom clusters can be produced by the malfunction of a single module (as in Figure 4.4) and by the malfunction of two modules. But if two modules are malfunctioning then both will have to be repaired if the disorder is to be dealt with.

that in Capgras subjects this is absent, or at least very permissive. Stone and Young argue that similar combinations of disordered affective response and belief-formation problems may underlie Cotard's Delusion, in which one forms the belief that one is dead. If these speculations are correct, then there is, in Capgras' Delusion, a part of the visual system that is working as designed, but receiving only one of the two sorts of input that it needs and passing its own output on to a central system which is also, perhaps, abnormal.

Since the Darwinian modules posited by evolutionary psychology can utilise input from non-proprietary stores of information, it can also happen that a module produces a problem generating output because the non-proprietary information it needs is incorrect. A clear example of this is one of the hypotheses we have already mentioned – the idea that some dysthymic people may have a normally functioning reciprocal altruism module which is being fed with inappropriate data about the values of various acts in the patient's culture.

3.2   *Disorders that result from an environment different from what*
       Mother Nature intended

Natural selection has no foresight; it is concerned only with what works in the here and now. A central tenet of evolutionary psychology is that the human mind is designed to work in our ancestral, hunter-gatherer environment. Natural selection did not design it for the contemporary world. But, of course, a system may function admirably in one environment and work rather poorly in another. So it is entirely possible that the mind contains modules or other sorts of systems which were highly adaptive in the ancestral environment but which do not lead to functional behaviour in our novel modern environments.

For example, the social competition theory of depression (Price *et al.*, 1994; Nesse and Williams, 1994) is based on the idea that depression is an evolved response to loss of status or to an unsuccessful attempt to gain status. In response to such a loss, it might be adaptive to abandon the strategy you were previously using in your attempts at status enhancement. Similarly, perhaps you should change behaviours if your previous behaviours were tied to reproductive potential you have now lost. The social competition theory claims that depression provides an introspectable marker which indicates when switching strategies to seek another niche is in order. If you are living in a small group, as our ancestors typically did, switching strategies might well result in considerably greater success. Depressed mood is nature's way of telling you to accept that your current behaviour will not improve your reproductive lot and motivating you to try behaving differently. In the circumstances, you should evaluate your behaviour thoroughly, dwelling on the negative.[10] In addition, you might try to

---

[10] There seems to be good evidence that this happens in depression. In a review article, Pyszczynski and Greenberg (1987) found support for the idea that depressed individuals have elevated levels of self-focus and that self-focus increases following a loss in the personal, social or employment spheres. In addition, depressives have elevated levels of 'negative self-complexity' and lowered levels of 'positive self-complexity' (Woolfolk *et al.*, 1995). That is, depressives tend to think of themselves unfavourably in many different ways, and are quite sophisticated at drawing distinctions among different ways of not being terribly good; whereas they think with a very broad brush when assessing themselves in positive terms.

stay out of social situations altogether if you think you lack the resources to do well in them, and indeed we find that 'depressed individuals report being uncomfortable in interactions with others, often perceiving these interactions as unhelpful, or even as unpleasant or negative' (Gottlib, 1992, p. 151).

The social competition hypothesis sees our ancestral communities as miniature ecosystems in which individuals strive to find niches where they can excel and make a good living. In modern societies, though, your chance of excelling – of being the best at anything, or indeed anywhere near the best – are remote. If we have inherited a mechanism which is triggered when we believe ourselves to be outcompeted, then that mechanism will fire frequently as we are inundated with information about accomplished people. But, of course, in the modern world it is far more likely that the mechanism will fail to achieve the goal it was selected to attain. If the mechanism is set off by the realisation that one is not even close to being the best at anything in the global village of the information age then getting depressed is not likely to be an effective reaction. For it is typically the case that there is no other strategy to adopt – no other niche one could fill – which would do significantly better than the present one in that global competition. Moreover, the mechanism will frequently be set off even though its owner is actually doing very well in the *local* environment. You can be the most respected and admired real estate developer in Sioux Falls without being Donald Trump.[11]

The social competition hypothesis is not the only explanation for depression which sees it as a formerly adaptive trait which causes problems in our current environment. The defection hypothesis, proposed by Watson and Andrews (1998), Hagen (1998, MS) and others maintains that in the ancestral environment postpartum depression was an adaptive response which led women to limit their investment in the new child when, because of social, biological or environmental factors, a major investment in the infant would be likely to reduce the total number of offspring produced by that woman during her lifetime who would reach reproductive age and reproduce successfully. Among the social conditions in the ancestral environment that would have been good cues for triggering a sharply reduced

[11] One question often asked about the social competition hypothesis is why it does not entail that just about everyone in modern societies should be depressed, since almost all of us are aware that there are lots of people who are better than us in just about anything that we do. Part of the answer, we think, is that different individuals will have different levels of sensitivity to the cues that trigger this sort of depression. We will say a bit more about individual differences in 'trigger' sensitivity in our discussion of panic disorders at the end of this section. Another factor that might be relevant is that in some important ways modern societies may not be all that different from ancestral communities. For as Dunbar (this volume) has shown, the social networks that individuals maintain in contemporary societies are similar in size to the social networks of individuals in surviving hunter-gatherer communities.

maternal investment would be insufficient investment from the father and/or other appropriate kin. Biological cues would include problems with the pregnancy or birth, or other visible indications that the infant was not likely to be viable and healthy. Environmental cues would include harsh winters, famine conditions and other indications that material resources would be inadequate. In modern societies, with elaborate support systems provided by the state and other organisations, it may be much less likely that these cues are reliable indicators that a mother who 'defects' and sharply reduces her investment in her baby will increase her own reproductive fitness. But there is a growing body of evidence suggesting that these situations are indeed significantly correlated with postpartum depression (Hagen, 1998, MS). So it may be that postpartum depression is yet another example of a condition produced by an adaptive mechanism that is functioning just as it was designed to function, though in an environment that is quite different from the one in which it evolved.[12]

One of the morals to be drawn from these two hypotheses about depression is quite general. The environment in which selection pressures acted so as to leave us with our current mental endowment is not the one we live in now. This means that any mental mechanism producing harmful behaviour in the modern world *may* be fulfilling its design specifications to the letter, but in an environment it was not designed for. In the disorders that result, there is nothing in the mind which is malfunctioning.

Some anxiety disorders provide another possible example of disorders that result from a mismatch between the contemporary environment and the environment in which our minds evolved. Marks and Nesse (1994) note

---

[12] Some theorists have proposed generalising the defection hypothesis to cover many more (perhaps *all*) cases of depression. On this account, the adaptive function of depression is to negotiate a greater investment from other people with whom one is engaged in collective activities when one's own investment seems unlikely to have a positive payoff. Depression, on this view, functions a bit like a labour strike. The depressed person withdraws his or her services in an effort to get a better deal in some co-operative enterprise. It is our view – though at this point it is little more than a guess – that it is counterproductive to seek a single account of the adaptive function of depression. Rather, we suspect, there may be several quite different kinds of depression, each with its own set of triggers and its own characteristic symptomatology. Thus, for example, we noted earlier that Woolfolk *et al.* (1995) found that people who are depressed have elevated levels of 'negative self-complexity'. This is a symptom that makes perfect sense if the episode of depression is triggered by the sort of perceived failure or loss of status that plays a central role in the social competition account of depression. People in that situation need to think hard about what they are doing wrong. But the symptom makes less sense if the episode is triggered by a situation in which an individual's reproductive interests require re-negotiation of the expected levels of investment in a collective activity. It would be very interesting indeed to know whether women suffering from postpartum depression exhibit negative self-complexity. On the pluralistic account of depression that we favour, it would be predicted that episodes of postpartum depression triggered by inadequate paternal and family investment are not marked by high levels of negative self-complexity.

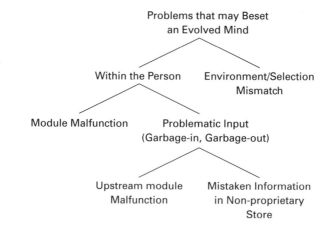

Fig. 4.6 E-M Problems. A taxonomy of the main categories of problems that may beset an evolved mind.

that in the ancestral environment fear of public places and fear of being far from home might well have been adaptive responses 'that guard against the many dangers encountered outside the home range of any territorial species' (p. 251). Similarly, a fear of heights accompanied by 'freezing instead of wild flight' (p. 251) would have had obvious adaptive value to our hunter-gatherer forebears. Moreover these traits, like most traits, could be expected to show considerable phenotypic variation even in a population of individuals who are genotypically identical with respect to the relevant genes. Individuals who are toward the sensitive end of these distributions – those who become anxious more readily when far from home or when they find themselves in high places – might well have functioned quite normally in ancestral environments. In a modern urban environment, however, people who become extremely anxious when they are away from home or when they are in public places will find it all but impossible to lead a normal life. And people who become extremely anxious in high places will find it difficult or impossible to travel in aeroplanes, ride in glass-enclosed elevators or work on the higher floors of modern buildings. Thus, because the modern environment is so different from the ancestral environment, people who are towards the sensitive end of the distribution of phenotypic variation may be incapable of coping with many ordinary situations despite the fact that all of their mental mechanisms are functioning in just the way that natural selection designed them to function.

Figure 4.6 indicates the main categories in our proposed taxonomy of problems that may beset an evolved mind.

4 The causes of disorder

In the previous section we saw how the evolutionary psychology model of the mind suggests a theoretically motivated strategy for classifying mental disorders. We also noted some of the ways in which this taxonomy might prove useful in planning therapeutic interventions. In our taxonomy, the notion of a module malfunction played a central role. In this section we want to consider some of the factors that can *cause* a module to malfunction. The discussion will illustrate some of the ways in which an evolutionary motivated taxonomy of disorders can integrate with a variety of scientifically promising approaches to mental disorder.

When considering the causes of module malfunction, it is, we think, both convenient and theoretically well motivated to distinguish two importantly different kinds of case: (i) those in which a fully developed, normally functioning module begins to malfunction and (ii) those in which, as the result of some problem in the course of development, the module in question never functions in the way that it was designed to. We will consider these two kinds of case in turn.

4.1 How can a normal module become pathological?

Modules are computers and hence require some kind of physical substrate; in human beings, this substrate is the brain. Psychological disturbances may be a result of damage to the brain caused by strokes or injuries or by other kinds of physical trauma. Apperceptive agnosia, for instance, has often been noted in subjects who have undergone carbon monoxide poisoning (Farah, 1990). Various physical disorders can also cause fully developed minds to malfunction. Metabolic disorders which interfere with the synthesis of neurotransmitters are an obvious example. Autoimmune responses of the sort believed to be responsible for Multiple Sclerosis can lead to the demyelination of nerve tissue which slows up the transmission of impulses. Late-onset genetic disorders are still another example. Huntington's disease (a DSM-IV diagnosis) is a late-onset neurodegenerative disorder caused by an abnormally long CAG trinucleotide repeat in a dominant gene close to the tip of chromosome 4.

Earlier we urged adopting the idea that a disorder should be identified with a network of problematic modules. The physiological causes we have just discussed might have implications for more than one network. Indeed cognitive neuropsychology is bedevilled by the problem of understanding how to apportion to their proper diagnoses the variety of symptoms which typically follow one injury to the brain. How should our taxonomy take these causal factors into account? We propose a *two-dimensional* classification of disorders that arise from problems within the person. One dimension is the network of problematic modules, the other dimension is the aetiology of the malfunction – physiological, developmental and so on. It may seem that the two-dimensional approach generates disorders beyond necessity. However, aetiology is always important in medicine, which tends to regard information about causal history as vital to accurate diagnosis. The other possibility is to opt for a *one-dimensional* classification that identifies disorders with a network of problematic modules (and other sorts of mental mechanisms) and to note in addition that some disorders can be caused in quite distinct ways. The two-dimensional picture is richer and probably more in keeping with medical practice generally, but the question whether to adopt a one- or two-dimensional picture should be decided on grounds of utility. Whichever emerges as the more useful approach should be adopted.

4.2   *Problems that can prevent a module from developing properly*

In the last section we briefly considered some of the causes that might lead to a malfunction in a fully developed Darwinian module that was functioning normally to begin with. All of the factors we mentioned – brain damage, stroke, physical trauma, physical disorders and genetic disorders – can also occur in infancy or childhood. However, when a module functions improperly in the course of development, it can lead to a suite of problems that are quite different from the sorts of problems that would arise if the same module were damaged in an adult. One reason for this is that modules may require appropriate input to develop normally. Thus if a downstream module is supposed to be getting input from another module further upstream, and if the upstream module is damaged and fails to provide appropriate input, the downstream module may never develop properly. By contrast, damage to the upstream module in an adult might leave the downstream module unscathed.

In a series of recent publications, Baron-Cohen has proposed a theory of the origin of autism that fits this pattern (Baron-Cohen, 1995; Baron-Cohen and Swettenham, 1996). On Baron-Cohen's account, normal development of the theory-of-mind module (ToMM) requires that three upstream systems be in place: an Intentionality Detector, an Eye Direction Detector, and a Shared-Attention Mechanism. In autism, a variety of biological hazards, most notably prenatal problems, damage the Shared-Attention Mechanism. As a result, the downstream ToMM is deprived of the input it needs to develop properly.

Blair's theory of psychopathy provides another illustration of the way in which a malfunction of one mechanism early in development can prevent other mechanisms from developing properly. In Blair's theory, the Violence Inhibition Mechanism (VIM) generates an aversive affective response to signs of pain or distress, and this response is required if the systems responsible for empathy and for moral emotions such as guilt and remorse are to develop properly. Blair claims that in psychopaths the VIM is absent, due to a physiological deficit or poor socialisation early in development, and as a result young psychopaths never acquire a capacity for empathy and are never able to experience the moral emotions.

There is another reason why module malfunction early in development can lead to problems that are quite different from those that result when a functional adult module is damaged. To see this, we must first explain a distinction between two importantly different sorts of modules. All of the modules that we've considered so far have, as their main function, subserving some capacity which, once in place, will typically remain intact for the rest of a person's life. Following Segal (1996) we will call these *synchronic modules*. However, theorists who advocate a highly modular account of mental architecture also posit a quite different sort of module which, again following Segal, we will call *diachronic modules*. The computational program and proprietary information embedded in some synchronic modules may be largely insensitive to environmental variation. Synchronic modules of this sort will end up with the same program and information in any normal environment. In many other cases, however, natural selection has found methods of exploiting information available in the environment to fine-tune the workings of a synchronic module in a way that would be adaptive in the environment in which our minds evolved. Thus some synchronic modules can develop in a variety of different ways, resulting in adult modules that compute different functions or use different proprietary information. Diachronic modules are one of the mechanisms responsible for this process of fine-tuning. Many diachronic modules function only in development, though others may be operative throughout life. Their job is to monitor the environment and to set the switches and dials of developing synchronic modules in appropriate ways. Perhaps the best-known example of a diachronic module is the Language Acquisition Device (LAD) posited by Chomsky and his followers. Its job is to set the parameters of the Language Competence System thereby determining which of the large number of languages compatible with Universal Grammar the child will come to know. If a diachronic module malfunctions in the course of development, the synchronic module that it services may be set improperly or, in extreme cases, it may not function at all.

Though there is still much research to be done, Specific Language Impairment might well turn out to be a developmental disorder that results from a malfunctioning diachronic module (Gopnik, 1990a, 1990b; Gopnik and Crago, 1991).

In a well-known series of experiments, Mineka *et al.* (1980, 1984, 1989) showed that young rhesus monkeys who have never seen snakes are not afraid of them, though they develop an enduring fear of snakes after only a few observations of another rhesus reacting fearfully to a snake. Rhesus monkeys do not, however, develop fear of flowers when they see another rhesus reacting fearfully to flowers. This suggests that rhesus may have a diachronic module (a Fear Acquisition Device, if you will) whose function it is to determine which of the switches on an innately prepared fear system get turned on. It is entirely possible that humans have a similar Fear Acquisition Device (FAD). If we do, then it may well be the case that some phobias (or some characteristic symptoms of phobias) are caused by a malfunction in the device which toggles an enduring terror of snakes or spiders, say, despite the fact that the person with the phobia has never seen anyone injured or frightened by snakes or spiders. In other cases phobias may arise when a properly functioning FAD is triggered inappropriately. If, for example, a child sees his parent reacting fearfully in response to something that looks like a snake or a spider, he may acquire a phobia even if the parent's fear was feigned or provoked by something else entirely. Still another intriguing possibility is that there are people whose FAD is defective in the other direction; instead of being too active, it is not active enough. These people would fail to develop fears or anxieties that they ought to develop (cf. Marks and Nesse, 1994). They would be unlikely to come to the attention of psychiatrists or clinical psychologists, though they might be more likely to come to the attention of coroners, since the disorder may have a negative impact on their life expectancy.

5   Disorders that may not be

We noted above that the environment, especially the social environment, may change in ways which render well-designed systems pathological. However, an important possibility is that certain forms of what we currently take to be pathology are in fact straightforwardly adaptive in the current environment, just as they were in the ancestral environment in which our minds evolved. To put the point starkly, some people may be designed to be antisocial.

Personality disorders are patterns of experience and behaviour which are culturally very deviant, persistent, inflexible, arise in adolescence or early adulthood and lead to distress or impairment. However, it is not clear that antisocial behaviour of this sort is always bad for the individual who engages in it, rather than the people who are on the receiving end. McGuire *et al.* (1994) suggest that two personality disorders in particular may represent adaptive deviant behavioural strategies. The first, antisocial personality disorder, is characterised by a disregard for the wishes, rights or feelings of others. Subjects with this disorder are impulsive, aggressive and neglect their responsibilities. 'They are frequently deceitful and manipulative in order to gain personal profit or pleasure (e.g. to obtain money, sex or power).' Typically, they show complete indifference to the harmful consequences of their actions and 'believe that everyone is out to "help number one"' (DSM-IV, p. 646).

The second disorder McGuire and his colleagues discuss is histrionic personality disorder. Subjects diagnosed as having this disorder are attention-seeking prima donnas. Often lively and dramatic, they do whatever is necessary to draw attention to themselves. Their behaviour is often sexually provocative or seductive in a wide variety of inappropriate situations or relationships (DSM-IV, p. 655). They demand immediate satisfaction and are intolerant of or frustrated by situations which delay gratification. They may resort to threats of suicide to get attention and coerce better caregiving (DSM-IV, p. 656). Both antisocial and histrionic personality disorders are characterised by manipulativeness, although antisocial subjects manipulate others in the pursuit of material gratification and histrionics manipulate to gain nurture.

Now, on the face of it you might think that being able to manipulate other people so that they nurture you or further your material ends would be quite a useful trait to have, moral qualms aside. And of course one of the more annoying facts about such people is that they don't have moral qualms about their behaviour. That makes it easier for them to commit the sorts of acts which occasionally lead to their arrest or undoing. To be classified as suffering from the relevant personality disorder, people must manifest a pattern of behaviour that involves these undesirable social acts, though to satisfy the diagnostic criteria set out in DSM-IV their behaviour must also 'lead to clinically significant distress or impairment in social, occupational, or other important areas of functioning' (DSM-IV, p. 633). To put the point more colloquially, their behaviour has to get them in trouble. However, it is quite likely that there are many people who are just as unsavoury and manipulative but who do not get in trouble or suffer adverse consequences. It is estimated, for instance, that fewer than 25% of those who commit non-violent crimes are apprehended (McGuire *et al.*, 1994). Such folk may cheat, deceive and manipulate but be good enough at reading social cues and understanding the structure of reciprocal exchange that they can exploit the social system successfully.

The natural way for philosophers to understand the function of a psychological mechanism, according to the conception of the mind we have presented, is in causal-historical terms (Neander, 1991; Millikan, 1993). This influential view construes the function of a psychological unit as the effect it has in virtue of which it is copied in successive generations. Now if it is indeed true that the disorders we have been considering are adaptive strategies, then we can give precisely this causal-historical explanation of the existence of the mechanisms which generate the antisocial behaviour of sociopaths. Antisocial behaviour is the proper function of these mechanisms. That pattern of behaviour enables enough sociopaths to make a good enough living to ensure that antisocial mechanisms are copied in subsequent generations. On the standard causal-historical view of functions, then, the antisocial behaviours of the sociopathic are produced as the proper, selected functions of their peculiar psychological mechanisms. So these people are, in this respect, functioning as they should; they do not have a broken module or any other sort of malfunctioning mental mechanism. Nor is there reason to believe that the environment has changed in relevant ways since the time when the system was selected. The relevant environment in this case is social, and the current social environment, like the ancestral one, offers many opportunities to cheat and exploit one's fellows.

It is true that some sociopathic individuals spend their best reproductive years incarcerated. However, statistically it may be that other things being equal (general intelligence, normal childhood environments and so on) sociopathic behaviour is quite adaptive – it is an effective way of getting one's genes into the next generation. Indeed, a population with a minority of sociopaths may be in an evolutionarily stable state. Skyrms has shown how this is mathematically possible for apparently bizarre strategies such as 'Mad Dog', which rejects a fair division of resources but accepts a grossly unfair one (1996, pp. 29–31); that is, Mad Dogs punish those who play fair. It is not hard to imagine the survival of more complex strategies which unfairly manipulate others.

These strategies will be useful provided two conditions apply. First, the subjects must often be able to disguise their cheating and deception, perhaps by exploiting and mimicking the signals which others use to convey co-operativeness (Frank, 1988). Second, the antisocial behaviours must be maintained at a comparatively low level in the population. If there are too many people who refuse to co-operate and deal fairly with others, then refusing to co-operate will gain one no dividends. We can expect an arms-race as sociopathic cheaters evolve to be even better at exploiting others, and the others evolve to become better at detecting cheaters and avoiding them.[13]

As we suggested earlier (footnote 6), we think there is an important distinction to be drawn between mental disorders and what, for want of a better term, we call *E-M problems* (problems that may beset an evolved mind). To count as an E-M problem, a condition must be located somewhere in the taxonomic structure sketched in Figure 4.6. And having an E-M problem is, we maintain, a *necessary* condition for having a mental disorder. But not all cases of E-M problems are or ought to be counted as mental disorders. Mental disorder is a partly normative notion; to count as a mental disorder a condition must cause problems for the people who have it or for those around them. A brain lesion that disrupts the normal function of some mental mechanism, but whose only enduring result is that those with the lesion develop an intense interest in gourmet food, would produce an E-M problem but not be a mental disorder.[14] In other cases, E-M problems do not count as mental disorders for a variety of historical, social or practical reasons. Thus, as we mentioned earlier, Huntington's disease is a disorder included in DSM-IV, but Multiple Sclerosis is not, nor are various agnosias and aphasias. If, as McGuire and others have suggested, the mechanisms underlying various sorts of personality disorders are adaptations that evolved in environments which were relevantly similar to the modern environment, then people with these conditions do not have E-M problems, and thus, we maintain, *they do not have mental disorders.*

These people are problems, of course. But they are problems to us, and so are lots of other people who do not receive diagnoses of psychopathology. We might perhaps be able to drug them into submission, but that is best viewed as punishment or pre-emptive social control, not therapy. Similarly, if we could devise ways of restructuring their motivational system, it would be inappropriate to call the process 'therapy'. Rather, we should simply recognise that we are trying to manipulate behaviour in the interests of social harmony. Unless we want to medicalise all deviant behaviour, we must acknowledge the possibility that apparently disordered behaviour, which receives a DSM diagnosis, can be produced by a psychological

---

[13] McGuire *et al.* are not the only theorists to have tried explaining a disorder in this way. Mealey (1995) thinks that primary sociopathy or psychopathy is an adaptive strategy. Her account is straightforwardly socio-biological, and, in contrast with Blair's theory, it neglects to go into any detail on cognitive mechanisms (Blair and Morton, 1995). However, the two are not entirely incompatible. Blair thinks that the VIM is missing due to neurological impairment or poor early socialisation. Mealey can be read as offering an alternative reason for the absence of the VIM; some people are just not designed to have one. The developmental consequences might then unfold as Blair envisages. We could treat Mealey as giving the 'ultimate' explanation and Blair the 'proximate' one (Mayr, 1976).

[14] This is not merely a hypothetical case. See Regard and Landis (1997).

endowment functioning exactly as it was designed to, in just the environ-ment it was picked to work in. One of the virtues of the evolutionary approach to psychopathology is that, in some cases at least, it provides a principled way of drawing the distinction between mental disorders and patterns of antisocial behaviour produced by people whose evolved minds are beset by no problems at all.

We are grateful to James Blair, Peter Carruthers, Andrew Chamberlain, Rachel Cooper, Fiona Cowie, Brian Loar, Richard Samuels, David Sloan Wilson, Terry Wilson and Robert Woolfolk for helpful feedback on the ideas developed in this chapter. Earlier versions of the chapter were presented to audiences at the California Institute of Technology, Central Michigan University, the University of California, Santa Cruz, the University of Sheffield, the University of Utah and Washington University. Comments and criticisms from these audiences have proved helpful in many ways.

5   Evolution of the modern mind and the origins of culture: religious concepts as a limiting-case

Pascal Boyer

The human cultural explosion is often explained in terms of 'liberating events', or of a newly acquired flexibility in mental representations. This chapter considers a domain where such flexibility should be maximal, that of religious representations, and shows that actual cultural transmission is in fact constrained by evolved properties of ontological categories and principles. More generally, this suggests that the 'cultural mind' typical of recent human evolution is not so much an unconstrained mind as a mind equipped with a host of complex, specialised capacities that make certain kinds of mental representations likely to succeed in cultural transmission.

1   Introduction

The hallmark of the modern human mind is that it is a *cultural* mind. Humans receive vast amounts of information from cultural elders and peers. They use that information to build conceptual structures, some aspects of which are group-specific and form the basis of what we usually call 'cultures'. What made the modern mind cultural? There are two complementary issues here. One is to describe the evolutionary emergence of cognitive capacities that made (and make) culture possible. Another is to examine how these evolved capacities have a constraining effect on actual human cultures; that is, how they make some cultural trends, and some types of cultural representations, more likely than others to appear in human groups.

In this chapter I suggest that the question of cultural evolution is all too often approached from the first angle only. As a result, we tend to see the appearance of a modern mind as a 'liberating event' whereby conceptual flexibility appeared in cognitive systems that were formerly constrained by evolution. Another consequence is that we are often all too prone to construe cultural evolution as a form of conceptual progress driven by an urge to produce a better, more efficient and truer world-view, however long the process that leads to such a world-view.

I focus here on a specific domain of cultural evolution: the appearance and spread of religious concepts. It is a limiting-case, because at first sight it may seem to support the notion that cultural concepts result from 'cognitive liberation'. I think the evidence supports rather a different interpretation, even in this limiting-case. Indeed, it may be the case that human culture is governed by evolved cognitive dispositions that have direct effects on some cultural concepts and indirect but real effects on most. If this is so, then evolving a cultural mind is a much more complex process than is commonly assumed.

This argument is based on an 'epidemiological' account of cultural evolution as developed by Sperber and a few others (Atran, 1990; Sperber, 1994a, 1996; Hirschfeld, 1996). What I want to describe here is why some cultural 'viruses', such as religious concepts, are so 'catching' that we find them in many different cultural settings, whilst other concepts of (seemingly) equal potential use or cognitive effect are very rare. The aim is to describe the constraints imposed by evolved capacities on the range of concepts likely to be culturally transmitted and to examine the consequences for cultural evolution in general.

2   Cultural evolution: cognitive liberation is only part of the issue

It is convenient to date the appearance of cultures of the modern type at the symbolic 'explosion' that occurs some time between 100,000 and 50,000 years bp, with an abrupt change in the number and quality of artefacts produced by modern humans, including the appearance of a great variety of new objects, some of which are of no practical utility, the use of ochre, the first cave-paintings, elaborate burial practices, etc. An important difference from earlier cultural manifestations lies in the diversity of objects and representations, which may indicate the emergence of those group-level similarities and between-group differences that are typical of human cultures as observed by anthropologists. What is the cognitive counterpart of this sudden change?

It is tempting to think of modern hominisation as some kind of *liberating* process, through which the mind broke free of evolutionary shackles and became more flexible, more capable of novelty – in a word, more open. Several scenarios of cultural evolution give pride of place to this kind of cognitive breakthrough, understood as a new capacity for symbolic reference and a newly acquired flexibility in 'off-line' mental representations (Donald, 1991). I will not discuss here all such scenarios but will focus on two accounts (Tomasello *et al.*, 1993; Mithen, 1996b) that are based on a fine-grained description of the cognitive processes involved.

In his impressive reconstruction of early to modern human transition, Mithen (1996b) offers a cognitive interpretation of the cultural explosion of the Upper Palaeolithic. Mithen accepts the general claims of evolutionary psychologists concerning a 'Swiss-army knife', multiple-module, cognitive architecture (Tooby and Cosmides, 1992). Evolution resulted in the accretion and complexification of a large number of pan-specific cognitive capacities geared to task-specific problem-solving. These 'Darwinian algorithms' have clear input conditions; that is, they attend to and handle information not only in a particular domain, such as intuitive physics, 'theory of mind', but also in more limited domains such as cues for parental investment, mate-choice, coalition-building, living-kind categorisation, etc. Mithen gives evidence of the first developments of a 'natural history intelligence' and a 'social intelligence' with consequences for the ways humans hunt and forage, and the way their groups are constituted and their habitats adapted. Mithen also argues that cultural explosion is the effect of significant changes in cognitive architecture, in particular the appearance of 'cognitive fluidity': that is, of multiple information exchanges between modular capacities. The difference between early and modern humans is not so much in the operation of each specialised capacity (intuitive biology, theory of mind, tool-making, intuitive physics) but in the possibility of using information from one domain in the course of activities monitored by another domain. So artefacts are used as body-ornaments, serving social purposes; biological knowledge is used in visual symbols; tool-making develops local traditions and makes efficient use of local resources, tapping information from 'natural history intelligence'; and so on.

Most strikingly, this is the period when visual symbols take a clear 'religious' appearance. For good reasons, Mithen does not want to read too much metaphysics into cave-paintings. His point is simpler and more relevant to cultural evolution. Cave-paintings and artefacts begin to include evidence of totemic and anthropomorphic representations. This only means that they include conceptual combinations (chimeras, for instance) that tap information from different evolved 'modules'. Mithen concludes that the Swiss-army knife of evolutionary psychologists has turned into a 'cognitively fluid' mind, typical of modern humans. This may not be a direct result of having language, for language may have been used exclusively for purposes of social interaction for a long time.

Mithen's description focuses on the capacities required to build new kinds of mental representation. A related argument concerns the capacities involved in the transmission of cultural information. For instance, consider Tomasello's notion of 'cultural learning' (Tomasello *et al.*, 1993). This emphasises the role of perspective-taking abilities in the acquisition of cultural knowledge. Tomasello *et al.* point to crucial differences between 'traditions' in various animal populations and human cultures: (1) human traditions include elements that are potentially acquired by every single individual in the population; (2) all members of the group tend to acquire a given cultural representation in the same way; (3) most importantly, 'human cultural traditions often show an accumulation of modifications over generations (i.e. the ratchet effect)' so that 'human children are born into a world in which most of the tasks they are expected to master are collaborative inventions' (Tomasello *et al.*, 1993, p. 508). A clear illustration of this can be found in the domain of technology – tools and tool-usage show incremental, cumulative change, not just a renewal of ephemeral and interchangeable 'fashions' as in the much-discussed cases of animal traditions. Tomasello *et al.* demonstrate that tool-making requires sophisticated perspective-taking capacities that are beyond the abilities demonstrated in apes. So 'cultural learning' is special in that it relies on 'theory of mind' principles. In most domains of acquired culture it is simply not possible for developing subjects to consider cues provided by cultural elders and to produce relevant inferences about them without representing those elders' communicative intentions.

Both Mithen and Tomasello point to plausible cognitive differences that account for the special features of modern human cultures. However, I would propose that a description of modern culture in terms of 'cognitive fluidity' might be somewhat misleading. Accepting Mithen's evidence and most of his conclusions, as well as Tomasello's description of cultural learning, I want to add a cautionary note as regards [1] the relative emphasis on Before and After cognitive liberation; [2] the scope of evolutionary explanations of culture; and [3] the connections between human cultures and evolved cognition.

Considering the first point, these models describe a new way of handling information that presumably triggered the cultural explosion. By saying that newly appeared 'cognitive fluidity' and 'cultural learning' are necessary conditions, these models certainly point to some salient differences between Before and After, as it were. But note that in these models 'After' is mainly described in *residual* terms. We are saying that modern cultural concepts are not quite as tightly shackled by domain-specific structures (as Mithen argues), and that they potentially encompass whatever information cultural elders happen to have (as Tomasello suggests). In other words, the main point of these models is that they give us a good description of what modern cultures are *not* or in what way they are *no longer* of a certain kind.

This leads me to the question of explanatory scope. Models of culture based on flexibility or fluidity give a plausible answer to the question, 'How do we explain an acquisition of group-specific representations and practices that requires information stored in other people's minds?' That is, how did humans become capable of acquiring culture at all? Now in this chapter I want to suggest that anthropological, cognitive and evolutionary evidence allow us to go further and ask the question, 'How is it that humans have the cultures they have, and not others?' That is, what cognitive underpinnings explain particular trends in the transmission of representations? This is obviously a different question, so it would be silly to criticise models that were not designed to address it. And it would be difficult to address, if we limited ourselves to these models.

This is where the question of evolved cognitive dispositions is relevant. If we consider that 'fluidity' is the main characteristic of culture, we suggest that, once we reach a particular watershed in cognitive evolution:

[1] all sorts of concepts or conceptual combinations can be entertained;
[2] as a result, cultures become extremely diverse;
[3] as a consequence of that, people's conceptual repertoire is massively determined by what is communicated by their cultural elders (culture becomes Lamarckian); and
[4] evolved dispositions for culture can be adequately captured in terms of a general capacity (and propensity) to adopt other people's concepts.

This view of human cultures is extremely popular among social scientists (see Tooby and Cosmides, 1992, for a thorough critique of its implications). In this chapter I want to suggest that it is unduly timid. Even in the limiting-case of religious concepts, it is possible to show that:

[1] cultural concepts are strongly constrained: the source of these constraints lies in evolved category-specific capacities;
[2] cultures are not that diverse: we find recurrent templates for religious concepts, not unbounded variation;
[3] some aspects of transmission are definitely non-Lamarckian: that is to say, although development of religious concepts is definitely triggered by cultural input, inevitable variations in that input do not seem to be equally heritable; and
[4] there is probably no single capacity for culture: that is, we cannot explain even the acquisition of religious concepts in terms of one capacity. (It is tempting to think that having a 'theory of mind' is sufficient to understand and acquire other people's religious concepts; however, even in this domain attention to and understanding of cultural input requires activation of various sources of category-level information.)

The main premise here, as in the models described above, is that cultural concepts are not 'downloaded' from one mind to another. They are built by inferences from cultural input (Sperber, 1990a; Tomasello et al., 1993). But this has important consequences. The processes in question do not reduce to 'decoding' other people's thoughts from their overt gestures or utterances. They create new representations (Sperber, 1994a). The way this happens is massively constrained by prior assumptions in memory. That communication consists of inferences rather than decoding would suggest that any communicative act can create extremely different representations in different individuals, and this is indeed the case. Communication in a group creates indefinitely many variants of people's representations. As Sperber (1996) puts it, mutation is the rule and replication the exception in cultural communication. So 'cultural' representations – that is, the ones that occur in roughly similar forms in members of a group – is transmission against the odds, as it were. It is evidence for the fact that cognitive processes 'nudge' the creation of variants towards particular types of representation. Whenever we try to account for cultural representations, we must address the questions of 'How are they acquired?' and 'What processes or structures give them this particular stability?'

These questions are examined here in the limited domain of religious representations. Religion is a limiting-case in human culture because (i) there is obvious between-group variation in the concepts people acquire and transmit, (ii) it has no clear referential constraints (whatever and wherever gods are, they do not cause our beliefs about them), and (iii) it would seem it has no clear adaptive value. True, some people have argued that it may have been of adaptive value to have *some* religion (to ensure co-operation, create social bonds, to enforce moral imperatives, etc.) but none of these arguments goes beyond post-hoc rationalisation.

3   Religious concepts, actual and potential

For some time, students of religion have tried to describe the general features of religious concepts by inductive generalisation from actual cultural concepts. That religious concepts are not constrained by their reference would imply that we will find unconstrained variety in this form of conceptual speculation. But this is not the case. Some concepts are found in most human cultures, so that their presence is commonly taken for granted by anthropologists. Consider, for instance, the notions that the minds of dead people linger after death in the form of immaterial 'souls' and that particular artefacts have cognitive capacities, such as statues that listen to people's prayers. Other concepts are found only in very few cultural settings, for example the concept of 'zombies', resurrected corpses that have no control over their movements and are 'piloted' by another agent. Such observations are not sufficient to formulate the problem, 'Why are some cultural concepts recurrent?' in empirically tractable terms. This is because inductive generalisations in this domain (i) do not specify a contrastive set of comparable concepts that are *not* found amongst religious concepts, and (ii) they do not suggest the *proximate mechanism* that would produce recurrence. As a result, it is difficult to determine how cultural recurrence is connected to evolved properties of human cognition.

Let me first consider the question of contrasts between recurrent and rare or non-existent cultural concepts. It is not too difficult to draw a list of concepts that are actually found in religious systems. Consider for instance the following:

(1) There is one omnipotent person who knows everything we do.
(2) Dead people's souls wander about and sometimes visit people.
(3) When people die their souls sometimes come back in another body.
(4) We worship this woman because she gave birth without ever having had sex.
(5) Some people are dead but they keep walking around. They cannot talk anymore; they are not aware of what they are doing.

This is not too impressive since the above propositions are all very familiar. However, familiarity is not important here. Consider another set:

(6) Some trees can 'store' conversations people hold in their shade. To 'retrieve' what was said, a diviner takes a twig from the tree, burns it and looks at the patterns formed by the falling ashes in a bowl of water.
(7) That mountain over there (*that* one, not this one) eats food and digests it. We give it food sacrifices every now and then, to make sure it stays in good health.
(8) There are invisible people around who drink cologne. If someone suddenly goes into a fit and screams for cologne, they are being possessed by one of these invisible people.
(9) Some people have an invisible organ in their stomachs. That organ flies away at night when they're asleep. It attacks other people and drinks their blood.

Most of these sound rather exotic. Yet it is intuitively clear that they are in the list of what we would call 'religious'. (Indeed, they are all taken from actual religious systems; see Boyer, 2000.) However, the criterion for a precise model is that it should exclude possible concepts that are never found in religious systems. This is where traditional understandings of religious concepts are less than satisfactory. For instance, it is often assumed that religion describes agents and situations that are 'strange', or 'unfamiliar', or in some way marked off from mundane occurrences. This is sufficient to exclude the following:

*(10) People get old and then one day they stop breathing and die and that's that.
*(11) If you drop this object it will fall downwards till it hits the ground.
*(12) Ghosts cannot go through walls because walls are solid.

However, this criterion is far too liberal, because all sorts of 'strange' or 'unfamiliar' material can be used to create concepts that are never found in religious systems, such as these:

*(13) Some people turn black when they are really thirsty.
*(14) We worship this statue because it is the largest artefact ever made.

*(15) We worship tigers that have no stripes because they are very rare.
*(16) We worship this woman because she gave birth to thirty-seven children.

One could try and fine-tune the criteria by saying that religious concepts invariably include 'supernatural' or 'superhuman' agents. Again, this is not sufficient. The following items all include supernatural agents, yet they are not found in any religious system:

*(17) There is only one omnipotent God! However, he is actually ignorant of what goes on in the world.
*(18) The gods are watching us and they notice everything we do! But they forget everything instantly.
*(19) There is only one God! He is omnipotent. He exists only on Wednesdays.
*(20) This statue is special because it vanishes every time someone thinks about it.
*(21) This statue will hear your prayers, but only if you're very far from the statue when you say them.

An anthropological model of religious concepts should make sense of these facts and provide a proximate mechanism that explains why *-marked concepts in the above lists do not seem to have much 'cultural fitness'. Note that they are not absurd, inconceivable, overly complicated or self-contradictory. This description should also give some indication of the proximate mechanisms that explain the apparent success of some types of conceptual information.

4   Templates for religious concepts

The anthropological model described here is an attempt to provide this connection (see Boyer, 1994a, 1994b, 1996 for more details). The main point of this account is that religious concepts are to a large extent constrained by their connection to *intuitive ontology*, that is, a set of categories and inference-mechanisms that describe the broad categories of objects to be found in the world (PERSONS, ARTEFACTS, ANIMALS, PLANTS) and some causal properties of objects belonging to these categories. These early developed, universal categories and inference-mechanisms deliver intuitive expectations about the likely states of such objects and the likely explanations for their changes. Intuitive ontology includes those domain-specific structures known in the literature as 'naive theories' of various domains: intuitive physics, intuitive biology, and theory of mind, for instance. (What intuitive ontology includes and why will be discussed below, in section 6.) Religious concepts are constrained by intuitive ontology in two different ways: [1] they include explicit *violations* of intuitive expectations, and [2] they tacitly activate a *background* of non-violated 'default' expectations.

To illustrate the first point: spirits and ghosts are commonly represented as intentional agents whose physical properties go against the ordinary physical qualities of embodied agents. They go through physical obstacles, move instantaneously, etc. Gods have non-standard physical and biological qualities. For instance, they are immortal, they feed on the smell of sacrificed foods, etc. Also, religious systems the world over include counter-intuitive assumptions about particular artefacts – for instance, statues which are endowed with intentional psychological processes, such as the ability to perceive states of affairs, form beliefs, have intentions, etc. In all these religious concepts we find a combination of [a] identification of the religious entity as belonging to a particular ontological category and [b] description of features that violate intuitive expectations for that category. This does not mean that the counterintuitive entities and situations described by religious concepts are not taken as real by most people who hold them. On the contrary, it is precisely in so far as a certain situation violates intuitive principles *and* is taken as real that it may become particularly salient.

To illustrate the second point: counterintuitive elements do not exhaust the representation of religious entities and agencies. Consider ghosts or spirits, for instance. They are construed as physically counterintuitive. At the same time, however, people routinely produce a large number of inferences about what the ghosts or spirits *know* or *want*, inferences which are based on a straightforward extension of 'theory of mind' expectations to the spirits. Indeed, most inferences people produce about religious agencies are straightforward consequences of activating those intuitive principles that are *not* violated in the representation of those supernatural entities.

So there are indefinitely many culturally specific religious *concepts*, but they correspond to a small number of more abstract *templates*. The templates all have the following structure:

[0] a lexical label
[1] a pointer to a particular ontological category
[2] an explicit representation of a violation of intuitive expectations, either:
     [2a] a *breach* of relevant expectations for the category, or:
     [2b] a *transfer* of expectations associated with another category
[3] a link to (non-violated) default expectations for the category
[4] a slot for additional encyclopaedic information.

For instance, the Western 'ghost' concept corresponds to this template:

[0] 'ghost'
[1] PERSON
[2a] breach of intuitive physics (e.g. goes through walls)

[3]   → 'theory-of-mind' expectations
[4]   (e.g.) 'ghosts like to come back to where they used to live'.

To consider a more exotic concept, take the following description:

> The [shaman's] song is chanted in front of two rows of statuettes [*nelekan*] facing each other, beside the hammock where the ill person is lying. These auxiliary spirits drink up the smoke, whose intoxicating effect opens their minds to the invisible aspect of reality, and gives them the power to heal. In this way [the statues] are believed to become themselves diviners. (Severi, 1993, p. 231)

This concept's template would be something like:
[0]   'nelekan'
[1]   → ARTEFACT
[2a] transfer of intentional psychology ('theory of mind')
[3]   → standard ARTEFACT expectations
[4]   (e.g.) 'statuettes need smoke to heal people'.

Now the major assumption in this account is that the reasons why certain concepts are stable within a culture, and the causes of recurrence between different groups, lie in the structure of templates rather than the structure of specific concepts. That is, what makes the Cuna statuettes or the Western 'ghost' culturally successful is not a series of contingent local details but a common structure that can be found in many other such concepts.

The template model produces specific predictions about the likely range of culturally successful religious concepts. The claim is (emphatically) *not* that religious ontological representations consist in any odd combination of 'something counterintuitive' and 'something intuitive'. The hypothesis is much more specific. Ontological categories and principles are not *ad hoc* stipulations. They are provided by independent evidence concerning the most entrenched, early developed, domain-specific structures of intuitive ontology.

This imposes constraints from which it follows that *there are not many possible types of religious ontologies* with good cultural fitness. This is because (i) intuitive ontologies comprise a limited range of broad ontological categories and associated principles, so that the number of assumptions that directly violate them are limited, too; and (ii) not all violations are compatible with maintaining an intuitive background that can support inferences.

Recall that counterintuitive representations stem from either *breach* or *transfer* of expectations. In the first case, the religious concept includes a description of an object that [i] belongs to an ontological category and [ii] has properties incompatible with inferences normally triggered by membership in that category. A 'god' is generally a PERSON with breach of *intuitive biology* properties, and so is the Mary of Christianity. A 'spirit' is a PERSON with breach of *intuitive physics* properties. You can combine several of these. An invisible spirit that feeds on cologne does just that.

In the second case, the religious concept includes a description of an object that [i] belongs to an ontological category and [ii] has properties normally inferred from membership of another category. Trees that recall conversations are PLANTS with a transfer of *theory-of-mind* properties. Mountains that digest food are NATURAL OBJECTS with transfer of *intuitive biology* properties. Statues that listen to people's prayers are ARTEFACTS with *theory-of-mind* properties.

Combining categories and associated inference engines in this way produces a variety of possible combinations, or a sort of catalogue of possible religious ontologies. Obviously, precisely how many types are generated depends on how many ontological categories or different types of inferences are selected in the first place. This is not a substantial issue. Whether you decide that trees are examples of LIVING THINGS or PLANTS will change the number of items in the 'catalogue' but has no consequences for the predictions of the model.

On this view, transmission of a religious ontology does not require that people transmit the whole conceptual package. Indeed, in most human groups cultural elders typically make available to their juniors the counter-intuitive elements of religious concepts ('spirits are persons that can go through walls') but do not transmit the background ('spirits have beliefs caused by their perceptions which are caused by what happens'). So to transmit a religious ontology all that is necessary is to give cues indicating which bits of standard expectations are violated. The rest is spontaneously inferred by people at the receiving end of cultural transmission. As a consequence, communication of religious concepts is invariably poorer than people's resulting representations of those concepts. Despite this fragmentary input, representations of religious concepts may be highly stable in a group, since a great part of the inferences people draw from cultural input are informed by an intuitive ontology that is common to them all.

5   Anthropological and experimental evidence for templates

On the whole, the anthropological evidence seems to confirm that, all else being equal, representations that combine counterintuitive assumptions and intuitive background in the way described here are more likely than others to be found in religious systems. Indeed, a 'catalogue' that uses only the categories PERSON, ANIMAL and ARTEFACT and includes only breaches of physical and cognitive properties associated with those categories virtually exhausts cultural variation in this domain (Boyer, 1996,

1998). To be more precise, we find that [1] all religious systems in the anthropological record are founded on one or several such combinations; [2] these are invariably central to the representation of religious concepts (that is, they are essential to what the religious entities are, to what marks them off from other types of imagined entities); and [3] there are virtually no systems based on concepts outside our short catalogue (such as would be the case in systems founded on the assumptions *17–*21 above).

Note that this is a claim about 'cultural fitness', not about 'conceivability'. Obviously, people can imagine all sorts of concepts that go beyond these kinds of combination. The point is that these concepts will have less cultural fitness and therefore less cultural spread, unless other factors boost their transmission. This is the case, for instance, in 'scholarly' or 'literate' religion as designed and transmitted by specialists (Brahmans, *ulema*, Christian theologians, etc.). These apparently provide counter-examples to the model above. The scholarly elite devise representations that go far beyond the breach-transfer system described here and, for instance, postulate an ontology that contradicts intuitions of identity (in the case of the Holy Trinity) or assumptions about agency (in the case of the non-anthropomorphic universe of literate Buddhism). Such cases in fact show that the 'violation + background' model is a rather good predictor of transmission. Anthropologists who study such cultural contexts have repeatedly shown that the scholarly version of religious ontology is transmitted through systematic training but also routinely ignored (in Christianity) or supplemented (in the case of Buddhism) by popular culture. In religion 'on the ground', we find a trinity of distinct persons (for Christians) and a rather familiar set of rather anthropomorphic gods and spirits (for Buddhists). So when cultural transmission does not receive the extra push given by literacy with long and systematic training, concepts tend to revert to the 'violation + background' mode.

Why are concepts that correspond to these templates successful? From an anthropological viewpoint, it would seem that both explicit counterintuitive and default background elements are necessary for cultural fitness (Boyer, 1994a). In order to have minimal cultural fitness, descriptions of religious entities found in the cultural input must be *attention-grabbing*, otherwise they will be forgotten or discarded. This quality is provided by violations of intuitive expectations. Also, the concepts built by subjects on the basis of that input must have some *inferential potential*, and this is provided by default assumptions.

So far, the anthropological model only shows that religious concepts do have recurrent features, if seen from the viewpoint of their ontological assumptions. This provides us with a plausible conjecture as concerns cultural fitness. The latter would depend on optimal combinations of salience and inferential potential. This naturally leads to the question of the *proximate mechanism* that would produce recurrence. Accepting that religious concepts correspond to templates with limited violations of intuitive expectations, how does this actually give such concepts an 'edge' in terms of transmission?

This is where we must turn to experimental studies on counterintuitive material. The anthropological model predicts that counterintuitive elements are better recalled or recognised than representations that conform to intuitive expectations. Second, it would predict that background assumptions (part [3] of our cognitive templates) are indeed activated by actual religious concepts. Both predictions are easily testable.

In several studies, Justin Barrett and I focused on one aspect that is crucial to differences of cultural survival, namely differences in *recall* (Barrett 1998; Barrett and Keil 1996; Boyer 2000). If we can show that concepts with the particular structure described above have an advantage in terms of recall, this should go some way towards explaining why they can be found in so many cultural systems. However, one of the few direct studies of recall for such material – Bartlett's famous study of transmission chains for mythical stories – seems to suggest the opposite. For Bartlett, subjects tend to normalise stories to familiar 'schemata' and discard their strange or exotic elements (Bartlett, 1932). So one could think that whatever conflicts with 'schemata' or intuitive ontology would be discarded as well. However, Bartlett's studies were very limited and could have confounded two causes for poor recall and distortion. More systematic transmission studies by Justin Barrett show that, once effects of cultural familiarity are controlled for, counterintuitive items do produce better recall.

Barrett used quasi-stories in which a variety of items (PERSONS, ARTEFACTS, ANIMALS) were described as exhibits in an inter-galactic museum. Barrett studied transmission of items on three 'generations' of subjects. Recalled items from each generation of subjects were used as stimulus material for the next generation. The stimuli came in three 'levels' of oddity: [1] conforming to intuitive expectations; [2] unfamiliar but not counterintuitive; and [3] counterintuitive (in the precise sense given above). In all categories, Barrett found a significant transmission advantage for counterintuitive items over standard ones, and in the PERSON category there was an advantage of counterintuitive over both standard and unfamiliar (Barrett 1996). These results were then confirmed by Boyer's studies of immediate recall (without transmission). Items that include either counterintuitive breaches or counterintuitive transfers of intuitive expectations were recalled better than standard associations (Boyer 2000). These controlled studies did not use material presented as 'religious', and post-study questionnaires showed that subjects did not assimilate them to religious concepts.

The template model also predicts that, whilst people hold counterintuitive material as explicit representations of religious entities, their inferences are governed by the 'background' of default assumptions that are not explicitly violated. A good illustration is Barrett and Keil's study of concepts of 'God' and other counterintuitive agents in both believers and nonbelievers (Barrett and Keil, 1996). Barrett and Keil first elicited explicit descriptions of God. These generally centred on counterintuitive claims for extraordinary cognitive powers. The subjects were then tested on their recall of simple stories involving God in various scenarios where these capacities are relevant. On the whole, subjects tended to distort the stories in ways that were directly influenced by their tacit principles of psychology, their 'theory of mind'. Barrett and Keil called this effect 'theological correctness'. Subjects strive to maintain theologically approved versions of religious agencies as explicit concepts, but experimental tasks that tap their intuitions reveal that the latter are influenced less by theologies than by ontological categories and principles, as predicted here.

Finally, the template model implies that religious concepts are influenced by a source of information (intuitive ontology) that is not itself culturally specific. This is required so that the model can work as an explanation of recurrent features across different cultural settings. Some experimental results suggest that this is indeed the case. For instance, Barrett and Keil found no difference in their results that would correlate with the participants' ethnic or religious background. Also, there is now direct cross-cultural evidence that shows that such effects are indeed similar in otherwise very different settings. Barrett tested the Theological Correctness effect with Hindus in Delhi and found patterns roughly similar to the Cornell campus results, with people using intuitive theory-of-mind principles to govern inferences and expectations about religious agents (Barrett, 1998). Also, Boyer and Ramble conducted a systematic replication of the recall experiments for counterintuitive and non-counterintuitive material in Gabon and Nepal (Boyer and Ramble, in preparation). They found recall patterns similar to those observed with Western subjects. Recall results show similar 'distinctiveness' effects for counterintuitive material. This is recalled better than common conceptual associations and also better than simple oddities (that is, violations of common expectations without violations of category-level information).

All this needs further testing, and more fine-grained study of other factors (mode of communication, difference between recall and recognition, measures of delayed recall, and so on). However, these are good results in that we seem to have here a model of religious concepts that is [i] consistent with the anthropological record and [ii] backed by independent evidence. Accepting that religious ontologies really are based on the conceptual combinations described here, I must now turn to more general issues concerning cultural representations in other domains.

6   What is evolved intuitive ontology?

Returning to the issues mentioned at the beginning, we can now chart in a more precise way the kind of mind you need in order to have (modern) culture. In my description of 'intuitive ontology' I made two assumptions that are essential to this depiction of cultural transmission. One assumption is that there is a special source of information ('intuitive ontology') that is distinct from other conceptual structures. There is a functional difference between expectations intuitively associated with categories like PERSON, ANIMAL, ARTEFACT, on the one hand, and the information associated with subordinate concepts (e.g. ACADEMIC, GIRAFFE, TELEPHONE), on the other. The second assumption is that intuitive ontology consists of domain- or category-specific principles and expectations. Both receive support from several independent sources of evidence:

[1]   Developmental studies have demonstrated the early emergence of categorical distinctions along ontological lines as well as their *theoretical* character (Gopnik and Meltzoff, 1997). These are described as 'skeletal principles' (Gelman, 1990), 'modes of construal' (Keil, 1994), or 'foundational theories' (Wellman and Gelman, 1992) in the literature.

[2]   In adults, inferences are governed by category-specific assumptions, that specify a range of non-obvious properties of the domain. For instance, we assume that membership of an ARTEFACT kind depends on structural properties that allow intended functional use. On the other hand, we tend to assume that membership of a LIVING THINGS category depends on a historical connection to other members of the kind.

[3]   Category-specific effects can be seen in the differential salience of cues. Consider the visual cues that facilitate face-recognition (distance between eyes and mouth, etc.) (Morton and Johnson, 1991). Clearly, a series of perceptual inferences are triggered by the identification of a visual display as human, and similar cues are not salient for other LIVING THING categories.

[4]   Also, different inferences can be triggered by similar cues in different domains. For example, a sudden change in the direction of motion for a solid object will lead to significantly different inferences, depending on whether the object is identified as an instance of LIVING THINGS, which typically move because they have particular goals, or as an

ARTEFACT, which is not intuitively understood as self-propelled (Premack, 1990).

[5] There are behavioural measures of the differences between conceptual associations retrieved at category-level and those available at the 'entry-level' (Jolicoeur *et al.*, 1984; Chumbley, 1986; Kosslyn *et al.*, 1995; see also Caramazza and Shelton, 1998).

[6] There is evidence for specific reactions to violations of category-level information. Material of this kind produces specific intuitions of sentence anomaly (Gerard and Mandler, 1983) and event-related potential studies show that semantic incongruities produce specific reactions (Polich, 1985) that are not obtained with syntactic anomalies (Ainsworth-Darnell *et al.*, 1998). The stimuli used in such studies are composed mainly, though not exclusively, of category-level violations as defined here.

[7] Some cognitive pathologies display a selective loss in specific domains of conceptual information (e.g. names for living things) that is not accompanied by a comparable loss of category-level (e.g. functional) information (see for instance Warrington and Shallice, 1984; Shallice, 1987; Sartori *et al.*, 1994; Moss *et al.*, 1997; Kurbat and Farah, 1998). Furthermore, loss of lower-level conceptual information can be specific to particular categories, for example damaged lexical access for living kinds or artefacts only (Warrington and Shallice, 1984).

All these studies confirm the presence, early development, and conceptual entrenchment of an *intuitive ontology*, that comprises not just a catalogue of possible types of objects in the world but also a series of automatic, spontaneous responses to the identification of objects as members of ontological categories. A crucial point in this account is that the contents and organisation of ontological categories and intuitive 'theories' are not culturally specific. There are, obviously, salient differences in cultural knowledge but these do not seem to concern category-level information. Categories such as PERSON, ANIMAL, and ARTEFACT, and associated expectations about agency, animacy, physics, or 'theory of mind' appear so early in cognitive development that there is little room here for cultural influences. With development children come to acquire all sorts of culturally specific information that enriches fundamental principles rather than changes them in most domains. (See Boyer, 1998, for an extensive discussion, as well as Walker, 1985, 1992a; Atran, 1989; Sperber, 1996; Bloch, 1998; Medin and Atran, 1999, for similar arguments.)

This description of an intuitive ontology, based on independent cognitive evidence, is on the whole consistent with the predictions of evolutionary psychology concerning evolved cognitive architecture as a 'Swiss-army knife' of independent, domain-specific cognitive adaptations (Tooby and Cosmides, 1992). The main point of evolutionary psychology is that the emergence of unprejudiced, domain-general inductive capacities would make neither computational nor evolutionary sense. Rather, evolutionary theory would predict the gradual complexification of specialised cognitive dispositions. Being complex adaptations, these are the outcome of gradual changes in pre-existing capacities and have evolved over a large number of generations, so that they are probably pan-specific.

7   Consequences for culture

This account of cognitive architecture has some important consequences for cultural inheritance. In the case of religious concepts, we see a spectacular illustration of the fact that, as I said at the beginning, cultural concepts are built by inferential processes, not by downloading of 'memes'. That is, to build a concept of 'spirit', for instance, people activate all sorts of background inferences that were not specified by cultural input. In this sense, religious concepts (like other cultural concepts) are *under-determined by cultural input*. The fact that people entertain roughly similar concepts is not so much determined by similarities in the input they are offered, as by similarities in the inferences they produce from a class of inputs. This, I would argue, is the case for most cultural concepts. It follows that we cannot understand recurrent patterns in culture unless we describe the source of such spontaneous inferences, i.e. intuitive ontology and its effects on the acquisition of cultural material.

Transmission requires that people attend to cultural input (consisting mainly but not exclusively of other people's utterances, gestures, images, etc.) and complement it to build a conceptual representation that is roughly similar to other people's. No communicator's output ever includes a complete description of the representation to be conveyed, so complex inferential processes are required (Sperber, 1990a). This two-stage process (understanding input and inferring a more complete conceptual representation) is still not precisely described in any domain of cultural knowledge (but see Atran, 1998, Medin and Atran, 1999, for concepts of living kinds). However, if we assume that an evolved source of categories and inference principles guides inferences from cultural input, we can at least delineate possible paths of transmission.

In particular, we can distinguish between three types of connection between cultural input and information supplied by intuitive ontology, that I call *enrichment*, *salient violations* and *displacement* respectively (see Boyer, 1998, for a more detailed presentation). The above argument about religious representations should be sufficient to suggest that salient violations exist and how they work. So now I must say a word about enrichment and displacement.

Enrichment means that some culturally provided information is attended to because prior principles specify that a domain exists, as well as constrain the type of information that will feed the developing domain. A simple illustration is the domain of NUMBER. Obviously, labels for numbers and counting systems are culturally specific (Crump, 1990). Acquiring the specifics of these systems, however, implies a set of prior principles that we find very early in development (Gallistel and Gelman, 1992; Wynn, 1992b). The combinatorial principles can vary from one place to another, but they are always consistent with these prior principles. In other domains, cultural input is enlisted to enrich a causal framework that is postulated but not specified by intuitive ontology. Consider folk-biology, for instance, most of which is continuous with early-developed intuitive principles in both the application of specific taxonomic principles and the activation of 'essentialistic' inferences (Gelman *et al.*, 1994; Medin and Atran, 1999). Cultural input certainly widens the scope of early biological understandings. Complex speculation about 'life', 'vitality', 'élan vital' and other such culturally specific concepts (see Karim, 1981, for instance) are also enrichments of the intuitive understanding that all members of living species share an inner causal essence.

Enrichment of intuitive categories and expectations also extends to cultural notions of the 'self' or the 'person', which can take very different forms in different social groups (Heelas and Lock, 1981). Theories of the person and of likely causes of behaviour enrich but do not modify tacit principles of intuitive 'theory of mind'.

Kinship categories provide a third example of this process, whereby culturally specific input can be acquired inasmuch as there are intuitive principles to generate relevant inferences on the basis of that input. Early developed intuitions include non-trivial expectations about human co-resident collections ('families') as distinct from other kinds of categories (Hirschfeld, 1989).

Displacement is an altogether different process that is, in fact, rather rare in cultural transmission. So far, I have described cultural concepts that (i) are acquired effortlessly and (ii) constitute either an enrichment of intuitive expectations or else a predictable combination of limited violation and tacit confirmation of expectations. This suggests strong conceptual predispositions. This argument is supported, conversely, by the special difficulties encountered in the transmission of cultural concepts that neither confirm nor violate intuitive ontology. The most salient illustration is scientific understandings that often challenge or displace intuitive expectations. This is typical though not exclusive of scientific concepts. In such domains, acquisition is effortful. Cultural transmission most often requires dedicated institutions with specialised personnel and systematic training extending over years. Also, transmission in these domains is boosted by literacy that allows external representation of cultural concepts (Goody, 1977; Donald, 1991; Lloyd, 1991).

To sum up, cultural concepts consist of ideas of various domains that are acquired along *domain-specific inheritance tracks*. All of these important properties – the properties of acquisition processes, the likelihood that cultural concepts will be stable or change rapidly, etc. – depend upon what ontological domains are activated and how. I will not go through the details of how many different domains and inheritance tracks there may be, that would not be of much interest for this discussion. What matters, on the other hand, is that if there are such domain-specific inheritance tracks, we do not need to posit any general 'capacity for culture'.

To return to the questions raised at the beginning of this chapter, Mithen and Tomasello showed that both inter-modular communication and theory of mind are involved in cultural transmission. They are a *necessary* condition for cultural transmission but not *sufficient* to predict trends in actual cultural transmission. For instance, theory of mind produces a relevant description of other people's representations only inasmuch as an intuitive ontology selects a relevant description of these representations. To take a few examples: acquiring a counting system on the basis of cultural cues certainly requires that we represent other people's thoughts about numbers, but we cannot do that unless we also activate an independent capacity for inferences about numerosity. Acquiring a folk-biology on the basis of people's utterances about plants and animals requires that we represent these people's thoughts about living things, but we cannot represent those thoughts unless we also activate intuitive tacit biological principles. Acquiring the concept GHOST requires that we understand other people's states of mind about religious agencies, which cannot be done unless we identify violations of intuitive physics as salient. So 'cultural learning' based on perspective-taking or theory of mind requires the prior contribution of other domain-specific capacities.

If cultural input is attended to and interpreted on the basis of prior principles supplied by intuitive ontology, then we have to take into account that intuitive ontology comprises domain-specific structures, and that the way these structures support inferences from cultural input may well be domain-specific too – with important consequences for our description of the modern human mind as a *cultural* mind.

In a selectionist, epidemiological framework, the origins of religious concepts are in conceptual propensities of the modern mind, and these can be investigated experimentally. Empirical studies of cognitive constraints on concepts suggest that accounts of cultural evolution based on a single 'liberating event' should not be taken too far. Religious concepts are the domain *par excellence* where unbound cultural variation should be observed. Demonstrating how they are constrained by intuitive ontology should *a fortiori* show that cultural concepts in general are constrained, too. The main difference between modern minds and what came before may be the emergence of *many* different domain-specific ways of partly transcending intuitive expectations.

The research summarised here was funded by a special grant from the Centre National de la Recherche Scientifique ('Aide à projets nouveaux'). A first version was presented at the 'Evolution of Mind' conference, Hang Seng Centre, University of Sheffield. I am grateful to the organisers for making this possible and in particular to Peter Carruthers for his comments and suggestions on several subsequent versions. Also Harvey Whitehouse, Justin Barrett, Robert McCauley, Thomas Lawson, Brian Malley, Steven Mithen and Dan Sperber helped me re-formulate the evolutionary and cognitive claims more clearly.

6 Symmetry and the evolution of the modular linguistic mind

Thomas Wynn

The archaeological record of hominid-imposed symmetry provides a direct look at evolutionary developments in the hominid mind. Well before the appearance of anatomically modern humans, and perhaps prior even to the appearance of *Homo sapiens,* hominid spatial cognition had become essentially modern. This development required the evolution of the hominid visual input module (in the sense of Fodor, 1983), but also developments in central processing. It did not, however, require language.

1   The archaeology of mind

The products of minds can provide clues to the organisation and working of the minds themselves. Most commonly, the products of minds are actions of some kind, and because action is ephemeral, it is necessary to observe or record it if we want to make inferences about the mind itself. This places obvious limits on our ability to make inferences about the minds of individuals who lived long ago; we cannot observe their actions. Some actions do affect material things, which as a consequence 'record' some features of the original action. Archaeology consists of a set of methods for reconstructing past action from patterns of material things that exist in the present. If the reconstructions of past action are reliable, they should allow inferences about the minds behind the action.

There are some obvious methodological caveats to an archaeology of cognition. The first is the problem of resolution. Most interpretations in cognitive science are based on experiments, in which particular problems are posed directly to subjects; or, in the case of ethology, on extensive observation of individuals in natural settings. Both methods emphasise control and replicability and require a large number of examples from similar, if not identical, circumstances. There is considerable disagreement in cognitive ethology, for example, about the usefulness of anecdotal evidence. If a primatologist observes a single instance of a chimpanzee smashing a rock and using the sharp pieces to cut a vine, must we add stone tool use to the natural repertoire of chimpanzees? Archaeologists confront this

113

problem regularly, because archaeological evidence is largely anecdotal. We have no control over the circumstances in which the actions occurred. We cannot take controlled samples of action streams, or attempt to duplicate circumstances, except in the most global sense (for example, we can sometimes determine that a stone tool was used for a particular class of task, say butchery, but cannot reconstruct the circumstances of a particular use). We must accept a great deal of latitude when we conclude that two tools or two reconstructed actions are the same. This problem is exacerbated by the problem of preservation. The vast majority of the material evidence of action is rapidly destroyed, leaving a non-random representation for later examination. And that which is not destroyed is subject to the serendipity of discovery. We do not have a continuous, coherent record of past action. An apt metaphor for the archaeological record is a jigsaw puzzle, most of whose pieces are missing. When archaeologists do a good job, we can describe one piece and place it somewhere in the vicinity of its position in time. If we are very lucky, this piece may fit with another. But local sequences or small-scale patterns of pieces are very rare. This does not mean that we cannot make interpretations of the past, but it does mean that our interpretations must always be relatively coarse-grained. We can often reconstruct the 'big' picture, but we can rarely detect fine-grained images.

A final caveat, with particular relevance to the archaeology of mind, is the problem of minimum necessary competence. Archaeologists can only assess the minimum abilities required to produce a particular pattern. We cannot logically eliminate the possibility that our prehistoric subjects employed simple reasoning when producing and using stone tools, and much more complex reasoning in archaeologically invisible domains. Our assessment becomes more reliable, however, if several lines of evidence point to the same abilities. If our reconstructions of foraging, tool manufacture, tool use, raw material selectivity, group size and size of home range all point to the same levels of cognitive ability, then our interpretation of minimum competence becomes more reliable. It is not always necessary to kowtow to the catchy phrase 'absence of evidence is not evidence of absence'. Sometimes absence of evidence is a very persuasive argument for absence.

The advantage that the archaeological record holds over other evolutionary methodologies is that it is able to provide long sequences of evolutionary development. These sequences are not predictions from comparative evidence, or interpolations from the spotty fossil record, but actual, chronologically ordered sequences of hominid products. The record of hominid tools is by far the most voluminous record we have from human evolution; archaeologists have recovered millions of stone tools. True, the record is not complete. There are chronological gaps, especially for the early periods, and there are geographic gaps, in areas where little or no archaeology has been done. But despite these gaps the archaeological record is more complete than the fossil record and presents a picture of technological change over a period of almost two and one half million years.

2   The archaeology of symmetry

This chapter focuses on the evolution of symmetry. There are two reasons for this choice. First, symmetry is a pattern and a concept that is recognised by everyone, which reduces the requirement for definition (but does not eliminate it entirely). Second, symmetry has been incorporated into most schemes of spatial cognitive development, and also into theories of perception, so that it provides a direct way to articulate the archaeological record with the cognitive science literature.

Symmetry actually documents two distinct threads in the evolution of human cognition. The first, and earlier, was the evolution of spatial perceptual–cognitive ability. Of particular interest here is the question of modularity. Does the archaeological record document evolutionary developments within a module of shape recognition and imagery, or is a central processor of some kind also implicated? It is this thread that is the focus of the present discussion. The second, and later, thread in the development of symmetry documents the appearance of symmetry as a transformational rule. While interesting in its own right, it is beyond the scope of this chapter.

2.1   Types of symmetry

There are several different patterns to which we apply the term symmetry. The most familiar is *bilateral symmetry*, also known as reflectional symmetry. Here one half of a pattern is duplicated and reversed on the opposite side. Implicit in the pattern is a central line, usually vertical, that divides the pattern into reflected versions of one another. Bilateral symmetry is 'natural' in the sense that we see this pattern in the natural world of plants and animals. A second symmetry is *radial symmetry*, in which a pattern repeats not across a line, but continuously around a point. Similar to radial symmetry is *rotational symmetry*, in which a pattern is not reflected across a line, but rotated around a point; here the pattern is not reversed or inverted. Finally, there is *translational symmetry*, in which a pattern is repeated in a sequence, without reversal or rotation. Are all of these symmetries the same; that is, do they all share some quality? Or are they different phenomena? Some might argue, for example, that translational symmetry is not symmetry, but simply repetition. However, a similar objection could be made about rotational symmetry, which few would reject. This heterogeneity in the concept of symmetry is at the heart of the current argument, for the archaeological record documents a clear evolutionary sequence in the development of symmetry, a sequence that can be exploited when interpreting cognitive evolution.

The argument begins with a discussion of chimpanzee drawing and painting. The bulk of this section then presents a chronological sequence of prehistoric products.

2.2   Chimpanzee drawing

Non-human primates do not produce symmetries. The only possible example of symmetry produced by apes in the wild is the chimpanzee sleeping nest, which has a kind of radial symmetry that is produced when the individual reaches out from a central position and pulls branches inward. Here the symmetry is a direct consequence of a motor pattern, and one need not posit some idea of symmetry. There are no other ethological examples, at least to my knowledge. However, there has been a significant amount of research with captive apes, especially chimpanzees, including a fascinating literature concerning chimpanzee art and drawing.

Work with ape art has been of two kinds. In the first, researchers present an ape with appropriate media (finger paints, brushes and paint, etc.) and encourage it to create. In the second, researchers control the productions by supplying paper with pre-drawn patterns. The former is the more 'archaeological', in that researchers have not tried to coax particular pattern productions. Perhaps not surprisingly, these spontaneous productions are patterned primarily by motor patterns. Fan shapes are common, as are zigzags produced by back and forth arm motion. Desmond Morris (1962), the most well-known researcher in ape art, thought that these productions may demonstrate a sense of balance, and tried to test this idea with a series of experiments using sheets with stimulus figures already printed on, following the earlier lead of Schiller (1951). Morris's work led to a number of subsequent experiments by others using similar techniques. The results have been enigmatic at best. Most chimpanzees presented with a figure that is offset from the centre of the paper will mark on the opposite side, or on the figure itself. Morris suggested (cautiously) that this confirmed a notion of balance. Later Smith (1973) and Boysen (Boysen *et al.*, 1987) confirmed these results, but argued that the pattern resulted from the chimpanzee's placing marks toward the centre of the vacant space; balance was an accident.

It is hard to know what to make of this evidence. First, even with such few experimental subjects, there was a lot of individual variability. Indeed, each chimpanzee had an idiosyncratic approach both to the controlled and uncontrolled drawing. Second, most repetitive patterns resulted from repetitive motor actions. Nevertheless, the individuals did appear to place their marks non-randomly and did attend to features of the visual field. Other, non-graphic, experiments have indicated that chimpanzees can be taught to select the central element of a linear array (Rohles and Devine, 1967), so chimpanzees can clearly perceive patterns in which balance is a component. But true symmetry is nowhere evident.

2.3   The bio-mechanics and cognitive prerequisites of stone tool
        manufacture

In order to make a stone tool, the knapper[1] must control actions directed at a relatively small spatial field. In the simplest kind of knapping,[2] the knapper strikes a cobble with another, usually harder, stone (termed a hammer) (see Figure 6.1). This basic action yields two potentially useful products: a smaller, thin piece (termed a flake) that has a very sharp edge, and the larger piece from which the flake was removed (termed a core). This large piece now has at least a few sharper edges than it did before, edges that are also potentially useful. Even this simple hammering technique requires that the knapper direct blows toward particular locations on the target core. The physics of stone fracture and the limitation of a knapper's strength preclude fracturing edges that form an angle greater than 90°; one must place a blow over an acutely angled edge. This proscription had important consequences for the development of knapping techniques. Eventually knappers developed core preparation techniques in which the removal of small flakes modified the edges of a core in order to permit the removal of larger flakes. After removing one flake, a knapper can further modify the shape of the core by removing more flakes, and can modify the shape of the flakes by removing even smaller flakes from their edges. All such modifications require directing the hammer blows to particular locations. Some knapping techniques that appeared late in human evolution required very precise placement indeed, such that a minor error could destroy the entire tool.

    Knapping requires both strength in delivering blows and precision in the placement of blows. Not surprisingly, there are features of human anatomy that appear to have evolved as an adaptation to stone knapping. The human hand presents the most salient of these; long thumbs relative to fingers, broad fingertip pads and a suite of features in the central palm that make it more robust and stable compared to those of apes (Marzke, 1996). Marzke argues that these features are an adaptation to the 'intrinsic and

[1] Knapping is the controlled fracture of stone by hand.
[2] One can fracture stone by simply throwing a core down onto a hard surface. While this can produce useful products, and may well have preceded more formal techniques, it is not knapping per se and reveals little about spatial cognition.

A

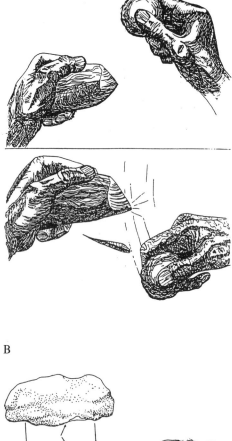

B

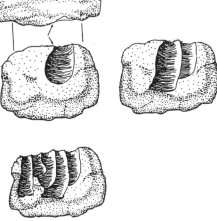

Fig. 6.1 A. The basic action of stone knapping. B. Patterns of 'negative scars' produced by successive blows.

extrinsic forces associated with the grasp and manipulation of stones in pounding' (1996, p. 131), and has identified many of these features on two-million-year-old hominid fossils, suggesting that selection had been in place for some time before then. Toth (personal communication) has suggested, based on his own experience in knapping and his observation of knapping done by a bonobo (see below), that there must also be anatomical features of the human shoulder that are adapted to delivering powerful, directed blows with a hand-held object.

Unfortunately, little has yet been published on the cognition of stone knapping. If one takes the perspective of evolutionary psychology, one might expect some dedicated cognitive module to have evolved in support of knapping; the presence of anatomical adaptations, after all, attests to the evolutionary importance of stone tool manufacture. However, no one has proposed such a specific module. Mithen (1996b) has argued for a more general tool manipulation module, and there is at least some support for this hypothesis from studies of modern technology. It is clear, for example, that people learn tool use largely by observation, replication and repetition (apprenticeship), and that language plays only a minor role (Gatewood, 1985; Wynn, 1991; Keller and Keller, 1996), so that it is reasonable to suppose that there is some cognitive encapsulation. This is, however, a long way from a detailed description of a cognitive module. Moreover, there has been no attempt to incorporate spatial cognition into a model of technical cognition, even though spatial knowledge had to have been incorporated from the very beginning of stone knapping. After all, knapping is a directed action in space. Studies of the evolution of spatial cognition have instead borrowed directly from psychology, where there is an extensive literature, and have modified the concepts for use in studying stone tools (Wynn, 1979, 1989; Robson Brown, 1993).

The cognitive requirements of stone knapping are within the abilities of apes, at least at the basic level of using a hammer to remove a flake. Nick Toth and Sue Savage-Rumbaugh have taught a bonobo to flake stone, and the results of their research help identify what might have been different about the cognition of the earliest stone knappers (Toth et al., 1993). Kanzi, a bonobo also known for his ability to understand spoken English and use signs, learned how to remove flakes from cores by observing a human knapper; he also learned to use the sharp flakes to cut through a cord that held shut a reward box. After observing the procedure, Kanzi perfected his technique by trial and error. His initial solution, interestingly, was not to copy the observer's action, but to hurl the core onto a hard surface and then select the sharp pieces from the shattered remnants. He clearly understood the notion of breakage and its consequences. When experimenters padded the room, he then copied the hammering technique used by the knapper. From this experiment (and an earlier one by Wright, 1972), it is clear that fracturing stone is within the cognitive abilities of apes. However, Kanzi is not as adept as human knappers. '(A)s yet he does not seem to have mastered the concept of searching for acute angles on cores from which to detach flakes efficiently, or intentionally using flake scars on one flake of a core as striking platforms for removing flakes from another face' (Toth *et al.*, 1993, p. 89). These abilities are basic to modern knapping and, more telling, are evident in the tools made two million years ago. Toth *et al.* suggest that this represents a significant cognitive development, though they do not specify just what cognitive ability may have evolved. Elsewhere (Wynn *et al.*, 1996) I have suggested that it may represent an evolutionary development in 'spatial visualisation', which is the ability to discriminate patterns in complex backgrounds. If true, this would represent a minor cognitive development, of interest primarily because it is a cognitive ability tied to tool manufacture and use.

Kanzi's inability to recognise acute angles is a feature of his spatial perceptual–cognitive repertoire. He is also not very accurate in delivering blows, and this is harder to assess. It could simply be a matter of biomechanical constraint; he does not have the necessary motor control. It could also result from his inability to organise his action on the small spatial field of the core. It is the organisation of such action, fossilised as patterns of flake scars, that developed significantly over the two million years following the first appearance of stone tools.

While spatial perceptual–cognitive abilities affected many characteristics of stone tools, it is the development of symmetry as an imposed pattern that most clearly documents the evolution of this component of human cognition.

2.4   The earliest stone tools

The earliest tools exhibit no convincingly symmetrical patterns. Archaeologists assign these tools to a category termed 'Oldowan,' because of their first discovery at Olduvai Gorge in Tanzania. A better label was proposed several decades ago by Graham Clark (1977), who termed them a Mode 1 technology, a term based on technological characteristics, with no time-space implications. Mode 1 tools first appeared about 2.5 million years ago in what is today Ethiopia, and were the only kind of stone technology in evidence for the next one million years. After 1.5 million years ago, Mode 1 technologies continued to be produced in many areas and, indeed, were made into historic times. As such Mode 1 represents a common, 'generic' stone tool industry. It was also the earliest (see Figure 6.2).

The emphasis of Mode 1 tools is on the edges. Simple stone flakes can

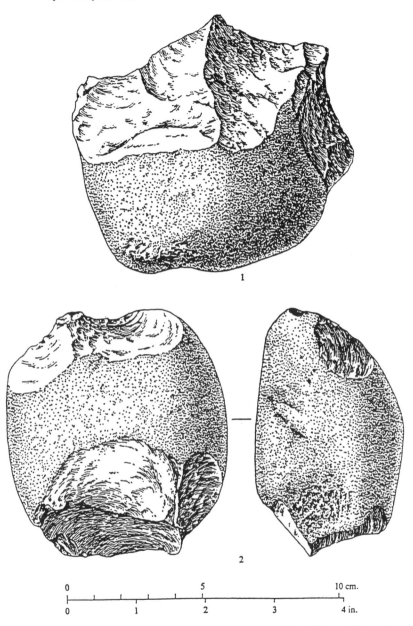

Fig. 6.2 1.8 million-year-old stone tools from Olduvai Gorge, Tanzania
(Leakey, 1971). The knapper placed blows adjacent to earlier blows, but
there is no reason to believe that the overall shape of the artefact was the
result of intention.

have very sharp edges, and are useful cutting tools without further modification. The cores from which the flakes were removed also have useful edges. These are not as sharp as the flakes, but the cores are usually heavier, and the result is a tool that can be used for chopping, crushing and heavy cutting. Mode 1 tools exhibit little or no attention to the overall shape of the artefact. The only possible examples of a shaped tool occur in relatively late Oldowan assemblages, where there are a few flakes with trimmed projections (termed awls). Here a two-dimensional pattern of sorts has been imposed on the artefact, but it is a very 'local' configuration, one that is very much tied to the nature of the edge itself.

There is nothing about these tools that required a concept of symmetry, or even of balance. The topological concepts of boundary, proximity and order constitute the minimum spatial concepts necessary to produce these tools. All are in the spatial repertoire of apes (Wynn and McGrew, 1989).

2.5   The first hominid-imposed symmetry

The earliest possible examples of a hominid-imposed symmetry occur on artefacts termed bifaces. These are core tools that have bifacial trimming around much or all of the margin. This trimming results in a single edge that is usually sinuous in profile, at least on the early examples. Bifaces are longer than they are wide. The core was often a very large flake that had been removed from a boulder-sized core by a two-handed hammering technique (Jones, 1981). There are two major types of biface: handaxes, whose lateral edges converge to a rounded or pointed tip, and cleavers, whose lateral edges define a transverse bit.

Some of the earliest bifaces are bilaterally symmetrical, with one lateral edge 'reflecting' the other. Others are not at all symmetrical, except to the extent that any artefact with a continuous edge and that is longer than it is wide will be vaguely symmetrical (see Figure 6.3). Must the maker have had an idea of symmetry, or is the symmetry only in the mind of the archaeologist? This is a knotty problem, about which there is considerable disagreement, and about which I have myself flip-flopped on several occasions. I now maintain that there is intentional symmetry here, but that it is a very simple kind. On several of the bifaces, the trimming appears to have been placed in order to produce the symmetry, that is to say, one lateral edge has been trimmed to copy the other (see Figure 6.4). But the inverted copy is not a precise duplicate. It reproduces the qualitative characteristics of shape, but it is not a quantitative duplicate.

There is some evidence for radial symmetry contemporary with these early bifaces. These artefacts are termed 'discoids' precisely because they

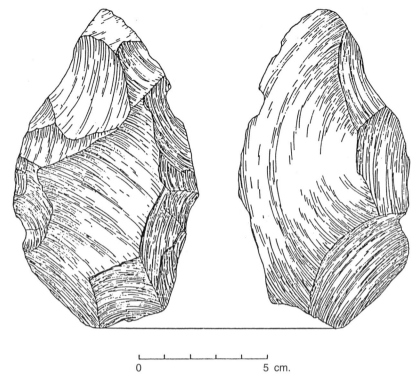

0   5 cm.

Fig. 6.3 1.4 million-year-old handaxe from West Natron, Tanzania. The artefact has a 'global' bilateral symmetry. The lateral edges mirror one another in quality of shape, but are not congruent.

have regular diameters (see Figure 6.5). One could also term them 'round' bifaces, because they differ from handaxes and cleavers only in having radial symmetry. Several discoids have been very extensively trimmed, and their shape is almost certainly intentional.

These earliest symmetrical artefacts first appeared about 1.4 million years ago in East Africa. They are the hallmarks of Clark's Mode 2 technology, which is also known as the Acheulean industry. Artefacts similar to these early African bifaces, and of similar age, have been found in Israel, but they were not as widespread geographically as the Mode 1 industries, which have been found in both Africa and Asia.

Over the next million years there were few, if any, developments in hominid-imposed symmetry. The symmetry of bifaces from the 700,000-year-old site of Olorgesailie is very like that of the earliest bifaces. However,

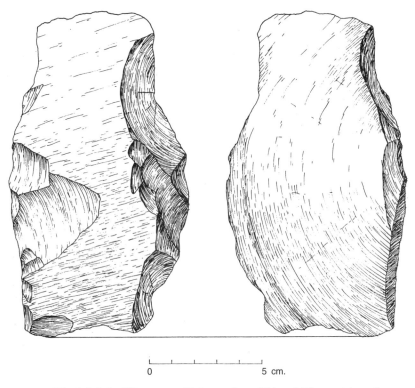

0   5 cm.

Fig. 6.4 1.4 million-year-old cleaver from Olduvai. The position of
negative flake scars indicates overall shape was probably intentional.

symmetry is far more common for the Olorgesailie bifaces; indeed, Glynn
Isaac (1977) once argued that there was a kind of cultural 'rule' for these
artefacts. Sometime after 500,000 years ago, however, some hominids
began producing bifaces with a much more striking symmetry.

2.6   Congruent and three-dimensional symmetries

Three developments in hominid-imposed symmetry appear in the
archaeological record sometime after 500,000 years ago. These are: (1) true
congruency; (2) three-dimensional symmetries; and (3) intentional violations of symmetry.

While the bilateral symmetry of early bifaces was rough and imprecise,
the symmetry of late examples clearly suggests attention to congruency.
The mirrored sides are not just qualitative reversals, but quantitative dupli-

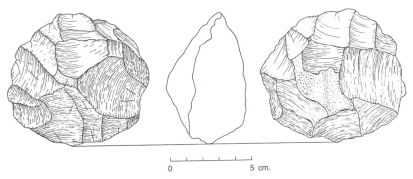

0   5 cm.

Fig. 6.5 1.4 million-year-old 'discoid' from Olduvai. The regularity of diameter suggests attention to a 'local' spatial quantity.

cates, at least to the degree that this is possible given the constraints of stone knapping. Many, but certainly not all, late handaxes and cleavers present such congruent symmetries, and this is one of the features that make them so attractive to us. Such a symmetry was not limited to a single shape. Late bifaces demonstrate a considerable amount of variability in overall plan shape. Some are long and narrow, others short and broad. Some have distinct shoulders, while others are almost round. Although there is some evidence that this variability was regional (Wynn and Tierson, 1990), much of it is related to raw material, and much appears to have been idiosyncratic. But in almost every assemblage of this time-period there will be a few bifaces with fine congruent symmetry, whatever the overall shape.

The second development in symmetry was the appearance of bilateral symmetry in three dimensions. Many of these bifaces are bilaterally symmetrical in profile as well as in plan. In the finest examples this symmetry extends to all of the cross-sections of the artefacts, including cross-sections oblique to the major axes, as we would define them (see Figure 6.6). Once again, this feature is not universally true, and many, many bifaces do not have it, but it is present in at least a few artefacts from most assemblages.

The third development in symmetry is not technically symmetry, but it is a feature of imposed shape in which symmetry plays a role. These are what I term 'violations' of symmetry, in which a bilateral pattern appears to have been intentionally altered into a non-symmetrical but nevertheless regular shape. Several cleavers from the Tanzanian site of Isimila appear 'bent,' as if the whole plan symmetry, including the midline, had been warped into a series of curved, parallel lines. These are invariably extensively modified artefacts, whose cross-sections are symmetrical, and the pattern is almost certainly the result of intention (see Figure 6.7). A better known example is

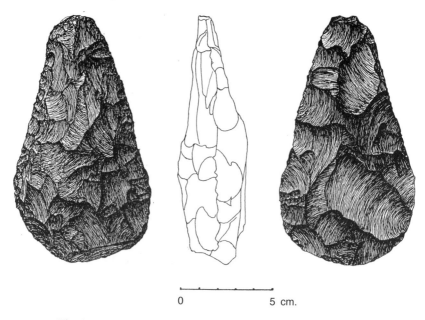

0   5 cm.

Fig. 6.6 A late European handaxe (age uncertain, probably 150–300,000 years). This artefact has congruent symmetry in three dimensions.

the twisted profile handaxe. These artefacts give the appearance of having been twisted around the central pole. The result is an S-shape to the lateral edges, as seen in profile. Again, these are extensively modified artefacts, and we must conclude, I think, that the pattern is the result of intention.

Several caveats complicate interpretation of these three developments. One is the problem of individual skill; some prehistoric stone knappers must have been more adept than others and better able to achieve congruent, three-dimensional symmetries in the intractable medium of stone. We have no way of knowing how common highly skilled knappers were. A second caveat is raw material. Some stone is much easier to work than others. I do not think it is entirely coincidence that twisted profile handaxes are invariably made of flint or obsidian, two of the most prized knapping materials. On the other hand, raw material is not as tyrannical as one might think. The 'bent' cleavers from Isimila are made of granite.

It is impossible to date these developments in symmetry precisely. Archaeological systematics place all of the examples in the late Acheulean (sometimes on morphological grounds alone, which leads to a circular argument). All were probably made after 500,000 years ago, perhaps even after 400,000 years ago. The Isimila artefacts, for example, date to between

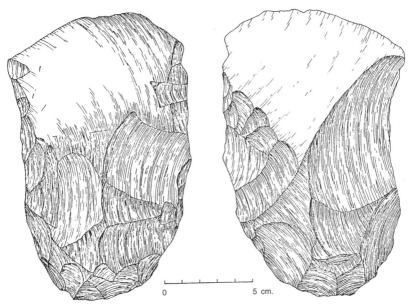

0   5 cm.

Fig. 6.7 A 'bent' cleaver from the Tanzanian site of Isimila (about
300,000 years old).

330,000 and 170,000 years ago (Howell *et al.*, 1972). The twisted profile
handaxes are probably no earlier than 400,000, and most may be much
later. Although 400,000 years is a long time in a historical framework, it
represents only the final 16% of technological evolution.

2.7   Symmetry in new materials

The examples I have used thus far have all been knapped stone artefacts.
While symmetry clearly can be and was imposed on many knapped stone
artefacts, the medium is not ideal for the imposition of form. It is not
plastic, and shaping can only be done by subtraction. Indeed, after the
appearance of the symmetrical patterns just discussed, no subsequent
developments in symmetry can be recognised in knapped stone. There were
developments in technique, and perhaps skill, but the symmetries imposed
on even very recent stone tools are no more elaborate than those imposed
on 300,000-year-old handaxes. As a consequence we must turn to other
materials.

It is not until very close to the present, indeed after 100,000 years ago,
that the archaeological record presents extensive evidence of artefacts

Fig. 6.8 Two bison from Lascaux (about 17,000 bp), a composition with reflection of elements.

made of perishable materials. Some archaeologists see this timing as entirely a reflection of preservation; others see it as evidence of new behaviours and abilities. The earliest such evidence is African and dates from before 90,000 years ago (Yellen *et al.*, 1995). These are worked bone points from a site in eastern Zaire. While these artefacts are quite important to several current arguments about prehistory, they reveal nothing new in regard to hominid-imposed symmetry.

The European Upper Palaeolithic provides the best-documented examples of hominid-imposed symmetries for the time period between 40,000 and 10,000 years ago. Here we find extensive evidence of symmetry in materials other than stone. Perhaps most widely known are cave paintings of Franco-Cantabrian Art, especially in compositions that are about 15,000 years old. Here we can see symmetries as patterns of elements in a composition, not just inherent in a single object. The example of bison from Lascaux is one of the better examples of reflection within a composition (see Figure 6.8). There are also examples of rotational symmetry (e.g. the Axial Gallery cattle, see Figure 6.9) and translational symmetry (swimming stags, see Figure 6.10). In addition to the art, there are examples of symmetry imposed on bone tools. The best examples are Magdalenian antler harpoons, some of which have barbs arranged in a reflection–translation

Fig. 6.9 Three bison and a horse from the ceiling of the Axial Gallery, Lascaux. Rotational symmetry may have guided the composition.

Fig. 6.10 'Swimming' stags from Lascaux. This is an example of translational symmetry.

pattern. In these examples symmetry arranges elements which are figural in their own right, but unlike the symmetry in the early stone tools, this symmetry is not a quality inherent in the figures. Instead, it arranges the figures.

2.8   *The appearance of modern symmetry*

On the scale of human evolution, 15,000 years was not long ago. Nevertheless, most prehistorians and historians acknowledge that a great deal has happened since then. There have certainly been major technological developments and it is appropriate to ask if there have been any developments in symmetry as an imposed pattern. Of course, the closer to the present an artefact was made, the more likely it is to be preserved and discovered. Perhaps more importantly, certain new technologies are more amenable to the imposition of form, because they are based on a malleable medium; ceramics and metallurgy come immediately to mind. People living during recent millennia were simply more able to impose form on artefacts.

Modern symmetrical patterns appear in the archaeological record with the Neolithic. Decorative patterns on ceramic pots, for example, commonly consist of simple shapes manipulated by symmetrical transformations (bilateral, rotational, translational and combinations), resulting in complex patterns. Here symmetry is not simply a perceptual pattern; it results from the application of a transformational rule. If we accept the evidence that the reflective/translational pattern of barbs on Magdalenian harpoons must also have resulted from the application of a symmetrical rule, then we can push the appearance of modern symmetry back into the late Palaeolithic (15,000 years ago). In either case, modern symmetry appeared late in human evolution.

3   Discussion

I believe it is possible to make two generalisations about the evidence. First, it documents a real trend in the nature of symmetry over time. By real, I mean that it is not a trend created by my interpretation, nor is it a trend in the concepts defined by cognitive psychology. Rather, it is an identifiable trend in the pattern itself. Over time artefactual symmetry became more regular and more complex. 'More regular' simply means that the symmetry more closely approximates the ideal of duplication and reflection. 'More complex' means that more elements came into play. Early symmetry was less regular and less complex than the symmetry of modern artefacts. I do not see this as resulting from some kind of inevitable progress, or any kind of orthogenetic striving. Rather, I believe that the evolution of symmetry reflects (but was not central to) developments in hominid cognition. The second generalisation that can be derived from the evidence is that symmetry does not seem to have developed in a slow, continuous way. There were immense spans of time during which no development occurred. For over one million years, for example, the symmetry of bifaces remained unchanged.

In order to bring this evidence to bear on the evolution of cognition, it is necessary to interpret it in the context of a theory of cognition. This can be done in three ways. The first is to use the archaeological evidence to check the explicit or implicit evolutionary predictions of cognitive theories. I have taken this approach in an earlier paper, 'Evolution of sex differences in spatial cognition', which assesses some of the predictions of evolutionary psychology using the paleoanthropological record (Wynn *et al.*, 1996). A second approach is to incorporate the evidence into an established theory and use the concepts of that theory to understand the evidence. This is the approach I have most often taken, as in my 1989 book *The Evolution of Spatial Competence*, which takes an explicitly Piagetian approach to the evolution of spatial thinking. A third approach is to make the archaeological evidence central to the argument, employing different theories to make sense of different aspects of the archaeological record. I have generally avoided this latter approach because it encourages a superficial eclecticism that has little interpretive power. Nevertheless, it is the approach that I will take below, largely because my previous interpretations have been unable to account for certain real features of the archaeological record.

The vast majority of the archaeological record of symmetry, chronologically speaking, reflects the evolution of hominid spatial perception–cognition. This evolution included both developments in perceptual–cognitive abilities and developments in skill. The earliest stone tools have no imposed symmetries. Basic spatial patterns like proximity and boundary are the minimum necessary concepts. In this the early stone knappers were very ape-like. Recall that apes can attend to nearness of existing elements and also the boundaries of figures, but they have never produced a symmetrical construct. There is enigmatic, anecdotal evidence that chimpanzee artists have a sense of balance, but 'space filling' seems a more parsimonious explanation. Concluding that the spatial patterns imposed by early stone knappers lacked symmetry, and were therefore ape-like, does not mean that these hominids were indistinguishable from chimpanzees. They may well have had, and probably did have, bio-mechanical abilities not found in modern apes, but this is not the point. Their spatial abilities *were* indistinguishable from those of a chimpanzee.

The first arguable symmetrical artefacts appeared about 1.4 million years ago, which post-dated the appearance of *Homo erectus*, the presumed artisan, by several hundred thousand years. This early symmetry is not regular, and indeed seems more akin to a balance of the halves of a spatial field. Nevertheless, it marks an imposition of overall form unknown in earlier artefacts, and this may well reflect developments in spatial perception–cognition. Much later, about 1,000,000 years later in fact, this rough symmetry was augmented with a fine congruent symmetry in three dimensions. These bifaces are very pleasing to the modern eye, and their quality of symmetry has never really been improved upon in stone knapping.

It is tempting to interpret this evidence in simple Gestaltist terms. The symmetrical target became more regular and refined over time, and one possible interpretation is that a neurologically based 'good Gestalt' of bilateral symmetry had evolved as a feature of the hominid perceptual–cognitive repertoire. Symmetry is an especially salient pattern in human perception (Uttal, 1996). Infants as young as four months discriminate symmetrical patterns better than asymmetrical patterns. Moreover, the pattern-perception abilities that children use to detect and remember symmetry develop during ontogeny. Initially children attend to the global pattern characteristic of symmetries; that is, they recognise and reproduce from memory the qualitative features of the pattern. Later they attempt to reproduce the pattern with precision (Bornstein and Stiles-Davis, 1984). There is a similar sequence of development in the symmetries imposed on stone tools. Initially it was a global symmetry of reflected shape; later precise congruent symmetries appeared. Children attend earliest to symmetries around a vertical axis, followed by recognition of symmetry around a horizontal axis, and only much later symmetries across oblique axes (Bornstein and Stiles-Davis, 1984). Once again, stone tools document a similar sequence. For a million years stone tools had only bilateral symmetry around a longitudinal axis; later there are symmetrical cross-sections across imagined oblique (and invisible) axes. 'Symmetry, a higher-order organising principle in pattern perception, aids children in both discrimination and memory . . .' (Bornstein and Stiles-Davis, 1984, p. 647). As a principle organising perception, it clearly develops in ontogeny. Stone tools indicate that it also evolved significantly between 2 million and 500,000 years ago. While reference to 'good form' has a certain aesthetic appeal, it is not an element in most current theories of perception or cognition, and it is to these that we must turn for greater interpretative insights.

The archaeological evidence corroborates some of the predictions of Piagetian psychology (which has some affinities with Gestaltist theory). Many aspects of Piaget's theory have been challenged over the last two decades, especially his ideas concerning infancy, but the basic outlines of his account of spatial development remain sound. Piaget and Inhelder (1967) argued that Euclidean concepts, including congruency and precise symmetries, appear late in childhood and are built out of earlier projective and topological concepts as the child reorganises his spatial conception of the world. Among these earlier concepts is the ability to reverse a configuration (global symmetry). The earlier appearance of roughly symmetrical artefacts in technological evolution is, then, predictable from a Piagetian developmental perspective. In addition, Piaget and Inhelder argued that the ability to conceive of regular cross-sections resulted from a child's ability to imagine a visual perspective not directly available to the perceiver, and that this projective ability develops in later childhood. Such an ability is obviously required to conceive of and produce the three-dimensional symmetries of later bifaces.

Symmetries imposed on artefacts also document the development of ability in visual projection and mental rotation. Reith and Dominin (1997) have recently documented children's ability to remember scenes projected onto a two-dimensional screen. The results corroborate, in general, some of the results of Piaget and Inhelder. It is not until the age of eight or nine that children reliably remember how a scene appears from a specific point of vision; earlier they recall global relations, ignoring changes in size and masking inherent in the view from a specific perspective. The ability to conceive of the invisible cross-sections of artefacts requires the same ability to 'record mentally a projection' that the eight- and nine-year-olds reliably employ, but it is an ability that appeared relatively late (after 500,000 years ago) in the archaeological record. A related ability is that of mental rotation (Linn and Petersen, 1986), which is the ability to rotate a three-dimensional image in the mind (e.g. the rotated block task on many intelligence tests). Success at these tasks varies greatly, even late in ontogeny, and it is one of the spatial abilities that consistently demonstrates a sex difference in performance (Wynn et al., 1996). The ability to rotate an image in the mind was almost certainly required for the manufacture of the very fine three-dimensional symmetries, and the violations of symmetry, true of some bifaces after 500,000 years ago.

Other specific spatial abilities required for the imposition of some symmetries are frame independence (also known as spatial perception) and spatial quantity. Even the earlier bifaces, with only a global symmetry, required that the stone knapper 'see past' the local spatial frame constituted by the core blank. This ability to impose a shape was not required for the earliest artefacts, and is nowhere clearly evident in the products of non-human primates. It also develops in ontogeny. The concept of spatial quantity also clearly evolved. Early symmetries were global, qualitative reversals of a shape; later bifaces with congruent symmetry add a notion of equivalent spatial *quantity*.

Models of the neurological underpinnings of imagery corroborate this important distinction between shape and spatial quantity. Kosslyn (various, e.g. 1994) has used PET scan studies and evidence from brain trauma patients to investigate the neural basis of visual recognition and imagery. One of the most reliable conclusions of his study is that recognition of shapes is largely independent of the recognition of spatial relations. The brain processes shape information in the lower temporal lobe but spatial information (size, left-right, etc.) in the parietal lobe. While there appears to be some direct neural connectivity between these regions, it is minimal. In other words, at the level of visual recognition, there are two separate neural networks. Information from these networks passes to associative regions of the frontal lobe where they are available for higher level processing. Complicating the picture further is the brain's apparent reliance on two spatial subsystems. The first, linked anatomically to the left parietal, processes 'categorical' spatial information such as left-right, above-below and inside-outside. Most of the 'topological' concepts discussed earlier in this chapter fall under this rubric. The second subsystem, which is linked more to the right parietal, processes metrical relations of size, co-ordinates, and so on. While the two subsystems are more directly linked than either is to the shape-recognition network, they process information separately and, again, pass it to higher functions. The processing of global symmetry appears to occur in the shape-recognition subsystem and does not require higher level processing. Congruent and three-dimensional symmetry are considerably more complex. In order to generate an image of a congruent symmetry, the brain must co-ordinate information from the shape-recognition network (temporal lobe) with information from the spatial network and the metrical subsystem in particular (right parietal). This co-ordination probably occurs in the associative regions of the frontal lobe.

In sum, the archaeological record of symmetry documents a clear development of spatial cognition over the million-year-period between 1.5 million years ago and 500,000 years ago. Essentially modern spatial cognition, at least in the sense of a perceptual–cognitive system, evolved relatively early in human evolution, certainly prior to the appearance of anatomically modern humans and perhaps earlier than the first *Homo sapiens*. But what was the context of this evolution? What selected for this impressive ability to conceive of and manipulate complex three-dimensional patterns?

To answer these questions, an evolutionary psychologist would undoubtedly look to the design features of the cognitive ability and match them to the specific behaviours they facilitate, on the methodological assumption that evidence of design and efficacy must be linked through natural selection. What is the perceptual saliency of symmetry, ability to remember projected images, mental rotation, etc., good *for*? There is some evidence that body symmetry is, in fact, related to reproductive success for males (Gangestad, 1997). According to Gangestad, observable phenotypic asymmetry (away from the bilateral symmetry coded genetically) correlates with developmental stress, so that asymmetry marks lower health. If a potential mate could detect this, he or she could avoid a reproductively costly (in an evolutionary sense) mating. But presumably this is true generally, and not just for humans; so why would our hominid ancestors have acquired such an exquisitely fine sense for symmetry, beyond that known for other animals? Perhaps symmetry gained added importance as a clue to general health when hominids lost thick body hair; condition of coat is also a good indicator of general health, and its absence forced selection for a heightened ability to detect variations away from symmetry.

Projective ability and mental rotation are harder to account for in evolutionary-psychological terms, but not impossible. Both are aspects of an ability to manipulate images and scenes. Navigation immediately comes to mind as a possible selective agent; but unfortunately, many animals are fine navigators without an ability to manipulate images, a fact that immediately weakens a navigation hypothesis (though see below). Other than navigation, these excellent spatial skills seem limited almost exclusively to cultural products of one kind or another (tools, houses, monuments, etc.), so perhaps the selective key lies here. An individual who could produce a more regular (symmetrical) artefact would be cueing his or her skill and worth as a potential mate. Other things being equal, a stone knapper who could produce fine three-dimensional bifaces was smarter and more capable, with better genes, than one who couldn't. So here the saliency of symmetry moves out of the phenotypic to the cultural, but the selective advantage is the same.

I hope that I have not been too convincing. I have made these selective guesses partially to demonstrate how easy it is to spin selectionist tales (Gould and Lewontin, 1979). The current weakness of evolutionary psychology is not so much in its tales (many of which are more convincing than mine), but in its failure to follow them up with testing against the actual evidence of evolution. As an evolutionary anthropologist, I know that this next step can and should be taken, primarily through an examination of the actual context of human evolution. Paleoanthropologists know a good deal about the anatomy of earlier hominids, including the size and overall shape of the brain. Archaeologists have, as we have seen, supplied useful information about the cultural products of these hominids. Both have provided extensive evidence of age and geographic location of finds, including the paleogeographic context. From all of this, anthropologists can put together an outline of actual sequences of development and the circumstances of this development. Certainly this is relevant to any discussion of the evolution of mind.

From this paleoanthropological perspective, the evolution of hominid spatial thinking appears to have coincided with an important shift in adaptive niche. About 1.8 million years ago, with the advent of *Homo erectus*, hominids finally broke from the woodland–riparian adaptations of their predecessors and moved out onto the open grasslands. Not only did they invade more open country, with dramatic anatomical consequences (Walker and Leakey, 1993), they also invaded higher and colder terrain (Cachel and Harris, 1995). The choice of 'invade' is apt, because the most striking feature of this new niche was that it was expansionistic. *Homo erectus* rapidly spread to occupy much of the tropical and sub-tropical Old World (e.g. Georgia at 1.6 million, Java as early as 1.8 million). Cachel and Harris have described *Homo erectus* as a 'weed' species (1995) – never numerous as individuals, but able to expand into new areas very rapidly. The generalised adaptation required of a weed species was, for *Homo erectus*, partially technological (reliance on tools and fire), but there is also evidence of a more sophisticated array of spatial concepts than any known for apes, including global symmetry imposed on artefacts and a rudimentary concept of spatial quantity (regular diameters of discoids, a round biface). These spatial patterns appeared on artefacts *after* the shift in niche, suggesting that something in the new niche selected for spatial thinking.

Presumably, better navigation skills would have provided a clear advantage to an expansionistic 'weed' species. Unfortunately, Kosslyn's study of perception and imagery, discussed above, challenges such a facile conclusion. While Kosslyn rarely addresses evolution, the implications of his results for evolutionary reconstructions are significant. If the brain processes information about space independently of information about shape, then selection for navigational ability is unlikely to have had a direct effect on shape recognition skills. Shape recognition (and, probably, imagery) must have been an aspect of the neural processing invoked in tool manufacture, especially edges and angles, but also symmetry. Here the archaeological record presents a puzzle for cognitive science. Eventually, metrical considerations came into play in the production of tools, and in Kosslyn's scheme metrics are processed by the spatial net in the right parietal. If Kosslyn's model is at all reliable (and there is strong evidence for its general features, at least), then the application of spatial information to shape images must occur in the higher processing regions of the brain, associative memory in particular.

This conclusion has implications for a modular view of intelligence in general, and for the evolution of a modular mind in particular. At first blush, developments in symmetry would appear to document the evolution of the hominid visual input system, to use Fodor's (1983) classic definition of a cognitive module. Even incorporating Kosslyn's more detailed characterisation of visual recognition and imaging (1994), it is possible to conceive of an encapsulated visual imaging module that is made up of shape and spatial subsystems. If true, what the archaeological record may document is the increasing complexity of the outputs of this cognitive module. However, there are good reasons for rejecting this idea. Features of 'advanced' symmetry, congruency in particular, simply do not fulfil the requirements laid out by Fodor (1983). Congruency, for example, is not fast, mandatory or limited in access. Even modern adults trained in geometry cannot automatically compute congruency, and when they do make such an assessment, it is not a rapid, at-a-glance recognition. It is a conscious (painfully so for many adolescents) cognitive process. All of this implies the operation of a central processor. Whether this is Kosslyn's associative memory, or Fodor's diffuse central processor, or Mithen's (1996b; this volume) cognitive fluidity is perhaps simply a difference in semantics. What seems clear is that the ability to recognise and conceive three-dimensional, congruent symmetries is not simply the output of an encapsulated visual system. It also requires the services of a more general neural processor that can integrate the outputs of several information subsystems. In other words, the archaeological evidence documents the evolution of higher brain function, not just spatial ability or shape imagery. And what selected for a more powerful general intelligence may have been very different, even unrelated, to what selected for spatial ability or shape recognition ability.

The evolutionary scenario just summarised presents no clear implications for language. At the level of sensory input and initial processing, spatial cognition and shape recognition appear to be largely independent of language. If associative thinking is language dependent, then the incorporation of spatial information into shape recognition would imply language. However, humans are not unique in possessing associative memory; and the archaeological record, particularly of congruent symmetry, only implicates associative memory in the most general sense. If, on the other hand, congruent symmetry requires an *abstract concept* of symmetry, then there may be an argument. According to Noble and Davidson (1996) abstract concepts can only exist in a symbolic communicative milieu, so that evidence for an abstract concept is evidence for words and language. This is precisely the reason they go to some lengths to argue that biface shape was an unintended consequence of a flaking procedure. If the knapper invoked an intended shape when making a biface this would require, according to Noble and Davidson, a concept, and a word, and language, placing language much earlier than they are willing to accept.

But must an intended shape have required a concept? To put it another way, does the association of shape and metrical spatial information into an image require abstract thinking? If so, then the congruent symmetries of late bifaces imply language. Kosslyn (1994) suggests that such links in associative memory do require some generalisation and abstraction (otherwise recognition would occur earlier in modality-specific pattern-activation subsystems), so the question hinges on whether all such abstraction requires words and language. This is, of course, a long-standing debate in philosophy, linguistics and psychology, for which there is as yet no resolution. I suspect that the kinds of generalisations necessary to construct congruent symmetrical images are comparatively low-level generalisations and incorporate associations between concrete, sensory-based information. Yes, this may tell us something interesting about developments in human associative memory, but it does not necessarily implicate linguistic ability.

The application of developmental theories has led to a paradoxical conclusion: by 300,000 years ago spatial perceptual–cognitive thinking was modern. The ability to conceive and execute regular three-dimensional congruent symmetries in flaked stone was in place three hundred millennia ago, at least. But very little else about the archaeological evidence from this time-period looks modern. Despite having a repertoire of modern spatial abilities, these hominids did not produce modern culture. Perhaps, as I once argued, cognition was modern, but culture was not (Wynn, 1979). I now suspect that this conclusion was naive, and that cognition continued to evolve after 300,000. Spatial perception–cognition, however, was not an important component of this evolution. Once again symmetry gives us a clue, not as an element of spatial thinking, but rather as a transformational rule.

When we examine the basic forms of patterns produced by modern people, they are often very simple. Yes, modern people produce artefacts with regular three-dimensional symmetry as impressive as that of 300,000-year-old bifaces. But we also delight in complex patterns produced by the iterative application of transformational rules. This results in symmetries, but the underlying cognition is very different from that of spatial perception and cognition. I believe that the complex symmetries of the Neolithic document a different kind of thinking from that underpinning handaxes, even the twisted profile variety. It is a kind of thinking that is largely, if not entirely, cultural and which relies on linguistic transmission. It appeared late in human evolution and is one of the hallmarks of modernity. It is not, however, a component of spatial cognition *per se*.

4   General conclusion

The archaeological record of symmetry documents the evolution of human spatial perception–cognition. Between 1.5 million years ago and 500,000 years ago, hominid ability to recognise and conceive of spatial patterns evolved away from a generalised ape ability and acquired the features of modern human spatial thinking. These included such specific spatial abilities as projection of shapes from alternative perspectives, mental rotation and congruency. The later developments almost certainly required central neural processing of some kind, so this evolutionary story is not simply one of developments within a single cognitive module. Whatever evolutionary process lay behind human spatial thinking, it worked relatively early in human evolution, certainly long before the appearance of anatomically modern humans. It did not, however, require language.

I would like to thank Peter Carruthers for inviting me to participate in the Hang Seng workshop on the evolution of mind and for his helpful criticisms and suggestions. Of the many other scholars who have provided useful comments on the matter of symmetry I note especially Charles Keller, Iain Davidson and Dorothy Washburn.

7 Evolution, communication and the proper function of language

Gloria Origgi and Dan Sperber

Language is both a biological and a cultural phenomenon. Our aim here is to discuss, in an evolutionary perspective, the articulation of these two aspects of language. For this, we draw on the general conceptual framework developed by Ruth Millikan (1984), while at the same time dissociating ourselves from her view of language.

1   Biological and cultural evolutionary processes

The phrase 'evolution of language' refers to two related but quite distinct processes: the biological evolution of a language faculty, and the historical-cultural evolution of languages. The historical-cultural evolution of languages itself requires the repetition across populations and over generations of the individual process of language acquisition. Individuals who have acquired the language of their community can engage in verbal communication. Through a myriad of acts of communication, they achieve a variety of effects, intended or unintended. The aggregation of these effects explains both the biological evolution of the language faculty and the historical-cultural evolution of languages.

The biological evolution of a language faculty and the historical-cultural evolution of languages are related in interesting ways. If we assume, with Chomsky, that human languages require, to be acquired, a language faculty, it follows that the biological emergence of this faculty is a precondition for the cultural emergence of any human language. On the other hand, if we think, without Chomsky this time, of the language faculty as a biological adaptation, then presumably its function – at least its proximate function on the successful performance of which other functions depend – is to make language acquisition possible. A language faculty is adaptive only in an environment where languages are spoken and where, therefore, inputs indispensable for language acquisition are found. Adaptations *qua* adaptations emerge only in an environment where they are adaptive. So it seems that the existence of a spoken language is a precondition for that of a language faculty. But then, the language faculty and a spoken language are each a precondition for the other. There are various ways to finesse this boot-strapping problem. We will conclude this paper by proposing a possible way to resolve it.

Even if the proximate function of the language faculty is to permit the acquisition of language, what makes *this* adaptive is the adaptive value of language use itself. In fact, most adaptationist explanations of the biological evolution of the language faculty just take for granted or ignore its obvious proximate function, that of permitting language acquisition. They explain the emergence and stabilisation of the language faculty by the adaptive value of language use, that is, in terms of quite remote functions of the language faculty itself.

How, then, does language use contribute to biological fitness? Language use consists in the expression and communication of thoughts. Expression without communication, as when we think in words, may be adaptive because of its contribution to cognitive performance (Chomsky, 1980, pp. 229–30; Bickerton, 1995, chapter 3; Carruthers, 1996b). We will not consider this (possibly important) aspect of the adaptiveness of language use in this discussion. The adaptive value of public languages is, we assume, mostly due to their use in communication. But what makes communication itself adaptive? Communication has a great variety of effects. It allows individuals to benefit from the perceptions and inferences of others and increases their knowledge well beyond that which they could acquire on their own. It allows elaborate forms of co-ordinated planning and action. It can be used for manipulation, deceit, display of wit, seduction and maintenance of social relationships, all of which have fitness consequences.

Many of the debates on the biological emergence and evolution of the language faculty revolve solely around the relative importance of these diverse functions of linguistic communication (e.g. Dunbar, 1996; Hurford *et al.*, 1998, part I). Even accepting the implicit move from language faculty to language use, there is something missing here. It is as if the evolution of organs of locomotion such as wings or legs were discussed only in terms of the effects of locomotion such as fleeing predators, finding food or finding mates, without considering the proximate function of these organs, namely locomotion itself. Different organs of locomotion determine qualitatively and quantitatively different performances. The evolution of these organs cannot be properly understood without taking into consideration these specific performances, i.e. the ways in which these organs perform their proximate function of locomotion. In much of the literature, verbal communication is treated as a well-understood process, the character of which can be taken for granted rather than examined when discussing evolutionary issues. This, however, is an illusion. The mechanism of verbal communication is contentious. Different views of this mechanism have different evolutionary implications, and this is one of the two main issues we want to investigate here.

A language faculty is an adaptation because it permits the acquisition of linguistic competence, which permits verbal communication, which can be used in a great variety of ways, some with beneficial effects. Identifying those remote effects of the language faculty that have contributed to the biological fitness of language users should provide some essential pieces of the overall puzzle. However, this is unlikely to help much with the specifics and the articulation of the two evolutionary processes involved: the biological evolution of a language faculty and the cultural evolution of languages. The proper way of describing this articulation is the second main issue we want to discuss here.

There have been, in the past twenty years or so, interesting discussions of the relation between biological and cultural evolution. On the one hand, processes of gene–culture co-evolution have been hypothesised. It is reasonable to surmise that solving the boot-strapping problem we mentioned at the outset would involve modelling such a co-evolutionary process between languages and the language faculty. On the other hand, various conceptual frameworks for dealing in a unified manner with both biological and cultural evolution have been proposed (Dawkins, 1976, 1982; Cavalli-Sforza and Feldman, 1981; Lumsden and Wilson, 1981; Millikan, 1984; Boyd and Richerson, 1985; Durham, 1991; Dennett, 1995; Sperber, 1996); the best known is probably Dawkins'. The conditions for undergoing Darwinian selection, Dawkins argues, can be fulfilled not only by biological replicators such as genes, but also by artefacts such as computer viruses, or by bits of culture that get copied again and again and which he calls 'memes'. If one accepts this framework, then languages, or at least linguistic devices such as words or grammatical forms, can be seen as paradigmatic examples of memes. There are problems, however, with the meme framework: either the Darwinian model of selection is applied *as is* to cultural evolution – and this is too rigid, as many including Dawkins himself have noted – or else the meme framework must be loosened, but it is unclear how this should be done, and to what extent the explanatory power of the approach might survive such loosening (see Sperber, 1996, chapter 5).

In this presentation, we will consider another conceptual framework, more familiar to philosophers than to evolutionary theorists, that of Ruth Millikan. It is intended from the start to approach biological and cultural phenomena in the same basic way, and it is, in this respect at least, both more precise and less rigid than Dawkins'. Moreover, in her book *Language, Thought and Other Biological Categories* (1984), Millikan uses this framework to discuss in detail the case of language. Her not-at-all-hidden agenda, in so doing, is to debunk a view of verbal communication defended in particular by Paul Grice (1957, 1989) that has gained not universal, but wide acceptance among philosophers of language and linguists. According to the Gricean view that Millikan attacks, comprehension systematically involves identifying an intention of the speaker. According to the view Millikan defends, comprehension typically consists in coming directly to believe what is being asserted or in coming directly to want to comply with what is being requested. Here we will articulate our discussion of the evolution of language around Millikan's proposals. Specifically, we will attempt to pry apart her conceptual framework, which we find well worth exploring further (in particular in reflecting about the case of language), from her own view of language, with which we very much disagree.

2   Millikan's teleofunctional framework

In her 1984 book, Millikan presented a general account of biological and cultural items in terms of 'proper functions' historically responsible for the reproduction and proliferation of these items. She proposed a particularly interesting distinction between direct and derived proper functions. (We will ignore several other conceptual distinctions that she introduced in this book and made little use of thereafter. Generally, our goal is not to present a critical exegesis of Millikan's work, but to reconcile aspects of her basic approach with a view of language she opposes.) Millikan's theory of proper functions is a way of explaining different cases of reproduction, in particular biological and cultural, within a single framework. Linguistic devices, purposive behaviours, artefacts and body organs provide examples of such cases.

What is a proper function? Quite standardly, Millikan distinguishes the proper function of an item from its actual effects, that is, what in fact it succeeds in doing on various occasions, and from the functions that various users intend it to perform on various occasions. She then defines, quite originally, not one but two types of proper function: direct and derived. For an item A to have a *direct* proper function F it has to fulfil the following condition:

Direct Proper Function
A originated as a 'reproduction' [. . .] of some prior item or items that, *due* in part to possession of the properties reproduced, have actually performed F in the past, and A exists because (causally, historically because) of this or these performances. (Millikan, 1993, p. 12)

An item may typically have a great many recurring effects: its *direct* proper function is the one that is *historically* responsible for its reproduction. A heart makes noise, contributes to the body's weight and pumps blood. Only the latter effect is its proper function. Even a malfunctioning heart still has the direct proper function to pump blood, because it has been reproduced through organisms that, thanks in part to their own heart pumping blood, have had descendants similarly endowed with blood-pumping hearts. Millikan's notion of direct proper function is a rendering of the biological notion of function as used in evolutionary theory, but without any reference to the particular conditions of biological reproduction and selection. As we will see, it applies equally well to an item such as a word.

A device having a direct proper function may perform it by producing items that are adapted to specific environmental circumstances. For instance the pigment-arranging device of the chameleon's skin performs its functions of hiding the chameleon by producing colour patterns matching the background on which the animal is sitting. When the chameleon is sitting on a matching surface, the function of hiding it from predators is performed by a particular colour pattern. It is reasonable to say that this pattern, though it may never have been produced before, has a proper function. However, this should be ascribed not a direct, but a derived proper function. For an item A to have a *derived* proper function *F* it has to fulfil the following condition:

Derived Proper Function

A originated as the product of some prior device that, given its circumstances, had performance of *F* as proper function, and that, under those circumstances, normally causes *F* to be performed by *means* of producing an item like *A*. (*Ibid.*)

Whereas, by definition, a direct proper function is performed by a great many items with the same causally relevant properties, a derived proper function may be performed by individual items that each have different causally relevant properties. An item with a derived proper function is one that has been produced by a device (for instance, the chameleon's pigment-arranging device) that produces different items in different contexts (for instance, different colour patterns depending on the surface on which the chameleon happens to be sitting). To take another example, the gosling's imprinting mechanism has the *direct* proper function of allowing each and every gosling to fix an image of its mother so as to follow her. The fixation by gosling George of an image of his mother Samantha is a product of this imprinting mechanism in the special circumstances of George's birth. This particular imprinting, unique to George, has the *derived* proper function of helping George follow Samantha.

Note that the derived proper function of a given item can be given two descriptions, one general, the other specific. A general description is without reference to the particulars of the case. For instance any particular colour pattern on the skin of a chameleon has the derived function of making it less visible on the surface on which it is sitting; any imprinting in the brain of a gosling has the derived function of helping it follow its mother. A specific description refers to the particulars of the case and may be different for each item. For instance *this* pattern has the derived function of making *this* chameleon less visible on *this* surface on which it is sitting; the imprinting in George's brain has the function of helping him follow Samantha. Under its general description a derived proper function is one typically shared by many items. Under its specific description, a derived proper function may be a one-off affair: the particular colour pattern of a chameleon sitting on an improbable background may occur only once in the history of the species, and therefore the derived proper function of hiding this chameleon on this background may be a function that, under this description, is performed only once.

Roughly, the distinction between direct and derived proper functions explains respectively how an item stabilises due to the function its ancestors have performed, and how a new particular item, not reproduced from any ancestral model, is nevertheless generated to perform a proper function – though an indirect one.

3   Millikan, language and communication

Culture is comprised of all items that are reproduced and proliferated through communication in the widest sense, including unintentional transmission of information. (For a more elaborate characterisation of culture, see Sperber, 1996.) The direct cultural function of a cultural item is, unproblematically, the effect that prior items of the same type have performed in the past and that have caused the item to be reproduced again and again. For instance, a hammer, even if it is actually used as a paperweight, has the direct cultural function of helping to drive nails, because it is the repeated and successful performance of this effect by hammers (helping to drive nails) that has caused them to be produced again and again.

Linguistic items are cultural items, and it is sensible to ask what direct proper functions of a cultural kind they have. In Millikan's terminology, language is a complex of different devices. A 'linguistic device' can be a word, a surface syntactic form, a tonal inflection, a stress pattern, a system of punctuation and 'any other significant surface elements that a natural spoken or written language may contain' (Millikan, 1984, p. 3). A linguistic device has proliferated because it has served a describable, stable, proper function.

Language use is a purposeful activity that needs some regularity for its successful performance. More specifically, there must be a regular pattern of correspondence between a speaker's purpose in uttering a given language device and the hearer's response to this utterance. It is this reliability that accounts for the device being used again and again. Among the effects that may be correlated with a linguistic device, its direct proper function is what keeps speakers and hearers using and responding to the linguistic device in a standard way and therefore stabilises the device. What is often called the 'conventional use' of a linguistic device corresponds to this *stabilising direct proper function*. Thus the stabilising direct proper function of a given word is to contribute its conventional meaning to the meaning of the utterances in which it is used.

The use of a given linguistic device on a given occasion, by a speaker with his or her own purposes, endows this token of the device with a derived proper function. This derived proper function may be a mere tokening without modification of its direct proper function (as when a word is used to convey just its conventional meaning) or it may be different from its direct proper function (as in the case of an indexical, or of a non-conventional metaphor). For example, at first blush (and we will propose a different account later), the indexical 'now' has the stabilising direct proper function of referring to the time of utterance, and this direct function is performed through each token of 'now' performing the derived proper function of referring to a specific time.

Though Millikan does not develop this, linguistic devices also have derived proper functions of a biological kind. A word, say the English word 'now', has both public tokens (one every time it is uttered) and mental tokens. The mental tokens themselves are at two levels. There is a mental token each time the word 'now' is uttered or comprehended, i.e. a mental representation of the uttered word. There is also, at a more fundamental level, an entry for 'now' in the mental lexicon in all individuals capable of using the word, which is part of their knowledge of the English language. This mental lexical entry is a mental version of the public language word. It is a cultural item, with a cultural direct proper function. At the same time, it is a device produced by the individual's language faculty or Language Acquisition Device performing its direct function in the particular environment of an English-speaking community. The direct biological function of acquiring a language is performed by producing mental devices adapted to the local language community. Therefore the mental 'now' in a person's mental lexicon (and all the mental linguistic devices of English or of any other language) have biological derived proper functions, just as does George the gosling's imprinting of his mother Samantha's image. The difference is that the gosling's imprinting mechanism fulfils its direct biological function by producing a single item with a derived biological function and no cultural function at all, whereas the Language Acquisition Device fulfils its function by producing tens of thousands of items with derived biological functions and direct cultural functions.

Here, then – thanks to the notion of derived function – is a way of describing linguistic devices as belonging simultaneously to biological and cultural histories. A linguistic device in the mind of an individual belongs to biological history in being the product of a biologically evolved language faculty that performs its function by producing such devices, adapted to the local linguistic community. The same linguistic device belongs to a cultural history: it has been reproduced in the mind of the individual, as in that of all the members of the linguistic community, because of its past and repeated performance of a specific linguistic function. The proliferation and stability of linguistic devices can be explained through a combination of cultural and biological (more specifically cognitive) factors. This seems to us much more insightful than a strictly cultural story.

Note that this account differs from a meme model of linguistic evolution in two respects. In the meme model, linguistic (and more generally cultural) evolution is homologous to biological evolution in that it, too, is essentially driven by a process of Darwinian selection. Biological and cultural evolution, however, are not otherwise articulated (apart from the obvious point that cultural evolution requires a species with biologically evolved capacities that makes it capable of culture). In contrast, by using Millikan's distinction between direct and derived proper functions, we can describe the articulation between biological and linguistic evolution. Also, whereas the meme model assumes that memes are typically replicated by 'imitation', there is no postulation of a copying process in the present account. Generally, the word 'reproduction' is ambiguous between a sense of *repeated production* and a sense of *copying*. Items of the same type can be produced again and again without being copied from one another, for instance by being produced from the same mould.

As Chomsky pointed out long ago, members of the same linguistic community do not learn to speak by copying the sentences they have heard. Most sentences of a language are uttered, if at all, only once, and therefore the overlap between the sets of sentences heard by two learners of the same language is quite small. If they learned their language by copying, language learners would end up speaking not just languages quite different from one another, but also languages quite different from those humans speak.

In fact, language learners sift, sort and analyse linguistic inputs, and use them as evidence for grammar construction. From quite different inputs sets, they converge on similar grammars – they 'reproduce' more or less the grammar of their community – thanks to a biologically evolved disposition to treat linguistic inputs to precisely this effect. A similar point can be made at the level of the lexicon. The contextual evidence on the basis of which a meaning can be attributed to a new word tends to be different in every case, and moreover, a word is quite often used with a contextual meaning different from its 'literal meaning'. Still, language learners converge on the same meanings for the same words, not by copying – and what exactly is there to copy on the semantic side? – but by deriving converging conclusions from quite different and sometimes divergent pieces of evidence. It may be assumed that the conclusions language learners derive about word meanings are guided by the language faculty, which constrains the kinds of words that can occur in the lexicon (count nouns, mass nouns, transitive verbs, intransitive verbs, prepositions, etc.), and also, possibly, by cognitive constraints on the structure of concepts. To sum up this point, the stabilisation of linguistic devices is explained, not by some kind of imitation of linguistic behavioural inputs, but by the constructive processing of these inputs by a biologically evolved language faculty. Such an account, though not exactly Millikan's own, fits much better within Millikan's conceptual framework than within the standard meme framework.

Millikan's motivation in developing her theory of proper functions and in applying it to language was, primarily, to give an original account of meaning and intentionality, and to defend a certain view of linguistic communication that we do not share. Here is a stark statement of this view: 'Speech is a form of direct perception of whatever speech is *about*. Interpreting speech does not require making any inference or having any beliefs [. . .] about the speaker's intentions' (Millikan, 1984, p. 62). According to Millikan, it is a sufficient condition for linguistic communication that the linguistic devices used succeed in performing their stabilising proper functions. For example, in the case of indicative sentences:

speakers proliferate tokens of the indicative mood mainly insofar as these tokens produce, at any rate, *beliefs* in hearers [. . .] For this to be true it is not necessary that speakers should explicitly "intend" that their hearers believe what they say in a sense of "intend" that would require thinking of these beliefs or even having concepts of beliefs. [. . .] A proper function of speakers' acts in speaking could be to produce true beliefs in hearers even if the speakers had no concept of mental states and no understanding of the hidden mechanism whereby rewards result from speaking the truth. (1984, p. 58)

Similarly, Millikan argues, the direct proper function of imperatives is to produce compliance. Thus, an imperative utterance such as 'Eat!' performs its proper function when it causes the hearer to intend to eat and to act accordingly.

Until very recently, all explanations of the very possibility of communication were based on one version or another of the idea that a communicator encodes a content into a signal, and that the audience decodes the signal back into more or less the original content. After Grice, a second, wholly different mechanism was identified that also made communication possible: a communicator could communicate a content by giving evidence of her intention to do so, and the audience could infer this intention on the basis of this evidence. Of course, the two mechanisms, the coding-decoding, and the evidence-inference one, can combine in various ways. Today, most students of linguistic communication take for granted that normal comprehension involves a combination of decoding and of Gricean inference processes. By rejecting the Gricean approach (or confining it to an occasional and marginal role), Millikan must, willy-nilly, fall back on some version of the coding-decoding explanation of verbal communication. There just is not to this day, in Millikan's work or anywhere else, a third type of explanation of the very possibility of communication.

In many respects, Millikan's view of verbal communication is a highly original one. Still it is, we claim, a version (however atypical) of the code model of human communication (this is not, of course, Millikan's terminology). A code can be viewed as a systematic pairing of stimuli and cognitive responses shared by communicators, such that the production by a communicator of a stimulus belonging to the code has (both for communicator and audience) the function of producing the associated response in the audience. We do not dispute that human languages are codes in this sense. We do not dispute that the use of a shared code provides a sufficient explanation for many forms of communication. Indeed, it does explain how non-human animal communication works. But is what makes human communication possible the sharing of a common linguistic code? According to the code model, it is. According to the alternative inferential model we will elaborate below, the sharing of a common linguistic code is what makes human communication so complex and powerful. What makes human communication possible at all, however, is human virtuosity in attributing intentions to one another.

In its standard form, the code model assumes that a human language is a pairing of sound and meanings, and that the meanings encoded by the sounds are – at a sentence level – propositional contents and attitudes, and – at a sub-sentential level – constituents of these propositional contents and attitudes. Mililkan takes a different and original view of the cognitive responses paired with linguistic stimuli. In a nutshell, the responses she envisages are closer to perception on one side, and to action on the other side, than the more abstract responses envisaged by standard accounts. Still, her model is a true code model of communication in that it explains communication by the systematic pairing of linguistic stimuli and responses. The representational resources of bees and their code are extremely different from the representational resources and language of humans, but some of the basic aspects of communication are, in a

Millikanian perspective, the same. In both cases communication is typically a form of belief and desire transfer: cognition by proxy – or to use Millikan's phrase 'natural teleperception' – made possible by a reliable pairing of stimuli and responses.

Most current discussions of the evolution of language give little or no place to pragmatics, and explicitly or tacitly accept the code model of linguistic communication. Human languages are seen as, precisely, a rich kind of code that allows for the encoding and decoding of any communicable thought.

A perfect code is one without ambiguity: each stimulus-type is paired to only one response-type. Simple perfect codes are common in animal communication. However, the code model does not require such perfection. Ambiguities do not necessarily compromise the model, provided that there is some method for automatically resolving them. Thus tokens of the same bee dance give, at different times of day, different indications regarding the location of food, but bees readily integrate relevant information about the position of the sun in their decoding of the dance and understand the dance unambiguously. Human languages are obviously not perfect codes. Typical sentences contain multiple ambiguities. Thus, the one-word sentence 'Eat!' might be interpreted as an order, a request, an encouragement or a piece of advice. It could be metaphorical, or ironic, etc.

As Millikan acknowledges, 'understanding a language is never just decoding' (Millikan, 1998b, p. 176). There must be further processes that use the output of decoding and information about the situation to fix the contextual meaning of the utterance. For Millikan, these further processes consist in strict disambiguation (except in marginal and untypical cases) – that is, in the selection of one of the possible decodings of the utterance. All the possible contextual meanings of a linguistic device (in normal language use) must be conventionally associated (in the sense of Millikan, 1998a) with this device. This actually implies truly massive ambiguity of nearly all linguistic expressions. As Millikan puts it:

A language consists in a tangled jungle of overlapping, criss-crossing traditional patterns, reproducing themselves whole or in part for a variety of reasons, and not uncommonly getting in each other's way. Places where these patterns cross can produce ambiguities. These are sorted out not by conventions, but by the hearer managing to identify, by one means or another, the source of the pattern, that is, from which family it was reproduced. (1998b, p. 176)

Although she does not dwell on the issue, Millikan's view implies, we insist, massive ambiguity. The idea closest to that of massive ambiguity is probably that of massive polysemy currently explored, for instance, in the work of Pustejovsky (1996). However, the idea of polysemy is that of many senses being generated in context and according to grammar-like rules, rather than that of many conventional senses each belonging to a distinct, reproductively established family. (Polysemy would deserve an elaborate discussion from an evolutionary point of view, but we cannot pursue it here.) The task of the hearer of the utterance 'Eat!', say, on the polysemy account, is to *generate* a contextually appropriate meaning for the lexical item 'eat'; whereas, according to Millikan, the hearer's task is to *recognise* to which one of the many families that proliferate phonetically indistinguishable but semantically different tokens of 'eat' this particular token belongs. (And the same problem has to be resolved with the imperative mood: to which of the many syntactically indistinguishable but semantically different tokens of the imperative does a particular token belong?)

4   Massive ambiguity versus Grice's 'Modified Occam's Razor'

Massive ambiguity and associated disambiguation processes (or, for that matter, massive polysemy and associated sense-generation processes) are not the only way to try and accommodate the fact that the same linguistic expression can convey many different meanings. In fact, Millikan's approach was developed as an alternative to Paul Grice's. Grice's influential approach is guided by a methodological principle he called Modified Occam's Razor: 'Don't multiply senses beyond necessity.' From a Gricean point of view, linguistic meanings provide indications, and not necessarily full encodings, of speakers' meanings, and the same words *used with the same linguistic meaning* can quite ordinarily serve to convey different speaker's meanings. Comprehension is not only a process of decoding and disambiguating, but also a process of inference that goes beyond disambiguation.

In all modern pragmatic approaches inspired by Grice – and in particular in Relevance Theory (Sperber and Wilson, 1986/1995), which is the approach we favour and will adopt in the rest of this chapter – three ideas go together: the goal of semantic parsimony expressed in Modified Occam's Razor, the distinction between sentence meaning and speaker's meaning, and the claim that to understand an utterance is to discover the speaker's meaning (using sentence meaning merely as a means towards that end). Millikan, rejecting the view that understanding an utterance is understanding what the speaker meant in uttering it, has to give up the goal of semantic parsimony.

It might seem that, in accounting for the richness of communicated meanings, there is a balanced choice between two possible approaches. According to a first approach – which was, for Grice, exemplified by Ordinary Language philosophers at the time when he wrote on the issue – communicated meanings are, with marginal exceptions, meanings linguistically encoded. For instance, if the English word 'and' can be understood sometimes as the corresponding logical connective, sometimes as *and then*, and sometimes as *and therefore*, there must be at least these three meanings in the mental lexical entry that English speakers have for 'and'. Reacting against Ordinary Language Philosophy, Grice pioneered another approach aimed at explaining the richness of communicated meaning, not at the linguistic-semantic level in terms of disambiguation, but at the pragmatic level in terms of inference. Thus, Grice argued, 'and' semantically has just the logical-connective meaning, and all other interpretations are pragmatic speaker's meanings derived inferentially in context.

In fact, it is questionable whether the disambiguation and inferential derivation approaches really provide two alternative accounts of the richness of communicated meanings, more or less on par with each other. Grice's ideas have given rise to a whole field of research – pragmatics – pursued more and more within the framework of cognitive psychology. On the other hand, the disambiguation approach to the richness of communicated meanings consists in little more than theoretical hand-waving. To quote Millikan again, hearers resolve ambiguities 'by one means or another'. True, but then, the more massive the ambiguity implied by the theory, the less plausible that human minds can deal with it. Any theory that implies massive ambiguity faces a problem of psychological plausibility and is betting on the outcome of future scientific development. Present studies of disambiguation in psycholinguistics (which tend to show that all the senses of a lexical item are unconsciously activated) and in pragmatics (which point the Gricean way) do not support the view that the richness of communicated meanings is based on massive ambiguity. This argument is, incidentally, similar to the sensible argument levelled by Millikan against Grice: that his account of the recovery of speaker's meaning involves psychologically implausible complex reasoning.

Of course, it is often a wholly open empirical question whether a given interpretation of a given lexical item or of some other linguistic device is linguistically encoded or contextually inferred. On the other hand, there is a clear and ready answer to the empirical question of whether the meanings that, in general, a word or a linguistic device may serve to convey form a small finite set. The answer, we would argue (and will shortly illustrate) is a resounding 'No'. If indefinitely many new meanings can be communicated by means of the same linguistic device used in a normal way, then the very notion of disambiguation (or, in Millikan's terms, of identifying from which family a linguistic token was reproduced) is of limited use in explaining the contextual aspects of comprehension. Meanings are not just disambiguated, they are in part disambiguated, in part constructed in context.

Let us illustrate. Julia puts a piece of cheesecake in front of Henry and says: 'Eat!' In so doing, she intends him to find it desirable to eat the cheese-cake there and then. Linked to the use of the imperative mood, Julia's utter-ance may have the character of a permission if it is manifest to the interlocutors that Henry would want to eat the cheesecake but might fear that it would be impolite to do so without having been invited; it may be an encouragement if it is manifest to the interlocutors that Henry's desire to eat the cheesecake is weak; or it may be an order, an enticement, or some less easily definable form of request, wish, advice, etc. Millikan would assume that every distinct force that the imperative serves standardly to convey must be one of the conventional meanings of the imperative, and that the hearer somehow (and without attending to the speaker's beliefs and intentions) infers which of these meanings is being reproduced in the situa-tion. Relevance theory assumes, on the other hand, that the imperative encodes merely desirability (whether to the speaker or to the hearer), and that its use in a given utterance and context allows the hearer to infer what specific form of desirability is meant by the speaker.

Say Julia intends that Henry should recognise that she is encouraging him to eat the piece of cheesecake. She intends that his recognition of her intention to encourage him should indeed encourage him. If, as a result of Julia's utterance, Henry understands that she is encouraging him to eat the cheesecake, then comprehension has been successful. This is so whether or not Henry complies: Julia's communicative intention is fulfilled by Henry's comprehension, that is, by his recognition of her meaning. Of course the goal that she was pursuing *through* communication, her 'perlocutionary' intention, to use Austin's term – *viz.* to cause Henry to eat the piece of cheesecake – may be frustrated, but this is another story: understanding an encouragement or request, and complying with it, are two different things. Similarly, from the speaker's point of view, securing comprehension and causing compliance (or, with other types of utterances, other perlocution-ary responses) are two distinct purposes, achieving the first being a means towards achieving the second. The speaker, however, is much more in control of the hearer's comprehension than of the hearer's further cognitive or behavioural responses. So, of the two effects, securing comprehension and causing further responses, the first, being more regular, is more likely to play a stabilising role in the evolution of linguistic devices. More about this later.

'Eat!' can also serve to convey an ironical or a metaphorical speaker's meaning. Imagine for instance that, to highlight the thickness of a stout beer Henry has ordered, Julia tells him 'Eat!' instead of 'Drink!' An ambi-guity-based analysis might consist in having 'eat' be ambiguous between (among many other senses) ingesting solid food and ingesting thick drinks, and having the hearer somehow disambiguate. But this would be a case of multiplying senses beyond necessity. A Gricean approach would consist in assuming that only the standard linguistic sense of 'eat' is involved here. According to Grice's own analysis of metaphor, Henry, encountering a linguistic meaning incompatible with what he can presume of Julia's communicative intention, searches for a meaning related to, but different from the literal one, a meaning she could have intended and expected to convey by means of her utterance (namely, drink a drink so thick that it resembles regular food). Henry then infers that this must indeed have been Julia's meaning. According to relevance theory, the same example would be explained by assuming that Henry accesses, in his mental lexicon, the standard entry for 'eat' and uses the information thus activated as a starting point for constructing a contextually relevant meaning that he then attributes to Julia. Millikan can treat such metaphors – which are neither dead nor out of the ordinary, neither clearly conventional nor particularly creative – either as ambiguities, or else as Gricean exceptions to the normal flow of verbal communication. If such metaphors are cases of ambiguity, then every word has a great many stably attached metaphorical senses. If these are Gricean cases, then communication is much more Gricean than Millikan would have it.

In any case, a Millikanian speaker-hearer has in his or her memory many more senses for each lexical item (or for other linguistic devices such as the imperative mood) than does a Gricean or a relevance-guided speaker-hearer. Is this extra weight in memorised lexical information compensated by a lighter inferential task in comprehending utterances? Gricean inferential patterns involve using higher-order meta-representations of the speaker's beliefs and intentions as premises, and are notoriously cumbersome. Relevance theory departs from Grice precisely in assuming and describing a much lighter inference-pattern where only the conclusion, but not the premises, need be about the speaker's intention. Since Millikan gives no indication of the inferential pattern involved in the kind of massive disambiguation she is hypothesising, there is no reason to assume that it would be lighter than relevance-based, or even than standard Gricean, inference. In fact, the only plausible accounts of context sensitive disambiguation are to be found in Grice-inspired pragmatics and involve standard forms of pragmatic inference.

Moreover, even massive disambiguation may not be sufficient for the task at hand. If Henry had simply decoded Julia's utterance and disambiguated it (by whatever means) as, say, a literal request to eat, he would still not know what and how much was to be eaten, nor when. He might just eat a crumb, and thereby fulfil Julia's request literally interpreted. Even if Henry, somehow, disambiguated 'Eat!' in this case as containing a reference to a direct object, and if, somehow, he inferred that the referent was the piece of cheesecake, this would not suffice. Should Henry take home the cheesecake, put it in his freezer, and eat it a month later, he would have acted in such a way as to render true the decoded, disambiguated and referentially specified meaning of Julia's utterance; but, of course, he would neither have understood her nor complied with her intention. In all these respects, it is hard to see how Henry could understand Julia's utterance without paying attention to what Julia means by the utterance. Millikan asserts that comprehension is just a belief or desire transfer, but she does not begin to address decisive empirical issues in the study of comprehension that have been highlighted in modern pragmatics.

Let us qualify the last statement. In fact, Millikan does provide a highly Gricean pragmatic account of the word 'this' (used as a whole noun phrase and without gestural demonstration as in: 'this is how to live!'). She writes:

'this' often holds a place for improvisation. [. . .] the speaker has the hearer's capacities, viewpoint, and dispositions in mind as he utters 'this' and utters it purposing that the hearer supply a certain referent for it, that is, that he translate it into an inner term having a certain referent. This referent is to be something proximate, or a sign or reminder of which is proximate, but beyond that the hearer is often pretty much on his own. He picks up his cues from the rest of the sentence and from his knowledge of what he and the speaker both know of that it would be reasonable for the speaker to expect him to think of first. When all goes well, speaker and hearer thus achieve a co-ordination, but not a co-ordination that results from the speaker's and the hearer's speech-producing and understanding abilities having been *standardised* to fit one another. (1984, p. 167)

Clearly, Millikan equates standardisation and full-fledged determinate meaning, and all the rest is mere 'improvisation'. We would argue, on the one hand, that there is some modicum of standardisation involved in the use of 'this' that makes it a word of English rather than of Italian, and a word different from 'that'. 'This' does not encode, but is indicative of, the speaker's meaning in a standardised way. The indication is weak, it leaves a lot to be inferred, but it does indicate to an English hearer that what is to be inferred is an easily accessible referent. We would argue, on the other hand, that even when the words used do have a full-fledged meaning, their use still leaves room for what Millikan calls 'improvisation' and which is just the inferential part of communication. So, for instance, the word 'square' has a definite meaning, but when a speaker says 'This field is square', she does not commit herself to the field actually having exactly four right angles and four equal sides. What she does is give an effective indication from which the hearer can infer her meaning, which, depending on the context, may involve a greater or lesser degree of approximation to squareness.

5   Comprehension as recognition of speaker's meaning

Comprehension, as understood in modern pragmatics, crucially involves the recognition by the hearer of a specific intention of the speaker, the 'speaker's meaning'. The fact that the hearer is seeking to reconstruct the speaker's meaning is what focuses, constrains and indeed makes possible inferential comprehension (and, to begin with, inferential disambiguation, the necessity of which Millikan well recognises). We won't here give more positive arguments for the view that comprehension is recognition of speaker's meaning. The whole of modern pragmatics is predicated on this assumption, and its findings are arguments in favour of it. Of course, this does not make the assumption right, but those who deny it, are, in effect, implying that pragmatics as currently pursued is a discipline without an object, somewhat like the study of humours in ancient medicine. The burden is surely on them to show how pragmatics fails and to provide a better alternative to explain comprehension.

We will, however, address the view expressed by Millikan, that there is some serious implausibility in the very idea that comprehension is about speaker's meaning. Millikan does not deny the existence of speaker's meanings, but she sees their communication through linguistic means, not as the normal form of linguistic communication, but as a departure from this normal form. 'The truth in Grice's model', she says, 'is that we have the ability to interrupt and prevent the automatic running on of our talking and our doing-and-believing-what-we-are-told equipment'. We do this when we have discovered 'evidence that the conditions for normally effective talking and for correct believing-on-the-basis-of-what-we-hear are not met' (Millikan, 1984, p. 69). In ordinary communication, she claims, going the Gricean way would be incredibly inefficient. However, for all we know, disambiguation that would not involve attending to the intentions of the speaker – if possible at all, which we doubt – might be even more dramatically inefficient.

Still, we do share Millikan's worry that comprehension as described by most Griceans is indeed implausibly cumbersome. There are two aspects to this. On the one hand the process of comprehension as described by Grice involves, in many cases, fairly sophisticated reasoning about the speaker's mental states. As we have already mentioned and will discuss again below, this is not the case in relevance theory, where the speaker's meaning is normally inferred without using as premises assumptions about the speaker's mental states. On the other hand the very notion of speaker's meaning can be seen as implausibly complex. In Grice's original account (1957) a speaker's meaning involved a moderately complex two-level intention: roughly the intention to achieve a certain effect on the audience by means of the audience's recognition of this intention. In order to accommodate some objections from, in particular, Strawson (1964) and Schiffer (1972), Grice (with some reservations) and others (more resolutely) embraced the idea that communicative intentions involve many – even infinitely many – levels, or are infinitely nested. Millikan objected at length, and rightly, against the psychological implausibility or irrelevance of communicative intentions so understood.

However, a Gricean-inspired approach to communication need not be committed to these complexities. Relevance theory's account of a communicative intention takes the objections into account but, just like Grice's original account, involves only two levels. According to this particular approach, a speaker has two intentions. She has the informative intention to make it manifest to the hearer that a certain state of affairs is actual or is desirable, and she has the communicative intention to achieve this informative intention by making it mutually manifest to the hearer and herself that she has this informative intention. (For a detailed defence of this account and arguments that it is sufficient and genuinely involves only two levels, see Sperber and Wilson, 1995, 1996.)

It might still be felt that there is some implausibility in attributing to speaker-hearers, and in particular children, the ability to represent, as a matter of course, second-order meta-representational intentions. However, to represent a second-order meta-representational intention does not mean representing its internal structure each and every time. We standardly attribute to speakers of English the knowledge that *John killed Bill* entails *John caused Bill to die* without assuming that they mentally represent the latter each and every time they understand the former. Still, this attribution of knowledge is psychologically relevant: we assume that an English speaker who believed that Bill was alive, or that John had not caused anyone to die, would not be inclined to believe that John had killed Bill. Similarly, Henry can merely represent that Julia means that he should eat the piece of cheesecake now, without expanding the meaning of 'means', except when needed.

Imagine the following scenario: Julia puts a piece of cheesecake in front of Henry and another one in front of Paul. Henry exclaims 'This looks delicious!' and Paul sneers 'Cheesecake again!' Henry looks at Paul and hears Julia say 'Eat!' Henry knows that Julia intends both of them to eat, but he – rightly as it happens – takes her meaning to be that Paul should. Without any difficulty, Henry thus dissociates Julia's informative intention to cause both of them to find eating the cheesecake desirable (already manifested by her putting the pieces of cake in front of them) from her communicative intention to make it manifest to Paul that she intends him to find eating the cheesecake desirable (manifested by her saying 'Eat!'). Let us stress the relevant particulars of this case. Henry is not looking at Julia and therefore has no behavioural cues to the fact that Julia is addressing Paul. The utterance would be perfectly interpretable if understood as addressed to Henry, or to both Henry and Paul. Yet it is quite natural for Henry to infer that the utterance is addressed to Paul only and that the unexpressed subject of 'Eat!' is Paul. His inference is guided, we would argue, by considerations of relevance. Given the circumstances, Julia's utterance best achieves the expected level of relevance if understood as addressed to Paul. We take this example to illustrate the fact that hearers are capable, as a normal part of the process of comprehension, of inferentially discriminating different levels of intention in the speaker. We have no evidence regarding the age at which a child would be likely to perform such inferences and to interpret Julia in the way Henry does, but there is nothing implausible in assuming that this would occur quite early in the development of verbal abilities (more about this below).

6   Fitting (post-)Gricean pragmatics into Millikan's conceptual framework

Assume that verbal comprehension is recognition of speaker's meaning. Assume that what a linguistic utterance does is not to encode speaker's meaning, but to provide rich evidence from which the audience can infer speaker's meaning. Could languages playing such a role be described within the general conceptual framework put forward by Millikan? What would then be the direct and derived proper functions of linguistic devices? Before giving a general answer, let us take three examples, that of 'now', of 'eat' and of the imperative.

It is a misleading over-simplification to say that the indexical 'now' refers to *the* time of utterance. Even ignoring various complications, and in particular the use of 'now' in free indirect speech, the time indicated by 'now' can be any time-span, long or short. For instance, 'now' in 'I feel great now' could refer to the very minute of utterance, to a period of a few days, or to a period of many years. 'Now' does not encode any one of these time-spans, nor is it ambiguous among them. Rather, it is indeterminate. The speaker's meaning, however, although it may be vague, is generally determinate. Therefore, in order to understand the speaker's meaning, the hearer must discover which time-span is intended. So, we suggest, the direct proper function of 'now' is to give evidence of the fact that the speaker's meaning includes a reference to a certain time-span within which the utterance occurs. This direct function is performed through each token of 'now' performing the derived proper function of indicating a specific time-span.

Unlike the adverb 'now', the import of which *must* be contextually specified for it to contribute to the meaning of any utterance in which it occurs, the verb 'eat' has a full-fledged meaning. On occasions, it is used to convey just this meaning. For instance, in 'Henry ate a piece of cheesecake', the meaning of 'ate' seems to be just that of 'eat' (plus some specification of the past tense). However, quite often, 'eat' is used to indicate a meaning that may be more specific, less specific, or more specific in certain respects and less specific in other respects, than the lexical meaning of 'eat'. For instance, a person declining an invitation to join a dinner party by saying 'I have eaten' is indicating not just that she has eaten, but also that she has eaten a quantity such that she has no desire to eat any more (having eaten just a peanut would make her utterance literally true, but would nevertheless make her a liar). In this case, the meaning conveyed by means of 'eat' is more specific than the lexically encoded meaning of 'eat' (this example is discussed in greater detail in Wilson and Sperber, forthcoming). In the example of Julia saying metaphorically 'Eat!' to Henry, who has ordered a thick stout, the lexicalised meaning of 'eat' has to be made less specific (by ignoring the restriction to 'food' in the sense where 'food' is opposed to 'drink') in order to understand Julia's meaning. Imagine now that Henry was asked if he would like to join a dinner party and he answered: 'I have had three stouts. As far as I am concerned, I have eaten.' In this case, Henry's meaning conveyed by means of the word 'eat' would be less specific than the lexical meaning of 'eat' in being extended to the ingestion of thick drinks. At the same time, it would be more specific than the lexical meaning of 'eat' in that it would indicate that he has ingested a quantity such that he had no desire to eat any more. Thus the direct proper function of 'eat' is to give evidence of the fact that the speaker's meaning includes a concept best evoked by 'eat', a concept which may, but need not be, the very concept lexically encoded by 'eat'. This direct function is performed through each token of 'eat' performing the derived proper function of evoking, in the context, a specific concept which is part of the speaker's meaning on that occasion.

The imperative mood, we argued, does not encode any particular illocutionary force such as request or advice, nor is it ambiguous among all the particular forces it may serve to convey. (That is, speakers and hearers don't have a mental list of possible forces among which they must choose each time the imperative mood is tokened.) The imperative mood merely indicates desirability. Indicating that the action or the state of affairs described in the imperative mood is desirable typically falls short of yielding, by itself, a relevant enough interpretation. On the other hand, given expectations of relevance and contextual information, desirability may be understood as desirability for the speaker (as in the case of a request), or for the hearer (as in the case of an advice), or for both (as in the case of a wish). When desirability is understood as being for the speaker, the use of the imperative may further be understood as indicating expectations of compliance (as in the case of an order), or preference for compliance (as in the case of an entreaty), and so on. So, we suggest, the direct proper function of the imperative mood is to give evidence of the fact that the speaker is presenting the action or the state of affairs described as desirable in some way. This direct function is performed through each token of the imperative mood giving evidence that, together with contextual information, indicates which specific form of desirability is intended by the speaker.

The description of these three examples – 'now', 'eat' and the imperative mood – can be generalised to all meaning-carrying linguistic devices. (See Carston, 1998; Sperber and Wilson, 1998; Wilson and Sperber, forthcoming, for a thorough discussion from a pragmatic point of view.) A linguistic device does not have as its direct proper function to make its encoded meaning part of the meaning of the utterances in which it occurs. It has, rather, as its direct proper function to indicate a component of the speaker's meaning that is best evoked by activating the encoded meaning of the linguistic device. It performs this direct function through each token of the device performing the derived proper function of indicating a contextually relevant meaning.

We follow Millikan in considering that the direct proper function of a linguistic device is what keeps speakers and hearers using and responding to the linguistic device in a reliable way, thus stabilising the device in a community. Our disagreement with her has to do with the level of processing at which linguistic devices elicit the reliable response to be identified as their direct proper function. For Millikan, this reliable response is to be found at the level of belief or desire formation, or even at the behavioural level in the case of compliance. In particular, the function of a word is to contribute its 'conventional meaning' to the overall meaning of an utterance which will then be accepted as a belief or a desire (depending on the mood) by the hearer. The function of the imperative is to cause desire and compliance, and so on. The problem, we argued, is that the same linguistic stimulus may elicit a great many different responses at the belief or desire level. In other words, at that level, responses are not reliably paired to stimuli. To invoke massive ambiguity and say that indistinguishable phonological or syntactic forms are, in fact, tokens of many different linguistic devices, is a way to shift the problem, not to resolve it. It amounts to saying that the reliability of linguistic stimuli is contingent on the ability of the hearer to identify the type to which the token belongs. As long as there is no account of how this can be reliably achieved, the very existence of reliable responses to linguistic devices at the level of belief or desire formation is in doubt, and so is the claim that the direct proper function of these devices is to be found at this level.

What is the alternative? Linguistic devices produce highly reliable responses, not at the level of the cognitive outputs of comprehension such as belief or desire formation, and even less at the level of behavioural outputs such as compliance, but at an intermediate level in the process of comprehension. Linguistic comprehension involves, at an intermediate and largely unconscious level, the decoding of linguistic stimuli that are then used as evidence by the hearer, together with the context, to arrive inferentially at the speaker's meaning. The same unambiguous linguistic item, decoded in the same way each and every time, can serve as evidence for quite different meanings in different contexts. (We do not, of course, deny the existence of true linguistic ambiguity, but there is much less of it than the code model of linguistic communication ends up implying; and moreover, the same inferential processes that explain other aspects of inferential comprehension explain disambiguation.) Linguistic devices have proliferated and stabilised because they cause these highly reliable cognitive responses *at this intermediate level*. Linguistic devices provide speakers and hearers with informationally rich, highly structured and reliably decoded evidence of speaker's meaning. Note that this proper function of linguistic devices is not one speakers and hearers are aware of, let alone something they choose.

There could, in principle, be an intelligent species that communicated the way Millikan believes humans do: with speakers using utterances directly to cause belief or desire transfer, and hearers merely decoding and disambiguating these utterances and automatically turning the resulting interpretation into a desire or belief of their own. The language of such a species should present many fewer ambiguities than actual human languages, and those ambiguities should be easily resolved – either on the basis of the linguistic context (the 'co-text') or by applying simple rules to pick out the pertinent piece of information from the environment (as, for instance, in replacing the first person pronoun with a reference to the actual speaker).

The reaction of a hearer to a speaker in such a species, using a language *à la* Millikan, would look very much like that of a hypnotised person to the hypnotist, where belief and desire transfers do actually occur. This raises, of course, the problem of explaining how hearers could escape being systematically deceived and manipulated by speakers. Communication is a form of co-operation. Co-operation is vulnerable to free-riding, which, in the case of communication, takes the form of manipulation and deception. In the study of any communicating species, explaining how it is that the benefits of communication are not offset by the cost of deception is a major problem (Krebs and Dawkins, 1984; Dawkins and Krebs, 1978; Hauser, 1996).

In the case of human communication, explaining how the costs of possible deception are contained crucially involves the fact that comprehension and acceptance are two distinct steps in the overall process. It may be (at least in some socio-cultural contexts) that people believe most of the things they are told, but this is not because they are hypnotised or gullible. It is rather that they mostly interact with relatives and friends with whom they co-operate and from whom sincerity can be expected in ordinary conditions. People are typically distrustful of information provided by strangers, or by competitors, or even by relatives and friends in situations of conflict. Communicated information is sifted, rather than automatically accepted as Millikan argues. Another part of the explanation of the viability of human communication is the fact that comprehension is, *pace* Millikan, a form of mind-reading and links easily with attending to the speaker's benevolence and competence. (For a more thorough discussion of the meta-representational mechanisms involved in sifting communicated information, see Sperber, forthcoming.)

So, yes, assuming that the problems raised by ambiguity and deception were somehow avoided or solved, there could be a species that communicated in the way Millikan believes humans do. On the other hand, there is nothing in Millikan's teleofunctional framework that implies that communication can only evolve in the way she claims it did. There could be a species that communicated in the way Grice or relevance theory says humans do, and, in fact, we believe that humans are such a species. At this point we have reached one of our goals: to pry apart Millikan's overall framework from her view of language, and fit this framework together with a view she opposes and according to which linguistic comprehension is a form of mind-reading. In the next two sections we explore some of the evolutionary implications of this view of language.

7   Linguistic communication and mind-reading

In the past twenty years, the study of the capacity to attribute mental states such as beliefs or intentions to others has become a major focus of cognitive science under names such as 'theory of mind' or 'mind-reading' (e.g. Carruthers and Smith, 1996). There is a growing body of evidence and arguments tending to establish that a mind-reading ability is an essential ingredient of human cognition and is, moreover, a domain-specific evolved adaptation (rather than an application of some general intelligence, or cultural competence). What are the relationships between mind-reading and the language faculty? Millikan argues that linguistic communication is independent of mind-reading, whereas Grice and post-Griceans assume that linguistic communication involves a form of mind-reading where, by speaking, the speaker helps the hearer read her mind. These two views of comprehension as a cognitive process fit differently with developmental and evolutionary considerations.

At the developmental level, Millikan assumes that linguistic abilities develop before mind-reading, and sees this as further evidence against a Gricean view of linguistic communication. At first blush, the evidence might seem to be in her favour. Whereas language comprehension starts developing in the second year of life, it is only around the age of four that children pass the much-studied 'false-belief task' (in which they are asked to predict where a character will look for an object that she falsely believes to be in one location when, in fact, it has been moved to another). Success at the false-belief task is often treated as the criterion establishing mind-reading abilities. Indeed, success at the task is a clear demonstration of mind-reading abilities. Failure, however, is by no means a demonstration of total lack of such abilities. Mind-reading is not an all-or-none affair. It develops in stages from infancy (Baron-Cohen, 1995; Gergely *et al.*, 1995). People with autism – a condition now understood as involving a deficit in mind-reading abilities – lack the ability to a greater or lesser degree (Frith, 1989; Happé, 1994).

The attribution of a meaning to a speaker and the prediction that a person with a false belief will act on this belief are two very different performances – though both involving mind-reading. The formal resources involved in the two cases are not the same. In the case of speaker's meaning, what is needed is the ability to represent an intention of someone else about a representation of one's own – a second-order meta-representation of a quite specific form. (From a modularist point of view, it is quite conceivable that children might develop the ability to represent speaker's meaning before being able to deploy other types of second-order meta-representations.) In the case of false beliefs, a first-order meta-representation of a belief of someone else is sufficient, but what is needed is the ability to evaluate the truth-value of the meta-represented belief and to predict behaviour on the basis of false belief. We are not aware of any argument to the effect that the ability needed to pass the false-belief task is a precondition for the ability needed to attribute speaker's meaning. There is nothing inconsistent or paradoxical, therefore, in the idea of an individual capable of attributing speaker's meaning and incapable of attributing false beliefs (and conversely).

There are, on the other hand, functional reasons to expect the ability to attribute false beliefs to develop after the ability to communicate verbally. The attribution of false beliefs to others plays an obvious role in the capacity to filter false information communicated by mistaken or deceitful speakers. It plays an obvious role also in the ability to deceive others by communicating false information. These abilities are asymmetrically dependent on the ability to communicate. Suppose, moreover, that comprehension consists in the attribution of a meaning to the speaker, as we have argued. Then there are reasons to expect attribution of false beliefs to develop after attribution of speaker's meaning.

The fact that success at the false-belief task occurs three years or so after the beginnings of verbal comprehension is no evidence against the view that comprehension is a form of mind-reading. Are there, though, positive arguments or evidence to the effect that, say, two-year-olds (who fail the false-belief task) do attribute meaning to speakers? We would be tempted to say that we all *know* that they do. As speakers, we take for granted that when we say something we mean something, and that people – including very young children – who understand what we say, understand what we mean (understand *us*, in an ordinary sense of the expression). But of course, this may be a piece of mistaken naïve psychology. A scientifically more compelling argument is this: young children do disambiguate, identify referents and understand implicatures. As we argued before, the only actual explanations of such achievements (as opposed to hand-waving in the direction of unspecified explanations) draw on (post-) Gricean pragmatics and presuppose a capacity on the part of the comprehender to attend to speaker's meaning. Further positive evidence of an experimental kind is provided by Paul Bloom's work, which shows that the acquisition of lexical meanings – which is involved very early in language acquisition – requires attention to speaker's intentions (Bloom, 1997).

At an evolutionary level, the biological evolution of language is, for Millikan, quite independent from that of mind-reading. From a Gricean viewpoint, the evolution of language should be linked to that of mind-reading, since utterances are encodings of speaker's thoughts and are typically recognised as such by the audience (Pinker, 1994). Linguistic communication enhances mind-reading abilities (and even, some might argue, makes true mind-reading possible in the first place; see Dennett 1991a), while also exploiting these abilities in complex cases where Gricean inferences must supplement linguistic decoding. It is reasonable therefore, from a Gricean point of view, to assume a co-evolution of language and mind-reading, without committing oneself any further.

From the point of view of relevance theory it is also reasonable to assume a co-evolution of language and mind-reading, but there are reasons to commit oneself to a more precise articulation of the two. In standard Gricean approaches, inference is seen as needed in discovering the implicit part of the speaker's meaning, while the explicit part is seen as decoded (and disambiguation is not much discussed). Accordingly, there could have been an initial stage in the evolution of language where utterances were wholly explicit and decoded, with Gricean inferences about implicit content evolving only at a later stage. In other terms, Gricean communication could result from a partial change of function of what might have been, at an earlier stage, a strict code. According to relevance theory, on the other hand, human verbal communication is never a matter of mere decoding. In fact, in its basic structure, inferential communication does not even depend on linguistic stimuli: other behavioural stimuli – e.g. improvised mimes – may provide adequate evidence of a communicator's intention. Linguistic utterances, however, provide immensely superior evidence for inferential communication. They can be as richly and subtly structured as the communicator wishes, and they are reliably decoded by the audience at an intermediate level in the process of comprehension. The function of linguistic utterances, then, is – and has always been – to provide this highly precise and informative evidence of the communicator's intention. This implies that language as we know it developed as an adaptation in a species already involved in inferential communication, and therefore already capable of some serious degree of mind-reading. In other terms, from the point of view of relevance theory the existence of mind-reading in our ancestors was a precondition for the emergence and evolution of language.

8   The boot-strapping problem and its solution

Most evolved domain-specific cognitive abilities have a specific domain of information (a 'proper domain' – see Sperber, 1996, chapter 6) available in the environment well before the ability develops, and they can be seen as adaptations to that aspect of the environment. For instance, different individuals have distinctive faces; an evolved face-recognition ability is an adaptation to the prior presence of these faces in the environment and an exploitation of their informational value. A mutant endowed with a face-recognition ability could benefit from it, even if he or she were the only individual so endowed. Some cognitive abilities, however, have a specific domain of information that is initially empty and that gets filled only by the behaviour of individuals who already have and use the ability in question. For instance, an ability to enter into reciprocal exchanges is an adaptation to the opportunities offered by other individuals who are also endowed with this ability. A unique mutant endowed with a reciprocal exchange ability could not benefit from it until other individuals became also so endowed. Thus the emergence in evolution of abilities that need to be shared by several individuals in order to be adaptive raises a specific boot-strapping problem.

Innate codes found in non-human animals are cases in point. What would be the use of an innate code in a single individual, as long as other members of its species, lacking such a code, could neither decode its signals nor send it signals of their own? To point out that any actual code is likely to result from several mutations, and to have evolved in small steps, spreads the problem but does not resolve it. There are, however, at least three ways to tackle this puzzle. The first is to assume that an innate code spread in a population as a neutral trait, initially without benefit but also without significant cost, so as not to be selected out. The trait then became advantageous and was selected *for* (Sober, 1984), when enough individuals sharing it could use it in their interactions and benefit from it. Such a development can occur rapidly, say among the offspring of the initial mutant individual endowed with the trait. Another plausible speculation is that the trait was initially selected for thanks to some other beneficial effect, and that its function as a code emerged as a new function, added to or substituted for some previous one. A third, more controversial speculation is that the signals of the code emerged first as 'cultural' items, transmitted through learning and not through genes; it then became advantageous to possess them innately, sparing the cost of learning. (This strictly Darwinian but Lamarckian-looking possibility is known as a 'Baldwin effect'.)

Human languages, however, are not innate codes. The human language faculty is not an ability to produce and interpret signals, it is an ability to acquire culturally transmitted languages. Thus the boot-strapping problem raised by the emergence of the human language faculty is not as easily speculated away as that raised by the innate codes involved in most animal communication. Even if a Language Acquisition Device, starting as a neutral trait, became shared by a number of individuals, this would not be advantageous to them, since there would still be no language to acquire. The argument applies not just to the initial emergence of a rudimentary language faculty, but also to any later biological development of this faculty. The emergence of an ability to acquire a different, presumably richer language, is not advantageous in the absence of such a language to be acquired.

This boot-strapping problem is at its worst if one accepts the code model of verbal communication. Coded communication works at its best when the interlocutors share exactly the same code. Differences in code typically lead to communication failures. Now, a modification in the language faculty of one individual, if it had any effect at all on the structure of her internalised language, would introduce a mismatch between her linguistic code and that of other people, and would have a detrimental effect on her ability to communicate. An individual endowed with a language faculty different from that of others, even if it were 'more advanced' in some sense, would stand to suffer rather than to benefit from it.

If, on the other hand, we adopt the inferential model of communication, the puzzle becomes much more tractable. Inferential communication is a matter of reconstructing the communicator's informative intention on the basis of the evidence she provides by her utterance. Successful communication does not depend, then, on the communicator and addressee having exactly the same representation of the utterance, but on having the utterance, however represented, seen as evidence for the same intended conclusion. Different decodings may provide evidence for one and the same inferential interpretation. Here a metaphor may help. Think of meanings as points in semantic space. Then according to the code model, any device encodes such a point (or several such points when it is ambiguous). According to the inferential model, on the other hand, a linguistic device encodes a *pointer* in semantic space (or several such pointers when ambiguous) that makes accessible, with ordered saliencies, a series of points. According to the code model, a mismatch between the codes of interlocutors must result in the selection of different points – i.e. different meanings – by the communicator and audience. Not so according to the inferential model: differently situated pointers may point to the same meaning. The inferential model is thus compatible with a much greater degree of slack between the codes of interlocutors.

Acquiring and using a non-standard version of the common code need not involve any cost, and it may even be advantageous. In particular, a language faculty that leads to the internalisation of a grammar that attributes more structure to utterances than they superficially realise (that project onto them 'unexpressed constituents', for instance) may facilitate inferential comprehension (Sperber, 1990b).

Imagine a stage in linguistic evolution where the languages available consisted in simple sound-concept pairs, without any higher structure at all. 'Drink' in such a primitive language encoded the concept *drink* and nothing else, 'water' encoded the concept *water* and nothing else, and so on. With such a limited code, the decoding by a hearer of a concept encoded by a speaker falls far short of achieving communication between them. An addressee associating, for instance, the concept *water* with the utterance 'water' is not thereby being informed of anything. Even a concatenation of expressions in such a language such as 'drink water' does not have as its decoded interpretation what we all understand from the homonymous English expression. It does not denote the action of drinking water. Rather two concepts, *drink* and *water*, are activated without being linked either syntactically or semantically. The mental activation of one or several concepts without syntactic linkage does not describe a state of affairs, whether actual or imagined. It does not express a belief or a desire.

If, however, the people using such a rudimentary code were capable of inferential communication, then the activation in their mind, through decoding, of a single concept might easily have provided all the evidence needed to reconstruct a full-fledged, propositional speaker's meaning (see Stainton, 1994, for a related point). Imagine two individuals of this ancestral species walking in the desert. One points to the horizon and utters 'water'. The other correctly infers that the speaker means *here is some water*. They reach the edge of the water, but one of them collapses, exhausted, and mutters 'water'. The other correctly infers that the speaker means *give me some water*. To the best of our knowledge, there is no evidence that the signals of animal communication ever permit such an open range of quite diverse interpretative elaborations.

Imagine now a mutant whose language faculty is such that she expects elementary expressions of the code she is to acquire to be either arguments or one- or two-place predicates. She classifies 'drink' as two-place predicate, 'water' as an argument, and so on. When she hears her collapsing companion mutter 'water,' what gets activated in her mind as a result of decoding is not just the mere concept *water*, but also a place-holder for a predicate of which *water* would be an argument. Her decoding, then, goes beyond what had been encoded by the speaker, who, not being a mutant, had spoken the more rudimentary language common in the community. This mismatch, however, far from being detrimental, is beneficial to the mutant: her inferential processes are immediately geared towards the search for a contextually relevant predicate of which *water* would be an argument.

When she talks, our mutant encodes, by means of signals homonymous with those of the community, not just individual concepts but predicate-argument structures. When she utters 'water', her utterance also encodes an unexpressed place-holder for a predicate; when she utters 'drink', her utterance also encodes two unexpressed place-holders for two arguments; when she utters 'drink water', her utterance encodes the complex concept of *drinking water* and an unexpressed place-holder for another argument of *drink*, and so on. These underlying linguistic structures are harmlessly missed by her non-mutant interlocutors, but are useful to other mutants, pointing more directly to the intended interpretation. In the language of these mutants, new symbols – for instance, pronouns for unspecified arguments – may then stabilise. This illustrates how in an inferential communication system, a more powerful language faculty, which causes individuals to internalise a linguistic code richer than that of their community, may give them an advantage and may therefore evolve (whereas in a strict encoding-decoding system, a departure from the common code may be harmful or harmless, but not advantageous).

This line of reasoning applies to the very emergence of a language faculty: being disposed to treat an uncoded piece of communicative behaviour as a 'linguistic' sign may have facilitated the inferential discovery of the communicator's intention and led to the stabilisation of this stimulus-type as a signal.

9 Conclusion

Millikan's conceptual framework allows one effectively to articulate various issues raised by the biological and cultural evolution of language. At the same time, her own view of language makes it more difficult to deal with these issues. In particular, it leaves one with an extra problem of massive ambiguity, and it makes the boot-strapping problem, if anything, less tractable. Fortunately, Millikan's conceptual framework can be dissociated from her view of language. It can be applied to Gricean or relevance-theoretic approaches to language, with – we hope to have shown – some interesting results.

We thank Peter Carruthers, Andrew Chamberlain, Ruth Millikan and Deirdre Wilson for their most useful comments on earlier drafts of this chapter.

8   The evolution of knowledge

David Papineau

Human beings are one of the great success stories of evolution. They have spread over the globe and refashioned much of it to their own convenience. What has made this possible? Perhaps there is no one key which alone explains why humans have come to dominate nature. But a crucial part has surely been played by our high potential for theoretical rationality. Human beings far surpass other animals in their ability to form accurate beliefs across a wide range of topics, and many aspects of human civilisation rest on this accomplishment. My aim in this chapter will be to explain this ability from an evolutionary perspective. I want to understand how creatures with our biological history came to be so good at theoretical rationality.

1   Introduction

The claim that humans are good at theoretical rationality is not entirely uncontroversial. Much recent psychological research suggests that humans are far less good at forming accurate beliefs than you might initially suppose. I shall discuss this research at some length below. It raises many interesting issues and will force me to be more specific about the precise sense in which humans possess a high level of theoretical rationality. But this research does not in the end undermine the claim that humans do have a high degree of theoretical rationality, nor that this has played an important role in human development.

   Evolutionary explanations do not always account for traits in terms of selective advantages they provide. Some biological traits have not been selected because of their effects. Rather they are by-products of other traits which have been so selected. They do not serve any function themselves, but have been carried along by different traits that do yield advantages. Such evolutionary side-effects are 'spandrels', in the sense made familiar by Stephen Jay Gould (Gould and Lewontin, 1979).

   My explanation of human theoretical rationality will in the first instance be spandrel-like. I shall not explain theoretical rationality directly. Instead I shall argue that it piggybacks on other traits. In particular, I shall argue that it piggybacks on the evolution of cognitive abilities for 'understanding of mind' and for means-end thinking. I shall argue that once these other abilities are in place, nothing more is needed for humans to achieve high levels of theoretical rationality.

However, at the end I shall add a twist. Even if theoretical rationality didn't initially arise because of its biological advantages, there seems little doubt that it does provide such advantages. Given this, we would expect it to be encouraged by natural selection, even if it wasn't natural selection that made it available in the first place. So maybe there have been biological adaptations for acquiring knowledge, so to speak, alongside the other cognitive adaptations bequeathed to us by natural selection. I shall explore this thought at the end of this chapter, not only for the light it throws on theoretical rationality itself, but also because it seems to me to point to some general morals about the evolution of human cognition.

I shall approach these issues via a discussion of the 'rationality debate' in contemporary psychology. As I said, the claim that human beings display high levels of theoretical rationality is not as straightforward as it may seem, since there is now a good deal of evidence that human beings are in fact surprisingly prone to theoretical *irrationality*. Subjects in a well-known series of psychological experiments tend to produce highly inaccurate answers in many situations where we might expect them to do better.

In the next section I shall point out that these experimental data raise two immediate problems. First, there is an *evaluative* problem about the status of our standards of rationality. Second, there is the *explanatory* problem of how humans are capable of adherence to such standards.

The following two sections, 3 and 4, will be devoted to the evaluative problem. In the end there is nothing terribly deep here, but a lot of confusing undergrowth needs to be cleared away. Once this has been done, then an obvious answer to the explanatory issue will become apparent; accordingly, in section 5 I shall account for the ability of humans to achieve high levels of theoretical rationality, the experimental data notwithstanding.

In sections 6–10 I shall place this answer to the explanatory problem in an evolutionary context. I shall show how my answer assumes that theoretical rationality is a by-product of two other intellectual abilities which we have independent reason to regard as evolutionarily explicable, namely, understanding of mind and means-end thinking. The final section, 11, will then explore the possibility that natural selection may also have fostered theoretical rationality directly and given us certain inborn inclinations to seek out true beliefs as such.

Before we start, one terminological simplification. Theoretical rationality, the rationality of the beliefs you adopt, contrasts with practical rationality, the rationality of the choices you subsequently make. Since I shall be focusing on theoretical rationality for the next few sections, it will be helpful to drop the 'theoretical' for now, and refer to 'rationality' simpliciter. When I do discuss practical rationality later in the chapter, I shall make the distinction explicit.

2   Widespread irrationality

Consider these three famous puzzles.

(1) Linda studied sociology at the London School of Economics. She reads the Guardian, is a member of the Labour Party and enjoys experimental theatre. Which of these is more probable? (A) Linda is a bank teller. (B) Linda is a bank teller and an active feminist.

(2) You are worried that you have a not uncommon form of cancer. (It is present in 1% of people like you.) There is a simple and effective test, which identifies the cancer in everyone who has it and only gives a false positive result in 10% of people without it. You take the test, and get a positive result. What is now the probability you have the cancer? (A) 90% (B) 9% (C) 50% (D) 89%.

(3) A pack of cards each has a letter on one side and a number on the other. The following four are dealt one side up. Which cards should you turn over to test whether *every vowel has an even number on the other side*?

|t| |4| |3| |e|

Most people are terrible at these problems. There is now a huge amount of experimental data showing that only a small minority give the appropriate answers in tests of these kinds. (The appropriate answer in (1) is (A): a conjunction cannot be more probable than its conjuncts; in (2) it is (B); in (3) it is |e| and |3|.[1] For two useful surveys of such studies, see Evans and Over, 1996 and Stein, 1996.)

Of course, many questions can be raised about the interpretation of experiments like these, and we shall raise some of them below. However, let us assume for the moment that these experiments do point to widespread deficiencies in human theoretical rationality. Two obvious questions then arise.

(A) *The Evaluative Question.* What is the status of the normative standards according to which some judgements and inferences are rational and others not? One natural answer would be that these normative standards

---

[1] Why isn't |4|, which many subjects choose, another appropriate answer? This answer mightn't be capable of falsifying the hypothesis, as |3| is, but it does at least promise to add support by instantiating it. This is a reasonable point, but the fact remains that most subjects choose |4| *instead* of |3|. It may be appropriate to view |4| as an answer, but it is not appropriate to think that |3| isn't one.

are a distillation of our best intuitions about rationality. On this view, a set of normative principles about rationality should be viewed as a kind of theory, a theory whose job is to accommodate as many as possible of our basic intuitions about rationality. However, this answer seems to be in tension with the experimental data, since these data suggest that the intuitions of ordinary people diverge markedly from orthodox standards of normative rationality. So, if we take the experimental data at face value, then we will need a different account of the source of these orthodox standards of normative rationality, an account which will make room for everyday intuitions to diverge from those standards.

(B) *The Explanatory Question.* A further puzzle is that many human activities seem to improve on the dismal performances in the psychological experiments. As it is often put, 'If we're so dumb, how come we sent a man to the moon?' The experimental data suggest that most people are irrational much of the time. But if this is right, then we need some further account of how these limitations are transcended in those many modern human institutions that seem to rely on a high degree of accuracy and precision.

3   The evaluative question

Let me begin with the evaluative question. One possible line of attack is to argue that the experimental data should not be taken at face value. Perhaps the intuitive judgements of ordinary people do not stray as far from orthodox assumptions about normative rationality as the experiments at first suggest. If so, then perhaps we can equate standards of rationality with the intuitions of ordinary people after all.

L. Jonathan Cohen, for example, has argued that, if we pay due attention to the distinction between intellectual *competence* and *performance*, then the apparent gap between ordinary practice and real standards can be made to disappear. 'Competence' here refers to underlying capacities, to basic reasoning procedures. 'Performance' refers to actual behaviour, which might not reflect competence for any number of reasons, such as momentary inattention, forgetfulness, drunkenness or indeed the distractions of undergoing a psychological experiment. Once we make this distinction, then it is possible to argue, as Cohen indeed does, that, while the *performance* of ordinary people often deviates from normative standards of rationality, the match between ordinary intuitions and normative standards is restored at the level of *competence* (Cohen, 1981).

Indeed, argues Cohen, how could it be otherwise, given that our normative theory must in the end answer to our best intuitions about the right way to judge and reason? Since our judgmental behaviour will also be guided by these intuitions (when inattention, drink or strange experimental settings do not intrude), there is no real room for a mismatch. Our underlying competence cannot fail to conform to our normative theory.

Cohen's position might seem plausible, but it has some odd consequences. Imagine that human beings really were incompetent in the ways suggested by the above experiments. That is, suppose that their underlying intellectual capacities, and not just failures of performance, made them take some conjunctions to be more probable than their conjuncts; made them commit the 'base rate fallacy' of ignoring the prior probability of some event when considering the relevance of new information; and, again, made them fail to see that possible counter-examples are more informative about a putative generalisation than positive instances. Now, if humans really were like this, would different standards of rationality then hold, would it then be rational to judge conjunctions more probable than their conjuncts, and so on? Surely not. Standards of rationality are not relative in this way. It is an objective matter whether or not a given intellectual move is rational, quite independent of whether people intuitively take it to be rational. Yet it is difficult to see how Cohen can avoid making rationality such a relative matter. If people did think as just hypothesised, then the theory that their thinking was rational would fit their intuitions about rationality perfectly, and so, by Cohen's argument, would be fully vindicated.

This thought-experiment (adapted from Stich, 1990b) bears directly on the interpretation of the actual experimental data. If it is *possible* for the underlying intellectual competence of human beings to incline them to irrationality, then surely the best explanation of the *actual* performance of human beings is that they have just such an irrational intellectual competence.[2] The experimental data indicate that human beings behave like the community in the thought experiment. So, in the absence of special arguments to the contrary, the obvious conclusion is that the basic intellectual inclinations of ordinary humans are indeed irrational.[3]

This now returns us to the evaluative problem. If the ordinary intuitions of ordinary people don't support objective standards of rationality, then

[2] Is such a community really possible? Some philosophers might argue on a priori grounds that such irrationality would be inconsistent with the supposition that the community have beliefs. However, while some minimal degree of rationality is no doubt required to qualify as a believer, it seems very doubtful whether this standard is high enough to rule out the postulated community (cf. Cherniak, 1986).

[3] Perhaps a match between orthodox notions of rationality and actual human practice can be restored by focusing on '*experts*', rather than the general run of humans. The difficulty here, however, is to identify the experts in a non-question-begging way (cf. Stich and Nisbett, 1980).

what is the status of those standards? What makes it right to reason in certain ways, even when reasoning in those ways seems unnatural to most people?

I would like to explore a very simple answer to this question. Suppose we say that a method of reasoning is rational to the extent that it issues in true beliefs. If we adopt this view, then there is no difficulty at all in understanding how the normal practice and intuitions of most people can be irrational. It is just a matter of their reasoning in ways which characteristically give rise to false beliefs (such as judging probabilities by reference to stereotypes, as in the Linda experiment, or ignoring base rates, as in the probability-of-cancer experiment, or failing to seek out possible counterexamples, as in the card-selection experiment).

This move is related to the 'reliabilist' strategy in epistemology. 'Reliable' in this context means 'a reliable source of true beliefs',[4] and reliabilists in epistemology argue that the notion of *knowledge* is best analysed as 'true belief issuing from some reliable method'. Some, but not all, reliabilists go further, and also analyse the notions of *justified* belief, and of a *rational* mode of thought, in terms of belief-forming methods which are reliable-for-truth. Now, there is a widespread debate about whether this reliabilist approach fully captures all aspects of the notion of knowledge, and *a fortiori* whether it is adequate to the further notions of justification and rationality. However, I shall not enter into these debates here, though many of the points made below will be relevant to them. Rather, my aim will merely be to show that *if* we adopt a reliabilist approach to rationality, *then* we can easily deal with the evaluative and explanatory problems generated by the experimental data on irrational human performance. I certainly think this lends support to a reliabilist approach to rationality (and to justification and knowledge). Whether other objections face the reliabilist programme in epistemology lies beyond the scope of this chapter.

A common first reaction to my reliabilist suggestion is that it cannot really help. For what does it *mean* to say that a belief is 'true', so the worry goes, other than that it is reachable by methods of rational thought? Given this, my reliabilist suggestion would seem to collapse into the empty claim that a method of thought is rational if it yields answers which are reachable by methods of rational thought.

I agree this would follow if 'true' meant something like 'rationally assertible'. However, I think that this is the wrong analysis of truth. I take it that truth can be analysed independently of any such notion as 'rational' (and

---

[4] Note that for inferential methods the relevant notion is *conditional* reliability. Inferential methods needn't always deliver true conclusions, but they should deliver true conclusions *if* their premises are true.

thus can be used to analyse rationality in turn, as in my suggested reliabilist account). These are, of course, matters of active controversy. My view, that truth can be analysed first, before we come to questions of rational assertibility, would certainly be resisted, *inter alia*, by neo-pragmatists like Hilary Putnam, by neo-verificationists influenced by Michael Dummett, and by the followers of Donald Davidson. There is no question of entering into this debate in this chapter. I have written about the issue elsewhere (Papineau, 1987; 1993, chapter 3; 1999). Here I can only invite readers to take my attitude to truth on trust and note how naturally it allows us to deal with the irrationality debate.[5]

4   More on the evaluative question

4.1   Further desiderata on modes of thought

I have suggested that we should equate the theoretical rationality of modes of thought with their reliability-for-truth. In effect this is to treat 'theoretical rationality' as a consequentialist notion. We deem a mode of thought to be rational to the extent that it is an effective means to the consequence of true beliefs.

Given this, however, an obvious further objection suggests itself. Why privilege truth as the only consequence that is relevant to the evaluation of belief-forming processes? There are a number of other consequences that might also be thought to matter. Most obviously, it will normally also be desirable that our belief-forming methods are *significant*, in the sense of delivering informative beliefs on matters of concern, and *frugal*, in the sense of not using large amounts of time or other resources. And we can imagine other dimensions of possible consequentialist evaluation of belief-forming methods, to do with whether they deliver beliefs that will make you rich, say, or are consistent with traditional values, or indeed pretty much anything,

---

[5] Even if 'true' doesn't *mean* 'rationally assertible', won't the suggested reliabilist strategy for assessing rationality still lack practical teeth? For, when we assess the reliability of our belief-forming methods, how else can we check their outputs except by using those selfsame belief-forming methods? So won't we inevitably end up concluding our methods are reliable? Not necessarily. For one thing, there is plenty of room for some belief-forming methods to be discredited because their outputs do not tally with those of other methods. And, in any case, assessments of belief-forming methods don't always proceed by directly assessing the *outputs* of those methods, but often appeal to theoretical considerations instead, which creates even more room for us to figure out that our standard methods of belief-assessment are unreliable. (For example, when I judge that newspaper astrology columns are unreliable sources of truth, I don't draw this conclusion inductively from some survey showing that astrological predictions normally turn out false, but from general assumptions about causal influences. For more on this, see Papineau, 1987, chapter 8.)

depending on who is doing the evaluating. To equate rationality specifically with reliability-for-truth would thus seem arbitrarily to privilege one dimension of theoretical rationality over others.

I don't think there is any substantial issue here. I agree that methods of belief-formation can be evaluated in all kinds of consequentialist ways. Moreover, I am happy to concede that reliability-for-truth is just one among these possibilities. While I think that truth is generally important for human beings, for various reasons, to which I shall return in my final section, I certainly do not want to argue that it is the only consequence of belief-forming methods which can be given evaluative significance. Indeed it is hard to imagine a realistic human perspective which ignores all other dimensions of possible evaluation in favour of truth. In particular, it is hard to imagine a realistic perspective that ignores significance and frugality. While we normally want to avoid error by having methods which are highly reliable-for-truth, we won't want to do this by restricting our beliefs to trivial and easily decidable matters, or by always spending inordinate amounts of time making sure our answers are correct. From any pragmatically realistic point of view, there wouldn't be much point in high levels of reliability, if this meant that we never got information on matters that mattered to our plans or only received it after the time for action was past.

Given these points, it will be helpful to refine our notion of theoretical rationality. Let us distinguish 'epistemic rationality' from 'wide theoretical rationality'. I shall say that a belief-forming method is 'epistemically rational' to the extent it is specifically reliable-for-truth, and that it has 'wide theoretical rationality' to the extent it produces an optimal mix of all the different desiderata imposed on it. I have no views about what this wide range of desiderata should be, and am happy to allow that different people with different interests may properly be concerned with different desiderata. In particular, therefore, I make no assumption that epistemic rationality is always more important than other aspects of wide theoretical rationality, nor that it should always be given any special weight in constructing an 'optimal mix' of different desiderata.

Having said all this, however, it is worth noting that 'epistemically rational' is not simply a term of art of my own construction, but is a component in such everyday notions as 'knowledge' and 'justified belief'. These everyday notions do focus exclusively on reliability to the exclusion of other desiderata. In particular, while frugality and significance are unquestionably significant aspects of our belief-forming methods, by anybody's standards, they are ignored by everyday epistemological notions like 'knowledge' and 'justified belief'.

To see that these everyday notions concern themselves only with reliability, and abstract them from further considerations of economy and importance, imagine a man who spends a month counting the individual blades of grass in his garden. We will no doubt feel that this is a complete waste of time and that the conclusion is of no possible interest to anyone, yet we will not say on this account that he does not *know* how many blades of grass there are, nor that his belief in their number isn't *justified*.

For the moment I offer this as no more than a terminological point. It is simply a fact about our language that we have words ('knowledge', 'justified') that we use to assess the sources of our beliefs purely from the perspective of reliability-for-truth, and in abstraction from such issues as significance and frugality. This linguistic fact does nothing to show that reliability-for-truth is somehow more basic or significant than these other desiderata, nor indeed is this something I believe. But I do take this linguistic fact to point to something interesting about our cognitive economy, and I shall return to the point in my final section.

4.2   *Perhaps humans are (widely) rational after all*

In section 3 I addressed the question of how far the data from psychological experiments show that ordinary people are 'irrational'. This question is complicated by the existence of further desiderata on belief-forming methods in addition to reliability-for-truth. Perhaps the allegedly poor performance of ordinary subjects in the psychological experiments is due to their using methods of belief-formation that *sacrifice* some degree of reliability-for-truth for further desiderata like significance and frugality. It is obvious enough that these further desiderata are in some tension with reliability, and indeed with each other, and that sensible belief-forming strategies will therefore aim to achieve some optimal balance between them. In particular they will generally trade in some degree of reliability-for-truth in the hope of gaining significant information while remaining frugal.

Given that such a trade-off is clearly a sensible strategy for dealing with the world in general, it would seem unreasonable immediately to condemn ordinary thinkers as 'irrational' just because they are using methods whose less-than-ideal reliability-for-truth is highlighted by the psychological experiments. Maybe their methods of thought characteristically give false answers in these settings, but this doesn't show that they don't embody an optimal mix of reliability, significance, economy, and other desiderata. In the terms introduced above, maybe ordinary people are 'widely theoretically rational' even if not 'epistemically rational'.

This is a reasonable point, but even so I have my doubts about whether ordinary methods of thought are 'rational' even in this 'wide' sense of yielding an optimal mix of reliability with other desiderata. It does not seem hard to imagine modes of thought which would get the right answers to the experimental puzzles, without sacrificing anything of frugality or significance across the board. However, I shall not press this point here, since there seems no principled basis for deciding how to weigh the ingredients in the optimal mix of reliability and other desiderata on belief-forming methods, and in any case the issue is of no importance to any of the questions we are interested in.

To see that it doesn't really matter for present purposes whether or not we end up calling ordinary people 'rational', note first that all my suggestions for *evaluating* belief-forming methods remain independent of whether actual human practice conforms to these evaluations. This is because the notions of 'epistemic rationality' and 'wide theoretical rationality' are both consequentialist notions. They both evaluate belief-forming methods in terms of whether they *actually* deliver certain results, be this truth alone, or some mixture of truth and other requirements. So whether a method is rational, in either of these consequentialist senses, is quite independent of whether ordinary people intuitively judge it to be rational, or whether they are naturally inclined to use it.[6]

Note also that the *explanatory* problem will remain a problem even if (which I am inclined to doubt) the practice of ordinary people is 'rational' in the wide sense that it optimises a mix of reliability, frugality, significance, and so on. For the psychological experiments certainly show that most people are bad in the specific dimension of reliability-for-truth, in that they characteristically give incorrect answers to the experimental puzzles. Maybe it is true that their high error rate in these situations is a necessary by-product of their modes of thought satisfying other sensible desiderata. But it is still a high error rate. So there is still a puzzle about how these imperfections in reliability are transcended in certain contexts, such as sending a man to the moon, where it is crucial that the kinds of mistakes made in the psychological experiments should somehow be avoided.

---

[6] This shows why, even given the complications introduced by different possible desiderata, my position on the evaluative question remains different from Cohen's. Where Cohen ties rationality to intuitions about rational thinking, I tie it to facts about which methods actually deliver which consequences. True, I have now in a sense admitted an element of relativism into judgements of 'wide rationality', in that I have allowed that it can be an evaluator-relative matter which desiderata are to count. But this is not the kind of relativism for which I earlier criticised Cohen's position. I allow that people and communities can have good reasons for differing on which desiderata they want belief-forming methods to satisfy. But it does not follow, as Cohen's position seems to imply, that whatever methods they practice will be rational for them if they *take* them to be so rational. For there will remain the question of whether those methods *actually* deliver the desired consequences, and nobody's merely thinking this will make it so.

*4.3   Human thought is suited to the environment of evolutionary
        adaptation*

There is a yet further dimension to assessments of rationality. As some of
the above remarks may already have suggested, assessments of rationality
are crucially sensitive to the *range of environments* against which modes of
thought are assessed. A mode of thought that scores badly within one
range of contexts may do well within another.

Note that this means that there is another way in which the performance
of ordinary people can be defended against aspersions cast on their 'rationality'. In addition to the point that they may be sacrificing reliability-for-
truth in favour of increased significance, frugality, and so on, there is also
the defence that they may score much better, on both epistemic and wide
theoretical rationality, if they are evaluated against a range of environments to which their abilities are well-suited. Maybe ordinary people can be
made to look stupid in the specific setting of the psychological laboratory.
But it does not follow that their intellectual performance will be poor across
a different range of environments, and in particular across the range of
environments in which they normally find themselves.

This point has been stressed by those writing within the tradition of
recent 'evolutionary psychology'. These evolutionary writers have set
themselves against the standard psychological understanding of the experimental data on irrationality. This standard response has come to be known
as the 'heuristics and biases' approach, and explains the data by arguing
that humans adopt certain *heuristic* strategies in solving theoretical problems, strategies which often provide useful short-cuts to reasonably accurate answers, but can be experimentally demonstrated to *bias* subjects
irrationally towards certain kinds of mistakes (Kahneman *et al.*, 1982).

Against this, the evolutionary psychologists (see Barkow *et al.*, 1992)
argue that our characteristic modes of thought must necessarily be well
suited to the range of environments in which they were originally selected.
In this sense, they argue, our modes of thought cannot help but be 'rational', even if they go astray when forced to work in unnatural contemporary
environments, including those of contemporary psychological experiments. This thought is normally presented in tandem with the evolutionary
psychologists' picture of the human mind as a 'Swiss-army knife', containing a number of self-contained and hard-wired *modules* each designed for a
specific cognitive task, such as visually identifying physical objects, thinking about other minds, selecting suitable mates, enforcing social contracts,
and so on. Since these modules have been developed by natural selection
over the last five million years, argue the evolutionary psychologists, we
should expect them to be good at satisfying the important desiderata, not

across all imaginable contexts, it is true, but specifically in the 'environment of evolutionary adaptation', in the range of contexts in which they were evolved by natural selection.[7]

An initial reservation about this evolutionary argument is that it assumes that natural selection always delivers optimal designs. This is simply not true, if for no other reason than that natural selection never designs things from scratch, but must build on structures already in place. (Thus, for example, the involvement of the emotions in cognition arguably derives from their role in the reptilian brain and may well have constrained modern cognition in distinctly sub-optimal directions.)

But suppose we let this point pass. A more significant observation is that there is far less distance between the evolutionary psychologists and their opponents in the 'heuristics and biases' tradition than might at first appear (cf. Samuels *et al.*, forthcoming). After all, both sides agree that the apparently poor performances in the psychological experiments are due to people using 'quick and dirty' cognitive techniques, which may work pretty well in some range of contexts, but which fail in the experiments. And there seems no reason why those in the 'heuristics and biases' tradition should not accept the suggestion that these 'quick and dirty' techniques are in fact evolved modules, whose neural underpinnings have been fostered by natural selection in the environment of evolutionary adaptation.

The only remaining issue is then whether all this shows that humans are 'irrational' or not. And here, too, there seems no substantial matter for disagreement. Both sides can agree that our modes of thought must have worked reasonably well in the range of environments where they were originally developed by natural selection. Maybe they aren't the best of all possible modes of thought, even in those environments, given that natural selection is often hampered by the blueprints it inherits from earlier stages of evolution. But they must have produced the goods often enough when it mattered, otherwise they wouldn't have been favoured by natural selection at all.

Similarly, on the other side, both sides can agree that our modes of thought fail in a wide range of modern environments. This is the inference that is normally drawn from the psychological experiments by those in the 'heuristics and biases' tradition. Sometimes it seems as if the evolutionary psychologists wish to deny this inference, in so far as they aim to defend 'human rationality' against the doubts widely thought to be cast on it by the

---

[7] The classic example of this approach is Cosmides' and Tooby's account of the Wason selection test (that is, puzzle (3) in section 2 above). They show that people are much better at this test when it is framed as a question about which individuals might be violating some social agreement, and they argue on this basis that the underlying abilities must be adaptations which are well-designed to detect social cheats (see their contribution to Barkow *et al.*, 1992).

experimental data. But on closer examination this impression dissolves. For, after all, the evolutionary psychologists defend human modes of thought by insisting that they must at least have worked well *in the environment of evolutionary adaptation*, even if they break down in modern environments. This shift of evaluative context, from the modern environment to the evolutionary one, would not be necessary if our modes of thought worked equally well in both, and so implicitly concedes that our biologically natural modes of thought do not work optimally in a wide range of modern situations.

5   The explanatory question

This now brings us back to the explanatory question. If it is agreed on all sides that human thinking depends on 'quick and dirty' problem-solving strategies which often go astray in modern environments, then how are we humans able to succeed in enterprises that demand a high level of accuracy across just such modern contexts? Or, as I put it before, 'If we're so dumb, how come we sent a man to the moon?'

The discussion so far suggests a natural answer to the explanatory question. As a preliminary to this answer, note that some people are better at the puzzles in the psychological experiments than others. In particular, I would expect those of my readers who had met versions of these puzzles before, and who understand their workings, to have had no great difficulty in avoiding the wrong answers.

I am not suggesting here that some people are innately smarter than others. On the contrary, my point is that nearly all humans are quite capable of *improving* their performance in such puzzles, if they prepare themselves appropriately. And the appropriate preparation is obvious enough. We can simply set ourselves to be more reliable sources of true belief. That is, we can identify and analyse different kinds of problem situation, figure out which methods of belief-formation will actually deliver true answers in those situations, and then set ourselves to practice these reliable methods. In this way we can 'transcend' the 'quick and dirty' modes of thought bequeathed to us by evolution. These 'heuristics' or 'modules' may work fine in a certain range of situations, or when speed is of the essence, but we can do much better when we want to make sure that we get the right answers, and are prepared to expend a significant amount of intellectual time and energy in finding them.

Thus some of us have learned to deal with the puzzles given above by applying the principles of the probability calculus and propositional logic. We 'calculate' the answers in accord with such principles, rather than relying on our intuitive sense of the right answer, precisely because we have learned that our intuitive judgements are an unreliable guide to the truth, and because we know that reasoning in line with the probability calculus and propositional logic is guaranteed to track the truth.[8]

I would be prepared to argue that this ability, to identify and deliberately adopt reliable methods of belief formation, has played a huge part in the development of human civilisation. Of course, it is not the only factor that separates us from other apes, and indeed I shall argue below that this deliberate pursuit of reliability rests on a number of further abilities which may also be peculiar to humans. But at the same time, it is clear that a wide range of advances in civilisation are simply special cases of the strategy of deliberately adopting methods designed to increase knowledge and eliminate error. Those ancient astronomers who first kept accurate records did so because they could see that this would enable them to avoid false beliefs about past events, and the same goes for every other kind of system of written records. Voyages of exploration, by their nature, are explicitly designed to gather accurate information that would otherwise be unavailable. The elaborate procedures adopted in courts of law and similar formal investigations have the overt function of minimising any chance of false verdicts. Arithmetic, geometry, double-entry bookkeeping, mechanical calculating devices, and so on, are all at bottom simply elaborate instruments invented in order to allow us to reach accurate conclusions on matters which would otherwise be left to guesswork.[9]

---

[8] Jonathan Evans and David Over distinguish 'personal rationality' ('rationality$_1$') from 'impersonal rationality' ('rationality$_2$'). They characterise the former as 'thinking . . . or acting in a way that is generally reliable and efficient for achieving one's goals', and the latter as 'thinking . . . or acting when . . . sanctioned by a normative theory' (1996, p. 8). It has been suggested to me, in various discussions, that this is similar to my distinction between 'quick and dirty' methods hard-wired by evolution and sophisticated methods deliberately designed to achieve the truth. I disagree. Even if we restrict Evans and Over's definitions to the subject area I am interested in, namely theoretical rationality, there remain crucial differences. Their 'personal rationality' is picked out as good for achieving personal goals. Some thinkers, especially those influenced by evolutionary psychology, may think this coincides with 'quick and dirty' thinking, but I don't, since I believe that 'quick and dirty' thinking often prevents us from achieving our goals in the modern world. Conversely, my sophisticated methods are themselves orientated to a particular personal goal, namely, the goal of true beliefs. For me, though not, it seems, for Evans and Over, any 'normativity' attaching to sophisticated methods is explained in terms of their being good routes to the personal goal of truth, and not in terms of some independent sense of normative correctness (cf. Papineau, 1999).

[9] To guard against one possible source of confusion, let us distinguish between *modern science*, in the sense of the institution that has developed in Western Europe since the beginning of the seventeenth century, and the general enterprise of deliberately seeking true beliefs, which I take to have been part of human life since before the beginning of recorded history. While deliberately seeking true beliefs is certainly part of science, the distinctively modern institution clearly rests on the confluence of a number of other factors, including distrust of authority, the use of mathematics and the expectation that simplicity lies behind the appearances.

Not everybody whose belief-forming strategies are improved by human civilisation need themselves have reflected on the advantages of these improvements. Once a certain technique, such as long division, or logarithms, or indeed the use of mechanical calculators, has been designed by innovative individuals in the interests of improved reliability-for-truth, then others can be *trained* in these techniques, without themselves necessarily appreciating their rationale. We humans have widespread institutions designed in large part for just this purpose – namely, schools and universities. Of course, it is to be hoped that many students will not only master the techniques, but also come in time to understand *why* they are good routes to the right answers. But this ideal is not always achieved (there are plenty of people who can use calculators, and indeed logarithms, without understanding how they work), and even when it is, it is normally only after at least some techniques have first been instilled by rote.

6   Transcending nature: the end of truth and the means to achieve it

From a biological perspective, the argument of the last section may seem only to have pushed the explanatory problem back. The explanatory problem was to understand how we can do such clever things as send a man to the moon, given the limitations of our biologically natural 'quick and dirty' modes of thought. My answer has been, in effect, that we can do another clever thing: namely, deliberately identify ways of thinking that are reliable for truth and set ourselves to practice them. But now it could reasonably be complained that I owe a further explanation, of how we can do this further clever thing, given our biological limitations. ('If we're so dumb, how come we can deliberately choose ways of thinking that are reliable for truth?')

This is an entirely reasonable challenge. I certainly don't want to argue that our ability deliberately to seek out the truth somehow requires us to transcend our biological natures. Fortunately, this is not necessary. We can indeed transcend the limitations of our innate 'quick and dirty' methods. But this doesn't depend on some non-biological part of our beings. Instead we use other abilities bequeathed to us by biological evolution to correct any failings in our innate belief-forming routines.

At first pass, two simple abilities would seem to suffice for the enterprise of deliberately seeking out reliable belief-forming methods. First, humans need to be able to identify the end of truth. Second, they need to figure out how to achieve it. After all, what are reliable belief-forming methods, except an effective means to the end of truth?

It may seem that the first of these sub-abilities – namely, identifying the end of truth – will present the bigger hurdle from a biological-evolutionary perspective. Surely, you may feel, it would beg all the interesting evolutionary questions simply to credit our ancestors with a grasp of a sophisticated notion like truth. On the other hand, if only our ancestors had been able to identify the end of truth, then wouldn't it be easy to explain how they figured out how to achieve it? For couldn't they simply have used general means-end reasoning to work out which means are an effective route to the aim of truth?

However, it is arguable that this may have things the wrong way round. Recent work on cognitive evolution suggests that acquiring a notion of truth may have been the easy part for our ancestors, by comparison with their identifying the best means to this end. This is because the notion of truth falls out of 'understanding of mind', and there is plenty of independent reason to suppose that our ancestors evolved such an understanding of mind. By contrast, the issue of means-end thinking is not at all straightforward, and it is not clear when, and in what sense, our ancestors acquired a general ability to identify effective means to given ends.

I shall consider these two topics in turn. First, in the next section, I shall make some remarks about theory of mind. Then, in the following two sections, 8 and 9, I shall turn to means-end reasoning. This latter will prove a large and unwieldy topic, and I will have to cut many corners. Still, it will be helpful to make some general comments, not least because it will cast some further light on my suggested solution to the explanatory problem. In particular, it will help us better to understand the way in which the deliberate pursuit of truth can *co-exist* with the older 'quick and dirty' belief-forming routines. This point will be discussed in section 10. The final section, 11, then considers the possibility that the deliberate pursuit of truth may not only be a spin-off from understanding of mind and means-end reasoning, but may itself be a biological adaptation.

7   Understanding of mind

The striking ability of humans to attribute a wide range of mental states to each other, and to use this to predict and explain behaviour, has been intensively discussed in recent years by philosophers and psychologists (Davies and Stone, 1995a and 1995b; Carruthers and Smith, 1996). However, the right analysis of this 'understanding of mind' is still a controversial matter, and it would be foolhardy for me to try and defend any agreed position here.

One popular contemporary view goes as follows. Normal adult humans have a *theory* of mind, which allows them to reason about beliefs, desires and other 'common-sense' mental states. Moreover, this theory resides in a 'module' which has been selected in the course of human evolution because of the specific advantages which derived from facility with psychological reasoning.

However, some dissenters doubt whether human understanding of mind consists in anything like a 'theory'; instead, they argue, it derives largely from our ability to *simulate* other human beings by running certain mental processes 'off-line'. A further question is whether understanding of mind is acquired during individual development via some more *general learning ability*, rather than from genes selected specifically to facilitate understanding of mind.

Fortunately, these intricacies are orthogonal to my concerns here. All that matters for present purposes is that at some point in evolutionary history all normal humans came to have an ability to think about each others' mental states. We can ignore such further questions as whether this understanding was itself an adaptation, or derived from some more general learning ability, or whether it required a 'theory' as opposed to simulation.

The important point here is that any being who has an understanding of mind, in any of these senses, will inevitably have a working grasp of the difference between true and false belief. To see this, recall that the diagnostic evidence for full possession of understanding of mind is the ability to pass the 'false belief test'. In this test, the experimenter tells a subject the following story. 'Sally puts her sweets in the basket. While Sally is out of the room her mother puts them in the drawer.' The experimenter then asks the subject, 'When Sally comes back, where will Sally look for her sweets?' If the subject has full-fledged understanding of mind, the subject will be able to answer that Sally will look in the basket. Even though the sweets are really in the drawer, subjects with an understanding of mind will know that Sally's actions are guided by her *beliefs* about the world, not by the world itself, and moreover that beliefs can represent the world as other than it is, as with Sally's belief about where the sweets are. There is now fairly clear-cut evidence that all normal human children acquire the ability to pass the false-belief test between the ages of three and four, but not before. By comparison, animals other than apes are clearly incapable of passing the false-belief test, while the situation with chimpanzees and other apes is obscure, not least because the experiment is very difficult to conduct if you can't talk to the subjects, and the results obtained with apes are therefore open to different interpretations.

Let us leave the chimpanzees and other apes to one side, and concentrate on the fact that, at some stage in evolutionary history, normal humans became cognitively sophisticated enough to pass the false-belief test. Once humans could pass the false-belief test, they would willy-nilly have been able to distinguish between true and false belief. They would have been able to think that *Sally believes the sweets are in the basket, when they are not,* and contrast that with the situation where *she believes them to be in the basket, and they are*. This would seem enough for them to be able to identify the end of true belief ('I don't want to be like Sally') and to start thinking about ways of achieving it.

Perhaps I am glossing over some different levels of sophistication here. It is one thing to note that Sally believes that the sweets are in the drawer, when they are, and that Ugh-Ugh believes the tiger is in the cave, when it is, and so on, and that Jane believes the cake is in the cupboard, when it isn't, and that Kargh believes the snake is in the hole, when it isn't, and so on. It is perhaps another thing to classify all the former beliefs together, as true, and all the latter together, as false.

Maybe so. Still, it doesn't seem all that big a step. In the rest of this chapter (after this sub-section), I shall accordingly assume that our ancestors were able to take this generalising step, and think of truth and falsity as such. After all, human beings clearly came to grasp these notions at some stage, even if not immediately upon acquiring theory of mind. Moreover, this assumption will allow me to by-pass a number of unimportant complexities.

Still, it will be worth digressing briefly in the rest of this sub-section, to note that *general* notions of truth and falsity may not themselves be required for the sort of deliberate attempt to improve epistemic rationality that I am interested in. In this chapter I have been talking about 'reliability-for-truth' as such, because I have been considering the epistemic goodness of belief-forming methods from a general point of view, abstracting from any particular features to do with particular subject matters. However, particular epistemic agents concerned to improve themselves do not have to aim for truth in the abstract. Instead, they might simply want the answers to specific questions.

Thus they may want to know *whether* the tiger is in the tree, or more generally *where* it is, or perhaps *how many* tigers are in that copse. 'Whether', 'where' and 'how many' here point to disjunctive aims which are indisputably available to any being with a theory of mind, even if the more abstract aim of truth requires some extra sophistication. Thus, to want to know *whether* the tiger is in the tree is to want that: you believe the tiger is in the tree, and it is, *or* that you believe it is not in the tree, and it is not. Similarly, to want to know the *where*abouts of the tiger comes to wanting: you believe it is in the tree, and it is in the tree, *or* you believe that it is in the cave, and it is in the cave, *or* . . .; and, again, to want to know *how many* is to want that: you believe there is one, and there is one, *or* you believe there is two, and there are two, *or* . . .

Philosophers familiar with disquotation-style accounts of truth may note here how wanting to know 'whether' the tiger is in the tree ('where', 'how many', . . .) is rather like aiming for a restricted kind of disquotational-truth (truth-in-L, where L is restricted to terms for talking about the tiger and the tree). But, whether or not we take this notion of restricted truth seriously, it is clear enough that any being who can pass the false-belief test can set itself the aim of finding out whether such-and-such (or set itself 'where' aims, or 'how many' aims, . . .) Moreover, if it can devise a strategy for achieving these aims, then it will *de facto* have devised a strategy to bring it about so that it gains true beliefs and avoids false ones. This would be quite enough for the deliberate improvement of epistemic rationality I am interested in. Whether these epistemic agents also think of themselves as aiming to gain *truth* and avoid *falsity* is an optional extra. The important point is that the strategies they devise to achieve their aims will in fact improve their reliability-for-truth on certain matters, whether or not they explicitly think of it in these terms.[10]

8   Means-end reasoning

Let me now turn to what I regard as the more difficult issue, the availability of means-end reasoning to human beings. The notion of means-end thinking is so familiar that it may seem as if there can be no problem here. Isn't it obvious that humans often figure out which possible actions are the best means to their ends? Indeed, isn't it obvious that this is true of many animals too? Given this, surely there is no special biological puzzle about humans applying means-end thinking to the specific task of improving their reliability-for-truth. Aren't they just deploying an ability which emerged fairly early in evolutionary history, and which can therefore be taken for granted when we are trying to identify features which differentiate humans from other animals?

But I don't think we should take means-end thinking for granted in this way. I take it to be a genuinely open question whether non-human animals really perform means-end reasoning. Indeed I take there to be serious questions about the extent to which even humans do this. Of course, much hinges here on exactly what is required for 'really performing means-end reasoning'. But the issue is by no means solely a definitional one. However we resolve the definitional question, there will still remain relevant issues about which cognitive mechanisms are responsible for which behaviours in

---

[10] It is interesting to contrast truth with probability here. While we have had the intellectual resources to pursue truth for at least 100,000 years, and quite possibly a lot longer, the notion of probability has only been around since 1654 (cf. Hacking, 1975). I think that this is why our culture encompasses many everyday techniques designed to help us track the truth, but is very bad at teaching ordinary people to reason with probabilities. It is no accident that many of the 'irrationality' experiments trade in probabilities.

which animals, and about the emergence of these mechanisms in the course of evolution.

The best way to bring out these issues is to describe a cognitive system which lacks any component designed to perform what I am thinking of as 'means-end reasoning'. No doubt the model I am about to elaborate is a caricature of any serious cognitive system. Even so, it will help to focus the issues. In particular, it will be easier to address definitional matters once this model is on the table.

Imagine a cognitive system with a number of input modules designed to extract information about the particular circumstances of the organism. These could range from sensory systems designed to identify environmental features and identify physical objects, to more specialised systems for recognising animals and plants, or indeed to systems for recognising faces and detecting cheats. Some of these input modules would receive information from others. Perhaps some of them would also lay down their findings in memory stores.

Now suppose also that there is a battery of output modules which generate certain kinds of behaviour when triggered. These behaviours might again range from the relatively unspecific, such as reaching or walking, to more specific activities like making a sandwich or driving to work, or indeed to greeting a friend or chastising a cheat. Maybe there is some nesting of these output modules, with some more complicated modules being built up from simpler ones. The execution of most output modules will also need to be guided by real-time informational resources, which may derive either from special informational channels dedicated to that output module, or from the above-mentioned input modules.

Suppose also some system of links between the input modules and the output modules. These links will determine which output modules should be triggered, on the basis of the deliverances of the input modules, and perhaps also on the basis of information about levels of current needs. Maybe these links also play a role on determining activity in the input modules, directing them to process information when it is needed by output modules or is relevant to the triggering of output modules.

Now, I could continue adding a number of obvious bells and whistles to this basic picture. But they would not affect one crucial point, namely, that there is no place in this cognitive architecture where representations of *general* or *causal* or *conditional* facts play a role. As I am telling the story, the function of the input modules is to deliver more or less recondite *particular* facts about the organism's present and past environment, and to make them available to the linking system and output modules. But so far I have postulated nothing whose job is to identify facts of the form *whenever A then B* or *A causes B* or *if A then B*.

Now, there is of course a sense in which some general-conditional facts of this form are already implicit in the architecture of our cognitive system. When the visual object recognition module moves from fragmentary retinal data to the judgement *edge of a localised body*, it is in effect proceeding on the highly contingent assumption that *whenever those data, there is an edge*. Since this assumption has nearly always been true in our ancestral environments, natural selection will have favoured cognitive modules which make this inferential move. In this sense the inferential structure of the object recognition module will embody general information acquired in the course of evolution. The same point applies to output modules. Your disposition to exert your leg muscles a certain way when climbing up a hill can be viewed as embodying the general-conditional information *this exertion will carry me so high*. And the same point also applies, even more obviously, to the links between input and output modules. If a fruit-eating organism is disposed to shake a certain kind of tree whenever it is hungry, this disposition can in the same sense be said to embody the general-conditional information that *shaking those trees will yield fruit*.[11]

However, while such general-conditional information will in this sense be implicit in various parts of the postulated architecture, there is no one place where it is brought together and reasoned with. Thus, to make the point graphic, an organism may have something like *shaking those trees will yield fruit* implicit in one set of links, and something like *throwing missiles will repel bears* implicit in another, and yet no way of putting these together so as to figure out that it would be a good idea to shake a tree when a bear is prowling nearby and no missiles are yet to hand. Of course, this information may itself come to be embodied implicitly in some disposition, if natural selection instils a specific disposition to shake trees to get fruit to throw at bears. But the general point will still apply. While the organism will have various bits of general-conditional information implicit in its various modules and the links between them, it will have no system for combining them and using them to infer the worth of behaviour that is not already directed by its cognitive architecture.

Nor is this crucial point affected by the existence of *learning* during the course of individual development. Suppose I now add that the modules and their interlinkages are shaped during the course of individual development.

---

[11] There are many delicate questions about exactly how to characterise contents in different kinds of cognitive system, and in particular about whether the simple cognitive architecture described so far warrants all of the precise characterisations of content I have suggested. I shall gloss over this in this chapter, as nothing much will hang on it. In Papineau (1998) I explain how the teleosemantic approach to content that I favour can deliver precise contents for full-fledged means-end reasoners, but I suggest that nothing similar is justified for less sophisticated cognitive systems. I am no longer so pessimistic – I think there are cases and cases – but further work remains to be done.

The precise structure of each individual's walking module might depend on which behaviours produced successful walking in the individual's past, particularly during infancy. The judgements issuing from the object recognition module will perhaps depend in part on which cues have, via independent checks in the individual's past, proved to indicate physical objects. The links between the input and output modules can depend on which outputs have produced relevant reinforcing results in the past. Possibly we might even wish to speak of whole modules being grown, so to speak, in response to environmental encouragement.

Learning in this sense will mean that a lot more general-conditional information will be embodied in various parts of the cognitive architecture. Wherever some architectural element is present because, in the individual's past, activity A was found to lead to reinforcing event B, then that element can be said to embody the general-conditional information that *if A then B*. But the earlier point still applies. All these items of general-conditional information are still embodied in the specific dispositions of various parts of the architecture to make various moves given various conditions, and there is still no one place where these items of information can be put together to draw inferences about the worth of new kinds of behaviour.

Let me stipulate that a creature as so far described is '*unthinking*', in that it does no 'means-end reasoning'. I presuppose nothing here about what others may intend by the phrase 'means-end reasoning'. From now on I shall mean: a cognitive mechanism where different items of general-conditional information are brought together and used to select behaviour. Still, in defence of this usage, note that any practical reasoning worth the name will involve the individual's ability to infer general-conditional facts of the form *in circumstances C, action A will lead to desired result R* from a number of other general-conditional facts. In particular, it will be able to do this even though neither the individual nor its ancestors have ever previously experienced A leading to R in C.

Now, even unthinking creatures will certainly be able to display a wide range of sophisticated behaviours, despite their lack of means-end reasoning. Nothing stops such creatures from being sensitive to the most intricate features of their environment and performing extremely complex routines under the guidance of this information. Moreover, their informational sensitivity and behavioural complexity can be moulded by learning to fit the particular features of their individual environments.

Given this, it is no straightforward matter to decide which, if any, non-human creatures might be performing means-end reasoning. This is of course an empirical matter, about which I shall have things to say in the next section. But it is certainly not to be taken for granted that sophisticated animal behaviour requires anything more than unthinking cognition.

It is interesting, indeed, to consider how much human behaviour might be explained on an unthinking basis. I suspect that a great deal of human behaviour depends on nothing but the cognitive mechanisms which we share with unthinking creatures. Moreover, I shall suggest in section 10 that even means-end reasoning itself shouldn't be thought of as something that transforms all human cognition, but simply as an appendage hooked on to the side of a pre-existing unthinking architecture, as it were.

Still, it seems clear that humans do have the ability to perform means-end reasoning in the sense I have specified. Humans don't always think carefully about their actions, but nearly all of them do this sometimes and select actions on that basis. After all, there are many examples of human actions which clearly depend on our ability to infer the efficacy of some novel action from the mass of general-conditional information in our possession. How else could we know in advance that a rocket of a certain construction will go to the moon? Or, to pick a related example which bears directly on the overall topic of this chapter, how else could we know in advance that a computer programmed in a certain way will deliver the right answers to a certain range of questions?

A full understanding of human cognition thus requires us to recognise the existence of human means-end reasoning and to account for the evolutionary emergence of this ability. It is somewhat surprising that this topic has received so little attention in recent discussions by philosophers and psychologists, by comparison with the vast recent literature on understanding of mind, and the widespread debate, over a rather longer timescale, of human language. This is especially surprising in view of the fact that much of this discussion of language, and of understanding of mind, takes human means-end reasoning for granted in explaining the structure and function of these other abilities.

9   The evolution of means-end reasoning

I am taking it to be uncontroversial that human beings are able to do means-end reasoning in my sense of inferentially processing explicit representations of general-conditional facts, even if it is an open question whether other animals can. How exactly humans do this, however, and what evolutionarily evolved abilities they deploy, are further questions, on which I have avoided committing myself so far.

We can compare two extreme views about the evolutionary underpinnings of means-end rationality. At one end of the spectrum is the view that there is some complex and separate faculty in the brain, devoted exclusively to means-end reasoning, and which was selected specifically for that purpose. At the other is the view that means-ends reasoning is a 'spandrel', which rests on other abilities, but has been of no evolutionary significance itself.

I think that both of these views are unlikely, and that the truth lies somewhere in between. Let me start with the latter extreme. On this view, means-end reasoning would be like arithmetic or music. Proficiency at these practices may well have yielded a reproductive advantage in the period since they emerged, in the sense that adepts may have had more children on average. But we wouldn't on this account want to view these practices as evolutionary adaptations. Other abilities, with independent evolutionary explanations, fully enable us to explain the emergence and preservation of arithmetic and music, once they get into our culture.[12] And in any case, there probably hasn't been enough time since these practices started for any selection of genes favouring them to be selected.

On this model, then, means-end reasoning would rest on other abilities with a biological purpose, but would have no such purpose itself. The most popular candidate for this enabling role is language, with understanding of mind also having some support from current fashion. Once our 'language organ' had emerged (or, alternatively, our 'understanding of mind module') then, so the story goes, we would have had the intellectual wherewithal for means-end reasoning, along with other cultural spin-offs like verbal agreements and fictional narratives.[13]

I find this extreme 'spandrel' view quite implausible, for the following general reason. Means-end reasoning needs to issue in *behaviour*. However, unthinking cognitive architectures, of the kind outlined in the last section, have no place for anything to issue in behaviour except hard-wired or conditioned links leading from input modules and need indicators to output modules. Somehow means-end reasoning has to be able to set up *new* links to output modules (either temporary – 'Next time I see a post box I'll insert this letter' – or permanent, 'From now I'll eat fish instead of meat'). Without being able to alter our behaviour-guiding programme in this way, means-end reasoning wouldn't make any difference to what we *do*.

However, it is difficult to see how a new power to alter behaviour could be a purely cultural matter. It scarcely makes sense to suppose that cultural innovation alone could intervene in some unprecedented way in the biological systems that direct action. Prior to means-end reasoning, behaviour is controlled by a set of dispositions that are laid down either by genes or by

---

[12] Which is not to deny that these explanations themselves can be informed by biological facts. *Which* practices are preserved by 'culture' depends crucially on which dispositions have been bequeathed to us by natural selection (cf. Sperber, 1996).

[13] The line that 'means-end reasoning is a spandrel' is found more often in conversation than in print. Still, it is popular among a surprisingly wide range of theorists, from official 'evolutionary psychologists', through Dennettians, to neo-associationist experimentalists.

conditioning. Somehow means-end reasoning, however it is realised, involves the power to create new such dispositions. So there must have been some biological selection for this aspect of means-end reasoning at least, some alteration of our biological design which allowed the output of deliberative decisions to reset our dispositions to action.[14]

To say this is not yet to go to the other extreme of the spectrum from the beginning of this section, and postulate a complex purpose-built faculty which evolved specifically to do means-end reasoning. Indeed it is consistent with the point just made to suppose that the evolution of means-end reasoning depended heavily on the emergence of either language or understanding of mind. Maybe language or understanding of mind emerged first, and *then* a small genetic alteration allowed certain kinds of processing within these faculties to affect dispositions to behaviour. This would mean that means-end reasoning wasn't entirely spandrel-like, in line with the point just made, but it would still make it largely derivative from language or understanding of mind.

I have some more specific worries about this kind of suggestion. To take understanding of mind first, the problem is that this faculty seems to *presuppose* means-end reasoning. Even though this point often goes unremarked, the standard explanations of understanding of mind simply help themselves to the idea that 'mind-readers' are already capable of making inferences from general-conditional claims. This applies to both the standard stories, the 'theory-theory' which holds that understanding of mind derives from an articulated theory of mind, and the 'simulation-theory' which holds that it rests largely on the ability to simulate the mental processes of others. After all, the 'theory-theory' explicitly makes understanding of mind a special case of our ability to reason with general facts. And the 'simulation-theory' holds that we anticipate others' decisions by mimicking their means-end reasoning 'off-line', which presumably presupposes a prior ability to perform means-end reasoning on-line.

As to the idea that language was the crucial precursor, here too it is argu-

---

[14] Note how this model, in which means-end reasoning 'resets' our dispositions to action, can easily accommodate *plans*, that is complicated sequences of actions needed to achieve some end. This would only require that the means-end system be able to produce multiple action settings, settings which would trigger a sequence of behaviours as a sequence of cues were encountered (some of which might simply be the completion of previous behaviours). An interesting evolutionary conjecture is that the possibility of such multiple settings came first. Perhaps the first evolutionary step pushing humans down a different cognitive path from other mammals was the ability to *learn* complex sequences of action (an ability which could in turn be explained by tool use and other practices made possible by complex hands). Once this ability to learn complex patterns was in place, then perhaps it became useful for our ancestors to start doing means-end thinking, in a way that it hadn't been before, because then they could figure out and set themselves to perform complex plans. That is, maybe means-end thinking is only worth the trouble for animals who are already capable of *learning* complex behaviours, for only they will be able to use complex plans.

able, if not so conclusively, that means-end reasoning must come before language, rather than the other way round. The thought here would be that the primary biological purpose of language is to increase each individual's stock of information. But such extra information wouldn't be any use to creatures who can't yet do means-end reasoning, since they wouldn't be able to use it to draw any extra conclusions about appropriate behaviour.

But perhaps this is too quick. Maybe language first evolved as a device for passing around pieces of *particular* information ('a tiger is coming', 'there are fruit in that tree', . . .). Since even creatures with unthinking cognitive architectures are guided by particular information about their circumstances, the utility of this information doesn't yet call for any means-end reasoning. So maybe means-end reasoning only emerged after our ancestors had first developed a relatively sophisticated language for reporting particular facts. Building on this basis, perhaps language *then* evolved to report and process general-conditional claims, together with some corresponding alteration in the system that sets our behavioural dispositions, to allow the results of such processing of general-conditional claims to make a behavioural difference.

I have no definite objections to this last language-based model for the emergence of means-end reasoning. But I am equally open to the idea that means-end reasoning may have emerged prior to and independently of any evolution of specifically hominid language.

Of course, it is not to be denied that once language (and indeed understanding of mind) did evolve, then this would have vastly augmented any pre-existing means-end abilities. Indeed we should expect there to have been significant co-evolution here, with pre-existing means-end abilities undergoing further biological evolution once they received extra input from language and understanding of mind, and these latter faculties similarly being biologically encouraged because of the assistance they thus provided to means-end reasoning.

Even so, it seems entirely plausible to me that there should have been at least some level of means-end reasoning in creatures who lack any hominid-type language. After all, there seems to be a huge gulf between purely unthinking creatures, as defined in the last section, and creatures who can converse about general-conditional facts. This should make us wonder whether there are some elementary kinds of means-end reasoning in creatures who lack language. Perhaps some pre-linguistic creatures developed ways of drawing on general-conditional information to set new dispositions to behaviour. (This of course might make it easier to understand how linguistic reasoning could acquire the power to affect behaviour: maybe it routes its influence via this more primitive kind of means-end reasoning, whatever that might be.)

At this point we need more empirical information about non-human creatures. There are surprisingly few data in this area. Some work has been done on the ability of apes and other primates to appreciate the *causal* connections between items in their environment (Tomasello and Call, 1997, chapters 3 and 12). This experimental evidence is not clear-cut. While apes can certainly learn to use tools in novel ways, they don't seem to represent the causal connection between the tool and the result in a way that can inform means-end reasoning. Experts doubt whether information about the connection between some intermediary cause and some end result ever allows non-human primates 'to devise novel ways of producing the intermediary and thus the end result' (Tomasello and Call, 1997, p. 390).

A rather different tradition of research has investigated whether rats can put together separate pieces of information to infer the worth of novel actions. Anthony Dickinson and his associates have argued that they can, on the basis of experiments like the following. Take a rat which is hungry, but not thirsty, and teach it that pressing a bar will produce dry food pellets, while pressing a lever will produce a sucrose solution (which also satisfies hunger). Now make it thirsty, but not hungry. Will it now press the lever, rather than the bar, even though its thirst, as opposed to its hunger, has never been satisfied by the sucrose solution?

The answer is yes – provided that the rat has at some previous time been shown that the sucrose solution is a better satisfier of thirst than the dry food pellets (Heyes and Dickinson, 1990; Dickinson and Balleine, 1999). And at first sight this does look like a bit of means-end reasoning. The rat seems to be putting together the information that (a) lever-pressing yields the sucrose solution, with (b) the sucrose solution satisfies thirst, to infer the conclusion (c) that lever-pressing will satisfy thirst.

This is certainly interesting, but there is room to query whether it indicates genuine means-end reasoning. Maybe the role of the earlier exposure to the thirst-satisfying effects of the sucrose solution is not to instil knowledge of this causal connection in the rat, but rather to give it a new acquired 'need', namely, for sucrose solution as such. This possibility is supported by other experiments of Dickinson's, which suggest that such 'incentive learning' would not be quashed even if the rat's later experience indicated that the sucrose solution did not satisfy thirst after all. If this is right, and the rat has come to value the sucrose solution in itself, then its behaviour can be explained without supposing it is putting together different pieces of general-conditional information. Rather its new need for sucrose solution is simply triggering its disposition to press the lever when it needs sucrose solution. Still, there remains the fact that the rat seems to have acquired this disposition, to press the lever when it needs sucrose solution, even though it has not been so rewarded for pressing the lever, and this itself is worthy of remark.

This kind of neo-associationist research raises any number of fascinating questions, but this is not the place to pursue details. Let me conclude this foray into empirical speculation by considering a rather different kind of basis for means-end reasoning. So far I have not raised the issue of how far means-end reasoning needs to be 'domain-general' rather than 'domain-specific'. When we think of mature human means-end reasoning, we automatically think of a faculty which is capable of dealing with information on pretty much any subject matter. But there is nothing in my definition of means-end reasoning as such to require such domain-generality. All I specified was a system that can put together different items of general-conditional information to draw conclusions about the worth of novel actions. This is perfectly consistent with the system doing this only with information of a quite specific kind.

This points to the possibility of creatures who evolve a domain-specific form of means-end reasoning, which deals with limited kinds of information and informs specific kinds of actions. One obvious example would be spatial reasoning. Research on rats and other mammals indicates that they can use representations of their spatial environment to figure out which of various possible actions will comprise the solution to some novel spatial problem, such as finding their way through a simple maze. Despite the domain-specificity of this ability, it satisfies my definition of means-end reasoning, in that such creatures effectively have a wealth of information about what will happen *if* they move in various ways, which they can use in combination to figure out what to do in novel situations.

Perhaps some domain-specific reasoning of this proto-means-end kind will provide a missing link between unthinking animals and full-fledged human means-end reasoners. On this suggestion, spatial reasoning or something similar would have come first, and then this would then have been further adapted to allow reasoning over a wider range of subject matters. The tendency of humans to represent intellectual problems in geometrical terms is suggestive in this context. Another aspect of human reasoning that may repay further research is the use of visual imagination to anticipate the results of possible actions.

10   Means-end reasoning and theoretical rationality

Let me now return to theoretical rationality. Recall that I argued, in response to the 'explanatory problem', that humans can avoid doxastic error by deliberately aiming to improve their reliability-for-truth. However, I have yet to address the question, which I flagged in section 6, about how this deliberate pursuit of truth is supposed to *co-exist* with older 'quick and dirty' methods of belief-formation.

On the face of it, there certainly seems to be a problem here. If humans are innately predisposed to use certain 'quick and dirty' mechanisms to deliver answers when faced with certain problems, then how is it possible for them deliberately to *stop* these mechanisms operating? After all, it is a familiar philosophical point that our doxastic behaviour is not under the control of our will. So we might expect the automatic, older mechanisms to continue operating as before, even after we form the intention to improve our doxastic performance. But then, if this is right, it remains unclear how humans *can* improve their doxastic performance, given that the automatic mechanisms will continue to churn out the bad old answers as before.

The discussion of means-end reasoning in the last two sections can help here. Consider first my overall picture of the relation between means-end reasoning and the rest of our cognitive architecture. It is no part of my thinking to suppose that, once humans are able to do means-end thinking, then this will somehow permeate all their cognition and transform it with some higher intelligence. On the contrary, I am supposing that nearly all our activities will continue to be driven as before, with fast and frugal modules processing information about our particular circumstances, and with output modules being triggered as opportunity arises and need demands. The means-end system is simply added on to the side of the existing unthinking architecture, as it were, leaving the rest as before.

The only change we need postulate is that sometimes, when the stakes are high and time does not press, the means-end system will be prompted to identify the best course of action in the light of the general-conditional information available to it. This identification will then feed back into the pre-existing unthinking architecture, by setting new input-output links so as to trigger some particular output module when certain cues are next encountered.

This model now gives us room to manoeuvre on the issue of whether it is in our *power* to improve our doxastic performance, given that the hard-wired and automatic belief-forming 'modules' threaten to force beliefs on us willy-nilly. As a first step, note that a decision to improve doxastic performance in such-and-such circumstances ('do the sums, don't just guess') is itself a special case of an *output* of means-end-reasoning. Our general-conditional information implies that, if we want to avoid error, we had better do the sums, or whatever, and our desire to avoid error then leads us to set certain dispositions to action accordingly. We set ourselves to perform a certain sequence of actions (mental arithmetic, paper and pencil calculations, etc.) whenever we are triggered by the relevant problem situations (problems involving probabilities, logic, arithmetic, etc.).

If we look at it in this way, there is no suggestion that the new belief-forming methods need somehow *replace* or *abolish* the old fast and frugal modules. There are some interesting issues here, but the simplest assumption will be that the old modules will continue to run, quickly and frugally, alongside the improved belief-forming methods which we are now disposed to follow when triggered by the relevant problems. This means that in certain cases, the ones where the fast and frugal methods go astray, we will in a sense 'end up' with two conflicting answers. The fast modules will continue to 'tell us' that it is likely that Linda is a feminist bank teller, and that we have cancer, and that we needn't turn over the odd number, even while the deliberate methods deliver the contrary answers.

Described like that, it may sound weird, but I think that it is quite faithful to the facts. Consider the familiar case of knowingly experienced visual illusions. The Müller-Lyer lines are the classic example. The two lines look different lengths to you, and moreover continue to do so *even when you know they are the same length.* There is an obvious modular explanation for this phenomenon. We have a fast and frugal object-identification module, which delivers the conclusion that the lines are different lengths. We also have more deliberate and accurate ways of deciding the question, using measurements, which delivers the conclusion they are the same length. Deciding the question the deliberate way does not block the operation of the fast module, which is why the illusion persists even when you know it is an illusion.

As with the visual example, so in the more general case. Don't we continue to 'feel the pull' of the judgements that Linda is a feminist bank teller, that we have cancer, and that we needn't turn over the odd number, even when our more deliberate reasoning gives us the contrary answers? I would say that this is because our hard-wired modules are still generating their erroneous answers, alongside the more deliberate belief-forming processes that deliver the right ones. We know the quick answers are 'cognitive illusions', but our hard-wired modules continue to press them upon us.

There may still seem to be a problem. If I am now saying we *don't* in fact block the bad old modules when we decide to use better belief-forming methods, since the old modules are still running, then in what sense can I claim that we *succeed* in giving ourselves the new improved beliefs? After all, I have just insisted that the old modules continue to press their bad answers on us, while the new methods give us the contrary claims. So won't we end up with self-cancelling contradictions, rather than unequivocally improved new beliefs?

Here we need to distinguish between the different *uses* of module-driven and deliberate judgements, in addition to distinguishing their sources. The language of 'belief' starts to break down at this point. Consider the vision case again. Do I 'believe' that the lines are different lengths or not, when I 'knowingly experience' the Müller-Lyer illusion? Yes and no. Certain parts of my behaviour will be driven by the judgement that they are different lengths, as when I am asked to point quickly and without warning to the longer. But other behaviour, such as betting a large sum on their lengths, will be driven by the deliberative judgement that they are the same length. Similarly, I would suggest, with the other cognitive illusions. When we have to act in a hurry, our behaviour will standardly be driven by the fast illusory judgements. When we have time to think about what to do, we act on the basis of the deliberative judgements.

So the different sources of the two kinds of judgements are mirrored by the different uses to which they are put. At a first pass, we can expect that the fast module-derived judgements will continue to drive behavioural routines that are tied to those judgements by hard-wired or conditioned links, even when deliberation indicates that those judgements are illusory. By contrast, deliberative judgements will be distinguished, not just by being *outputs* of the means-end system, but also by providing distinctive *inputs* to that system. The main roles of deliberative judgements will be to feed further information back into the means-end system, and thus to improve future means-end decision-making. Of course, the means-end system will also acquire many judgements via the old fast modules, in cases where we have no reason to distrust those modules. But judgements issuing from the deliberate pursuit of truth will play a dominant means-end role, in that they will override doubtful modular judgements, within the means-end system at least, when there is any conflict.

11   Knowledge-seeking and biological design

So far I have simply presented our ability to achieve high levels of theoretical rationality as a spandrel. While I argued in the section before last that means-end reasoning in general must involve *some* genetic evolution (if only to explain how it has the power to influence behaviour), I have not claimed this about the deliberate pursuit of truth. If you can identify the end of truth (from your understanding of mind), and if you can figure out which strategies are the best means to this end (from your means-end system), then you will therewith have the ability to adopt reliable belief-forming methods in pursuit of true beliefs, without any further biological evolution needed.

In this section, however, I want to consider whether there has been any biological selection for truth-seeking itself. Have certain genes been favoured specifically because they make us better at seeking out reliable belief-forming processes?

One reason for pursuing this thought is that there has been a gap in my story so far. I have spoken of *identifying* the end of truth and have argued that this falls out of theory of mind. But note that what falls out of theory of mind is the concept of truth, if anything, not a desire for truth. To be able to think about truth isn't yet to *want* truth, but it is only wanting truth that will make you seek reliable belief-forming processes.

Why might people seek truth? One reason has been implicit in much of the argument so far, but has not yet been explicitly mentioned. If you act on true beliefs, you will generally get the results you want, but not if you act on false beliefs. So people who reflect on what's generally needed to satisfy their desires, and figure out that they need to act on true beliefs to be confident of this, will want truth as a means to satisfying their desires.

But this is rather a lot of reasoning to ask of our rather dull ancestors. They would need to start thinking about their aims, and about the general connection between possessing true beliefs and success in achieving what they want. Perhaps this connection will fall out of the theory of mind (it would be interesting to test small children on this), but it is not obvious that it should do so.

So, if it was not manifest to our ancestors that they needed true beliefs to succeed in action, then they may have had means-end thinking in general, yet mightn't have sought truth via reliable methods, for lack of thinking through the reasons for wanting truth as a means. Still, it seems clear that they would have been much more successful the more true beliefs they were able to feed into their means-end system. So any gene that made them desire truth in itself would have been strongly favoured by natural selection.

Note that this would just be a special case of the logic by which natural selection makes us desire anything. There is a perspective from which it can seem puzzling that natural selection has designed us to desire anything except reproductive success. After all, natural selection favours traits just to the extent that they contribute to reproductive success. So why should it be a biologically good idea to design us to pursue proximate goals like food and warmth and sex, rather than reproductive success itself? Why not just set us the single aim of reproductive success and leave it to us to figure out how best to achieve it?

The answer, of course, is that the relevant connections are often obscure, if not to us, then certainly to our ancestors. Natural selection couldn't trust our ancestors, so to speak, always to identify the best means to reproductive success. So instead it set them some more immediate goals, like food, warmth and sex, which had correlated reasonably well with eventual reproductive success in the evolutionary past, and which were immediate enough for our ancestors to figure out effectively how to pursue them.

Similarly, I would like to suggest, with truth. True beliefs will correlate well with reproductive success (since they will correlate with desire satisfaction which correlates with reproductive success). But if our ancestors were unable to discern this connection (or more to the point, discern the connection with desire satisfaction, given that evolution had already set them to pursue various proximate goals, rather than reproductive success *per se*), then it would have been greatly to their biological advantage to be instilled with a desire for truth *per se*. Then they would have pursued truth in any case, whether or not they saw the connection with further success in action, and so reaped the rewards of such further success as a side-effect (intended by evolution, so to speak, but not by themselves).

One obvious piece of evidence in support of this conjecture is the natural tendency of many human beings to seek out the truth on matters of no obvious practical concern. Consider investigations into the origin of the universe, or the evolution of species, or abstract metaphysics. It is not obvious, to say the least, how these investigations might be motivated by the thought that true beliefs will enable us to succeed in our practical projects. Of course, the tendency towards such research might be due to culture rather than any genetic selection. But we should not rule out the possibility that such pure research owes its existence to the fact that natural selection couldn't trust us to tell when the truth was going to be useful to reproductive success and so made us seek it willy-nilly.

How seriously should we take talk of evolution selecting certain *desires*? This depends in part on how we understand desire talk. For most of the past few sections I have avoided 'belief' and 'desire' talk, because of philosophical controversies surrounding its interpretation. But in this section I have not been able to resist the expository convenience. Let me now make this talk of 'desires' good by explaining that I mean nothing but the *preferences revealed by means-end thinking*. This notion was already implicit in my earlier discussion of a means-end system, which after all is a system which takes in beliefs, figures out what they imply for the consequences of the various actions available, and then selects one such option. Such a system, by its nature, favours certain consequences over others, and so to this extent can be said to embody a 'desire' for those consequences. This is all I mean when I say that natural selection may have instilled a 'desire' for truth in us. All I mean is that natural selection did something which increased the likelihood of our means-end reasoners selecting actions which would yield true beliefs.

At this stage it will be useful to make a rather different point about genetic selection for a trait like desiring the truth. So far I have presented this as an alternative to the view that the pursuit of truth was *invented* by some stone-age decision theorist, some prehistoric genius who saw for the first time that people who had true beliefs would generally be better at achieving their ends. But in fact the two possibilities are not in conflict; indeed, the invention scenario adds hugely to the plausibility of the genetic story.

Suppose, for the sake of the argument, that some prehistoric ancestor did first see that it would be useful to get at the truth. Perhaps the idea spread some way, to the family of the immediate inventor, or to his or her hunter-gatherer band. This would be a wonderfully useful practice, and those who cottoned on to it would fare well. Indeed those who cottoned on to it quickly would be at a huge reproductive advantage. So there would be immense selective pressure in favour of any genetically-based quirks of cognitive development which aided the acquisition of this trick.

One way to achieve this would be to jiggle the development of the means-end system slightly, in such a way as to make it more likely to acquire a preference for truth *when* the surrounding culture sets an example. It seems independently plausible that our adult preferences should depend upon our developmental experience, yielding derived preferences for things which in our experience have led to reinforcing results (cf. the discussion of Dickinson's rats in section 9). And it is also independently plausible that surrounding cultural practices will influence which such derived preferences get set up. Now, when some such culturally influenced derived preference is also biologically advantageous, then natural selection is likely to come to the aid of the party too, by favouring genes that make it easier for this particular preference to be acquired. This genetic alteration needn't be advantageous in the absence of the surrounding culture. It may not be selectively positive when, in the absence of a supporting culture, there is no real chance of developing a preference for truth. Yet, if such a genetic alteration were selected within the context of a surrounding culture, then this would still constitute selection of a desire for truth, in the sense I intend. For certain genes would have been favoured because they increased the likelihood that the means-end system would select actions which promised to yield true beliefs.

It is important not to think of all biological selection as requiring complexes of genes which on their own specify elaborate end-products, in the way an architect's drawings specify a building. All an advantageous allele need do is increase the likelihood that some advantageous trait will develop *in the normal range of environments*. Indeed all genes will depend on some features of the environment to help bring about the effects for which they are selected. In the special case of organisms with cultures, the features of the environment which might combine with the gene to help produce the advantageous effects might be very complex and specific. The gene 'in itself', so to speak, might have no obvious connection with a desire for truth, to return to our example, except that it causes some non-specific change in the brain that happens to make you better at learning to pursue the truth *when others in your society are already setting an example and encouraging you to follow it*. But once there is a culture with this last-mentioned feature, then this gene will be strongly selected for. (What is more, once it is selected for, then there will be scope for more elaborate developments of the cultural practice, since everybody has now become better at cottoning on to it, which will create extra pressure for genes which make you good at learning the more elaborate practice . . .)

Let me now conclude by briefly considering a rather different way in which natural selection may have favoured the pursuit of belief-forming strategies which are reliable for truth. Apart from fostering a desire for truth, it may also have given us an input module dedicated to the identification of reliable sources of belief. I do not intend this as an alternative to the hypothesis of a biologically enhanced desire for truth, but as something which may have occurred in addition. (Moreover, the points about culture-gene interaction just made in connection with the desire for truth will also apply to the biological selection of an ability to identify reliable sources of belief. Let me now take this as read, without repeating the story.)

This further suggestion should strike an immediate chord with philosophers. Anybody who has tangled with the baroque philosophical literature on the *concept of knowledge* will know that humans make unbelievably detailed and widely consistent judgements about which people count as *knowers*. They can judge, in a way that seems to escape any straightforward philosophical analysis in terms of necessary and sufficient conditions, whether true beliefs derived in all kinds of recherché ways are tightly enough linked to the facts to qualify as knowledge. I would like to suggest that these judgements issue from a biologically favoured input module whose task is to identify those routes to belief which can be trusted to deliver true beliefs. When we ask, 'Does X really *know* about p?', or 'Wouldn't we *know* whether p if we went and examined those tracks carefully . . ?', we are arguably deploying an notion which has been designed to help us decide whether some route to the belief that p is a reliable source of truth. From this perspective, then, judgements about knowledge are the products of an input module which has been encouraged by natural selection because it yields a fast and frugal way of identifying strategies which are reliable for truth.

Recall a point I made in section 4.1, that the everyday notion of 'knowledge' focuses exclusively on reliability-for-truth, and abstracts from the cost or significance of the belief in question. The man *knew* how many blades of grass he had, even if he was wasting his time on a trivial matter. This bears on one common objection to my suggestion that biological evolution may have favoured truth-seeking as such. A number of colleagues have contended (standardly citing Peter Godfrey-Smith's 'Signal, Decision, Action', 1991) that it is implausible that evolution should have encouraged the aim of truth as such. Since there are serious costs to a high degree of reliability, wouldn't we expect evolution to have balanced the worth of truth against the cost and significance of acquiring it?

This is a reasonable point, but we should not forget that evolution isn't a perfect engineer and often has to settle for less than the best. I conjecture that, once domain-general means-end reasoning was up and running, it was *so* important that it be stocked with accurate information that evolution started selecting for truth-seeking *per se*, in abstraction from cost and significance. Maybe an even better cognitive design would have avoided ever making truth *per se* one of our doxastic aims, but only truth weighed by some mix of cost and significance. But my suspicion is that evolution couldn't take the risk, so to speak, that the pursuit of truth might be diluted in this way. (Compare: maybe it would be even better if sex as such were never one of our aims, but only sex that is likely to lead to healthy offspring; here, too, evolution has clearly found it better not to be too fancy.)

I take the striking structure of the concept of knowledge to lend support to the idea that truth-seeking *per se* has been selectively advantageous in our biological history. This complex concept comes so easily to humans that it seems likely that there is some genetic component in its acquisition. Yet this concept focuses exclusively on reliability-for-truth, in abstraction from any other desiderata on belief-formation. If I am right to suggest that judgements about knowledge are the products of an input module which has been encouraged by natural selection, then this at least is one case where evolution has decided that the important thing is to get at the truth, whatever the cost or significance.

A prediction follows from the hypothesis that judgements about knowledge are the products of an input module. On this hypothesis, we ought to suffer 'cognitive illusions' with respect to judgements about knowledge. There should be situations where the quick but dirty module takes a view on whether some belief is or isn't 'knowledge', but our more deliberate reasoning disagrees on whether this belief stems from a reliable source.

I think there are cases just like this, and they will be familiar to philosophers. Consider the 'intuitions' that are standardly thought to count against reliabilist theories of knowledge. These are precisely cases where some true belief has been arrived at by a reliable process, and yet, in the immediate judgement of ordinary people, does not really qualify as 'knowledge', or vice versa. I have no view (nor do I really care) whether this disqualifies reliabilism as a philosophical theory of knowledge. But it does fit the hypothesis of a dedicated module whose function is to identify reliable sources of belief. For, like all fast and frugal modules, it will cut some corners, and end up making some judgements it ought not to make.

Philosophical epistemologists may wish to continue charting such mistakes in the pursuit of the everyday notion of knowledge. But naturalist philosophers of psychology will be happy to note how their existence perfectly confirms the hypothesis of a biological module dedicated to identifying reliable sources of truth.

I would like to thank Peter Carruthers, Peter Goldie, David Over, Kim Sterelny and Stephen Stich for comments on this chapter.

9 Mind, brain and material culture: an archaeological perspective

Steven Mithen

The fossil record for human evolution has provided a detailed picture for the course of brain enlargement from the *c.* 400cc brain size of early australopithecines at around 3.5 million years ago to the *c.* 1200–1500cc of modern humans. I discuss the relationship between this and the evolution of the human mind, arguing that neither brain size alone, nor arguments about changing networks within the brain, are sufficient to explain the patterns we can infer from the archaeological record about the development of human intelligence. The key event in the evolution of the modern mind appears to be when humans began to extend their minds by exploiting not just language, but also material culture and their social structures, as means of augmenting the mental capacities delivered by the brain alone.

1 Introduction

The last decade has seen a remarkable surge of interest in the evolution of the mind. This has arisen within a wide range of disciplines and been fostered by a considerable degree of inter-disciplinary cross-fertilisation at conferences and within edited publications (e.g. Barkow *et al.*, 1992; Mellars and Gibson, 1996; Mithen, 1996b; Noble and Davidson, 1996; Bock and Cardew, 1997; Pinker, 1997b; Crawford and Krebs, 1998). Each discipline has, of course, a unique contribution to make to our understanding of cognitive evolution – psychologists bring to this topic a specialised understanding of modern minds, while neuroscientists, armed with their latest brain scanners, seek to extend our understanding of how the brain works. Archaeology has the benefit of being able to study the behaviour of human ancestors and relatives. It attempts to draw inferences about the nature of their minds, some of which may have been precursors to the modern mind of today. Yet it does so under the severe constraints of poorly preserved evidence, evidence that is often open to multiple, equally valid, interpretations.

Within this chapter I wish to reflect upon this contribution of archaeology to the study of both past and modern minds. I do so because it appears to me that the most striking piece of evidence about the evolution of the mind that can be gleaned from the archaeological record has been neglected in much of this recent literature, including my own writings about the pre-history of the mind (e.g. Mithen, 1996b). This evidence is quite simply that between 100,000 and 30,000 years ago the evolution of the mind departed on a completely new trajectory by becoming extended beyond the brain. Both others and myself have previously argued that within this time period there was a major development in cognitive evolution, something that I have termed the emergence of cognitive fluidity (Mithen, 1996b).

But the new types of material culture and behaviour – notably art, ritual and symbolism – which have been used to support this view, have been seen as no more than the *products* of a new type of mind. This is, however, only half the story: the material culture, social structures and economic patterns were fundamentally *part* of the new mind, they themselves were as much the cause as the consequences of new ways of thinking. In this regard the archaeological record appears to provide substantial support to the notion of the 'extended mind' as has been favoured by Clark (1996; Clark and Chalmers, 1998), and detracts from arguments that there is an equivalence between the mind and the brain.

The key argument of this paper is that by examining the archaeological record we can gain a more effective appreciation of the extent to which human mental activity is dependent upon the external world. We can do this because the archaeological record provides evidence about other types of humans, such as the Neanderthals and archaic *Homo sapiens*. Their mental activity appears to have been substantially more reliant on their brains alone – brains that are unlikely to have been significantly different to those that we possess today. We can see that the range and scope of their mental activity was markedly constrained when compared to the way that we think today.

2   Brain and mind in evolution

One of the most striking patterns in the archaeological record is that modern brain sizes are reached long before there is any trace of modern human thought and behaviour. This has been frequently commented upon (e.g. Bickerton, 1995; Mithen, 1996b) but its full implications are rarely considered. The expansion of the brain in the hominid lineage is now known in considerable detail (Aiello, 1996; Ruff *et al.*, 1997; Lewin, 1999). Having had a volume of around 400cc in our earliest hominid ancestors, the australopithecines of *c.* 2.5–4.5 million years ago – a volume equivalent to that of the chimpanzee today – there was a substantial period of encephalisation around 2 million years ago. This resulted in some hominid species having brain sizes of up to 750cc, notably the specimen KNM 1470, the type specimen for *Homo rudolfensis*. This spurt in brain size appears, however, to be largely related to increases in body size. Although it has traditionally been used as one of the markers for the start of the *Homo* genus, Wood and Collard (1999) have persuasively argued that these large-brained hominids should remain with the australopithecine genus.

By 1.5 million years ago, specimens are found with brain sizes of 900–1000 cc, the most notable being the Nariokotome Boy, WT 15000 (Walker and Leakey, 1993), classified as *Homo ergaster*. As Aiello (1996) has stressed, after this date brain size seems to remain at a plateau, this coinciding with a period of considerable anatomical stability and cultural stasis. The most telling artefact of this period is the handaxe, found throughout the Old World (with the possible exception of southeast Asia) and providing a marker for the dispersal of this grade of early human into a variety of environments. It would appear, therefore, that the particular combination of anatomy, social structure and material culture of *Homo ergaster* and its immediate descendants, *Homo erectus* and *Homo heidelbergensis*, provided a remarkably successful adaptation to Pleistocene conditions. I have previously argued that this derived from having a mind constituted by multiple, specialised intelligences.

It is worth emphasising just how smart some of these early species of *Homo* were, in their domain-specific way. The handaxe is their most characteristic artefact, first appearing in the archaeological record 1.4 million years ago and remaining a pervasive element of that record for more than one million years. These are pear- or ovate-shaped artefacts, made by the bifacial flaking of stone nodules or flakes. Many display a high degree of symmetry. There can be no question that they were very challenging to make. Often non-archaeologists speculate that handaxes are equivalent to the complex artefacts made by other animals, such as a beaver's dam, a honeycomb or a spider's web: all complex artefacts with degrees of symmetry but which require neither intelligence nor conscious thought to produce. Well, such comparisons are ill-founded. A reductive technology is necessary to make a handaxe. One must begin with a nodule of stone and employ a range of different hammers and methods of fracture to achieve the final product. There is a great deal of unpredictability involved: unexpected contingencies arise, plans need to be continually modified. One simply cannot produce a handaxe by iterating a fixed action routine as a spider or beaver might use for their artefacts. Making a handaxe is a completely different mental ball game. It is one that requires intelligent thought.

One of the most critical periods in cognitive evolution occurred between 600,000 and 200,000 years ago. This marks a second, and far more dramatic, spurt of encephalisation resulting in hominids with brain sizes with a size range equivalent to those of modern humans today (1200–1750 cc) (Ruff *et al.*, 1997). The brain expansion of this period cannot be attributed to changing body size and is most likely related to the evolution of a linguistic capacity. The basis for this argument is simply that anatomical remains after 250,000 years ago provide various indicators for a degree of vocalisation similar to that of modern humans (Schepartz, 1993), and that the addition of a linguistic capacity to the human mind is likely to have required a larger brain. It seems likely, however, that language would have co-evolved with enhanced abilities of theory of mind – these piggybacking on each other during cognitive evolution (Gómez, 1998; Mithen, 1999a).

Although modern brain sizes and some form of language had evolved by 250,000 years ago, human behaviour appears quite archaic in nature. Those features that seem to define a uniquely modern mind – symbolic thought, religious beliefs, rapid and continuous cultural change – remain absent from the archaeological record (Mithen, 1996b). This is most apparent from the relatively well-preserved and studied record of the Neanderthals in Europe (Stringer and Gamble, 1993; Mellars, 1996). Although some enigmatic artefacts are often claimed to represent symbolic thought (e.g. the Berekhat Ram 'figurine' – Marshack, 1997; incised bones from Bilzingsleben – Bednarik, 1995), these appear far too few in number and ambiguous in form to substantiate such claims (Chase and Dibble, 1987; Mithen, 1996a). As I have previously argued at length, the most feasible interpretation of the Neanderthal record is that those humans had a mind not substantially different to their *Homo heidelbergensis* and *Homo ergaster* ancestors – one constituted by multiple, specialised, but isolated intelligences (Mithen, 1996b). As such the linguistic capacity must have differed from that of modern humans either in form, such as by lacking syntax (as argued by Bickerton, 1996) or by itself being constrained to the social domain, as I have proposed. We must not underestimate the significance of even a limited proto-language. This may have itself begun the extension of the mind beyond the brain in the manner that Clark (1996) proposed, and had a significant impact on the nature of human thought due to the intimate relationship between thought and language (Carruthers and Boucher, 1998).

This domain-specific mentality of the Neanderthals was a highly effective form of adaptation to late Pleistocene environments, as this species survives in the fossil record for more than 200,000 years and was able to exploit a diversity of environmental types. This type of mind appears to have been shared by late *Homo heidelbergensis* in Africa, and also by the first *Homo sapiens* appearing in Africa by 130,000 years ago and which had soon spread to the Near East, as represented in the caves of Skhul and Qafzeh. The archaeological record of these early modern humans looks strikingly similar to that of the Neanderthals (Mithen, 1996b). It differs by having occasional glimpses of new behaviour, as seemingly represented by the use of red ochre in the Middle Stone Age of South Africa (Watts, 1999); this ochre was most likely used for body-painting, although direct evidence for this remains elusive. The first evidence for the manufacture of bone harpoons is found at Katanda *c.* 90,000 years ago (Yellen *et al.*, 1995), while ritualised burials first occur at Skhul and Qafzeh caves, Israel, at *c.* 100,000–80,000 years ago (see Mithen, 1996b for a review of this evidence).

These are, however, mere glimpses, and it is not until between 60,000 and 30,000 years ago that the archaeological record is transformed in a sufficiently dramatic fashion to indicate that a distinctively modern type of behaviour and mind had evolved (Stringer and Gamble, 1993; Mithen, 1996b). The markers for this are the occupation of new and arid environments, resulting in New World colonisation; the appearance of the Upper Palaeolithic with its suite of technological developments; the appearance of art; and the pervasive presence of ritual and religious belief. Perhaps most telling is the dispersal of modern humans throughout the world and the loss of all other human types, seemingly having been edged into extinction by competitive exclusion. To many archaeologists, such dramatic behavioural developments can only reflect the appearance of a new form of mentality. But this appears in most peculiar conditions on two accounts: first, it is not associated with a speciation event, as *Homo sapiens* had appeared at least 70,000 years before modern behaviour and thought; second, it is not associated with any change in brain size.

3   Saving the brain

Within much of evolutionary psychology, and indeed other disciplines, there is an assumption that mind and brain are equivalent and hence the time lag between the appearance of the modern-size brain and the modern 'sized' mind has posed a severe problem (e.g. see Bickerton, 1996). But the central role of the brain in understanding the mind has been saved by the claim that there occurs a change in the structure, rather than the size, of the brain at 60,000 years and it is this that lies at the root of the modern mind. In its most extreme version this is claimed to be a mutation that allows new types of neural networks to develop and hence new types of thinking (e.g. Klein, 1995). That new types of thinking emerge cannot, I think, be doubted, and I am confident that these relate to cross-domain thinking – the integration of knowledge and ways of thinking that had previously been isolated within separate intelligences. The claim that such thinking arises from some neural mutation is one that cannot be tested: even if we were ever able to understand the neural networks within modern minds, we simply do not have those of archaic *Homo sapiens* or Neanderthals to use as our comparison.

I do not mean to diminish the significance of such arguments; indeed, I have considerable sympathy with them. Carruthers (1998b) has, for instance, made the very interesting proposal that the cultural developments of 60,000–30,000 years ago arise from the appearance of a very simple additional cognitive–affective mechanism – a disposition to engage in pretend play in childhood. Moreover, there has been an implicit suggestion in my own work that the change from a domain-specific to a cognitively-fluid mentality ultimately derives from a neurological change (Mithen, 1996b). I remain, however, cautious about invoking such arguments, not simply because of their ultimate unfalsifiability, but because there are several issues and evidence that pose severe problems for them.

Perhaps the most significant issue concerns the timing of the mutation. If we wish to align ourselves to the notion of a pan-human psychology then we would have to place this mutation happening at 100,000 years ago at the very latest. For after that date modern humans had become dispersed and most probably existed in fragmented populations throughout the world. Any universal biological trait would by necessity have had to have appeared before this date. But as I have just summarised, the archaeological evidence seems conclusive that modern mentality evolved after 60,000 years at the very earliest. My own previous attempt to resolve this paradox has been to invoke parallel evolution (Mithen, 1996b), while one might also invoke substantial migrations and population dispersals occurring throughout the Late Pleistocene and Holocene.

Yet those who wish to maintain changes in the brain as the key explanation for the cultural explosion between 60,000 and 30,000 years ago also have to account for the high degrees of plasticity within the brain. Quite simply, the areas of the brain that get most use become larger and have cells more densely packed; conversely, those areas that have little use shrink and their cells die off more quickly (Pascual-Leone and Torres, 1993; Schlaug *et al.*, 1995). It is quite apparent from studies of those who have suffered brain damage that parts of the brain can begin to undertake functions that had once been conducted elsewhere. There seems no reason why a similar degree of plasticity should not also be attributed to Neanderthals. Moreover, neural networks are constructed during childhood and adolescence and to some degree are constantly re-modelled during one's lifetime (Changeux, 1985). The large Neanderthal brain implies a similar period of rapid postnatal brain expansion, and hence we should expect similar patterns of neural development and plasticity as in modern humans.

Irrespective of these arguments about brain plasticity, invoking a change in the brain as the key explanation for changes in thought and behaviour in the late Pleistocene runs counter to our understanding of relationships between brain size and intelligence in modern humans. There appears to be no relationship between these within our species today, although examining this relationship is not easy (Byrne, 1996a). As the brain sizes of Neanderthals and archaic *Homo sapiens* fall into the same range as modern humans, it seems tenuous to place too great an emphasis on the brain itself when explaining the dramatic cultural changes between 60,000–30,000 years ago. Tenuous, but certainly not impossible, as the computational resources of one part of the brain might have become co-opted for a different purpose, or there may have been a computationally inexpensive change, such as the appearance of an innate disposition towards pretend play (Carruthers, 1998b). But here I wish to explore the possibility that any changes in the brain are essentially developmental responses to new environmental stimuli created by new material culture.

4   Extending the mind beyond the brain

Rather than interpreting the appearance of a complex and symbolic material culture as a product of a biological change to the brain–mind, we can alternatively see these as largely the means by which the mind was extended beyond the biological limits imposed by the brain itself. There has recently been considerable interest in this notion of an extended mind, this having been argued most persuasively by Clark (1996, Clark and Chalmers, 1998) and Gell (1998, chapter 9). Archaeologists have also drawn heavily on this idea, although principally with regard to the extension of memory by using artefacts as a form of external storage (Donald, 1991; Renfrew and Scarre, 1998).

Clark and Chalmers lay particular stress on the role of public language as the mechanism by which the human mind became extended beyond the resources that any one individual brain can muster. Once people communicate with language it makes little sense to conceive of the mind as being constituted within the body of a single person, as each person draws upon, exploits, and adds to, the ideas and knowledge within other people's minds. As Clark (1996, p. 206) describes, this can allow the 'communal construction of extremely delicate and difficult intellectual trajectories and progressions' that any one individual mind could never accomplish. Moreover, Clark and Chalmers (1998, p. 18) speculate that 'the intellectual explosion in recent evolutionary time is due as much to this linguistically-enabled extension of cognition as to any independent development in our inner cognitive resources'. One assumes that they are referring, here, to the cultural explosion of 60,000–30,000 years ago.

While this argument is theoretically highly persuasive, it runs into trouble with the substantial evidence that Neanderthals and other archaic humans had a degree of vocalisation that is most appropriately described as language. The major evidence for this has been derived from the fossil record, which suggests that the vocal apparatus of archaic humans was essentially indistinguishable to that of modern humans (Schepartz, 1993). Even though the type of language possessed by archaic humans may have differed substantially from that of modern humans, this evidence nevertheless undermines the argument that it is language which is the most significant means by which mind becomes extended beyond the brain.

A much more powerful means by which this is accomplished is by material culture. Artefacts can play precisely the same role as that of language in Clark and Chalmers' scenario: they allow ideas to migrate between minds, hence enabling new ideas to be developed which could never have emerged from a single mind alone. But material culture has additional qualities. Perhaps the most significant is that it endures: spoken (or gestured) utterances are quite transient. Hence we can look at artefacts made by people long ago in prehistory and use them to develop new ideas of our own – as have many modern artists, ranging from Picasso to Henry Moore. But we do not have their utterances to use in this fashion.

Material culture has two further qualities with regard to its efficacy as a means to extend the mind. First, it can act as a form of non-biological memory. This is, of course, widely recognised and has long been used by archaeologists to interpret the art of the Upper Palaeolithic (e.g. Marshack, 1972, 1991). It was, however, the psychologist Merlin Donald (1991) who developed this idea in greatest detail by arguing that artefacts are a form of 'external symbolic storage', and providing the basic ideas behind the collection of studies published in Renfrew and Scarre (1998) on this theme. Considerable methodological developments with regard to the study of incised Upper Palaeolithic objects from this perspective have been achieved by D'Errico (e.g. 1991; D'Errico and Cacho, 1994). Although we do not know precisely what information was being stored in such objects, there can be little doubt that these are no different in kind from the vast range of external storage devices that we use today, ranging from post-its to encyclopaedias and CDs. All of these extend our mind beyond the limits of our brain.

An equally important means by which material culture extends the mind is by providing 'anchors' to ideas that are 'unnatural' for our biologically evolved brains to possess. To understand this we must first appreciate the paradox facing those who adopt an evolutionary perspective on the mind. On the one hand the arguments put forward by Darwinists such as Pinker (1997b) and the authors within Barkow *et al.* (1992) that our brain–minds are to a large degree conditioned by our hunter-gatherer past are most persuasive. As I have argued, for the vast majority of our evolutionary past the human brain–mind appears to have spent no time engaging in science, or art or religious thought, and was structured in a highly domain-specific fashion, being adapted to solving those immediate problems of a hunter-gatherer existence. Many of those problems are precisely the same as we face today, such as those of social interaction, and consequently our minds are particularly well attuned to entertaining, communicating and developing ideas relating to such problems. But, in light of this evolutionary heritage, ideas about domains of activity quite alien to our hunter-gatherer ancestors are far more difficult for the mind to possess and manipulate – they have no natural home within the mind. Nevertheless, we still succeed within these domains.

The most obvious example of this concerns religious ideas. Within the corpus of Upper Palaeolithic art there are images of 'supernatural beings', such as the painting from Chauvet Cave of an entity with a human torso and legs and a bison head, or the Hohlenstein-Stadel figure of a lion head and male body. Such entities are biologically impossible and in this sense no different in kind from modern conceptions of supernatural beings, such as one that has a virgin birth, can walk on water and rise from the dead. Ideas about such beings can have no natural place within an evolved mind as species are single entities, which must obey basic laws of physics and biology. According to the arguments of evolutionary psychology as expressed by Barkow *et al.* (1992) we should expect individuals to have an intuitive knowledge of biology and physics which accords with the real world; and there is indeed substantial evidence to that effect (as reviewed within Mithen, 1996b). So while a biologically evolved mind may be able to conceive of such entities, they certainly cannot be easily discussed, communicated and developed. Hence the role of material culture is not simply to represent ideas formed within the mind–brain; artefacts are not simply a mirror of our inner states. These material images play a constant role in reformulating the ideas, allowing them to be recreated within the mind–brain by off-loading them into the external world (Mithen, 1999b). The same argument can apply to many other domains of thought which humans excel at today but appear quite alien to our hunter-gatherer ancestors, such as pure mathematics and indeed much of science in general. These depend upon material culture in a fundamental fashion, as evolved brains alone are simply inadequate to the task of thinking about such topics.

Mathematics provides a particularly good example of the extension of the mind beyond the brain. Butterworth (1999) has made a most persuasive argument for the existence of a distinct number module within the brain, seeking to identify its specific neurological location. This number module allows people to identify the numerosities of collections of objects – to recognise immediately whether there are one, two, three or four objects without needing to count. But as soon as collections go beyond a mere four items, one needs to begin to count the objects, as the number module is inadequate at immediately recognising numerosities of that size. In other words, the number module of the brain has remarkably limited abilities. Nevertheless, as Butterworth (1999) argues, once it is linked up with the body, such as by using fingers, toes and other body parts for counting, and more particularly with material culture, this number module provides the basis for the whole of mathematics. Butterworth (1999) argues that non-human primates may possess a similar number module, and it seems perverse to deny the existence of this to human species such as the Neanderthals. But neither the Neanderthals nor any other non-human species linked their number module to items of material culture, and hence remained constrained to what the brain alone is able to do – which with regard to recognising numerosities is not very much at all.

5   The evolution of material culture

My argument is that material culture plays as important a role as that of language in extending the mind beyond the limits of the brain alone. Our human ancestors were using material culture for at least 2.5 million years, and most probably substantially longer in light of the use of artefacts by modern primates. But for the vast majority of that time, the material culture appears to be no more than a product of the mind–brain. Hence the stone artefacts found in Oldowan, Acheulian, or Mousterian industries appear to be instruments for engaging with the natural and social world, the outcome of thoughts and decisions, 'mirrors of inner states'. In this regard the cultural complexity of archaic *Homo sapiens* and the Neanderthals is most likely the limit that a mind–brain the size of ours can achieve by itself alone.

The cultural and cognitive transformation that occurred between 60,000 and 30,000 years ago arose because humans learnt a clever trick. They learnt how to exploit material culture to extend their minds beyond the limits of their brains alone. By creating artefacts that represented ideas that could only have a transient existence within the mind, it became possible to regenerate those ideas, communicate those ideas, and allow for cross-fertilisation of ideas between individuals in such a way that completely new constructs could be developed. Similarly, by using material culture to store knowledge, the bounds of biological memory could be transcended.

Once material culture is used in this fashion, the cultural contexts within which children develop and mature are transformed. And hence their brains will be networked in new fashions, and this will facilitate the possibility of further extensions of mind into the material world. In this regard cultural and biological changes are intimately linked, but there is no need to invoke any neural mutation to get this self-amplifying process started. All that is needed is a 'discovery' of how to use material culture in a new fashion, as an extension of the biological mind.

6 The internal and external evolution of the mind

For the vast majority of human evolution, the evolution of the mind was synonymous with the evolution of the brain. Consequently as brain size enlarged, especially in relation to body size, our human ancestors exhibited new types of behaviour. It was only after brain size of *c.* 900cc had been exceeded that artefacts such as handaxes, which required design and were technically demanding, were manufactured. And it was only after modern brain sizes had evolved that we see the appearance of a Middle Palaeolithic technology using the demanding levallois technique. All of these early types of humans were constrained in mental capacity by the capacity of the brain, and that appears to have imposed a highly domain-specific form of mentality. Moreover the size of the brain has physiological limits – its high metabolic costs prevented it from simply getting bigger and bigger in human evolution. Hence when relying on the brain alone there have to be limits on human thought, and these limits are most likely to be those exhibited most clearly by the Neanderthals. The earliest members of our species between 130,000 and 60,000 years ago were similarly mentally constrained by the brain, with a few possible exceptions. But after this date, and after the discovery of using material culture to extend the mind, humans escaped those mental constraints imposed by the brain. By extending the mind into material culture a new evolutionary trajectory was initiated. This is precisely what Clark (1996, p. 63) argued: 'We manage our physical and spatial surroundings in ways that fundamentally alter the information processing tasks our brains confront . . . what makes this co-operative approach worthwhile is the difference in nature between the kinds of computations that come naturally to the free standing brain and ones which can be performed by parasitising environmental resources'. Moreover, there are no physiological constraints: when extended into the material world, the mind appears to have infinite limits. And hence in little more than 50,000 years, by having 'given up' their near-total reliance on the brain alone, humans have mentally evolved from having thoughts about no more than stone tools and, acquiring food to having thoughts about subjects no less than the origins of the Universe and the nature of the human mind itself.

I am most grateful to Peter Carruthers for inviting me to participate in the Hang Seng series of meetings regarding the evolution of the mind, and to both Peter and Andrew Chamberlain for comments on this manuscript and a previous version.

10   The evolution of strategic thinking

Adam Morton

The theme of this chapter is that some seemingly arcane philosophers' disputes about the nature of rationality are relevant to questions about the evolution of *strategic thinking* in our species. By strategic thinking I mean, roughly, the kinds of cognitive processes that an agent uses in order to choose an action or a strategy in a situation involving other agents, taking account of the fact that the others are also choosing acts or strategies in the light of the same factors. There is a fairly familiar connection between strategic thinking and evolution in terms of considerations governing the choice of strategies that species can adopt in their interactions among themselves, for example with Maynard Smith's (1982) concept of an evolutionarily stable strategy. A crucial question will be the relation between the criteria governing choice of strategy for an evolving species and for individuals in the species. The plan of the chapter is first to present reasons for dissatisfaction with the central tool of present theories of strategic thinking, the concept of an equilibrium. There are equilibria which it would seem that intelligent creatures should avoid rather than gravitate towards. Then I argue that there is really no alternative to thinking in terms of equilibria, but that by using the concept carefully we can see how evolving intelligent creatures could cope with the situations that make it problematic.

1   Strategy and equilibrium

When intelligent agents interact, the consequences of each agent's decisions depend not only on the state of the world and chance but also on the decisions that other agents make. Strategic thinking is the thinking that leads to decisions which take account of the factors that affect other agents' decisions. This is the standard meaning of the term in economics, game theory and philosophy, where strategic choice is contrasted with parametric, that is, non-strategic, choice. Biologists sometimes use 'strategic' so that the emphasis is instead on strategic deception, which is certainly an aspect of strategic thinking, but not central to it as it is understood by these other disciplines. (From the perspective of game

G1

I	II	
	Friendly	Unfriendly
Adventurous	(10,10)	(-100,5)
Defensive	(6,2)	(0,0)

Fig. 10.1

theory, deception presumably falls under the general topic of situations where agents have incomplete information, which is a very live but also rather controversial and unsettled part of the subject. See Myerson, 1991, chapter 2, sections 7 to 9, and chapter 4.) The most important thing to come to terms with about strategic thinking is this: *strategic choice cannot rely on beliefs or probabilities about the other agents' choices.* The reason is clear. The agent herself is thinking through what to do and so are the other agents. She does not know in advance what *she* is going to do, and as she deliberates her expectations about what acts she might choose may change completely. Moreover her decision depends on what she expects the others to do, and their decisions depend on what they expect her to do. So as everyone concerned thinks out what they and the others may do the probabilities of their actions change, until finally they crystallise in a decision. There are no stable probabilities to guide a decision; they only emerge once a decision has been made.

This basic fact has an important consequence: it is not evident what we might mean by saying that one strategic choice is rational or optimal. In non-strategic choice we have a vague handle on rationality in terms like 'the rational choice is the one which is most likely to maximise satisfaction of an agent's preferences'. But both 'most likely to' and 'maximise' here are implicitly probabilistic: the natural way of making the idea precise is in terms of expected utility. The best act is then the one whose average outcome is greatest, taking into account all possible future states of affairs but giving more probable ones more weight than less probable ones. To do this we have to think about what kinds of probabilities we are talking about, but with strategic choice we have deep problems before we have a chance to ask these questions. G1 (see Figure 10.1) is an example that brings out several basic points. It is a two-person game for two players, I and II, diagrammed in the usual matrix.

What should agent I choose? One line of thought runs: in the absence of probabilities she should act with extreme caution, choosing the act whose worst consequences will be least bad for her. This is the minimax strategy. In this case this means choosing $\underline{D}$, since the worst possible consequences of $\underline{A}$ are very bad. Or she might assign probabilities via an indifference principle: 50/50 that II will choose $\underline{F}$ or $\underline{U}$. Then the act with the higher expected pay-off will be $\underline{D}$, so again she will choose that. But both of these strategies have a serious flaw, when one adopts the strategic attitude. Agent I can consider what the situation looks like from II's point of view. Then she can see that he is very unlikely to choose $\underline{U}$, for whatever I chooses II will be better off if he has chosen $\underline{F}$. $\underline{F}$ is II's dominant choice; he will only choose $\underline{U}$ by mistake. So if I thinks that II is informed, intelligent and paying attention (I am avoiding 'rational'!) she will choose $\underline{A}$.

The combination $(\underline{A}, \underline{F})$ is an *equilibrium outcome* of the game in that if either player chooses their part of it then the best response of the other is to choose their part too. Or, equivalently, it is stable in that if either player knew that the other was going to choose their part, they would choose their own part too. (Perhaps of interest: the equilibrium outcome in this case is also each agent's best response to the other agent's minimax choice.) There are economists and others who equate the equilibrium outcome with the rational choice. But this is not a position that is at all forced on us; it smacks more of prescriptive definition than of analysis. (It was not the attitude in the early days of the subject, except perhaps in the special case of zero-sum games, and it is increasingly doubted among contemporary writers. It seems to have had a temporary semi-orthodoxy though. See Luce and Raiffa, 1957, chapter 2; Myerson, 1991, chapters 3 and 5; Skyrms 1996, chapter 2.)

Equilibria are particularly attractive when we move away from the original domain of game theory – one-off unrepeated choices by individuals whose earlier and later interactions are irrelevant – to consider situations in which agents make the same choices in the same situations repeatedly. Suppose that two agents meet in a situation like the one above and the combination of their choices is not an equilibrium. Then one or another of them would have done better by making a different choice. So it may be that next time that agent will make that different choice. Or both may. And so on. As a result it is plausible (*not* inevitable) that they may eventually gravitate to a combination of choices in which each agent's act is the best response to that of the other. This situation will be stable in that no agent will have a motive for deviating from it as long as the other does not deviate. (Note the qualification.)

Or imagine a different model: both agents tend to choose by considering their previous action and thinking how they could have done better. When this doesn't tell them what to do, they choose at random. Suppose that one way or another they arrive at an equilibrium. Then they will stick there, since neither can improve on the situation as long as the other acts as they did the previous time. The stability of the equilibrium will be greatest if it is strict, that is, if any agent will do strictly worse by unilateral deviation. The equilibrium is non-strict if unilateral deviation may get some agent an equally good result though not a better one. The standard equilibrium concept is non-strict, but we can obtain more stability while not moving all the way to strictness. We can do this by requiring that any unilateral deviation set off a series of changes which takes all agents back to the equilibrium. One agent shifts to a just-as-good alternative, which changes the situation of the other, who can now do better by herself shifting, putting both agents in a situation where they can do better by shifting back to where they started.

This can be put more formally (and also more off-puttingly; all that really matters is the informal explanation I've just given.) A combination (a,b) of choices for two agents I and II – the extension to n agents is no problem – is a *stable equilibrium* if (i), (ii) and (iii) are true.

(i) There are no choices x, y such that (a,x) is strictly better for I than (a,b) or (y,b) is strictly better for II than (a,b).

(ii) If there is a choice c such that (a,c) is as good for II as (a,b) then there is a choice d such that (d,c) is better for I than (a,c), and (a,b) is better for I and II than (d,c).

(iii) If there is a choice d such that (d,b) is as good for I as (a,b) then there is a choice c such that (d,c) is better for II than (d,b), and (a,b) is better for I and II than (d,c).

((ii) and (iii) are just I/II mirror images.)

A special case of stable equilibrium is well known in biology as an *evolutionarily stable strategy* (ESS). (The classic source is Maynard Smith, 1982. See also Skyrms, 1996, chapter 3.) We get an ESS if we imagine the interactions to be between biological individuals who gain or lose reproductive fitness relative to one another. We then imagine that all the individuals form part of one rough species-with-variants. We can then ask which variant will do best in interaction with others from this pool. Since individuals are part of the same rough species, we can have some idea of 'same' and 'difference' as applied to their actions. We can also suppose that the pay-offs are symmetrical in that the gain in evolutionary fitness to I, when she chooses strategy a against II's b, is the same as the gain to II, when she chooses a against I's b. Then the three conditions above reduce to two. A strategy x is an ESS if (i) and (ii) below are true, where $(z,w) > (t,s)$ means that the pay-off of (z,w) to the agent choosing z is greater than the pay-off to that agent of (t,s), and similarly for $=$, $\geqslant$.

(i) For any y $(x,x) \geqslant (x,y)$.

(ii) For any y if $(x,x) = (x,y)$ then $(y,x) > (y,y)$.

An ESS is a special case of a stable equilibrium, where the biological context allows us to simplify by assuming a symmetry in the payoffs and assuming that we can identify actions of one agent as the same as actions of the other. But the importance is the same: any deviation from equilibrium leads to a chain of deviations, which leads back to the starting point. The consequences are clearest when deviations are mutations. Start with animals interacting via some action x performed by all of some species and then introduce a mutation which interacts via a different act y. If x is an ESS (that is, x against x is a stable equilibrium) then the mutation is unlikely to get established. Conversely if we begin with animals interacting via some action y which is not an ESS then a mutation to an action x which is an ESS is likely to get established, and in fact to displace y. In this connection it is worth noting that a set of choices is an equilibrium, or a strategy an ESS, only with respect to a given set of alternatives. Add another choice and an equilibrium may cease to be so. Thus a strategy x may be an ESS as long as some rival y is not available, but as soon as a mutation makes y available then x may cease to be an ESS. It may be that no strategy then is.

It appears then that at a very abstract unrealistic level we can say that species tend to evolve towards ESSs, and that a long-term departure from an ESS is likely to be to another one. This is like saying that combinations of rational actions tend to be stable equilibria. But this latter claim is not clearly true. In fact, on the face of it, it seems false. For it seems to say that, in trying to choose for the best, rational agents will tend toward situations that are stable equilibria. The problem about this claim is that there are many stable equilibria which are decidedly *not* in the best interests of the agents concerned. Human agents very often do not choose them. So how could they be required by rationality, or be the inevitable results of trying to choose for the best?

The standard example to make this sort of point is the familiar prisoner's dilemma, or PD. The payoffs have the right kind of symmetry for there to be an ESS, and indeed **D** is an ESS (and thus a stable equilibrium). But it is not optimal, in the following sense: if a pair of agents both choose **D** they will do less well than if they both choose **C**. It *is* optimal in a different sense: whatever one agent chooses, the other will be better off choosing **D**. The sense in which it is not optimal is relevant to actual human choice, in that in many prisoner's dilemmas people do choose the action corresponding to **C**. They do so trusting that the other person will too, either from moral principle or because they see that it would be best for both of them if they both so chose. We have agreed you'll send me a first edition of *The Origin of Species*, if I send you £2,000. **C** is keeping one side of the deal and **D** is doing nothing, hoping the other will be suckered into sending for nothing. Most people most of the time will do what they have agreed

PD

	II	
I	Co-operate	Defect
Co-operate	(5, 5)	(0, 9)
Defect	(9, 0)	(1, 1)

Fig. 10.2

to. Especially if, as in a PD, it is worse for both if neither keeps their word than if both do.

It is worth remembering now the doubts expressed earlier about identifying rational choice with choice that conforms to an equilibrium. Those doubts had much less hold when we considered not what choices people would make one-off, but what choices they would make repeatedly. An equilibrium is then a situation which once reached is unlikely to be departed from. And many PDs do indeed have this quality. If in the past you have not sent the money for the transactions we have agreed, then the next time round I am not going to send the goods. Knowing this you won't send the money, and we won't do business.

Switch back now from individual choice to evolution. Both senses of optimality are relevant. The first sense applies when we have two populations of animals interacting in a PD, one of which interacts via **D** and one via **C**. Then the population interacting via **C** will do better than the one interacting via **D**. So the C-interactors will do better, have more grandchildren, than the D-interactors. The second sense applies when we have a mixed population of C- and D-interactors. Then, as long as everyone interacts with everyone else, the D-interactors will do better. The C-interactors may wish that the D-interactors were not around, but as long as they are, in any numbers, the best policy is to join them.

In fact, the first of these situations is unlikely to be sustained. It takes just a few D-interactors to have gotten within the walls – by invasion or mutation – to ruin the C-interactors haven. The situation can only be sustained either by some mechanism that constrains C-interactors to interact only with other C-interactors, or some fact of the situation that makes D-against C-interaction less good than it appears for D-interactors. (An example of the latter would be shared genes, so that in clobbering a C-interactor a D-interactor would be lessening the survival of its own genes in the long term. But this, like other similar facts, covertly changes the payoffs so that we no longer have a PD.) As a result a population of C-interactors is likely to evolve towards a mixture of C- and D- interaction, in which the proportion of C-interactors is likely to decline, even though this decline will result in a lessening of the general fitness of the population. (The matter of proportions is delicate – see Skyrms, 1996, chapters 1 and 4.)

Some stable equilibria, ESSs, are thus as much traps as improvements. They are like the situation of would-be traders who have no reason to trust one another enough to do business. Once a population finds itself in such a situation, there is a strong pressure to remain in it, in spite of the fact that there are combinations of actions that are better for all concerned. But these better combinations are not stable.

2   Choosing a choice-mechanism

We are facing some challenges to naïve convictions. We naïvely think that evolution results in better-adapted animals. And we naïvely think that rationality allows agents to choose the options that are in their best interests. So we might think that when an ESS has the trap quality of a PD, then somehow or other evolution will find a way to a situation in which combinations of better actions will have the stability they lack. And we might think that rational agents will find ways of co-operating in PDs and similar situations without running the risk of defection by others.

These are indeed naïve ideas. They do not follow from evolutionary theory or from any standard account of strategic decision. But putting them together, we might well make a conjecture about the evolution of rational decision. Ways in which individuals choose their actions are subject to evolution, like everything else. So we might conjecture that ways of choosing that avoid PD-like traps will be favoured in evolution. Creatures that develop them will have an advantage over creatures that do not.

The purpose of this section is to show that this conjecture is false, at any rate on one way of understanding it. What a pity. The argument is fairly abstract, and it leaves us roughly where we were. So if the question does not interest you, skip to the next section, which is less abstract and less disappointing.

Suppose we have an organism which interacts with conspecifics and mutants in strategic choice situations, and in its evolution all possible ways of making choices are tried out. Which ones will be selected? Put less carefully: what is the optimal way of making strategic choices?

My way of answering this question is a traditional 'backwards' one: I assume that there is such an optimal way and then I deduce what properties it must have. So suppose that we have a population of individuals, each of whom has preferences over a range of outcomes which can result from the effects of combining their actions with those of others. (The preferences may be for outcomes with greater reproductive benefit, though the argument does not assume this.) And suppose that each individual has an 'oracle' which, given information about the situation, including the preferences of other agents, pronounces on the action to choose. In the evolution of the species we can imagine that a variety of oracles have developed, and we can imagine that each oracle-bearing agent interacts with others bearing variant oracles. For example there is the oracle EQU which always suggests choosing an action which is an equilibrium solution to the game. (Suppose that if there is more than one equilibrium EQU makes a random choice between those which are best for the greatest number of agents.) There is the oracle MINIMAX, which always suggests choosing that action whose worst consequence is least bad; there is the oracle CO-OP, which says 'in a prisoner's dilemma, choose the co-operative option'. (CO-OP could be extended to an oracle giving advice about all games in many different ways.) And we can wonder what will happen when, say, MINIMAX-respecting individuals interact with EQU-respecting individuals.

Suppose then a strategic choice situation s involving two individuals and consider a 'meta-choice' between two oracles O and O* prior to choosing between the acts that s offers. This sets up a new situation $s[O, O*]$ in which the choices are which of O and O* to apply to s, and the outcomes are the outcomes that would result from the combinations of the choices between acts in s that would be made from these meta-choices. (First you decide which oracle to listen to, and then you do what it says.)

Sometimes given a situation s, and a prior choice of oracles O and O*, one of O and O* will clearly be an ESS of $s[O, O*]$. For example if s is PD as above, and the oracles are EQU and CO-OP, then both agents will choose **D** if they have first chosen EQU and **C** if they have first chosen CO-OP. The matrix of the resulting outcomes is another prisoner's dilemma with (EQU, EQU) as a strict equilibrium, so EQU is an ESS. On the other hand, if s is G1 above and the oracles are EQU and MINIMAX, then agent I will choose **A** if she has chosen EQU and will choose **D** if she has chosen MINIMAX, while II will choose **F** either way. (Note that the resulting matrix is not the same as that of G1.) There are two equilibrium outcomes of $G1[O, O*]$, (EQU, EQU) and (EQU, MINIMAX). So EQU is not an ESS of this two-stage situation.

This may seem slightly paradoxical. In the situation in which going for the equilibrium is on reflection the right thing to do (assuming the other player is rational), G1, EQU is not an ESS, while in PD, in which for most people the rationality of the equilibrium is somewhat puzzling, EQU is an ESS. The puzzle diminishes when you consider that an ESS is the situation that we can expect agents to gravitate to in the long run, if they are continually trying alternatives and sticking to them if they pay off. It is no surprise that a choice-procedure that leads to defection in a PD is like this. It may be more surprising that EQU in G1 is not an ESS. But this is really a limiting case. Choosing equilibria is clearly optimal for I in that it is a dominant strategy – it is better whatever II chooses – while II is strongly indifferent between the two choice-methods – they have exactly the same consequences for her. So if we begin with a population of equilibrium choosers interacting via G1 and consider possible mutations to minimax, then the individuals playing the II-role would mutate quite freely while the individuals playing the I-role would stick to equilibrium choosing. If individuals switched from II-role to I-role they would quickly cease mutating. The II-role mutations don't really count, in that the consequences for the agent of choosing the two methods are exactly the same. From the point of view of G1, EQU and MINIMAX are the same strategy.

This discussion suggests a general result, which is in fact true:

If in a given 2 person game s, EQU and some other method M lead to different acts for each of the agents concerned, then EQU is an equilibrium of the game s[EQU, M].

Proof: Suppose that we have a game s such that EQU is not an equilibrium of s[EQU,M]. Then there is an act a of s such that if one agent chooses M and as a result chooses a in s, and the other agent chooses EQU, then the outcome o is better for the first agent than the outcome e if they had both chosen EQU. So o is better for the agent than e. But the result of their both choosing EQU is an equilibrium of s, by definition of EQU. So e is at least as good for the agent as o, by the definition of an equilibrium. Contradiction.

If we are thinking in terms of evolution, then ESS has more interest than bare equilibrium. So we might wonder if EQU will in general be an ESS when oracles are being chosen and used. Not surprisingly, it will not always be. There are games s with a single equilibrium that is not a stable equilibrium such that for some O EQU is an equilibrium but not an ESS of s[EQU, O]. (I won't give details. For all I know this may be true of all such s.)

None of these results are very profound, and indeed there is a disappointing quality to them. It looks as if an evolution of choice mechanisms will favour some (realistic approximation to) an equilibrium-choosing procedure. And this makes it appear as if the advantages of non-equilibrium choice, for example in prisoner's dilemmas, can never evolve. That appearance is in part due to the naïve abstraction of the discussion so far.

3   Not taking ESSs too seriously

The argument for the conclusion that we can expect a species to evolve towards an ESS is simple. So are the reasons for expecting strategic thinking to evolve towards the choice of equilibria. But their premises are quite strong, and it is not obvious when they are satisfied. To see this, consider some consequences that do *not* follow from the idea of an ESS.

It does not follow that the species will evolve to the equilibrium *soon*. In fact the considerations that suggest that the equilibrium is a likely eventual destination also suggest that in some cases it may take a long time to get there. For example, suppose that starting from many particular combinations of strategies there are many alternative strategies that each participant can change to, which present advantages over the beginning combination. Then one possibility is a long migration from one combination of strategies to another, arriving at the equilibrium, if at all, after many intermediate stops. It may be that from some of these half-way halts the equilibrium is in actual biological terms rather remote. (From the starting point fairly simple mutations would get to the equilibrium. But if instead we mutate to an alternative, the mutations that would then produce the equilibrium may be much less simple, or biologically plausible. If you can get easily from A to B and from A to C it does not follow that it is easy to get from B to C. For example London, Bristol and Cambridge.)

It also does not follow that there could not be much better equilibrium outcomes for the species than the ESS. Suppose, for example, an ESS in mating behaviour in which males defend territories and females try to estimate which territory is biggest and best defended. Members of the species might do much better if males could produce infallible proof of their fortitude and females of their fertility. (Or if they could scan one another's DNA, or if they could register with a discreet mating agency.) But this is just not biologically possible for them: there is no pattern of mutation or learning, available to those animals at that time, that is going to get them there. To conclude that the species will tend to the ESS, we must assume that the situation of which the ESS is the equilibrium is composed of strategies which are biologically possible developments for the species. In fact we have to assume that the situation includes all the biologically possible developments for members of that species at that time. If not, there may be other combinations of strategies to which the species could move from its initial situation rather than to the ESS, or to which it could move after arriving at the ESS.

(This point combines powerfully with the observation above that accessibility of B and C from A does not entail accessibility of C from B. Suppose a fairly tight construal of what is biologically possible, so that the ESS is in fact a likely outcome of evolutionary forces. Suppose also a large number of possible strategies that the animals could adopt. Then there will be a great danger that though all of these strategies are possible starting from some actual initial situation, and although one of these is an ESS, that ESS is not itself possible starting from some of the alternatives. This would lessen the explanatory force of the model considerably. To avoid such worries, biological applications of game theory usually work with an extremely tight understanding of what is a biologically possible alternative to an existing situation.)

These two provisos should make us hesitate before using the arguments of the previous section to show that creatures involved in strategic choice will in any realistic sense gravitate towards equilibrium-choosing decision procedures. For there are many many ways of making decisions, some differentiated from others in subtle ways, with finely balanced advantages and disadvantages. And from some presumed starting point of a strategic species, most abstractly conceived decision-making methods will not be available. So what we should really expect is that decision-making procedures will move towards very local equilibria, stable only given a narrow range of alternatives. And we should expect that as other features of the species and of its environment change these will cease to be optimal and will shift to other equally local good-enough solutions. We cannot be surprised if sometimes the evolution to such a local equilibrium blocks the way to a more global one: an adequate decision-making method undermines the pressure to discover an ideal one. (It is for this reason that evolutionary theory is compatible with the contingency in evolution defended by Stephen Jay Gould. See Gould, 1989 and Sterelny, 1995.)

Now in this light reconsider prisoner's dilemma-type situations, in which the equilibrium is not the best outcome for any of the participants. Consider two extreme perspectives.

On the one hand, consider situations involving two animals with hard-wired social choice mechanisms: ants, for example. Suppose that the pay-offs for combinations of co-operative and defecting behaviour are as in the prisoner's dilemma, but that the choice of one behaviour or another is completely determined by which group (nest, colony or band) the individuals come from. Then individuals cannot but act co-operatively to individuals of the same group, and cannot but act defectingly to all others. What we have then is not accurately described as a prisoner's dilemma at all. For the options actually available to individual animals never form the required structure: on each occasion either co-operation or defection is simply not an option. And the mechanism that selects either behaviour on the basis of a classification of the other is, we may suppose, effective and stable. It is an ESS among the alternatives within evolutionary reach of the species.

At the other extreme, consider situations involving ideally rational agents. Again suppose that there are options available to them which define outcomes with the shape of a prisoner's dilemma. The situation of the agents only is a prisoner's dilemma, though, if these are *all* the options, and if the agents really are ideally rational, this is very rarely the case. A crude way to express this is to say that if agents are rational they will have created some of the social apparatus of rational social life: contracts and means of enforcing them, motives for third parties to react appropriately to violations of conventions, and so on. (*We* are not ideally rational agents, so we can only gesture at the apparatus of fully rational life.) So when two of them approach a potential prisoner's dilemma they can either take steps to make sure that the actual pay-offs do not fall into that pattern or there are other options besides co-operation and defection. (For example, they can do the former by tying behaviour in the PD-like situation to choices in later situations: if you defect now my friends will defect on you later. And they can do the latter by signalling their intentions to co-operate and to behave vindictively if co-operation is not matched. Signalling often requires preparation: in practice the two kinds of measure are hard to distinguish.)

There is a more subtle argument for the remoteness of prisoner's dilemmas for ideal agents. If they are ideally rational they can do game theory. And they can deduce what *would* be a set of institutions that would guide agents like themselves through problems of acting for mutual benefit. For example, they can think through the various conventions that could regulate future behaviour of third parties to someone who has defected in a prisoner's dilemma and come to conclusions about which ones are best. As a result, even without any explicit communication or convention, each agent will know what reactions, and alternatives, and sequels would be the object of a convention, and each agent will know that each other agent will know this and that she knows it. (It will be mutual knowledge.) The conclusion is surprising: if there were conventions which ideal agents would adopt in order to disarm prisoner's dilemmas (and other similar situations) before they arose, then such agents would not have to explicitly adopt them; the mere knowledge that they would be adopted can do all the work. Ideally rational agents would be pre-insulated against all but the most unforeseeable prisoner's dilemmas. (Arguments like this are sometimes presented with an ideological slant: smart people don't need governments. For a clean and unrhetorical expression of the attitude see Sugden, 1986.)

The prisoner's dilemma is thus not a major issue either for animals with fixed social routines or for ideally rational agents. It will only arise as a persistent feature of life for creatures who choose their actions on the basis of expectations about one another's choice, but bring an imperfect rationality to such choices. And that certainly sounds like us! But notice how the context has changed. We began by fearing that the evolution of strategic choice would converge on patterns that condemn agents to the consequences of double defection. Now we see that evolution can tend towards choosing equilibria, while making some uncomfortable equilibria very rare. For sufficiently evolved agents would make sure that they were rare. PD-like situations are a feature of the middle stages of evolution.

4   Coalitions

Creatures of active but limited rationality, such as human beings and many of their precursors, will make strategic decisions by a complex improvised combination of innate social routines and attention to the likely consequences of possible actions. There is an aspect of strategic choice where explicit strategic thinking and primate social capacities combine in a revealing way: that of the formation of coalitions. A coalition arises when two or more agents can, by choosing suitable actions, obtain a benefit in a situation involving a greater number of agents. What I shall argue is that the formation of coalitions – something which can be based on innate primate sociality – is systematically related to the measures by which rational agents can ensure that they are not caught in PD-like situations.

The analysis of coalitions plays a large role in the application of game theory to economics (see Myerson, 1991, chapter 9). The standard theories assume an interestingly richer apparatus than is usual in the game theory of individual agents. The basic assumption of the theory of coalitions is that each agent will perform an action which is part of a pattern of actions by some coalition which maximises the total pay-off to the coalition. This assumption bears a delicate relation to the simpler assumption that each agent will perform an equilibrium action. (It does not follow from it, without additional assumptions. Its consistency with it is not obvious. Their relations are worth investigating for their own sake.) Using it, though, we can get very plausible and common-sensical predictions about the coalitions that will form in particular situations. In particular, we can predict that people will co-operate with one another in order to form a profitable coalition against others, even when so doing requires them to forgo the advantages of free-riding or defection. In effect, in a coalition individuals find their way to co-operation in PD-like situations.

This standard theory leaves the basic question unanswered. It just assumes that individual rational actors can form coalitions, without explaining how. But in some cases it is not too hard to see how coalitions can work. Consider a case which illustrates how a coalition can solve a PD. Two proto-humans, Cain and Abel, are considering whether to fight over a carcass or to share it. Either could be aggressive (**D**) or pacific (**C**). If one is aggressive and the other is pacific, then the aggressor gets the carcass to himself and the other is badly beaten. If both are aggressive then both are bruised, but not badly beaten. If both are pacific then they share the carcass. They would both rather share the carcass than get bruised. Then the structure is that of a PD and seems to have the same sad consequences. If either is pacific then he will be beaten by the other. So they will both fight, and both will be bruised, though each would have preferred a peaceful division of the carcass.

Now add one more element: an old ferocious patriarch, Adam, who will hear any quarrel and interfere, beating both participants and taking anything worth having. In Adam's presence the situation is no longer a PD. Aggression leads to a worse outcome than pacificity, whatever the other does.

Now suppose that Cain and Abel see a carcass that they might share or fight over. They can sneak towards it or stride in a noticeable way which will catch Adam's attention. If they sneak, then they are in the original PD. If they stride, then they are in the variant situation in which Adam enforces co-operation. The predictable outcome of sneaking is thus mutual bruising and that of striding is an equal share of the carcass. (I'm assuming that they can share it and move off without bringing Adam down on them, but that a fight will make it impossible to avoid him.) So they will stride and share.

There is something magical about this simple conclusion. The presence of Adam allowed them to achieve exactly the co-operative outcome that they could not achieve in his absence, even though he did not perform any action or get any benefit. The fact that if they had acted differently he *would* have intervened does the trick, ensuring that they do not and he does not.

Notice, though, the calculation required. Cain and Abel must consider their actions several moves ahead, and each must consider how the other will consider their future actions. Each has to know that the other will see the advantage of making Adam aware of their presence. Moreover, they have to be able to stick to a plan once they have made it. Once they get to the carcass they have to be able to refrain from fighting. And each has to know that the other has this degree of resolution. Though the plan is simple, it requires quite a lot of thought.

The three-person game with Cain, Abel, and Adam could be written out as a fairly complicated-looking matrix with a PD like that in section 1 embedded in it. The complex action of striding and sharing would be an equilibrium, in fact a stable equilibrium. (To get everything to work out exactly right some more details would have to be specified. I am assuming the main point is easier to see without them.)

Cain and Abel have in effect managed to use Adam's presence as a way of making an enforceable contract between them. It is interesting how little of Adam's real physical presence is needed. A mythical Adam would do almost as well.

5   Stratification

Agents can form coalitions in the presence of third parties in ways that enforce co-operative behaviour. In this final section I shall argue that we have here a central feature of strategic thinking in all primates, and one which marks human social organisation in characteristic ways.

You are a subordinate male and you want to displace the dominant male, who is distressingly more powerful than you. So you make an alliance with another subordinate by grooming, sharing food and other small co-operative acts. Then in the showdown with the boss you call for help and (all going well) get it. You can make it more likely that you will get help if you advertise to the dominant male your alliance with your confederate, as it makes it more likely that the confederate will be also be the object of his aggression.

Or, you are a female and can see a future when you are going to have trouble feeding and protecting yourself. You have just given birth, and you raise your infant in such a way that she is devoted to you and very likely to take care of you later. You can make it more likely that she will remain bonded to you if you make common cause with her in bettering and defending your and her status.

In the first of these cases the two males transform each other by forming an alliance, in the second the mother transforms her daughter in the ways that parents have always transformed children. The mechanisms at work here are all evolved primate features. They are all shortcuts for strategic thinking, necessary for creatures which live by social strategies in which everyone has to take account of everyone else's plans, but which have limited powers to think through the resulting complexity. Thinking in terms of coalitions and bonding-inducing transformations seems to be a basic element of the primate approach to this problem. Let me put the problem in perspective.

All primates live deeply social lives, in that each lives their life in the company of others and at any moment is aware of the activities of others. In any primate group at any time there is a lot of watching going on, and a lot of it is triadic or more: a is keeping a careful eye on what b is doing to or with c (or with c and d and e, etc.). These n-adic trackings are cognitively demanding and account for part of the size of primate brains. They obviously set the stage for strategic thinking when we introduce any capacity to anticipate the actions of others. For if a is forming an expectation of b's action based on her information about b, that information will include the fact that b is keeping track of others, who typically include a. So a's expectations about b's actions must take account of the fact that b is also forming expectations, probably about a. (See Smuts *et al.*, 1987; Dunbar, 1988; chapter 13 of Byrne, 1996b; chapters 3 to 5 of de Waal, 1996; chapters 2 and 3 of Dunbar, 1996.)

There is a clear ratchet factor here. When an increase in the power to anticipate others in such a context becomes the norm, it makes the job of anticipating harder, necessitating more anticipatory power, and so on. We can expect then that, as primate social life becomes more complex, individuals will usually be at the limits of their cognitive capacity. In particular, the number of individuals whose possible strategies they can anticipate will be limited by memory and processing limitations. (With n agents, each of whom has m possible actions, there are m^n cells to the matrix – the complexity you have to think through rises as the power of the number of agents involved.) So individuals will be torn between on the one hand the advantages of co-ordinated actions, which increase with the number of co-ordinating individuals, and on the other hand the danger of getting into unmanageable complexity, which also increases with the number of individuals.

There is an obvious solution to the problem, which marks all primate social life from baboons to humans: stratification. Keep the coalitions no larger than required for the activity in question. Engage with a minimal number of individuals for the required purpose, while having a greater number of individuals available in case of need. To make this a bit more precise, suppose that the social tasks individuals in a species face come in kinds, and that for each kind the benefit to the individual in co-operating with others is linear in the number of individuals involved – so the benefit from co-operation with n others in task i is given by $b = k_i n$ – while the cognitive cost is exponential to the number involved – so the cost of interacting with n others is given by $c = K m_i^n$. (Perhaps m_i is determined by the number of actions each individual can perform in task i, as suggested above.) Then the advantage of approaching a task socially will be b-c, which will increase up to a crucial value of n (which will depend on k_i, K and m_i) and then decrease rapidly. So we can expect a stratification of social groupings, each no larger than it needs to be for some purpose.

There are two predictions here, which should hold across primate species. First, that the number of individuals co-operating on any task will be the minimum required for the task, so that we will find groupings of a number of discrete sizes, depending on the kinds of tasks and challenges that the species faces. Second, that co-operation between individuals will be shaped by specific devices for coalition formation, which will tend to be specific to a small range of tasks. The second prediction reinforces the first, in that the coalition-forming devices will tend to form alliances between small numbers of individuals. Since such devices evolve slowly, they will typically lag behind the general capacity for strategic thinking. So there may be more co-operation among smaller numbers, though with less flexibility in its aims.

And this is what we find. As Dunbar writes, introducing the general topic of primate social life:

a local population consists of a large set of animals who have relationships of varying intensity with each other. Certain individuals will associate with and interact frequently with each other. Certain individuals will associate and interact frequently, others only rarely, and in yet other cases the relationships may be purely antagonistic. . . . Where the sets of relationships of several individuals coincide and are reciprocated, a formal group emerges as a stable cohesive unit. Such groupings can be created at many different levels within the same population at the same time. [In the gelada] the patterns of association between individual animals reveal a hierarchically organised series of clusters at five levels [coalition, unit, team, band, community, population].

An analogous series of hierarchically structured grouping patterns has been described for the hamadryas baboon. . . . In this case, definable groupings occur in the form of one-male units, clans, bands, and sleeping troops. These groupings are similar to those of the gelada only in respect to the functional significance of one-male units and bands. Otherwise, they differ significantly from those of the gelada in size, composition, structure, dynamics and function. (Dunbar, 1988, p. 12)

The specific pattern of groupings found in any species will be a response to the kinds of tasks and problems that individuals in that species face, and the kinds of cognitive resource that they can bring to them. Dunbar later lists four very general categories of reasons for group formation: protection against predators, defence of resources, foraging efficiency and improved care-giving opportunities (see Dunbar, 1988, p. 106). Different species will have different strategies and face different problems in each of these areas, and the optimal social groupings will thus vary from species to species. Remember, though, the main thrust of the argument of this chapter: there is an optimal way of solving strategic problems, namely by identifying equilibria; and there is a unique cognitive strategy for doing this, namely by ascribing preferences to individuals and working out their possible reasoning. If there is anything to this, we should find a mutual pressure between increasing cognitive capacity and the development of routines for thinking through social problems in terms that are more and more explicitly along the lines of this optimal strategy.

One might apply this theme in a definitely speculative way to the comparison of human and chimpanzee social life. With chimpanzees the pattern of social grouping seems to be that individuals form bands which are parts of larger tribes. Bands are defined in part in terms of matrilinear descent: most members of a band are some sort of mother's-side cousins. Beneath the level of the band there is a formation of constantly shifting groups and parties, which have a very short-term and task-specific nature. In human societies, on the other hand, we have stable families, smaller in size than the next grouping upwards (which tend to be larger than chimpanzee bands). Thus for long-term groupings, the smallest human unit is smaller and the next unit larger than with chimpanzees.

We can explain this if we assume that the larger and the smaller grouping serve different purposes and are made possible by the solution of different strategic problems. Assume that the larger grouping is a general-purpose one requiring co-ordinated action. The paradigm strategic problem at this level would thus be one in which what most matters is that everyone perform the same one of some subset of the available actions (travel in some direction; act aggressively, evasively, or appeasingly to some threat; follow this would-be leader or that one). Assume that the smaller grouping serves different purposes, being focused on a few specific co-operative activities (such as the provision of food and the raising of young). The paradigm strategic problem at this level will be prisoners' dilemma-like, and it will typically be solved by forming some sort of coalition. If we make these assumptions, we can conclude that the greater cognitive power of humans will lead to greater group sizes at the larger level and smaller at the lower level.

The larger groups will be larger because the problem they present is typically one of keeping track of the benefits or losses to a number of individuals of a number of actions. The best co-ordination – the equilibrium for this kind of situation – is a pattern of action in which everyone gains if everyone conforms to it, and everyone loses if substantial numbers deviate. The limits to the number of agents with whom one can co-ordinate are thus defined by the limits on the number of outcomes that one can distinguish. In effect, by short-term memory. The more that can be distinguished and kept in mind, the greater the number of agents that can act in concert.

The smaller groups will be smaller because the problem they present is typically one of anticipating the patterns of motivation of others. For example if one fears the possible betrayal of another in a forthcoming confrontation with a third, then the conflicting effects of loyalty, desire for future alliance and the benefits of betrayal, all have to be weighed against one another. If one can imagine and ascribe more in cases like this, solutions become harder rather than simpler. As a result, though it is true that there are many-agent situations which a more intelligent agent can handle while a less intelligent agent can only handle the analogous situations for fewer agents, it is also true that there are simple problems where intelligence complicates co-ordination. There are many situations in which two agents can achieve a mutually profitable co-ordination as long as neither realises a subtle motive that the other might attribute to them: only creatures that can entertain quite complex thoughts will find their attempts at co-ordination blocked by such considerations.

Another factor tends in the same direction. With increased cognitive power a smaller group can sometimes do what would otherwise require a larger group given less intelligence. The crucial example is the formation of coalitions. As we saw in the last section, the presence of an additional agent can be exploited in a variety of ways to bind a coalition. The extra presence is just a device, and the more one can see ahead, communicate or make promises, the less need one has of it. So we can expect that in some situations more cognitive capacity will mean that larger groups are not necessary.

The other cause of the smaller size of the smaller grouping is the different functions of the smaller grouping in the two species. In chimpanzees the coalitions are directed at short-term food gathering and mating aims. In humans the aims are longer-term, since they involve raising vulnerable human children through their longer development. These longer-term aims require more delicate balancing of one short-term aim against another, and thus more thought. A larger grouping of people might perform these tasks more effectively, but it would require a social cognition that is beyond us. So our more demanding core social needs keep our smallest grouping fairly small.

(I am omitting an absolutely crucial factor: the interaction of strategic thinking and theory of mind. Some patterns of strategic thinking are only possible if one can articulate the thinking the other agents may be employing. For example problems of pure co-ordination, such as those I associated with the larger groupings, are less demanding of psychological cognition than problems of coalition formation, which I associated with the smaller groupings. Co-ordination requires that one think about outcomes and preferences, while coalition requires that one think about patterns of reasoning, which requires much more psychological sophistication. So rather than talk of human strategic thinking as being both facilitated and complicated by an amorphous cognitive capacity, it would be more helpful to consider how the development of theory of mind facilitates the transition between the 'hard wired' and the 'ideally rational' poles of the previous section. I believe that strategic thinking and theory of mind are two sides of the same coin, as I argue in my forthcoming book *Folk Psychology as*

Ethics. However, in this volume Carruthers and Chamberlain, chapter 1 and Dunbar, chapter 11, argue for related conclusions.)

This is speculation: neither the phenomena explained nor the premises used to explain it inspire total confidence. More important is the general primate strategy of producing co-operation through coalitions, and of basing coalition-formation on bonding processes linked to very specific tasks. We humans clearly do live our lives between social groups of several different sizes, serving different purposes and relying to different degrees on general strategic thinking and specific coalition-inducing factors. There are good reasons for expecting that there will be such a stratification of group activity in any creature that approaches strategic problems in the general way that we and other primates do. And there are good reasons for believing that the optimal sizes of these groups will be sensitive to the cognitive capacities of the animals concerned. How much fixity is there to the sizes of human groups and the mixtures of cognition that we can successfully bring to them? Important as the question is, we really do not know.

Versions of this chapter were read to the Hang Seng workshop and conference, and received a wonderfully useful discussion. I am particularly grateful to Alex Barber, Peter Carruthers, Andrew Chamberlain and Robin Dunbar for comments.

11   On the origin of the human mind

Robin Dunbar

Humans seem to lie on a different cognitive plane to the other primates. My aim in this chapter is to try to provide an explanation as to why and when this might have come about. First, however, I want to identify what seem to me to be crucial cognitive differences between humans and other primates: these I characterise in terms of theory-of-mind ability, though I do not want to suggest that this is all there is to the human–ape difference. I shall then go on to offer an explanation as to why humans should need these additional cognitive abilities and conclude by offering a suggestion as to when they might have evolved.

1   What makes us human?

While we undoubtedly share a great deal in cognitive terms with our primate cousins, there must be some features that set us apart. At least, this is the implication of our intuition that we are in some sense 'smarter' and socially more complex than our nearest relatives, the great apes. Although we do not have a particularly clear handle on this problem as yet, there are nonetheless some features that we can point to as promising candidates. One of these is Theory of Mind (ToM: the ability to understand another's mental state, sometimes also known as 'mind-reading') (Perner and Wimmer, 1985). Although I shall focus exclusively on ToM here, I want to emphasise the fact that there may be other features of our cognitive machinery that may also be important.

During the last decade or so, theory of mind (the ability to mind-read) has been of considerable interest to developmental psychologists for two reasons. One is that children do not possess it at birth, but rather acquire it sometime between the ages of three and five years. Second, some individuals (whom we conventionally identify as autistic) never acquire ToM. Considerable research effort has therefore been invested in studies of both the processes whereby children acquire ToM (e.g. Whiten, 1991; Astington 1994) and the question as to why a lack of ToM forms so crucial a part of autism and its associated syndromes, such as Asperger's syndrome (e.g. Happé, 1994; Baron-Cohen, 1995).

Briefly, this research suggests that children develop ToM at about the age of four years, following a period in which they engage in what has come to be known as 'Belief–Desire Psychology'. During this early stage, children are able to express their own feelings quite cogently, and this appears to act as a kind of scaffolding for the development of true ToM (at which point they can ascribe the same kinds of beliefs and desires to others). The crucial point about ToM *sensu stricto* is that children are able to recognise that another individual has a belief that they know to be false: they can, in other words, differentiate between their own beliefs about the world and someone else's to the point where they can recognise and accept that another person may believe something to be the case which they know is not true. False-belief tasks have thus become a standard marker for ToM.

ToM is formally what has been defined as second-order intentionality. Intentionality in this sense is a recursive sequence of mind states involving beliefs: 'I *believe* that you *believe* that I *believe* something to be the case' is an example of third-order intentionality. This highlights the point made by Dennett (1983) that this recursiveness of the levels of intentionality is in principle infinite. I shall have more to say about this in a moment, but it is important to appreciate that almost all the work that has been done so far has been restricted to second-order intentionality, because this has been seen as a benchmark for an important (and indeed crucial) stage in early human social development. In effect, when children acquire ToM, they acquire the ability to see the world from someone else's point of view.

Second-order intentionality (or ToM) is important because it paves the way for at least two forms of behaviour that are of particular interest, namely lying and fictional (or pretend) play (Leslie, 1987). Without the ability to see the world from someone else's point of view, it is impossible to feed another individual with information that you know to be false in order to get them to behave in a way that suits your purposes. By extension, the ability to believe that the world can be other than it really is necessarily underpins the ability to engage in pretend play (and ultimately, of course, to write fiction). These points acquire particular relevance in the context of autism because autistic individuals both lack ToM and can neither lie nor engage in pretend play (Leslie, 1987; but for an alternative view, see among others Carruthers, 1996a). It is, however, important to be clear that an absence of ToM is not necessarily the only deficit present in autistic individuals, even though it may be diagnostic of the condition. (It may, however, be the principal deficit in Asperger's syndrome, where sufferers may often be of average or even above average IQ.)

There are two issues that arise out of this body of work. One is the question of how other non-human primates compare with humans on the intentionality dimension. Are we the only species that can aspire to ToM? The second issue arises from the fact that the developmental literature has focused exclusively on second-order intentionality (ToM *sensu stricto*) and no attention has been paid to higher orders of intentionality, even though we know from everyday experience that adult humans are capable of working at higher orders of intentionality. We have no idea, however, what the normal distribution of intentionality abilities is in the adult human population. Folk wisdom suggests that humans may be capable of coping with five or six orders of intentional propositions (Dennett, 1983), but we have no hard empirical evidence for making such a claim. We do not know, if it comes to that, what levels of intentionality adults typically make use of in their everyday lives: we may be capable of sixth-order intentionality, but do we ever use it in real life? Is there individual variation in the levels that adults can aspire to? Are there sex differences in this ability? We do not even know how children build up towards these adult limits once they have achieved second-order intentionality at the age of four years.

I will deal with the second question in the next section. First, let me summarise the results of what, so far as I know, is the only published study of 'advanced' ToM in normal human adults. Kinderman *et al.* (1998) used a story format to test for higher orders of intentionality in normal adults. Subjects were read four stories that gave short vignettes on everyday experiences (someone wanting to date another person, someone wanting to persuade her boss to award a pay rise). The stories contained between three and five levels of embedded intentionality (in the limit, 'Jane *believes* that Peter *supposes* that Sarah *thinks* that Simon *believes* that Sarah *would like* to go out with Peter'). After being read the stories, subjects were asked to complete a series of questions graded by the levels of intentionality present in the story. Mixed in with the mind-reading questions were factual questions designed to check that any failures on intentionality questions were not simply due to failure to remember the material facts of the story.

In addition, subjects were given a parallel story that did not involve mind-reading, but was simply an account of a series of events: this story was intended to test subjects' abilities to handle causal embeddedness for purely factual events. These involved a simple account of a sequence of events in which 'A gave rise to B, which resulted in C, which in turn caused D, ... etc.' The aim was to mirror the kinds of recursive embeddedness in mind-reading tasks in order to determine whether the problem lay with mind-reading *per se* or with recursiveness. In retrospect, the design of the factual story may have failed to mimic the full recursiveness of mind-reading. However, the literature on intentionality does not make a clear distinction between sequential mind-reading ('Jane *thinks* that Peter *thinks* that Sarah *thinks* that Philip *thinks* that. . . .') and recursive mind-reading ('Jane *thinks* that Peter *thinks* that Jane *thinks* that Peter *thinks* that. . .').

The results of the study were, nonetheless, striking. Subjects had little problem with the factual causal reasoning story: error rates were approximately 5% across six levels of causal sequencing. Error rates on the mind-reading tasks were similar (5–10%) up to and including fourth-order intentionality, but rose dramatically to nearly 60% on fifth-order tasks. Apparently, subjects found anything above fourth-order ('Simon *believes* that Peter *supposes* that Simon *thinks* that Peter *wants* . . .') extremely difficult to do. We know that this failure on the mind-reading tasks is not simply a consequence of forgetting what happened, because subjects performed well on the memory-for-facts tasks embedded into the mind-reading questions.

This finding has important implications in at least one area of human cultural endeavour, namely literature. The fact that people seem to experience considerable difficulty with fifth-order intentional statements but not fourth-order ones may explain why writing fiction is much harder than reading it, and may thus in part explain why good writers are considerably less common than good readers. In other words, a novelist writing about relationships between three people has to '*intend* that the reader *think* that character A *supposes* that character B *wants* character C to *believe* that . . .' – five orders of intentionality. The reader, in contrast, has a much easier task: he or she merely has to '*think* that A *supposes* that B *wants* C to *believe* that . . .' – four orders of intentionality.

Sophisticated literature (i.e. something other than pure narrative) thus places very considerable demands on both writer and reader, but the demands placed on the writer are of an order that starts to create a very significant load on most people's cognitive abilities. Both science and religion must also fall into this category since they require us to suppose that the world is other than we perceive it to be. This must require at least second-order intentionality, but it seems likely that higher orders than this may also be required.

Second-order intentionality is also essential for language as we use it. A great deal of the way we use language in everyday contexts depends on metaphor. Many of the words we use, and much of what we do in the way of inventing new meanings for words, depend crucially on metaphor. In addition, much everyday speech (as opposed to written language) is telegraphic in style: sentences remain half completed, words are omitted and the phrase 'You know what I mean . . .?' litters conversations. What this points to is the fact that the success of our conversational activities depends crucially on the listener's ability to read the speaker's mind and understand what it is he or she intends to say. The important lesson here is that language is not simply a matter of the speaker intending to communicate something and broadcasting this lighthouse-like to a world of passive receivers. Much work has to be done by the recipients of our broadcasts: they have to read behind the mere form of the words to work out what it is that we mean to communicate. Sometimes, indeed, we are deliberately opaque and obscure, using forms of words that are open to misinterpretation and thereby deliberately making the listener's task even harder. We are now forced into fourth (possibly fifth?) order intentionality: I have to *realise* that you *intend* me to *believe* that you *want* something that you do not in fact *want*. The need to work at fifth-level intentionality may explain why deception is sometimes difficult to detect: the deceiver works at fourth-order, but the deceived has to work at that crucial level where normal individuals start to fall apart.

Irrespective of the details, it is clear that ToM is crucial for many of those phenomena that are most characteristic of our humanity – conversation, literature, religion. The question we now have to address is: are we alone in aspiring to these levels of cognitive complexity?

Note that there has been some disagreement about exactly how many levels of intentionality are involved in conventional theory-of-mind tasks. I here follow convention in assuming the theory of mind (*sensu stricto*) is equivalent to second-order intentionality. Some (e.g. Origgi and Sperber, this volume) argue that there are up to two additional levels of intentionality tacked onto those described above. Thus a child doing a conventional false-belief task (the benchmark for ToM) actually aspires to fourth-order intentionality: the child *believes* that the experimenter *wants* it to *think* that Sally *supposes* her ball is in the basket. Since these levels are almost always present (even for monkeys in conventional cognitive experiments), this claim may do no more than re-scale the orders of intentionality: ToM *sensu stricto* now requires fourth-order intentionality, and humans have a limit at about eighth-order.

2   What makes apes different?

The most obvious place to look for human-like cognitive abilities is our nearest relatives, the great apes (chimpanzees, gorillas and orang-utans). If these species do not possess ToM and other related cognitive traits, then it may be considered unlikely that other species will do so. So far, then, all attempts to evaluate the intentional status of non-human animals has concentrated on apes, and specifically chimpanzees (our sister species).

There have been four broad attempts to determine whether or not chimpanzees have ToM. Povinelli *et al.* (1991) have explored questions about chimpanzees' understanding of others' intentions and knowledge and have shown that chimpanzees can understand the difference between knowledge and ignorance, and between intention and accident. Povinelli's experiments, however, have not focused specifically on false beliefs. O'Connell

(1995) has carried out tests using a mechanical analogue of the false-belief tasks that have been the bedrock of mind-reading in the developmental literature. More recently, Whiten (unpublished) and Call and Tomasello (1999) have undertaken further experiments using language-trained chimpanzees.

By way of example, I will simply summarise O'Connell's experiment. In the developmental literature, the standard marker for ToM is the ability to solve a false-belief task – to recognise that another individual can hold a believe about the world which is different to your own (i.e. a belief that, in principle, you believe to be false). O'Connell presented four chimpanzee subjects with an apparatus that consisted of four drawers. The experimenter marked one drawer with a peg and then retired behind the apparatus to load the identified drawer with a food reward. From her position at the rear of the apparatus, the experimenter could not see the peg and the chimpanzees had to learn that the marked drawer was the one they should open to get the food reward when offered the chance to do so. Opening the wrong drawer resulted in no reward and no opportunity to have a second go on that trial. The chimpanzees learned to solve this task to a reliability criterion of six out of ten trials correct. (This criterion was chosen to give a performance that was significantly different from chance at $P < 0.05$.)

Once the subjects were performing to criterion, the test trial was introduced. In the test trials, the peg moved (apparently of its own volition) to come to rest above another box after the experimenter had retired behind the apparatus. In principle, then, the chimpanzee had to distinguish between the box now indicated by the peg (as seen by the chimpanzee) and the box which the experimenter had indicated before retiring behind the apparatus. The apparatus was benchmarked on a set of normal children aged three to six years old and on a sample of autistic adults. Both these populations were given the mechanical analogue task and a conventional false-belief task (the so-called Smartie Task).[1]

The children clearly found the mechanical analogue task harder to master than the more conventional false-belief task (it does, after all, offer four alternative answers [= boxes] against the two choices of conventional false-belief tasks), but they showed the same pattern: performance rose from chance levels at three years of age to more or less 100% correct by age

[1] The Smartie Task involves showing a Smartie sweet tube to a child and asking it to say what might be inside. The child will invariably say 'Smarties' (sweets similar to M-and-Ms), at which point the top is taken off the tube and the child shown that the tube actually contains pencils. The child is then asked: 'Your best friend [*name*] is now going to come into the room and we will ask him/her what is in the tube. What do you think he/she will say is in the tube?' Pre-ToM children will usually say 'Pencils', but post-ToM children will give the reply 'Smarties'.

six years. Conversely, the autistic subjects mastered neither the conventional false-belief task nor the mechanical analogue task. The chimpanzees were by no means perfect on the mechanical version of the task; however, they did perform significantly better than the autistic adults (Mann Whitney test, $n_1 = 4$, $n_2 = 11$, $z = 1.96$, $P = 0.05$ two-tailed). More importantly, the chimpanzees did about as well as the four- to five-year-old children, suggesting that they may be hovering just on the brink of theory of mind. However, on an individual basis, only one of the four chimpanzees demonstrated unequivocal evidence of ToM by doing significantly better than chance on the test trials ($P < 0.001$). This chimpanzee also performed at higher levels than the other three on the training trials.

These results are fairly typical. However, the consensus on the published projects is probably that, while there is prima-facie evidence to suggest that chimpanzees possess ToM, the evidence is not wholly unequivocal. In no case do the chimpanzees achieve the levels of performance that characterise six-year-old children (i.e. those that have fully mastered ToM). Further, Call and Tomasello (1999) reported that chimpanzees failed on their non-verbal ToM task even though the children passed. One of the problems here has always been that we can never be sure whether the chimpanzees' poor performance reflects a genuine cognitive limitation in respect of ToM tasks or a failure on their part to grasp the point (or relevance?) of the experiment. However, the fact that they are performing at levels significantly above those of autistic subjects suggests that they are at least on the threshold of second-order intentionality even if not fully over the doorstep.

Given that apes can only just aspire to second-order intentionality (and even that somewhat controversially), there seems little point in asking whether monkeys might do so. Although monkeys have never been tested on these kinds of tasks, the consensus based on circumstantial evidence is that they would fail. Povinelli and Nelson (1990) for example, were unable to find any evidence that monkeys could distinguish between knowledge and ignorance in another (human) individual. Similarly, Cheney and Seyfarth (1990) provide circumstantial evidence that monkeys cannot interpret other individuals' knowledge states correctly. They once observed a male vervet monkey deterring a rival male from joining his group by repeatedly giving leopard alarm calls (i.e. calls signalling the presence of a leopard) every time the rival tried to cross the open ground between its own grove of trees and that where the male and his group were located. This looks like bona fide deception and might thus be a candidate case for false belief. The male, however, eventually gave the game away by giving leopard alarm calls while himself walking nonchalantly across the open ground.

Cheney and Seyfarth (1990) describe monkeys as being good ethologists but poor psychologists. In other words, they are good at reading and interpreting behaviour (and at using this information for trying to deceive others), but they cannot read the mind behind the behaviour and therefore make crucial mistakes (as the male vervet did). In effect, they are like three-year-old human children who know enough about human behaviour to be aware that, if they lie with conviction, adults are likely to believe them, but who are not competent enough at ToM to realise that the chocolate smeared around their faces actually gives the game away.

One possible light on this issue is provided by Joffe and Dunbar (1997). They plotted the volume of the primary visual area (V1) against the rest of the neocortex for all primates for which data on these are given by Steffan *et al.* (1981). Unfortunately, it was not possible to partition the neocortex any further than this, because Steffan does not provide data on the size of other parts of the neocortex other than V1. Nonetheless, this does separate out the major area associated with primary analysis of visual input from those areas that are more concerned with the interpretation of sensory inputs and the planning and execution of behavioural responses. The plot shows that the size of V1 increases more or less proportionally to the size of the rest of the neocortex up to about the brain (body) size of the apes. At this point, it begins to level out.

What this seems to imply is that the value of primary visual processing reaches an asymptotic value beyond which there are only limited gains from investing further in signal-processing capacity. Further increases in overall brain (or neocortex) size beyond this result in spare capacity that can be more usefully directed elsewhere – presumably to the interpretation and meaning of signals rather than to the recognition of signals. While it is difficult to be more specific without fine grained data, one obvious implication is that additional neural processing capacity becomes available for difficult tasks like ToM only at about great ape brain sizes. More importantly, the marginal gains in terms of spare capacity increase with increasing size beyond this. In other words, humans are likely to be able to engage in deeper mind-reading than other great apes precisely because their larger brain allows them to set aside more computing power for these purposes. In contrast, monkeys, with their smaller brain volumes, are constrained into devoting more computing power to visual processing because there are still important gains to be made from doing so.

3   Why did theory of mind evolve?

Given that differences in cognitive capacities such as ToM did evolve, the next question we have to ask is why they did so. Our concern here is with the functional questions that imposed the pressure to evolve the additional computing power required to sustain them.

This question is of some evolutionary significance precisely because the brain is a very expensive organ to support (and thus evolve). Aiello and Wheeler (1995) point out that the brain consumes about eight times more energy than would be expected on the basis of its mass alone. This is mainly a consequence of the need to manufacture more neurotransmitters every time a neuron fires, plus the more general costs created by the sodium pump and its role in maintaining a neuron's readiness to fire. Given these costs, increases in brain size are expensive and correspondingly powerful benefits are required to balance the evolutionary equation.

The growth in neocortex size within the primates as a whole appears to be driven by the need to increase social group size (Dunbar, 1992). (There is some evidence to suggest that this relationship may extend beyond the primates to other mammals, including insectivores, carnivores and the cetaceans: Dunbar and Bever, 1998; Marino, 1996; Tschudin, 1998.) Extension of this argument to humans suggests that group sizes of about 150 would be predicted for a primate with the size of neocortex that modern humans possess (Dunbar, 1993). This prediction appears to be surprisingly well confirmed by the available data (Dunbar 1993, 1998).

Note that in humans, as in chimpanzees, the groups identified in these analyses are dispersed groups and have no physical instantiation in any conventional sense: in other words, you cannot 'see' these groups either in the sense that they leave an archaeological record of the community's presence (e.g. dwellings) or in the sense that their physical presence in one place allows us to point to them (as we can with the groups of most primate species). Rather, this is a group in the sense that the membership exists in the minds of the individuals concerned: they *know* who belongs and who does not. Modern hunter-gatherers, for example, typically forage in groups of thirty to fifty individuals ('overnight camps'); these foraging groups constantly change membership over time. However, the pool from which membership of these groups is drawn is always the same for any given individual: you do not form foraging groups (or overnight camps) with individuals drawn at random from the regional population as a whole, but only with a local subset whose members stand in a special relationship to you (signalled by levels of intimacy, duties of obligation, etc.). These two layers of grouping are thus arranged in an hierarchically inclusive pattern, a pattern that is almost identical to that seen in chimpanzees (where the respective groupings are usually labelled 'feeding parties' and 'the community').

We should note, however, that while group size is the ultimate effect that an increase in brain size is designed to achieve, it may do this via a number of different cognitive and behavioural mechanisms. There is evidence to support at least two processes in this respect. One is the fact that neocortex size correlates with grooming clique (i.e. coalition) size in anthropoid primates (including modern humans) (Kudo and Dunbar, in preparation). Since grooming clique size is very tightly correlated with total group size, it seems likely that grooming cliques are the proximate mechanism that allow the animals to support large group sizes: grooming cliques act as coalitions that buffer the individual against the centrifugal forces (ecological competition and reproductive suppression) that act to disperse groups. Second, there is evidence to suggest that neocortex size correlates with the frequency with which subtle social strategies are used: Byrne (1996) has shown that the relative frequency of tactical deception correlates with neocortex size in primates, while Pawlowski *et al.* (1998) have shown that the extent to which low-ranking males can use social skills to undermine the power-based strategies of dominant males so as to gain access to fertile females is likewise correlated with neocortex size.

Whatever the proximate mechanisms involved may be, the selection pressures favouring increases in brain size within primates as a whole seems to be the need to increase group size. This pressure, in turn, presumably reflects the need to solve some kind of ecological problem (in most cases, predation risk: Van Schaik, 1982; Dunbar, 1988). In other words, species invade new habitats or find their existing habitat undergoing rapid change (usually as a consequence of climate change) and, as a result, are faced with, among other problems, increased predation risk. At this point, they have a choice: they can either (i) move to a different area where the habitat remains similar to their original one; (ii) increase group size to compensate for the demands of the new conditions; or (iii) go extinct. Increasing group size, however, comes at a price (brains are costly) and it is likely to impose some additional foraging demands.

While we can be fairly sure that the increase in human brain size was driven by the need to increase social group size, it is less clear why humans should have needed larger groups. Increases in group size come at a significant cost both in terms of foraging (see for example Dunbar, 1988) and in terms of opportunities for free-riders to prosper (Enquist and Leimar, 1993; Dunbar, 1999). Thus, aside from the costs of evolving larger brains, there are additional (and very significant) costs associated with increasing group size in the first place.

The problem with trying to explain why the hominid lineage should have increased group size so much is that it is difficult to see why they should have needed groups that are significantly larger than those currently observed among primates in general if the factor(s) selecting for large groups are the same as those currently experienced by other primates. If increases in group size among primates seem to be associated with increases in predation risk, how can the predation risk experienced by ancestral humans have been so much greater than that already experienced by many terrestrial open country primates such as baboons (who solve the problem with significantly smaller groups)? Moreover, the steady increase in brain size through time within the hominid lineage implies a corresponding increase in group size, and this in turn implies that the selection pressure was itself increasing proportionately. What we are looking for is some way in which later hominids (at least) differ ecologically from the rest of the primates. It is possible to offer at least three suggestions as to why hominids might have needed bigger groups.

First, it is possible that hominids' foraging strategies began to take them increasingly into even more predator-risky habitats than those occupied by baboons and chimpanzees today. This might seem reasonable on the grounds that both baboons and chimpanzees are really woodland or forest edge species, whereas hominids have traditionally been considered open savannah dwellers. With few large trees to act as refuges, hominids occupying savannah grasslands might have been more dependent on group size for protection. One can point to the gelada as a possible example: this species occupies treeless high altitude grasslands where they are very exposed to high risks of predation, and seem to have responded by living in unusually large groups (by baboon standards).

There must be some doubts about this suggestion simply because it does not seem likely that hominids ever occupied truly open grassland habitats: most fossil sites seem to have been associated with something closer to gallery forest, woodland or wooded steppe. However, the most telling argument against this hypothesis is the fact that modern hunter-gatherers do not actually *live* in groups of 150 even though groups of this size are a crucial part of their social tool kit. In other words, for modern hunter-gatherers, the groups of 150 are not *ecological* groups but purely *social* groups. Most hunter-gatherers forage in much smaller groups of 30–50 individuals even in open country habitats, and their clan groupings of 150 come together only very occasionally (e.g. once every year or so, as in the jamborees of the Australian Aboriginals). This pattern is mirrored by that seen in chimpanzees: chimpanzees live in communities that average some 55 individuals, but most of their time is spent in much smaller foraging parties (typically 2–10 individuals in size). Since modern hunter-gatherers do not require groups larger than 35–50 to protect themselves from predators, it is difficult to see why their predecessors need have required groups of 150.

A second possibility is that with hominids moving into more open habitats, those with larger groups gained by being able to defend access to particular ecological resources. This really focuses on the alternative (but currently less favoured) explanation for the evolution of large groups in primates: Wrangham's (1980) proposal that group-living evolved to allow primates to defend access to food sources. It is again difficult to see how hominids could have had access to even more defendable food sources than other primates, the more so as the whole trend of hominid evolution has been to occupy more open (albeit wooded) habitats that tend to have fewer defendable resources. Most open country primates (e.g. baboons) do not defend food sources, even though they have large groups. Nonetheless, one possibility might be access to permanent water holes or other keystone resources. Access to water sources is not usually a problem that primates experience, but hominids who have started to travel over larger ranges (especially once the more migratory phase of human evolution began with *Homo erectus*) might well have done so. Access to water might have become especially acute for a species that ranged over a wide area either because such a species is likely to be less familiar with all parts of its territory or because the habitat it occupies is likely to have fewer permanent water sources.

One way to solve the access-to-water problem for a species that ranges widely would be to form co-operative alliances with neighbouring groups of individuals so as to trade reciprocal access to water-holes in times of climatic stress. These alliances might even have been formally cemented in place with exchanges of women as 'brides'. This suggestion has some prima-facie support from the fact that, in at least some hunter-gatherers (e.g. the !Kung San of the Kalahari), this is exactly the function of the large clans of 150. Many pastoralist nomads also operate similar alliances that provide access to water-holes, especially during droughts.

The third possibility, mooted by Alexander (1974), is that hominids themselves became a new source of predation pressure as population densities rose. In other words, the ancestral human populations would have been forced into an escalating war by the beginnings of inter-tribal raiding (e.g. for women). Since group size is a crucial factor affecting the likelihood of winning a fight, there would have been strong selection pressure for increased group size. This explanation has been used very cogently to account for the rise of villages and larger scale social units (see Johnson and Earle, 1987). The problem in the present context is that we really need to be able to see the beginnings of this pressure being exerted well back into the history of *Homo erectus*, namely at the point where hominid brain size starts to take off. We know nothing of likely population densities of early *Homo* populations, and the fact of trans-continental migration probably cannot be taken as evidence of migration forced by population pressure *per se*.

On balance, my sense is that the need to evolve alliances to provide access to limited ecological resources (almost certainly permanent water) was most likely to have been the key pressure selecting for increased brain size in ancestral hominids. This would have started to become significant once a more nomadic or migratory lifestyle had been adopted.

An alternative interpretation (suggested by Andrew Chamberlain) might be that increasing competition between human groups led to both enlarged groups and greater cognitive skills (e.g. 'advanced' ToM) as mechanisms for out-competing rival groups. An important point here is that fighting a mind-reader is a very different proposition to fighting a predator (which will typically only have first-order intentionality). The selection pressure imposed by mind-reading opponents may itself have enough impact to spur the evolution of higher orders of intentionality. This suggestion sees group size and mind-reading as two separate consequences of rivalry, whereas the preceding explanation assumes, in effect, that mind-reading is a by-product of group size (in the sense that the extra brain power generated by large groups allows the development of mind-reading abilities, which in turn are selected for because they are advantageous in ensuring the temporal cohesion of large dispersed groups). The important distinction between these two hypotheses is that the first sees mind-reading as being related to the internal dynamics of groups, whereas the alternative sees it as being related to the external dynamics of groups.

These analyses all assume that the impetus to the evolution of large brain size in primates (and humans in particular) is the need to evolve large groups in order to solve a particular ecological problem. It might be argued that the causal arrow runs in reverse: that large brains evolved to enable mind-reading abilities to evolve, and thus in turn facilitated large groups. However, such an argument falls foul of two biological considerations. First, only hominoids aspire to advanced levels of mind-reading and there is no evidence for powers greater than first-order intentionality among the other simian and prosimian primates, despite considerable changes in brain size. While the requirements of mind-reading (e.g. for obtaining mates: Miller, 1998) seem like a plausible explanation for the evolution of super-large brains in humans, they do not allow us to explain why brain size changes have occurred elsewhere among the mammals. We thus need to argue that humans are a special case, something that we ought to do only as a very last resort once we have excluded all other possibilities. Second, this interpretation assumes that large groups are formed merely because they can be formed, not because they have some function. However, this is biologically implausible: groups incur very considerable costs for primates (and other animals), in terms of both foraging competition (Van Schaik, 1982) and reproductive suppression (Dunbar, 1980; Wasser and Barash, 1983). These costs act as evolutionarily inertial forces, slowing down the rate at which group size can increase. As a result, costly features seldom evolve in reality unless the benefits they convey are disproportionately great.

4   When did theory of mind evolve?

The final question to ask is when the human mind in its modern form appeared. There have been a number of attempts to consider this problem over the years, the most recent (and perhaps most successful) being those by Merlin Donald (1991) and Steven Mithen (1996b, this volume). (For additional consideration of this issue, see chapters in Corballis and Lea, 1999.) Donald argued for a two-stage evolutionary process from the ancestral primates, each associated with a more sophisticated way of storing and manipulating knowledge. The first stage involved mimetic skills that allowed individuals to transmit information or skills by imitation learning in ways that appear to be beyond the scope of living non-human primates (Tomasello *et al.*, 1993; Tomasello and Call, 1997). The second stage was associated with the evolution of language which enabled an even more sophisticated and rapid transmission of information. Donald associated the first stage with *Homo erectus*, the second with the appearance of *Homo sapiens*. In contrast, Mithen sees the evolution of the human mind in terms of the interlinking of a set of cognitive elements, each dealing with different aspects of the world in which we live (natural history, technical, social): the final integration of all these previously independent units (and, more importantly, the ability to move easily and rapidly from one to another – what he terms 'cognitive fluidity') is again associated with language and the emergence of modern humans.

I shall take a different tack here and ask a somewhat different question, namely how did hominid group size and brain size change over time and what can this tell us about the evolving human mind? Aiello and Dunbar (1993) used the regression equation that relates group size to neocortex size in non-human primates to estimate group size for different fossil hominids. Neocortex size was estimated from cranial capacity using a regression equation that relates these two variables, based on data for all primates (including modern humans). The results are shown in Figure 11.1.

What these data suggest is that hominid group sizes did not rise substantially above those typical of living apes (typically around 50–80) until the appearance of *Homo erectus* (a little after two million years ago). Although there is a steady increase in projected group size with time, the increase is slow and of limited scale. Group size does not begin to show a sudden acceleration until the appearance of the earliest *Homo sapiens* specimens (about 500,000 years ago).

There is no reason to require a different kind of mind to support the group sizes predicted for the australopithecines because these are within the current range for great apes (albeit at the upper limits of the range in chimpanzee community size). The transition to early *Homo erectus* is associated

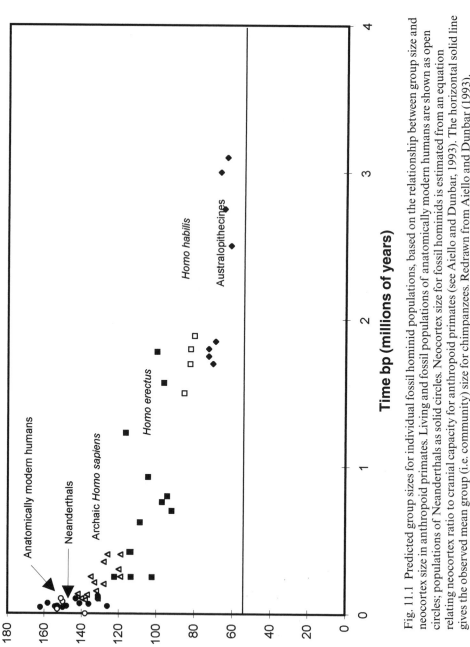

Fig. 11.1 Predicted group sizes for individual fossil hominid populations, based on the relationship between group size and neocortex size in anthropoid primates. Living and fossil populations of anatomically modern humans are shown as open circles; populations of Neanderthals as solid circles. Neocortex size for fossil hominids is estimated from an equation relating neocortex ratio to cranial capacity for anthropoid primates (see Aiello and Dunbar, 1993). The horizontal solid line gives the observed mean group (i.e. community) size for chimpanzees. Redrawn from Aiello and Dunbar (1993).

with what appears to be a step-like increase in typical group size from about 75 (in the australopithecines as a group) to about 100, taking them well out of the range of group sizes found in contemporary great apes. The transition to archaic (i.e. early) *Homo sapiens* is less step-like and more of an exponential upsurge, driving group size up from around 110 to 150 within a relatively short period of time (between *c*. 450,000 and 100,000 years ago). Prior to this, however, brain size had remained surprisingly constant across the whole span of the existence of *Homo erectus* (something in the order of 1.5 million years).

If there is a roughly linear relationship between spare neocortical capacity and levels of intentionality, we can make some rather rough and ready calculations based on the assumption that great apes can (just) aspire to second-order intentionality while modern humans can manage fourth-order (as a norm). Given this, then every increment of 50 in mean group size above that observed in living great apes corresponds to an additional level of intentionality. This is not necessarily a causal relationship; rather, it is simply a very rough scaling of ToM abilities in relation to neocortex size (here indexed by group size). If this is even roughly realistic, it implies that *Homo erectus* (the point at which the 100 group size mark was first breached) is marked by the development of the ability to engage in third-order intentionality, and anatomically modern *Homo sapiens* (dated to around 120,000 years bp) is marked by the appearance of fourth-order intentionality.

This is, of course, a very rough calculation and we should not put too much faith in it until there has been time to evaluate more closely the relationship between neocortex volume and cognitive skills. However, it does provide us with an approximate scale against which to interpret the likely changes in cognition and behaviour that we might expect across time between ourselves and the last common great ape ancestor.

12   The evolution of consciousness

Peter Carruthers

How might consciousness have evolved? Unfortunately for the prospects of providing a convincing answer to this question, there is no agreed account of what consciousness *is*. So any attempt at an answer will have to fragment along a number of different lines of enquiry. More fortunately, perhaps, there *is* general agreement that a number of distinct *notions* of consciousness need to be distinguished from one another; and there is also broad agreement as to which of these is particularly problematic – namely *phenomenal* consciousness, or the kind of conscious mental state which it is *like something* to have, which has a distinctive *subjective feel* or *phenomenology* (henceforward referred to as *p-consciousness*). I shall survey the prospects for an evolutionary explanation of p-consciousness, on a variety of competing accounts of its nature. My goal is to use evolutionary considerations to adjudicate between some of those accounts.

1   Drawing distinctions

One of the real advances made in recent years has been in distinguishing different notions of consciousness (see particularly: Rosenthal, 1986; Dretske, 1993; Block, 1995; Lycan, 1996). Not everyone agrees on quite *which* distinctions need to be drawn; but all are at least agreed that we should distinguish *creature* consciousness from *mental-state* consciousness. It is one thing to say *of an individual person or organism* that it is conscious (either in general or of something in particular); it is quite another thing to say *of one of the mental states* of a creature that it is conscious.

It is also agreed that within creature-consciousness itself we should distinguish between *intransitive* and *transitive* variants. To say of an organism that it is conscious *simpliciter* (intransitive) is to say just that it is awake, as opposed to asleep or comatose. Now while there are probably interesting questions concerning the evolution of the mechanisms which control wakefulness and regulate sleep, these seem to be questions for evolutionary biology alone, not raising any deep philosophical issues. To say of an

254

organism that it is conscious *of such-and-such* (transitive), on the other hand, is normally to say at least that it is *perceiving* such-and-such. So we say of the mouse that it is conscious of the cat outside its hole, in explaining why it does not come out: meaning that it *perceives* the cat's presence. To provide an evolutionary explanation of transitive creature-consciousness would thus be to attempt an account of the emergence of perception. No doubt there *are* many problems here, to some of which I shall return later.

Turning now to the notion of *mental-state consciousness*, the major distinction is between *phenomenal (p-) consciousness*, on the one hand – which is a property of states which it is *like something* to be in, which have a distinctive subjective 'feel' – and various functionally-definable notions, such as Block's (1995) *access consciousness*, on the other. Most theorists believe that there are mental states – such as occurrent thoughts or judgements – which are conscious (in whatever is the correct functionally-definable sense), but which are not p-conscious.[1] But there is considerable dispute as to whether mental states can be p-conscious without also being conscious in the functionally-definable sense, and even more dispute about whether p-consciousness can be *explained* in functional and/or representational terms.

It seems plain that there is nothing deeply problematic about functionally-definable notions of mental-state consciousness, from a naturalistic perspective. For mental functions and mental representations are the staple fare of naturalistic accounts of the mind. But this leaves plenty of room for dispute about the form that the correct functional account should take. And there is also plenty of scope for enquiry as to the likely course of the evolution of access-consciousness.[2]

But what almost everyone agrees on is that it is p-consciousness which is philosophically most problematic. It is by no means easy to understand how the properties distinctive of p-consciousness – phenomenal feel, or *what-it-is-likeness* – could be realised in the neural processes of the brain; nor is it easy to see how these properties could ever have evolved. Indeed, when people talk about the 'problem of consciousness' it is really the problem of p-consciousness which they have in mind. My strategy in this chapter will be to consider a variety of proposals concerning the nature of p-consciousness from an evolutionary standpoint, hoping to obtain some adjudication between them. Whether any of these proposals can provide a

[1] In my 1996b and 1998a I disagreed, arguing that occurrent propositional thoughts can only be conscious – in the human case at least – by being tokened in imaged natural language sentences, which will then possess phenomenal properties.

[2] In my 1996b, for example, I speculated that a form of higher-order access to our own thought-processes would have conferred decisive advantages in terms of flexibility and adaptability in thinking and reasoning.

successful *explanation* of the puzzling properties of p-consciousness must be a topic for another occasion (see my 2000).

2   Mysterianism and physicalism

There are those who think that the relationship between p-consciousness and the rest of the natural world is inherently mysterious (Nagel, 1974, 1986; Jackson, 1982, 1986; McGinn, 1991; Chalmers, 1996). Of these, some think that p-conscious states are non-physical in nature (Nagel, Jackson), although perhaps tightly connected with physical states by means of natural laws (Chalmers). Others think that while we have good general reasons for believing that p-conscious states *are* physical, their physical nature is inherently closed to us (McGinn). In respect of all of these approaches one might think: if p-consciousness is a mystery, then so will be its evolution. And that thought is broadly correct. If there is an evolutionary story to be told within these frameworks, it will be an account of the evolution of certain physical structures in the brain – structures with which (unknowably to us) p-consciousness is identical (McGinn); or structures which cause p-consciousness as an epiphenomenon (Jackson); or structures which are causally correlated with p-consciousness by basic causal laws (Chalmers). These will not, then, be accounts of the evolution of p-consciousness *as such*.

There is no good argument against mysterian approaches to p-consciousness to be found from this direction, however. To insist that p-consciousness must have an evolutionary explanation, and hence that mysterian theories are wrong, would plainly be question-begging, in this context. The real case against mysterianism is two-fold. First, it can be shown that the various arguments which have been presented *for* the inherent mysteriousness of p-consciousness are bad ones (Lewis, 1990; Loar, 1990; Tye, 1995; Lycan, 1996; Carruthers, 2000). Second, it can be shown that a successful explanatory account of p-consciousness can be provided (see below, and my 2000).

Since the focus of my interest, in this chapter, is on cases where evolutionary considerations may help to provide an adjudication between alternative explanations of p-consciousness, I propose to leave mysterian approaches to one side. In the same way, and for a similar reason, I leave aside theories which claim to explain p-consciousness by postulating a type-identity between p-conscious states and states of the brain (Crick and Koch, 1990; Hill, 1991). This is because such identities, even if true, are not really explanatory of the puzzling features of p-consciousness. The right place to look for an *explanation* of p-consciousness, in my view, is in the cognitive domain – the domain of thoughts and representations. Accordingly, it is on such theories that I shall concentrate my attention.

3   First-order representation (FOR) theory

A number of recent theorists have attempted to explain p-consciousness in first-order representational (FOR) terms (Kirk, 1994; Dretske, 1995; Tye, 1995). The goal of such accounts is to characterise all of the phenomenal – 'felt' – properties of experience in terms of the representational *contents* of experience. So the difference between an experience of green and an experience of red will be explained as a difference in the properties represented – reflective properties of surfaces, say – in each case. And the difference between a pain and a tickle is similarly explained in representational terms – it is said to reside in the different properties (different kinds of disturbance) represented as located in particular regions of the subject's own body. In each case, a p-conscious experience is said to be one which is *poised* to have an impact on the subject's beliefs and practical-reasoning processes in such a way as to guide behaviour.

It seems plain that there will be no special problem for such accounts in providing an evolutionary explanation of p-consciousness. I suggest that the task for FOR theory is just that of explaining, in evolutionary terms, how the transitions get made from (a) organisms with a repertoire of behavioural reflexes, triggered by simple features of the environment; to (b) organisms whose innate reflexes are action-schemas guided by incoming quasi-perceptual information; to (c) organisms which can also possess a suite of learned action-schemas, also guided by quasi-perceptual information; to (d) organisms in which perceptual information is made available to simple conceptual thought and reasoning.

As an example of (a) – an organism relying only on environmental triggers – consider the tick, which drops from its perch when it detects butyric acid vapour (which is released by the glands of all mammals) and then burrows when it detects warmth. These are fixed action-patterns released by certain triggering stimuli, but which do not seem in any sense to be *guided by* them. As an example of (b) – an organism with a set of innate action-schemas guided by quasi-perceptual information – consider the Sphex wasp, whose behaviour in leaving a paralysed cricket in a burrow with its eggs seems to be a fixed action-pattern, but an action-pattern the details of whose execution depends upon quasi-perceptual sensitivity to environmental contours. (The states in question are only *quasi*-perceptual because, by hypothesis, the wasp lacks a capacity for conceptual thought; rather, its 'percepts' feed directly into behaviour-control, and only into behaviour-control.) For examples of (c) – organisms with learned action-patterns – one can probably turn to fish, reptiles and amphibians, which are capable of learning new ways of behaving, but which may not yet be capable of anything really resembling practical reasoning. Finally, as an example of (d) – an organism with conceptual thought – consider the cat, or the mouse, each of which probably has simple conceptual representations of the environment generated by perception and is capable of simple forms of reasoning in the light of those representations.

It should be obvious that the evolutionary gains, at each stage, come from the increasingly flexible behaviours which are permitted. With the transition from triggered reflexes to perceptually-guided ones you get behaviours which can be fine-tuned to the contingent features of the organism's current environment. And with the transition from a repertoire of perceptually-guided action-patterns to conceptual thought and reasoning, you get the possibility of subserving some goals to others, and of tracking and recalling the changing features of the objects in the environment in a much more sophisticated way.

There is no good argument to be found against first-order representation (FOR) theories from this quarter. Quite the contrary is true, as the ability of FOR theory to provide a simple and elegant account of the evolution of p-consciousness is one of its strengths. According to FOR theory, the evolution of p-consciousness is really just the evolution of perceptual experience. There are powerful objections to FOR theory from other quarters, however; some relating to its failure to draw important distinctions, and others arising from its failure really to explain the puzzling features of p-consciousness (Carruthers, 2000). I shall not pursue these here. Instead, I shall focus my discussion on a variety of higher-order representationalist (HOR) accounts of p-consciousness, in connection with which evolutionary considerations really do start to have a significant impact in guiding choice.

4   Higher-order representation (HOR) theory

HOR accounts of p-consciousness may be divided into four general types. First, there are 'inner sense', or higher-order experience (HOE), theories, according to which p-consciousness emerges when our first-order perceptual states are scanned by a faculty of inner sense to produce HOEs (Armstrong, 1968, 1984; Lycan, 1996). Second, there are higher-order thought (HOT) accounts, according to which p-consciousness arises when a first-order perceptual state is, or can be, targeted by an appropriate HOT. These HOT theories then admit of two further sub-varieties: *actualist*, where it is the actual presence of a HOT about a perceptual state which renders the latter p-conscious (Rosenthal, 1986, 1993; Gennaro, 1996); and *dispositionalist*, where it is the *availability* of a perceptual state to HOT which makes it p-conscious (Carruthers, 1996b). Then finally, there are higher-order description (HOD) accounts (Dennett, 1978, 1991a), which are like HOT theories, except that linguistically-formulated descriptions of the subject's mental states take over the role of thoughts.

Each kind of higher-order representational (HOR) account can make some claim to *explaining* p-consciousness, without needing to appeal to intrinsic, non-representational, properties of experience (qualia). I have developed this claim in some detail with respect to dispositionalist higher-order thought (HOT) theory in my 1996b (section 7.6), and so do not intend to repeat it here; and I think that it is fairly obvious that this form of explanation generalises (with slight variations) to any kind of HOR account. It is perhaps important, however, to give at least some flavour of the approach, before turning to adjudicate between the four different varieties. So let me just outline why subjects whose experiences are available to HOTs might become worried by inverted and absent qualia thought-experiments (assuming, of course, that they have sufficient conceptual sophistication in other respects – such as a capacity for counter-factual thinking – and have the time and inclination for philosophy).

Any system instantiating a HOT model of consciousness will have the capacity to distinguish or classify perceptual states according to their contents, not by inference (that is, by self-interpretation) or relational description, but immediately. The system will be capable of recognising the fact that it has an experience *as of red*, say, in just the same direct, non-inferential, way that it can recognise red. A HOT system will, therefore, have available to it recognitional concepts of experience. In which case, absent and inverted subjective feelings will immediately be a conceptual possibility for someone applying these recognitional concepts. If I instantiate such a system (and I am clever enough), I shall straight away be able to think, '*This* type of experience might have had some quite other cause', for example. Or I shall be capable of wondering, 'How do I know that red objects – which seem red to me – don't seem green to you?' And so on.

5   The evolution of HOEs

How might a faculty of inner sense have evolved? A prior question has to be whether it would *need* to have evolved? Or might inner sense be a 'spandrel' (Gould and Lewontin, 1979) – that is, a mere by-product of other features of cognition which were themselves selected for? The answer to this question will turn largely on the issue of *directed complexity*. To the extent that a faculty of inner sense exhibits complex internal organisation subserving a unitary or systematically organised causal role, it will be plausible to postulate evolutionary selection.

5.1   The complexity of inner sense

HOE theories are 'inner sense' models of p-consciousness. They postulate a set of inner scanners, directed at our first-order mental states, which construct analog representations of the occurrence and properties of those states. According to HOE theorists, just as we have systems (the senses) charged with scanning and constructing representations of the world (and of states of our own bodies), so we have systems charged with scanning and constructing representations of some of our own states of mind. And just as our 'outer' senses (including pain and touch, which can of course be *physically* 'inner') can construct representations which are unconceptualised and analog, so too does 'inner sense' ('second-order sense') construct unconceptualised and analog representations of some of our own inner *mental* states.

The internal monitors postulated by HOE theories would surely need to have considerable computational complexity, in order to generate the requisite HOEs. In order to perceive an experience, the organism would need to have mechanisms to generate a set of internal representations with a content (albeit non-conceptual) representing the content of that experience, in all its richness and fine-grained detail. For HOE theories, just as much as HOT theories, are in the business of explaining how it is that one aspect of someone's experiences (e.g. of colour) can be conscious while another aspect (e.g. of movement) can be non-conscious. In each case a HOE would have to be constructed which represents just those aspects, in all of their richness and detail.

As a way of reinforcing the point, notice that any inner scanner would have to be a physical device (just as the visual system itself is) which depends upon the detection of those *physical* events in the brain which are the output of the various sensory systems (just as the visual system is a physical device which depends upon the detection of physical properties of surfaces via the reflection of light). It is hard to see how any inner scanner could detect the presence of an experience *qua* experience. Rather, it would have to detect the physical *realisations* of experiences in the human brain, and construct, on the basis of that physical-information input, the requisite representation of the experiences which those physical events realise. This makes it seem inevitable, surely, that the scanning device which supposedly generates higher-order experiences (HOEs) of visual experience would have to be almost as sophisticated and complex as the visual system itself.

Now one might think that HOE theory's commitment to this degree of complexity, all of which is devoted to the creation of p-conscious states, is itself a reason to reject it, provided that some other alternative is available. This may well be so – indeed, I would urge that it is. But for present purposes, the point is that mechanisms of inner sense would need to have *evolved*. The complexity of those mechanisms makes it almost inevitable that the devices in question would have evolved, in stages, under some steady selectional pressure or pressures.

5.2   *Perceptual integration as the evolutionary function of HOEs*

What, then, might have led to the evolution of a faculty for generating HOEs? The answer had better not turn on the role of HOEs in under-pinning and providing content for higher-order thoughts (HOTs), on pain of rendering a faculty of inner sense redundant. For, as we shall see shortly, HOT theory can provide a perfectly good explanation of p-consciousness and a perfectly good explanation of its evolution, without needing to intro-duce HOEs. So even if some or all creatures with inner sense are *de facto* capable of HOTs, a HOE theorist would be well advised to find some dis-tinctive role for HOEs which need not presuppose that a capacity for HOTs is already present.

One suggestion made in the literature is that HOEs might serve to refine first-order perception, in particular helping to bind together and integrate its contents (Lycan, 1996). The claim seems to be that HOEs might be nec-essary to solve the so-called 'binding problem' in a distributed, parallel-process, perceptual system. (The problem is that of explaining how representations of objects and representations of colour, say, get bound together into a representation of an object-possessing-a-colour.) But this suggestion is highly implausible. So far as I am aware, no cognitive scientist working on the binding problem believes that second-order representations play any part in the process. And in any case it is quite mysterious how such second-order processing would be presumed to work.

Suppose that I am viewing an upright red bar and a horizontal green bar, and that my visual system has constructed, separately, representations of red and green, and representations of upright and horizontal bars. Then the binding problem is the problem of how to attach the redness to the uprightness and the greenness to the horizontalness, rather than *vice versa*. How could this problem possibly be helped by adding into the equation a HOE of my experience of red, a HOE of my experience of green, a HOE of my experience of uprightness, and a HOE of my experience of horizontal-ness? Those HOE states look like they would be just as discrete, and just as much in need of appropriate 'binding', as the first-order experiences which are their targets.

5.3   *Mental simulation as the evolutionary function of HOEs*

Another suggestion made in the literature is that the evolution of a capacity for 'inner sense' and for HOEs might be what made it possible for apes to develop and deploy a capacity for 'mind-reading', attributing mental states to one another, and thus enabling them to predict and exploit the behaviour of their conspecifics (Humphrey, 1986). This idea finds its analogue in the developmental account of our mind-reading abilities provided by Goldman (1993) and some other 'simulationists'. The claim is that we have introspective access to some of our own mental states, which we can then use to generate simulations of the mental activity of other people, hence arriving at potentially useful predictions or explanations of their behaviour.

I believe that this sort of evolutionary story should be rejected, however, because I think that simulationist accounts of our mind-reading abilities are false (see my 1996c). Rather, 'theory-theory' accounts of our abilities are much to be preferred, according to which those abilities are underpinned by an implicit *theory* of the structure and functioning of the mind (Stich, 1983; Fodor, 1987; Wellman, 1990; Nichols *et al.*, 1996). Then since all theories involve concepts of the domain theorised, it would have to be the case that mind-reading abilities coincide with a capacity for higher-order thoughts (HOTs). However, it is worth setting this objection to one side. For even if we take simulationism seriously, there are overwhelming problems in attempting to use that account to explain the evolution of a faculty of inner sense.

One difficulty for any such proposal is that it must postulate that a capacity for 'off-line thinking' would be present in advance of (or at least together with) the appearance of inner sense. For simulation can only work if the subject has a capacity to take its own reasoning processes 'off-line', generating a set of 'pretend' inputs to those processes, and then attributing the outputs of the processes to the person whose mental life is being simulated. Yet some people think that the capacity for 'off-line' (and particularly imaginative) thinking was probably a very late arrival on the evolutionary stage, only appearing with the emergence of *Homo sapiens sapiens* (or even later) some 100,000 years ago (Bickerton, 1995; Carruthers, 1998b). And certainly the proposal does not sit well with the suggestion that a capacity for higher-order experiences (HOEs) might be widespread in the animal kingdom – on the contrary, one would expect that only those creatures with a capacity for 'mind-reading' and/or a capacity for 'off-line' imaginative thinking would have them.

Another difficulty is to see how the initial development of inner sense, and its use in simulation, could even get going, in the absence of some mental *concepts*, and so in the absence of a capacity for HOTs. There is a stark contrast here with outer sense, where it is easy to see how simple forms of sensory discrimination could begin to develop in the absence of conceptualisation and thought. An organism with a light-sensitive patch of skin, for example (the very first stages in the evolution of the eye), might become wired up, or might learn, to move towards, or away from, sources of light; and one can imagine circumstances in which this would have conferred some benefit on the organisms in question. But the initial stages in the development of inner sense would, on the present hypothesis, have required a capacity to simulate the mental life of another being. And simulation seems to require at least some degree of conceptualisation of its own inputs and outputs.

Suppose, in the simplest case, that I am to simulate someone else's experiences as they look at the world from their particular point of view. It is hard to see what could even get me started on such a process, except a *desire* to know what that person *sees*. And this of course requires me to possess a concept of *seeing*. Similarly at the end of a process of simulation, which concludes with a simulated intention to perform some action *A*. It is hard to see how I could get from here, to the prediction that the person being simulated will do *A*, unless I can conceptualise my result *as* an intention to do *A*, and unless I know that what people intend, they generally do. But then all of this presupposes that mental concepts (and so a capacity for HOTs) would have had to be in place *before* (or at least coincident with) the capacity for inner sense and for mental simulation.

A related point is that it is difficult to see what pressures might have led to the manifest complexity of a faculty of inner sense, in the absence of quite a sophisticated capacity for conceptualising mental states, and for making inferences concerning their causal relationships with one another and with behaviour, and so without quite a sophisticated capacity for HOTs. We have already stressed above that a faculty of inner sense would have to be causally and computationally complex: in which case one might think that a steady and significant evolutionary pressure would be necessary, over a considerable period of time, in order to build it. But all of the really *interesting* (that is, *fit*, or evolutionarily fruitful) things one can do with mental-state attributions – like intentional deceit – require mental *concepts*: in order to *deceive* someone intentionally, you have to think that you are inducing a false belief in them, which in turn requires that you possess the concept *belief*.

I conclude this section, then, by claiming that 'inner sense' accounts of p-consciousness are highly implausible, on evolutionary (and other) grounds. The take-home message is the following: we would never have evolved higher-order experiences (HOEs) unless we already had higher-order thoughts (HOTs); and if we already had HOTs then we did not need HOEs. The upshot is that if we are to defend any form of higher-order representation (HOR) theory, then it should be some sort of HOT theory (or perhaps a higher-order description, or 'HOD', theory), rather than a HOE theory.

6   Evolution and actualist HOT theory

The main objection to actualist forms of HOT theory is at the same time a difficulty for evolutionary explanation. The objection is that an implausibly vast number of HOTs would have to be generated from moment to moment, in order to explain the p-conscious status of our rich and varied conscious experiences. This objection has been developed and defended in some detail in my 1996b (section 6.2), so I shall not pause to recapitulate those points here. I shall for the most part confine myself to exploring the further implications of the objection for the evolution of p-consciousness.

One aspect of the 'cognitive overload' objection should be briefly mentioned here, however. This is that it is not very plausible to respond by claiming – in the manner of Dennett (1991a) – that the contents of experience are themselves highly fragmentary, only coalescing into a (partially) integrated account in response to quite specific internal probing. This claim and actualist HOT theory would seem to be made for one another (although Rosenthal, for example, does not appear to endorse it; 1986, 1993). It can then be claimed that the p-conscious status of an experiential content is dependent upon the actual presence of a HOT targeted on that very state, while at the same time denying that there need be *many* HOTs tokened at any one time. Yet some attempt can also be made at explaining how we come to be under the *illusion* of a rich and varied sensory consciousness: it is because, wherever we direct our attention – wherever we probe – a p-conscious content with a targeting HOT coalesces in response.

Yet this sort of account does not really explain the phenomenology of experience. It still faces the objection that the objects of attention can be immensely rich and varied, hence requiring there to be an equally rich and varied repertoire of HOTs tokened at the same time. Think of immersing yourself in the colours and textures of a Van Gogh painting, for example, or the scene as you look out at your garden – it would seem that one can be p-conscious of a *highly* complex set of properties, which one could not even begin to describe or conceptualise in any detail.

6.1   Actual HOTs and mental simulation

Now, what would have been the evolutionary pressure leading us to generate, routinely, a vast array of HOTs concerning the contents of our conscious experiences? Not simulation-based mentalising, surely. In order to attribute experiences to people via simulation of their perspective on the world, or in order to make a prediction concerning their likely actions through simulation of their reasoning processes, there is no reason why my own experiences and thoughts should actually give rise, routinely, to HOTs concerning themselves. It would be sufficient that they should be *available* to HOT, so that I *can* entertain thoughts about the relevant aspects of my experiences or thoughts when required. All that is necessary, in fact, is what is postulated by dispositionalist HOT theory, as we shall see shortly.

I think the point is an obvious one, but let me labour it all the same. Suppose that I am a hunter-gatherer stalking a deer, who notices a rival hunter in the distance. I want to work out whether he, too, can see the deer. To this end, I study the lie of the land surrounding him, and try to form an image of what can be seen from my rival's perspective. At this point I need to have higher-order access to my image and its contents, so that I can exit the simulation and draw inferences concerning what my rival will see. But surely nothing in the process requires that I should *already* have been entertaining HOTs about my percepts of the deer and of the rival hunter *before* initiating the process of simulation. So nothing in a simulationist account of mind-reading abilities can explain why p-consciousness should have emerged, if actualist HOT theory is true.

6.2   *Actual HOTs and the is–seems distinction*

Nor would a vast array of actual HOTs concerning one's current experiences be necessary to underpin the is–seems distinction. This distinction is, no doubt, an evolutionarily useful one – enabling people to think and learn about the reliability of their own experiences, as well as to manipulate the experiences of others, to produce deceit. But again, the most that this would require is that our own experiences should be *available* to HOTs, not that they should routinely give rise to such thoughts, day-in, day-out, and in fulsome measure.

Again the point is obvious, but again I labour it. Suppose that I am a desert-dweller who has been misled by mirages in the past. I now see what I take to be an oasis in the distance, but I recall that on previous occasions I have travelled towards apparently-perceived oases, only to find that there is nothing there. I am thus prompted to think, 'Perhaps that is not really an oasis in the distance; perhaps the oasis only *seems* to be there, but is not.' I can then make some sort of estimate of likelihood, relying on my previous knowledge of the area and of the weather conditions, and act accordingly. Nothing here requires that my initial (in fact delusory) percept should already have been giving rise to HOTs. All that is necessary is that the content 'oasis' should prompt me to recall the previous occasions on which I have seemed to see one but have been proved wrong – and it is only at this stage that HOTs first need to enter the picture.

I conclude this section, then, with the claim that we have good evolutionary (and other) grounds to reject actualist HOT theory, of the sort defended by Rosenthal. Greatly preferable, as we shall see, is a form of dispositionalist HOT theory.

7   Evolution and dispositionalist HOT theory

The account of the evolution of p-consciousness generated by dispositionalist HOT theory proceeds in two main stages. First, there was the evolution of systems which generate integrated first-order sensory representations, available to conceptualised thought and reasoning. The result is the sort of architecture depicted in Figure 12.1, in which perceptual information is presented via a special-purpose short-term memory store (E) to conceptualised belief-forming and practical reasoning systems, as well as via another route (N) to guide a system of phylogenetically more ancient action-schemas. Then second, there was the evolution of a theory-of-mind faculty (ToM), whose concepts could be brought to bear on that very same set of first-order representations (see Figure 12.2, in which 'E' for experience is transformed into 'C' for conscious). A sensible evolutionary story can be told in respect of each of these developments; and then p-consciousness emerges as a by-product, not directly selected for (which is not to say that it is useless; it may be maintained, in part, as an *exaptation* – see below).

The first stage in this account has already been discussed in section 3 above. Here just let me emphasise again in this context how very implausible it is that perceptual contents should only be (partially) integrated in response to probing. For many of the purposes of perception require that perceptual contents should *already* be integrated. Think, for example, of a basketball player selecting, in a split-second, a team member to receive a pass. The decision may depend upon many facts concerning the precise distribution of team members and opponents on the court, which may in turn involve recognition of the colours of their respective jerseys. It is simply not plausible that all of this information should only coalesce in response to top-down probing of the contents of experience. ('Am I seeing someone in red to my right? Am I seeing someone in yellow coming up just behind him?' And so on.) Indeed in general it seems that the requirements of on-line planning of complex actions demand an integrated perceptual field to underpin and give content to the indexical thoughts which such planning involves. ('If I throw it to him just *so* then I can move into *that* gap *there* to receive the return pass', and so on.)

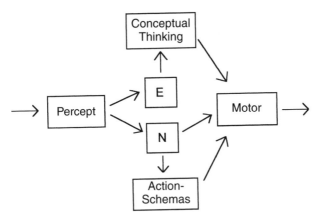

Fig. 12.1 First-order perception

At any rate, this is what I shall assume – that it is the task of the various sensory systems to generate an integrated representation of the environment (and of the states of our own bodies), which is then made available to a variety of concept-wielding reasoning, planning and belief-generating systems (some of which may be quasi-modular in structure – see my 1998b, and Mithen, 1996b).

7.1   The evolution of mind-reading and p-consciousness

Now for the second stage in the evolution of p-consciousness, in a dispositionalist HOT account. There seems little doubt that our mind-reading (or 'theory of mind') faculty has evolved and been selected for. First, there is good reason to think that it is a dissociable module of the mind, with a substantive genetic basis (Baron-Cohen, 1995; Hughes and Plomin, this volume). Second, precursors of this ability seem detectable in other great apes (Byrne and Whiten, 1988; Byrne, 1996b), having a use both in deceiving others and facilitating co-operation with them. And there seems every reason to think that enhanced degrees of this ability would have brought advantages in survival and reproduction. Consistently with this, however, we could claim that what really provided the pressure for development of the highest forms of mind-reading ability was the need to process and interpret early hominid attempts at speech (Carruthers, 1998b; Gómez, 1998), which would probably have consisted of multiply-ambiguous non-syntactically-structured word-strings (what Bickerton, 1995, calls 'proto-language').

Now the important point for our purposes is that the mind-reading

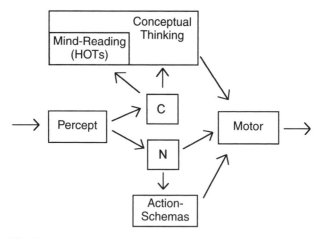

Fig. 12.2 Dispositionalist HOT theory

faculty would have needed to have access to a full range of perceptual representations. It would have needed to have access to auditory input in order to play a role in generating interpretations of heard speech, and it would have needed to have access to visual input in order to represent and interpret people's movements and gestures, as well as to generate representations of the form, 'A sees that P' or 'A sees *that* [demonstrated object/event]'. It seems reasonable to suppose, then, that our mind-reading faculty would have been set up as one of the down-stream systems drawing on the integrated first-order perceptual representations, which were already available to first-order concepts and indexical thought (see Figure 12.2).

Once this had occurred, then nothing *more* needed to happen for people to enjoy p-conscious experiences, on a dispositionalist HOT account. Presumably they would already have had first-order recognitional concepts for a variety of surface-features of the environment – *red, green, rough, loud*, and so on – and it would then have been but a trivial matter (once armed with mentalistic concepts, and the is–seems distinction) to generate higher-order recognitional concepts in response to the very same perceptual data – *seems red, looks green, feels rough, appears loud*, and so on. Without the need for any kind of 'inner scanner', or the creation of any new causal connections or mechanisms, people would have achieved higher-order awareness of their own experiential states. And then once armed with this new set of recognitional concepts, subjects would have been open to the familiar and worrisome philosophical thought-experiments – 'How do I know that red seems red to you? Maybe red seems green to you?' and so on.

Once people possessed higher-order recognitional concepts, and were capable of thoughts about their own experiences generally, then this would, no doubt, have had further advantages, helping to preserve and sustain the arrangement. Once you can reflect on your perceptual states, for example, you can learn by experience that certain circumstances give rise to perceptions which are illusory, and you can learn to withhold your first-order judgements in such cases. This may well be sufficient to qualify p-consciousness as an *exaptation* (like the black-heron's wings, which are now used more for shading the water while fishing than for flight; or like the penguin's wings, which are now adapted for swimming, although they originally evolved for flying). But it is important to be clear that p-consciousness was not originally selected for, on the present account. Rather, it is a by-product of a mind-reading faculty (which *was* selected for) having access to perceptual representations.

7.2   *HOT consumers and subjectivity*

It might well be wondered how the mere *availability* to HOTs could confer on our perceptual states the positive properties distinctive of p-consciousness – that is, of states having a subjective dimension, or a distinctive subjective 'feel'. The answer lies in the theory of content. I agree with Millikan (1984) that the representational content of a state depends, in part, upon the powers of the systems which *consume* that state. There is a powerful criticism here of 'informational' or 'causal co-variance' accounts of representational content, indeed (Botterill and Carruthers, 1999, chapter 7). It is no good for a state to carry information about some environmental property, if – so to speak – the systems which have to consume, or make use of, that state do not know that it does so. On the contrary, *what* a state represents will depend, in part, on the kinds of inferences which the rest of the cognitive system is prepared to make in the presence of that state, or on the kinds of behavioural control which it can exert.

This being so, once first-order perceptual representations are present to a consumer-system which can deploy a theory of mind, and which contains recognitional concepts of experience, then this is sufficient to render those representations *at the same time* as higher-order ones. This is what confers on our p-conscious experiences the dimension of subjectivity. Each experience is at the same time (while also representing some state of the world, or of our own bodies) a representation that we are undergoing just such an experience, by virtue of the powers of the mind-reading consumer-system. Each percept of green, for example, is at one and the same time a representation of *green* and a representation of *seems green* or *experience of green*. In fact, the attachment of a mind-reading faculty to our perceptual systems completely transforms the contents of the latter.

This is a good evolutionary story that dispositionalist HOT theory can tell, it seems to me. It does not require us to postulate anything beyond what most people think must have evolved anyway (integrated first-order perceptions, and a mind-reading faculty with access to those perceptions). Out of this, p-consciousness emerges without the need for any additional computational complexity or selectional pressure. So other things being equal (assuming that it can do all the work needed of a theory of p-consciousness – see my 2000 for a full discussion), dispositionalist HOT theory is the theory to believe.

8   Evolution and HODs

The only real competitor left in the field, amongst higher-order representation (HOR) theories, is the higher-order *descriptivism* espoused by Dennett (1978, 1991a).[3] On this account, p-conscious states are *those perceptual contents which are available for reporting in speech* (or writing, or for representing to oneself in 'inner speech'). Dennett can (and does, in his 1991a) tell a perfectly good evolutionary story about the evolution of the required cognitive structures, in a number of stages.

8.1   HODs and evolution

First, hominids evolved a wide variety of specialist processing-systems for dealing with particular domains, organised internally along connectionist lines. Thus they may well have evolved specialist theory-of-mind systems; co-operative exchange systems; processors for dealing in naive physics and tool-making; processors for gathering and organising information about the living world; systems for selecting mates and directing sexual strategies; and so on – just as some evolutionary psychologists and archaeologists now suppose (Barkow *et al.*, 1992; Mithen, 1996b; Pinker, 1997b). These systems would have operated independently of one another, and at this stage most of them would have lacked access to each other's outputs. Although Dennett himself does not give a time-scale, this first stage could well have coincided with the period of massive brain-growth, lasting two or more million years, between the first appearance of *Homo habilis* and the evolution of archaic forms of *Homo sapiens*.

Second, hominids then evolved a capacity to produce and process natural language, which was used in the first instance exclusively for purposes of inter-personal communication. This stage could well have coincided with the arrival of *Homo sapiens sapiens* in Southern Africa some

---

[3] Note that I shall abstract from the major differences between these works – particularly the claim in the latter that facts about consciousness are largely *indeterminate* – focusing just on the alleged connection with language.

100,000 years ago. The resulting capacity for sophisticated and indefinitely complex communication would have immediately conferred on our species a decisive advantage, enabling more subtle and adaptable forms of co-operation, and more efficient accumulation and transmission of new skills and discoveries. And indeed, just as might be predicted, we do see *Homo sapiens sapiens* rapidly colonising the globe, displacing competitor hominid species, with Australia being reached for the first time by boat some 60,000 years ago. The evidence is that our species was more efficient at hunting than its predecessors and soon began to carve harpoons out of bone, beginning fishing for the first time (Mithen, 1996b, pp. 178–83).

Finally, a new and clever trick caught on amongst our ancestors, giving rise to what is distinctive of the conscious human mind. As Dennett (1991a) tells the story, we began to discover that by asking ourselves questions, we could often elicit information which we did not know that we had. Each of the specialist processing systems would have had access to the language faculty, and by generating questions through that faculty and receiving answers from it, these systems would have been able to interact quite freely and access one another's resources for the first time. The result, thinks Dennett, is the *Joycean machine* – the constant stream of 'inner speech' which occupies so much of our waking lives, and which amounts to a new *virtual processor* (serial and digital) overlain on the parallel distributed processes of the human brain. This final stage might well have coincided with the explosion of culture around the globe some 40,000 years ago, including the use of beads and necklaces as ornaments; the burying of the dead with ceremonies; the working of bone and antler into complex weapons; and the production of carved statuettes and paintings (Mithen, 1996b).

8.2   *HODs versus HOTs*

This is a perfectly sensible evolutionary account, which can be made to fit the available archaeological and neuropsychological data quite nicely. But what reason does it give us for thinking that p-conscious states are those which are available to (higher-order) linguistic description (HOD), rather than to higher-order thought (HOT)? After all, Dennett himself is eulogistic about HOT theories of consciousness, except that he thinks it unnecessary to insert a *thought* between an experience and our dispositions to describe it linguistically (1991a, chapter 10); and he also allows that quite sophisticated mind-reading capacities would probably have been in place prior to the evolution of language, and independently of it in mature humans (personal communication). The vital consideration, I think, is that Dennett denies that there exists any thought *realistically construed* independently of language; and so, *a fortiori*, there are no genuine HOTs in the absence of language, either – it is only when those higher-order contents are formulated linguistically that we get discrete, structured, individually-causally-effective states; prior to that stage, it is merely that people can *usefully be interpreted as* entertaining HOTs, from the standpoint of the 'Intentional Stance' (on this, see Dennett, 1987).

In arguing against Dennett's HOD theory, then, I need to do two things. First, I need to argue that a mature capacity for HOTs *would* involve discrete, structured states, and to argue this independently of any considerations to do with natural language. And second, I need to show that such a capacity is in fact independent of linguistic capacities – in evolution, development and/or mature human cognition.

8.3   The case for structured HOTs

For the first stage of my case I borrow from Horgan and Tienson (1996), who show how the standard arguments for the view that thoughts must be carried by discrete structured states (generally thought to be sentences of an innate and universal symbolic system, or Mentalese) can be considerably strengthened. (The standard arguments are that only the Mentalese hypothesis can explain how thought can be *systematic* and *productive*; see Fodor, 1987.) Horgan and Tienson ask just *why* propositional attitudes should be systematic. Is it merely a brute fact about (some) cognisers, that if they are capable of entertaining some thoughts, then they will also be capable of entertaining structurally related thoughts? They argue not and develop what they call *the tracking argument* for Mentalese. Any organism which can gather and retain information about, and respond flexibly and intelligently to, a complex and constantly changing environment must, they claim, have representational states with compositional structure.

Consider early hominids, for example, engaged in hunting and gathering. They would have needed to keep track of the movements and properties of a great many individuals – both human and non-human – updating their representations accordingly. While on a hunt, they would have needed to be alert for signs of prey, recalling previous sightings and patterns of behaviour, and adjusting their search in accordance with the weather and the season, while also keeping tabs on the movements, and special strengths and weaknesses, of their co-hunters. Similarly, while gathering they would have needed to recall the properties of many different types of plants, berries and tubers, searching in different places according to the season, while being alert to the possibility of predation and tracking the movements of the children and other gatherers around them. Moreover, all such hominids would have needed to track, and continually update, the social and mental attributes of the others in their community (see below).

Humans (and other intelligent creatures) need to collect, retain, update and reason from a vast array of information, both social and non-social. There seems no way of making sense of this capacity except by supposing that it is subserved by a system of compositionally structured representational states. These states must, for example, be formed from distinct elements representing individuals and their properties, so that the latter may be varied and updated while staying predicated of one and the same thing.

This very same tracking-argument applies – indeed, applies *par excellence* – to our capacity for higher-order thoughts (HOTs), strongly suggesting that our mind-reading faculty is set up so as to represent, process and generate structured representations of the mental states of ourselves and other people. The central task of the mind-reading faculty is to work out and remember who perceives what, who thinks what, who wants what, who feels what, and how different people are likely to reason and respond in a wide variety of circumstances. And all of these representations have to be continually adapted and updated. It is very hard indeed to see how this task could be executed, except by operating with structured representations, elements of which stand for individuals and elements of which stand for their mental properties, so that the latter can be varied and altered while keeping track of one and the same individual. Then on the assumption that a mind-reading faculty would have been in place prior to the evolution of natural language, and/or that it can remain intact in modern humans in the absence of language, we get the conclusion that HOTs (realistically construed) are independent of language.

The demand for structured representations to do the work of the mind-reading faculty is even more powerful than the above suggests. For HOTs are characteristically relational (people have thoughts *about things*; they have desires *for things*; they have feelings *about other people*; and so on) and they admit of multiple embeddings. (I may attribute to John the thought that Mary does not like him, say; and this may be crucial in predicting or explaining his behaviour.) In addition, HOTs can be acquired and lost on a one-off basis, not learned gradually following multiple exposures, like a capacity to recognise a new kind of object.[4] When I see John blushing as Mary smiles at him, I may form the belief that he thinks she likes him. But then later when I see her beating him furiously with a stick, I shall think that he has probably changed his mind. How this could be done without a system of structured representations is completely mysterious, and the chance that it might be done by some sort of distributed connectionist network – in which there are no elements separately representing John, Mary and the *likes*-relation – looks vanishingly small.

---

[4] Pattern-recognition is what connectionist networks do best, of course; but they normally still require extensive training regimes. One-off learning is what connectionist networks do worst, if they can do it at all.

8.4   The independence of HOTs from language

How plausible is it that such structured higher-order representations are independent of natural language? Many theories of the evolution of language – especially those falling within a broadly Gricean tradition – presuppose that they are. On these accounts, language began with hominids using arbitrary 'one-off' signals to communicate with one another, requiring them to go in for elaborate higher-order reasoning concerning each other's beliefs and intentions (Origgi and Sperber, this volume). For example, in the course of a hunt I may move my arm in a circular motion so as to get you to move around to the other side of our prey, to drive it towards me. Then on Grice's (1957, 1969) analysis, I make that movement with the intention that you should come to *believe* that I *want* you to move around behind, as a result of you *recognising* that this is my *intention*. Plainly such communicative intentions are only possible for beings with a highly developed and sophisticated mind-reading faculty, capable of representing multiple higher-order embeddings.

A number of later theorists have developed rather less elaborate accounts of communication than Grice. For example, Searle (1983) argues that the basic kind of intention is that I should be recognised as imposing a particular truth-condition on my utterance. And Sperber and Wilson (1986/1995) explain communication in terms of intentions and expectations of *relevance*. But these accounts still presuppose that communicators are capable of higher-order thought (HOT). In the case of Searle, this is because the concepts of truth and falsity – presupposed as already possessed by the first language-users – would require an understanding of true and false *belief* (Papineau, this volume). And in the case of Sperber and Wilson, it is because calculations of relevance involve inferences concerning others' beliefs, goals and expectations.

On a contrasting view, it is possible that there was only a fairly limited mind-reading capacity in existence prior to the evolution of language, and that language and a capacity for structured HOTs co-evolved (see Gómez, 1998, for an account of this sort). Even if this were so, however, it would remain an open question whether language would be implicated in the internal operations of the mature mind-reading faculty. Even if they co-evolved, it may well be that structured HOTs are possible for contemporary individuals in the absence of language.

In so far as there is evidence bearing on this issue, it supports the view that structured HOTs can be entertained independently of natural language. One sort of evidence relates to those deaf people who grow up isolated from deaf communities, and who do not learn any form of syntactically-structured Sign until quite late (Sacks, 1989; Goldin-Meadow and Mylander, 1990; Schaller, 1991). These people nevertheless devise systems of 'home-sign' of their own and often engage in elaborate pantomimes to communicate their meaning. These seem like classic cases of Gricean communication; and they seem to presuppose that a capacity for sophisticated HOTs is fully intact in the absence of natural language.

Another sort of evidence relates to the capacities of aphasics, who have lost their ability to use or comprehend language. Such people are generally quite adept socially, suggesting that their mind-reading abilities remain intact. And this has now been confirmed experimentally in a series of tests conducted with an a-grammatical aphasic man. Varley (1998) reports conducting a series of mind-reading tests (which examine for grasp of the notions of belief and false belief) with an a-grammatic aphasic. This person had severe difficulties in both producing and comprehending anything resembling a sentence (particularly one involving verbs). So it seems very unlikely that he would have been capable of entertaining a natural language sentence of the form, 'A believes that P'. Yet he passed almost all of the tests undertaken (which were outlined to him by a combination of pantomime and single-word explanation).

It seems, then, that a capacity for HOTs can be retained in the absence of language. But we also have the tracking-argument for the conclusion that a capacity for HOTs requires discrete, structured, representations. This gives us the conclusion that higher-order thought, realistically construed, is independent of language, even in the case of human beings. And so there is reason to prefer a dispositionalist HOT theory over Dennett's dispositionalist HOD theory.

9   Conclusion

Evolutionary considerations cannot help us, if our goal is to argue against mysterian views of p-consciousness, or against first-order representational (FOR) theories. But they do provide us with good reason to prefer a dispositionalist higher-order thought (HOT) account of p-consciousness, over either actualist HOT theory, on the one hand, or higher-order experience (HOE) theory, on the other; and they also have a role to play in demonstrating the superiority of dispositionalist HOT theory over higher-order description (HOD) theory.

I am grateful to George Botterill, Andrew Chamberlain, Susan Granger and two anonymous referees for Cambridge University Press for comments on earlier drafts of this chapter. This chapter extracts, re-presents and weaves together material from my 2000, chapters 1, 5, 8 and 10, with thanks to the publishers, Cambridge University Press.

13 Evolution, consciousness and the internality of the mind

Jim Hopkins

The problem of consciousness seems to arise from experience itself. As we shall consider in more detail below, we are strongly disposed to contrast conscious experience with the physical states or events by which we take it to be realised. This contrast gives rise to dualism and other problems of mind and body. In this chapter I argue that these problems can usefully be considered in the perspective of evolution.

1 Evolution, mind and the representation of mind

Among other things, an evolutionary perspective brings to the fore a contrast between human and (other) animal minds. Many animals seem to have minds, at least in the minimal sense of a system of internal states which represent the environment, and so enable them to attain goals intelligently, that is, in light of a wide variety of information relevant to this task. A striking thing about human beings, however, is that we also represent our own minds, via the various ways of thinking about internal states encompassed in our concept of mind.

This difference seems linked to one in adaptive function. While the advantages of possessing a mind apparently derive from representing the self in relation to the environment – which of course includes other creatures and their behaviour – those of possessing a concept of mind would seem to flow from representing these representations themselves, and so further anticipating and controlling the behaviour they govern. We apparently do this, for example, when we deliberate about our own motives, or seek to anticipate or influence those of others. How far animals besides ourselves enjoy these further advantages remains unclear.

2 An apparent difficulty for the evolution of a concept of mind

We take the behaviour-governing representations described by our concept of mind to be realised in the nervous system. This means both that they are normally out of sight, and that their causal and functional roles could not be rendered transparent to perception in any case (as shown by the fact that even with all our science we are scarcely beginning to fathom them). So, as we can say, the human species – or the human nervous system – has had to evolve the capacity to represent behaviour-governing states and events in nervous systems *blindly*, that is, without drawing on perceptual information about neurons as disposed in space and having features perceptibly related to the operations of computation and control which they perform.

This seems part of the reason why in employing our concept of mind we do not represent the neural causes of behaviour as such, but rather as it were from the outside, that is, by relation to observable behaviour and the environment. In thinking of persons as having minds we construe their behaviour as action stemming from desires, beliefs and other motives, which are directed to the environment and which serve to render both speech and non-verbal action rational (logical) and so intelligible. The capacity for thinking this way evidently develops together with that for using language from early childhood; and we can plausibly regard both as parts of a natural system for understanding and influencing human behaviour precipitated in the course of evolution.

3   Having a mind: representing environmental goals and information
     relevant to their attainment

Let us now consider the causal role played by the representation of a goal in intelligent behaviour. Roughly, the representation should function so to govern behaviour as to bring about (cause) the attainment of the goal, and in addition the creature should register (cf. Bennett, 1976) that this has happened; and this should cause the cessation of this process. Thus consider a beaver whose goal is to stop a potentially erosive flow of water through his dam, and who succeeds in this task. Designating this animal agent by 'A' and the causal relations involved in perception and the regulation of behaviour by '-[causes]->', we have overall:

A acts with goal that *A stops that flow* -[causes]-> *A stops that flow*.

And when the creature registers the attainment of this goal, we should have:

A registers that *A has stopped that flow* -[causes]-> A ceases to act with goal that *A stops that flow*.

These formulations display a familiar ambiguity, as between external and internal, in the way we speak of goals. We describe representations via what they represent; so the highlighted sentence '*A stops [+ tense] that flow*' serves to specify both the alteration in the environment which is the animal's goal, and the behaviour-directing representation of this which we take to be realised in its nervous system. The same holds for the use of the sentence to describe the internal registration of the event or situation in which the goal is attained. So on this account the process by which a creature ceases to seek a goal once it is attained is one in which the representation of the attainment alters that of the goal so that it ceases to direct behaviour.

Let us call the event which renders the goal-specifying sentence (in this case 'A stops that flow') true the *satisfaction* of the goal, and the termination of further goal-directed activity by the representation of this the *pacification* of the goal. Then the characteristic case of successful action will be that in which the satisfaction of a goal causes its pacification. Using 'G' for 'goal' and 'P' as a schematic letter for representation-specifying sentences, we can write this as follows:

D: A has G that P -[causes]-> P -[causes]-> A registers that P -[causes]-> A's G that P is pacified.

This schematises the life-cycle of a single goal in successful action; and the same schema also applies to human desire, as becomes clear if we substitute 'desires' for 'has goal' and 'believes' for 'registers', as we shall do in considering the human case. These processes also include the veridical registration of information about the environment. For as part of the schema we have:

P -[causes]-> A registers that P

If we take it that the creature perceives and so experiences its own success, then this expands to:

B: P -[causes]-> A perceives (e.g. sees) or experiences that P -[causes]-> A registers that P

This schema describes an animal analogue of perception-based veridical belief; and we take animal goal-seeking to be informed by perception and memory of the environment in an analogous way. Thus if a beaver has the goal of stopping a certain flow of water, and perceives or otherwise registers that if it moves a certain branch then it will stop that flow, then it may form the subsidiary goal of moving that branch. In this case the animal's goals are related to its information about the environment in a familiar and logical way, which we can set out as follows:

Initial Goal: A has G that P (that it stops that flow).

Information: A registers that if Q then P (if it moves that branch then it stops that flow).

Derived Goal: A has G that Q (that it moves that branch).

Here the form of the goal- and information-specifying sentences mirrors that of a truth-preserving deductive argument; and this marks the way such an amplification of goals is satisfaction-preserving as well. As substitution again makes clear, this is analogous to human practical reason, and we can schematise it as follows:

PR: A has G that P and A registers that if Q then P -[causes]-> A has G that Q.

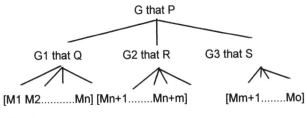

Fig. 13.1

Animal action is commonly driven by numerous goals related by complex information. Thus even in a very simple case a creature may have the goal that P (that it stop that flow) and register that it can do this if Q and R and S in that order (if it fells a certain sapling, gnaws off a branch, and moves the branch to the point of flow). We can indicate such structured goals by a derivational tree, as in Figure 13.1.

Such a tree runs from its aerial root down through a series of goals to the lowest level of behaviour (here marked as the series of bodily movements M1 through Mo) which we take to be ordered in this way. The ordering of goals manifest in such a tree thus corresponds to an ordered series of instances of **G**, nested in accord with complex instances of **PR**. Each tree relates the goal-representation at its root to a sequence of hypothesised effects, which, insofar as the animal is successful, should also be ultimately describable as a bringing about of the associated goal-situation, and thence of the registration of the attainment of the goal, and thence of its pacification. When we interpret an animal's movements in this way, we tacitly relate them to a series of such trees, and in this we impose a hypothetical structure which is highly constrained and predictive, and so comparable to a powerful empirical theory. This is particularly so when, as in the human case, the assignments of sentences to non-verbal trees and actions can also be related to those manifested in speech.

4   **Representing minds: a possible advantage of representing inner causes as opposed to regularities in behaviour**

This provides a minimal sketch of the kind of ordering and modification of goals in which we take animal intelligence to be manifested. A creature with a conception of this kind of intelligence, in turn, will be capable of representing such trees of representations, and hence of manifesting intelligence in relation to them. We can get some further sense of the value of representing inner causes as such by considering Andrew Whiten's (1993, 1996)

Fig. 13.2

adaptation of an argument by which Neal Miller (1959) sought to convince behaviourists to take account of causes concealed in the brain.

Suppose we are studying the behaviour of some creature, whose body we represent by an opaque sphere, with question marks signifying that we cannot readily determine what is going on inside, as in Figure 13.2. We can represent our information about input–output correlations relating the creature's behaviour to the environment by arrows. In the case of a laboratory rat, for example, we might have something resembling Figure 13.3. Now clearly we might want to explain these correlations by introducing the hypothesis that they are mediated causally, by a state within the creature. We can illustrate this by replacing the inner opacity with the hypothesised state, so that we have the structure depicted in Figure 13.4.

This simple theory is both plausible, and, as Whiten stresses, also a more economic representation of the correlational data on which it is based. Roughly, adding one element to the representation (the intermediate inner cause) in effect enables us to drop three others (three correlation-marking arrows). This illustrates the idea that representations which postulate inner causes may enable us to *compress* (in the computational sense; compare Dennett, 1991b) correlational data relating to the environment, so that there is cognitive and hence possible reproductive advantage in representing them in this way.

Also it seems reasonable to hypothesise (or speculate) that some such mode of representation would be produced in the course of evolution. The internal states which are involved in the possession of environmental goals and information are also keyed to a variety of other externals – for example characteristics of gaze, posture, facial expression and bodily configuration generally – which therefore carry significant information about probable behaviour. Since anticipating such behaviour would be advantageous, we might expect networks of neurons to evolve to make use of this information; and these, as the argument suggests, would improve their performance by triangulating among the relevant externals, so as to track the internal

Input   **Output**

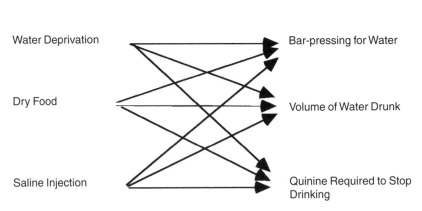

Fig. 13.3

states themselves. This would be a form of tracking causes via the external situations which it is their adaptive role to produce (as in the case of goals or desires, cf. Millikan, 1984) or reflect (as in the case of registration of information, or belief, or thought). A further possible improvement would be the development of more explicit representations of these causes; and this could partly be effected by explicitly linking them to the external situations by which they are tracked and which give them their significance. In *Homo sapiens*, it seems, this development can be observed in concert with a particular use of natural language.

5 Sentential descriptions of goals and information as a semantic mode of presentation of inner causes and their role

Above we described animal representations via representations of our own, that is, sentences from natural language which specify the situations in which goals are satisfied, and thereby the internal representations of these situations. This is also the way we represent our own motives. Our vocabulary for describing the mind includes a stock of words for motives, such as 'desires', 'believes', 'hopes', 'fears', etc., each of which admits complementation by a further sentence. So we speak of the desire, belief, hope, fear, etc., *that P*, where 'P' can be replaced by any sentence suitable for specifying the object, event or situation towards which the motive is directed.

In this we as it were re-cycle our sentential descriptions of the world as descriptions of the mind. We can think of this – artificially but usefully

Input   Internal Cause   Output

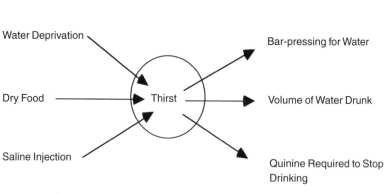

Fig. 13.4

– as effected in two stages. First, and as a matter of basic linguistic understanding, we learn to map our sentences to the perceptible objects and situations which constitute their conditions of truth. Thus each of us comes to master an unbounded correlation of sentences to worldly situations, which encompasses such instances as:

'Snow is white' is true just if snow is white.

and which we can schematise as:

T: 'P' is true just if P.

Second, we learn to relate these sentences to our motives in common-sense psychological ascription, together with the situations now linked to them via the concept of truth. In learning to connect sentences with motives in this *that P* way, we perforce learn to link the sentences with the states of our brains – say, the imperceptible patterns of neural connectivity and activation – by which the motives are realised. Just as a person who learns to eat thereby learns to fill her stomach, whether she knows about stomachs or not, so also a person who learns to describe motives by embedded sentences learns to map these sentences to the appropriate mechanisms in her brain, whether she knows about brains or not. Since the sentences now mapped to the inner states are already linked to the environment, we can see this mode of description as overlaying – and consolidating, systematising, extending and refining – such an in-built tendency to represent these states by linking them with their environmental *relata* as we considered just above.

This mode of description, in turn, enables us to represent the *causal role* of the inner states via our linguistic understanding of the sentences we use to describe them. Thus consider the schema above, as related to human perception and belief:

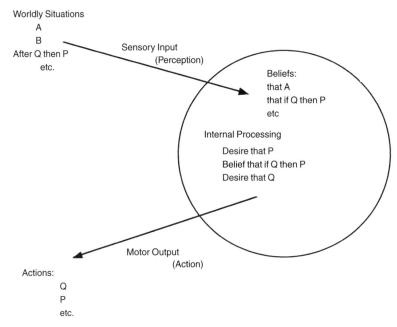

Fig. 13.5 The sentential images of the mind–brain.

B: P -[causes]-> A sees that P -[causes]-> A believes that P

In thinking in accord with this schema we use repetitions of the sentence 'P', and hence our grasp of the truth-conditions of that sentence, to mark successive stages in the transfer of information from the environment to the brain. This runs from the environmental situation described by 'P', through the perception described by 'P' as applied to information in the visual apparatus, to the belief described by 'P' as realised in the brain. Likewise, in thinking in accord with **PR** and **D,** we use sentences to mark stages in internal processing and motor output. And as we have seen, sentences in this use specify the complex and concatenated dispositions relating behaviour and environment by which we understand human (and other animal) behaviour generally. We can partly represent this by a diagram of inputs, internal causes and outputs, as in Figure 13.5.

The internal states or mechanisms described in this way can equally be taken as those of mind or brain. So we can regard the system of sentence–world mappings informing our common-sense concept of motive as, among other things, a linguistic or semantic *way of thinking* or *mode of presentation* of the neural mechanisms which realise belief, desire and action. The norms of truth for our world-describing sentences, as schematised in **T,** function in such forms as **B, D,** and **PR** as normative–functional descriptions by which we track aspects or phases in the neural governance of action. In this guise the brain appears to us as a *virtual semantic engine*, that is, one whose causal workings we specify via sentences and the situations they describe, and so by using the notions of truth, reason and the satisfaction of desire.

This provides an initial indication as to how we represent the brain – and represent it *as a mind* – through the use of perceptible information from outside the body. Such a representation, as in accord with Whiten's proposal, serves to compress correlations relating behaviour to the environment; in particular, this use of language enables the relevant correlations to be specified and processed via our understanding of whole sentences, and thus with a maximum of flexibility and power. So our exegesis also suggests that this representation evolved in a particular way, namely via the involvement of neural mechanisms also adapted for communication.

6   Two problems of explanation: the precision and certainty of linguistic understanding, and first-person authority

We have described this kind of representation as having the strength of a powerful empirical theory. Such strength is evidently required, for our mutual understanding includes that of language, and most of what we know seems registered in language or understood through our use of it. Collaborative science, for example, rests on our understanding of the linguistic and non-linguistic activities of scientists, mathematicians and many others; and this is part of the sentential understanding of motive which we have been considering.

Again, and more clearly related to our present topic, we take it that we have first-person authority about our own inner states. This is an important component of our notion of consciousness, which, as it seems natural to assume, gives us full and immediate access to the introspectible items of which we are aware. But first-person authority also applies, for instance, to the meanings of our words, the contents of our thoughts, and the nature of our intentions in acting; and these are central to our conception of ourselves as thinkers and agents more generally.

All this, however, presupposes that a person understands the sentence–world correlation schematised in **T** coherently and correctly, and links its instances with his or her own neural mechanisms in the right way. That anyone does all this is a weighty empirical claim; and because articulate thinking presupposes this claim, no one can investigate it without circularity 'from inside', that is, in his or her own case. Still we determine that it holds for others insofar as we understand their language and action, and the same applies when others understand us. What assures us that we understand our own sentences and selves is thus that we share this understanding, or at least could do so, with others. So there is a sense in which there is nothing we understand better than our own language, and hence those we take to share it with us.

7   An approach to these problems: crosschecking the interpretation of language and non-verbal action

We take the precision and certainty of linguistic understanding for granted, but this is surely something which should admit of explanation. It seems that we can sketch a part of the required explanation by attending to the contrasting roles of verbal and non-verbal action.

Speech seems a kind of action which we can interpret with particular clarity and certainty; and it is through understanding speech that we attain our precise and extensive understanding of the motives of others. But it is worth noting that speech is a kind of behaviour which we could *not* understand in isolation from the rest of the behavioural order of which it is a part. If we could not regard people's productions of sounds or marks as part of a larger pattern of action and relation to the environment, we could not make disciplined sense of them. (One can get a sense of this point by imagining trying to interpret radio broadcasts of foreign speech, without, however, being able to know anything about what the programmes are about.)

By contrast, we can understand a lot of non-linguistic behaviour without relying on language, at least up to a point. We can generally see the purposive patterns in people's behaviour in terms of their performance of commonplace intentional actions, as in accord with **D** and **PR** above, taken in terms of belief and desire. But unless we can link such actions with language, we cannot, in many cases, know the precise contents of people's beliefs and desires; and in the absence of language it would be doubtful how far we could ascribe precisely conceptualised thoughts to people at all.

This yields a general claim about interpretative understanding. Words in isolation are unintelligible, and deeds without relation to words are inarticulate. Hence the understanding we actually attain, in which we take persons' deeds to spring from motives with determinate and precisely conceptualised content, requires us to integrate our understanding of verbal and non-verbal behaviour, and hence to correlate and co-ordinate the two. This enables us to link the complex structure of utterance to particular points in the framework of action and context, and thereby to interpret language; and this in turn enables us to understand the rest of behaviour as informed by experience and thought which, like that expressed in language, has fully articulate content.

In our interpretative integration of verbal and non-verbal behaviour we systematically relate the motives we take to be expressed in speech – including desires, beliefs and experiences – to those upon which we take speakers to act. We thus, in effect, triangulate between verbal and non-verbal behaviour to focus on their common causes, that is, on motives which we can specify by relation to uttered sentences, but which also drive non-verbal action. In this, therefore, we constantly and tacitly crosscheck the motives we assign via speech against those we assign via non-verbal action; and this constitutes an empirical method of particular power.

This can be illustrated with a simple example. Suppose that I competently frame hypotheses as to the motives upon which you are presently acting and also about what the sounds in your idiolect mean. Then suppose that you also make sounds which, according to my understanding of your idiolect, constitute authoritative expressions of the motives upon which I take you to act, and your further behaviour bears this out. Then questions of sincerity aside, this tends to show (i) that my hypotheses about both the meanings of your utterances and the motives for your present behaviour are correct, and (ii) that you have first-person authority about these things. So the more I can do this in respect of your non-verbal actions, then the higher a degree of confidence I can attain about the hypotheses which constitute my understanding of the contents of your motives and utterances, and also about your possession of first-person authority.

In this, moreover, everything is confirmed empirically, so that I would be taking nothing simply on trust. My confidence in my interpretations would be due to their success in explaining and predicting what you did and said, and my confidence in your first-person authority would be based upon its coinciding with my own independent understanding of the utterances and actions which expressed it. The same, of course, would hold for your understanding of my utterances and actions. In these circumstances, furthermore, each of us could in principle take any of our countless interpretations of the other's non-verbal actions, and seek to pair it with an appropriate self-ascription from the other; and by this means each interpretation of non-verbal action, provided it was correct, could also be made to count in favour of each's understanding of the other's idiolect. This potentially infinite correlation between verbal and non-verbal action could thus be exploited indefinitely often, to move confirmation of the hypothesis that each understood the idiolect of the other steadily upwards. So by this means, it seems, we could in favourable circumstances come to regard our possession of mutual linguistic understanding as confirmed to the highest degree. (The principles illustrated here are discussed more fully in Hopkins, 1999a and c, and apply to more complex cases.)

Triangulation of this kind presupposes an interpreter with a capacity to think in an effective hypothetical way about motives which explain both verbal and non-verbal actions, and an interpretee who can provide both non-linguistic and linguistic behaviour, where the latter accurately expresses, and so serves to specify, the motives which explain the former. Given these materials, it seems, an interpreter could come to understand the contents of an interpretee's motives with a degree of accuracy which was potentially very high. In the process, moreover, the interpreter could constantly check both her own ability to interpret and the first-person authority of the interpretee, and hence continually test the presuppositions of successful interpretation of this kind. So the fact that each of us is *both* a potentially accurate interpreter *and* a potentially authoritative interpretee would appear to enable us to calibrate our interpretations of verbal and non-verbal behaviour continuously and cumulatively, so as to give both something like the degree of precision and accuracy which we observe them to enjoy.

8   A conclusion from this approach: interpretation, evolution and first-person authority

According to this line of thought, it is no coincidence that we should both possess first-person authority and also be able to interpret one another as accurately as we do, for these apparently distinct phenomena are inter-related. Taken this way, moreover, first-person authority does not seem solely or primarily directed to the self. Rather it appears as a social achievement, which complements the ability to interpret. It is the foundation of the ability to manifest the kind of correlation between utterance and action which makes precise and fully grounded interpretation possible, and thereby to make oneself understood.

This dovetailing of abilities, however, also seems to have been shaped by evolution. As we have already noted, we should expect that an increase in the ability to understand and anticipate the behaviour of others should be an advantage to members of a species who possess it; and the same holds for an increase in the ability to determine the way in which one is interpreted by others, that is, the ability to make oneself understood in one way rather than another. So we might expect that there would be circumstances in which evolution would cull and save in favour of both these abilities, interactively. There seems reason to hold that such a process has been accelerated among the social primates, and particularly in our own species (see e.g. Deacon, 1997). If we take this together with the development of the mode of presentation of motive considered above, it seems we might start to frame an account of the processes by which we have become able to express (and hence to describe) our own motives with the accuracy manifest in first-person authority. And such an account would not presuppose the idea of introspection, but rather might be used in explanation of it.

9   A further aspect of our representation of inner causes of behaviour: the internality of the mind

Now it is a striking and further aspect of our conception of the mind that we also regard the states or events about which we have first-person authority as in some sense *internal* or *inner*. If we consider the visual experience of perceiving a tree, for example, we think of the experience as *internal* to the mind, whereas the tree which is the object of the experience is part of the *external* world. This notion of internality permeates both everyday and philosophical thinking. We speak, for example, of knowing what experience is like *from the inside*, and of the *inner* life of the mind. This includes the *inner* aspects of experiences and sensations, our *innermost* thoughts and feelings, and so forth. And part of this notion of the internal is the idea that we have access to our own minds by *introspection*, that is, a kind of internal perception or 'looking into' this inner locus, which seems particularly direct, accurate and revealing.

We apparently have this sense of internality from early in life. Children of three, for example, already distinguish between a physical item such as a dog and its corresponding visual image, holding that the latter is 'just in the mind', where only one person can see it (Wellman, 1990). Although this presumably somehow reflects the fact that the events we describe as mental are realised in the nervous system, it nonetheless remains puzzling. For when we consider mental events in introspection, their innerness does not *seem* to be that, or only that, of being physically inside the body. A visual image, for example, may seem to be somewhere behind the eyes; but it also seems to have spatial aspects or regions of its own, which are not those of anything inside the skull.

This applies even to events which have a precise internal bodily location, such as pain. We feel the pain of an aching tooth as *in the tooth*, but we also hold that no examination of the physical space occupied by the tooth will reveal the pain itself which we feel there. The felt quality of the pain seems to be in an internal locus which is introspectible only by the person who actually has the toothache, and which therefore seems distinct from the public physical space inside the tooth and body. Indeed, as the case of pain in a phantom limb makes clear, this space can apparently be occupied even at a locus at which nothing real exists. And as is familiar, the introspectible quality apparently manifest in this internal space seems to be the defining or essential feature of sensations such as pain.

10   Internality and the problem of consciousness

This brings us to a further aspect of the internality of the mind, namely that it is bound up, via the notion of introspection, with the problem of consciousness. The qualities which are internal and hence introspectible seem to us to be *phenomenal* as opposed to *physical*, in the sense that it seems (at least to many) to be unintelligible or inexplicable that such qualities should be possessed or realised by a physical thing.

As the consideration of pain above indicates, this opposition between the phenomenal and the physical seems part of a series, related to the internality of the mind. As noted, qualities which are internal and so introspectible seem *private*, in the sense that a particular instance can be introspected by just one person; whereas externally perceptible qualities are *public*, in that more than one person can perceive them. Again, such qualities also seem *subjective*, in that their nature seems wholly and fully presented in how they seem in introspection, so that there is no clear distinction between how they seem and how they really are. This contrasts with qualities which are externally perceivable, for these can differ from how they seem and hence are *objective*. If we represent the internality of the mind by a circle, we can diagram this series of oppositions, as in Figure 13.6.

These oppositions are partly defined by negation, and it seems that no one thing could satisfy both of any pair of them. It seems that no one thing or property could possibly be internal to the mind in the way experiences are, and also external to the mind in the way physical things are. Again, it seems that no one thing could be both introspectible and externally perceivable, or both phenomenal and physical, or both private and public. So these oppositions naturally give rise to *dualism*, the view that experience is distinct in nature from the physical world, and via this to further problems, such as the problem of other minds.

A main problem presented by consciousness is that of understanding this series of oppositions. States and events as given in consciousness seem inner, phenomenal, subjective and private, whereas states and events of the nervous system are apparently outer, physical, objective and public. So how can the latter be identical with, realise or constitute the former? This problem is clearly not solved by accepting that mental events are in fact events in the brain, for the difficulty is precisely that of understanding *how* this can be so. Again it is clearly not solved by holding that neural events can have aspects or properties which are phenomenal, etc., since this also is a version of what requires to be explained. Finally, the problem is not solved by holding that we have first-person ways of thinking or modes of presentation which represent experience in these problematic ways, although this certainly seems to be the case. For we still require an account

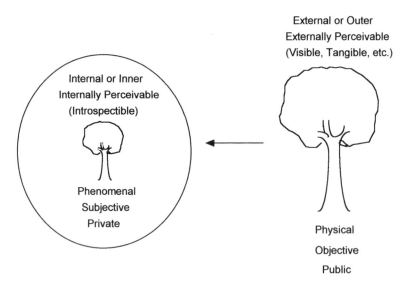

Fig. 13.6 An image of the internality of the mind.

of these modes of presentation, and an explanation as to how they render experiences phenomenal, subjective and private – or make them seem so – despite their physical nature. This is what we can now start to consider.

11   The internality of the mind as a mode of presentation of experience

No doubt, as noted above, our thinking of the mind as internal reflects the fact that the events we describe as mental actually occur inside the body. Still, the mere physical location of these events does nothing to explain how we manage to represent them as internal, much less how we do this in the particular ways we do. Further, it seems that we take the way we depict experiences as inner to provide a way of thinking, or a mode of presentation, of these events. For we distinguish, for example, between apprehending or thinking of experience (as we say) *from the inside* and doing so *from the outside*, where the former mode of apprehension, as opposed to the latter, is unmediated by the observation of behaviour or body, and shows first-person authority. We thus apparently identify this first-person way of thinking by the internality which we ascribe to the mind.

This suggests that our way of representing the mind as internal may itself be the mode of presentation in which the problem of consciousness is rooted; and indeed the other oppositions which we have taken to constitute the problem seem systematically related to this. The subjectivity and privacy of phenomenal things or qualities seems entailed by their existing in an internal private space, so that they are introspectible by just one person, and from just one point of view; and this is the space we think of ourselves as inhabiting when we think of experience from the inside. The objectivity and publicity of physical things, by contrast, seem entailed by their existing in an external public space, and so being observable by more than one person and from more than one point of view; and this is the space we think of ourselves as inhabiting when we think from the outside. It is as though in representing experiences as internal, we somehow split them off from the public space of the world, depicting them as in a virtual space (or spaces) of their own; so that in consequence the inner seems marked by features which are negations of those of the world from which it is divided. If something like this is true, then understanding our representation of internality may be the key to understanding these further features and hence to the problem of consciousness.

12   The example of conceptual metaphor

We saw above how mapping internal (neural) states and events to sentences and thus to environmental situations serves as a mode of presentation of these states and their causal role. So here it seems worth noting that we already make use of another mapping from the environment, by which we represent certain mental states or events as internal. Recently George Lakoff, Mark Turner and a number of others have argued that we frequently represent via *cognitive metaphor*. In this we systematically map one domain of objects and properties (the *source domain*) to another (the *target domain*), and use the one to represent, or think about, the other (see Lakoff, 1993). To take a relevant example, we often represent the mind in terms of the *inside of a container*, where this container can *also* be taken as the body (the mind–body container, as we can say).

Metaphors from this family appear in many contexts, as when we say that someone who has failed to keep something concealed has *spilled the beans*, i.e. let things spill out of his mind–body container, in a way that makes them difficult or impossible to replace. They are, however, particularly common in our conceptualisation of emotion (see, e.g., Koveces, 1990). Thus, for example, we seem to conceive certain emotions as *fluids* in the mind–body container. We think of anger, for example, as a *hot* fluid: the feelings of someone who is angry may *seethe* or *simmer* and so are *agitated*. A person who is *hot under the collar* in this way may be *fuming* as the anger *rises*, or *wells up* in him; and so he may have to *simmer down*, or *cool down*, so as not to *boil over*. If he doesn't manage to *let off steam*, he may *burst with anger*, or *explode with rage*. We thus represent the spectrum of feeling between

calmness and uncontrollable anger relatively strictly in terms of the temper-
ature of the emotion-liquid, which may be cool (no anger), agitated or hot
(some degree of anger), or boiling (great anger); and the pressure caused by
the emotion–heat may ultimately cause the mind–body container to burst.
By contrast, a source of fear may make one get *cold feet* or make one's *blood
run cold,* so that, in the extreme case, *cold fear* or *icy terror* may render one
frozen to the spot and so unable to move. Here the opposition in the nature
of feelings is marked by an opposition in the properties of the metaphorical
fluids to which we map them. This is one of very many examples of representation of the mind as an inner space or container, and indicates something of the tacit systematic nature of such thinking (see also Hopkins,
1999b).

13   Metaphoric representation and the internality of experience

This metaphoric thinking can be seen as similar in nature to the sentential
mode of presentation discussed above. In both cases, as it seems, we represent the causal role of internal neural states or processes by systematically
relating them to things external to the body. In this latter case, however, the
relation represents the internality as well as the causal role of the processes
to which it is applied. The emotions are represented as acting as a fluid
might, and this activity is represented as *inside* the mind–body container, as
a fluid acts *inside* a vessel.

While the mapping to sentences and situations provides a powerful representation of the causal role of the neural mechanisms to which it is applied,
it yields no image of their internality, nor of important internal aspects of
their causal role. This is a lack which we can think of as addressed by the
kind of mapping we are now considering. In the metaphor of the
mind–body container we represent events which are (i) *perceptually and
causally inscrutable* and (ii) *hidden inside the body* by linking them to others
which are (i) *perceptually intelligible* but which may be (ii) *hidden in containers in the external environment.* We thus use information about *contained
events in the external environment* to create an image of *events contained in
an inner space,* which we use to represent the neural events involved in
emotion as both internal and intelligible.

We can think of such conceptual metaphor as a process by which the
brain makes use of existing prototypes to bring new domains into its representational scope. Above we speculated that a similar process – in which the
capacity to represent one domain provides a basis for, and is also partly
retained in, the capacity to represent another – takes place in evolution
(on this see also Pinker, 1997b, pp. 353ff). Either of these processes, or
some combination of both, could yield domains in which something like
metaphor constitutes the basic fabric of our thought. I think this applies

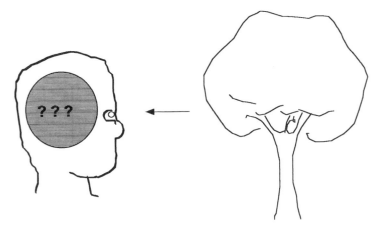

Fig. 13.7 The lack of a representation of internal visual experience.

not only to thinking about desire, belief and other sententially conceived motives, but also to our basic image of the internality of the mind. For we can see this image as partly formed by a mapping of *the external process and space of perception* into *the space internal to the body* and thus to *the internal neural events which realise conscious experience.*

14   Experience and virtual internal space

This can be illustrated by a cartoon related to the diagrams above. Suppose we initially had no way of representing the internality of visual experience, and so were in the situation depicted in Figure 13.7.

A straightforward way to remedy this, via information available in the environment, would be to map the physical space of perception itself inwards to that of the as-yet-unrepresented internal (and neural) events. This would yield a representation of visual experience as occurring in a quasi-spatial inner visual field – a kind of virtual inner space – which we could illustrate as in Figure 13.8. This seems essentially the same representation as that involved in the conception of the internality of the mind illustrated in Figure 13.6 above. So this may indicate something of the path by which we have built up an image of a space (or spaces) within, whose function as a mode of presentation of neural events in the physical space inside our bodies we now find hard to recognise.

Now of course this is only a cartoon, and not an explanation which purports to do justice to the full complexity of our sense that the mind is internal. Still, the conception which it illustrates – that of a visual image, or the visual field, as 'in the mind or head' – seems to apply to a range of other

294   *Jim Hopkins*

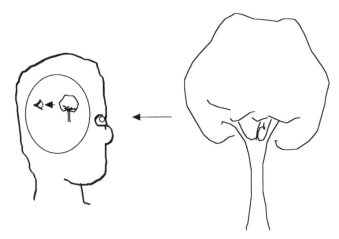

Fig. 13.8 A representation obtained by mapping the external causes of experience inwards.

cases, in all of which we regard experience as presented in something like internal perception (introspection) and in one or another kind of internal space. As well as visual space, we think in terms of auditory space, olfactory space, the space in which we feel pain, the space of kinaesthetic sensations, and so forth. The common feature of these modes of representing experience seems to be that we take them to be somehow spatial and inner, even if they are distinct in many other ways.

Often we envisage the relevant spaces very vaguely and align them only roughly with the body. Thus we think of visual space as having to do with the eyes and hence, perhaps, as somewhere behind them; we think of auditory experiences as having to do with the ears and so, perhaps, as somewhere inside them; and so on. Hence we naturally tend to conceive visual experience as a sort of inner seeing, auditory experience as a sort of inner hearing, olfaction as a sort of inner smelling, pain as a sort of inner and vision-like perception of painfulness, and so on. All this, it seems, is just as it would be if the representation of the inner spaces involved had been derived from our experience of space external to the body, in such a way as to yield partial images of that space within.

15   Virtual inner space and the non-physicality of the mind

The argument is thus that evolution has provided us with a fundamentally metaphorical way of apprehending the neural events which realise experience *as internal*, which draws upon the way we represent things in space outside the body. This, however, is also a potential source of confusion. For we present aspects of these events to ourselves as in one or another internal analogue of space, and we do not present them to ourselves by other means, such as sight and touch. So nothing compels us to recognise that this inner analogue of space is a mode of presentation of neural events in the physical space inside the body. Rather we may think of these events as unseeable, intangible and housed in an alternative kind of space.

This possibility is connected with a more general feature of metaphoric representation. For it is a striking fact that in thinking in terms of such mappings as we have been considering, we tend automatically and unconsciously to delete aspects of the source domain which would lead us to think of the targets in an incoherent way. Lakoff calls this the *invariance principle* (1993, pp. 216ff), and we can regard this as an in-built aspect of the capacity for comparative thinking which it regulates. We can see this in our use of the metaphor of the mind–body container. For example, if we think of anger as a hot fluid inside us, and so actually feel the anger in this way, we still do not think that if someone's anger *wells up, boils over* or *spills out*, this anger will subsequently be found spattered on the carpet. To use the metaphor thus would clearly be to think of anger and its locus in too concrete a way, and most people automatically do not do so. (There are exceptions, as in autism and schizophrenia; and in these disturbances concrete thinking, or difficulty in understanding metaphorical mappings, tends to go with difficulty in understanding the internality of the mind.) Rather we subtly and systematically *de-concretise* and so *de-physicalise* both the virtual space occupied by the anger-as-fluid and the metaphoric fluid itself.

We thus tacitly treat the anger-space as a *non-physical space*, not to be confused with the actual internal space with which, nonetheless, it may phenomenologically overlap; and likewise we treat the anger-fluid as a *non-physical fluid*, not to be confused with physical things actually inside us. We represent mental states via virtual entities derived from physical ones, but which, as coherence requires, we also think of as not fully physical. Nonetheless this representational de-physicalisation actually involves nothing which is really non-physical. It flows from the tacit imposition of a requirement of coherence upon a mapping which has both physical sources (physical fluids and containers) and physical targets (changes inside the body involved in emotion). Since nothing which is both real and non-physical actually comes into question, we can say that the apparent non-physicality of the anger-space and anger-fluid are *cognitive illusions*, engendered by this spatial mode of representing the inner. So it seems that a comparable process might likewise account for the apparent non-physicality of the inner space and contents involved in our everyday conception of the mind.

16   Virtual inner space and the problem of consciousness

This suggests the possibility of an account of those features of consciousness which we find problematic, and which are dependent on our notion of the internality of the mind, as sketched above. As a first approximation, such an account might run as follows. We naturally conceive the internal by tacit mapping from the external, and coherence in this may require us tacitly to distinguish the internal target domain from the external source via which it is conceived. Hence just as we tacitly distinguish the internal anger-space and fluid from the physical spaces and fluids upon which the conception is based, so we may also tacitly distinguish introspection and its locus and objects from the physical sources of this mapping, and hence from physical things generally.

This way of thinking of the internal, therefore, would naturally predispose us to distinguish the mental from the physical. As long as such thinking remained tacit – as it may have done for most of human history – so also might the disposition to distinguish the internal from the external latent in it. Once we started to develop our thinking about the mental and the physical, however, we would also be bound to elaborate this intuitive difference of domains. We can see a simple and perhaps basic instance of this in the way a child, upon being pressed, will distinguish internal images from external objects – thus, as it were, starting to de-physicalise the images – while still conceiving the former in terms of the latter.

Such elaboration, indeed, seems to have been a feature of thinking about the mind since the scientific revolution. For example Leibniz (1973, p. 171) contributed to the development of the present problem by arguing:

Suppose that there were a machine so constructed as to produce thought, feeling, and perception, we could imagine it increased in size while retaining the same proportions, so that one could enter as one might a mill. On going inside we should only see the parts impinging upon one another; we should not see anything which would explain a perception. . . .

The mill which Leibniz cites is an example of the metaphor of the mind–body container (cf. the *house* of reason, the *windows* of the soul, etc.); except in this case the container is visibly occupied by an internal physical mechanism. So here the metaphor carries naturally to events in the brain, which we compare to those we take as internal to the mind. The former are physical events in the body, whereas the latter – once we make the comparison explicit – seem events of a different kind, in a different internal space. We can see this, according to the present account, as a response comparable to that by which we think of the anger-space and anger-fluid as non-physical. Here, however, the response holds for the more basic and pervasive structure of introspectible inner space illustrated above (Figure 13.8). Paradoxically, the more we make the targets of our natural mode of presentation explicit, the more the mode seems to be presenting events of an entirely different kind.

Leibniz focuses on the qualities of perceptions; and he seems to have thought of these partly as Locke did, that is, as involving versions of shape and colour, which, being internal, were non-physical. This conception, in turn, was later to be modified by arguments that internal sensations could not actually possess such external properties (compare Berkeley's 'nothing but an idea can be like an idea'). Accordingly, more recent accounts have tended simply to postulate mappings which enable us to conceive internal properties by linking them to external ones – for example to conceive the visual field via mappings to planes, shapes and colours – while allowing that the internal targets do not actually share properties with the external sources (see, e.g., Peacocke, 1983). But then if we accept that the cognitive mechanisms which impose these mappings might also yield a kind of internalised and so de-physicalised image of their sources, we may be able to account for the apparent inner realms and properties themselves.

This idea, of course, requires to be developed in more detail. But it suggests how something like the reflex of clarification which we find in a child's thinking about visual images may have taken us to the conception of consciousness which we now find problematic. In this we are tempted to construe conscious events as occurring in an internal locus which is somehow non-physical, and which is populated by instances of properties which we conceive mainly as the ghosts of the departed external properties by which we map them. Since the items represented as perceived within this virtual region are not shown as having existence apart from it, their *esse* seems *percipi*, so that they are also subjective; and since they are shown as having their being in the space (or spaces) making up a single consciousness, they also seem private.

It is no wonder that we find this conception problematic, for it is hard to suppose that there really is such an internal space (or set of spaces) as, in thinking of the mind in this way, we take it to be. Rather the conception of the internal which we employ here seems an artefact of a mode of representation. If the present account is on the right lines, we may be able to understand ourselves as having constructed this artefact by intelligible cognitive operations on mappings which involve only physical sources and targets, and hence in terms of the computational and physicalistic view of the mind–brain which it seems to contradict. If so, we may be able to understand the 'explanatory gap' between the phenomenal and the physical in a way similar to that in which we have already understood the supposed gap between physical causes and mental reasons. Just as our sentential mode of presentation of the causal role of motives can wrongly suggest that this role is semantic as opposed to causal, so our spatial mode of presentation of the internality of mental states could wrongly suggest that this innerness is phenomenal as opposed to physical. If this is the source of the gap, we need no more bridge it than we need to weigh the rainbow. We come to understand such oppositions by recognising that their place in nature is not as it appears, and so by studying them as forms of illusion.

I would like to thank the British Academy for Research Leave which made it possible to write this paper as well as the others which appear in the bibliography. I am grateful to discussants at the Sheffield conference on Evolving the Mind, and in particular to Professor Peter Carruthers, for penetrating and helpful comments on an earlier draft.

References

Aiello, L. (1996). Hominine preadaptations for language and cognition. In P. Mellars and K. Gibson (eds.), *Modelling the Early Human Mind*, pp. 89–99. Cambridge: McDonald Institute Monographs.

Aiello, L., and Dunbar, R. (1993). Neocortex size, group size and the evolution of language. *Current Anthropology*, 34, 184–93.

Aiello, L., and Wheeler, P. (1995). The expensive tissue hypothesis. *Current Anthropology*, 36, 199–211.

Ainsworth-Darnell, K., Shulman, H., and Boland, J. (1998). Dissociating brain responses to syntactic and semantic anomalies: evidence from Event-Related Potential. *Journal of Memory and Language*, 38, 112–30.

Alexander, R. (1974). The evolution of social behaviour. *Annual Review of Ecology and Systematics*, 5, 325–83.

American Psychiatric Association. (1980). *Diagnostic and Statistical Manual of Mental Disorders (DSM III)*. Washington: American Psychiatric Association.

(1987). *Diagnostic and Statistical Manual of Mental Disorders (DSM III-R)*. Washington: American Psychiatric Association.

(1994). *Diagnostic and Statistical Manual of Mental Disorders (DSM IV)*. Washington: American Psychiatric Association.

Anderson, M. (1992). *Intelligence and Development*. Oxford: Blackwell.

Armstrong, D. (1968). *A Materialist Theory of the Mind*. London: Routledge.

(1984). Consciousness and causality. In D. Armstrong and N. Malcolm (eds.), *Consciousness and Causality*, pp. 103–192. Oxford: Blackwell.

Astington, J. (1994). *The Child's Discovery of the Mind*. London: Fontana.

(1996). What is theoretical about the child's theory of mind? A Vygotskian view of its development. In P. Carruthers and P. Smith (eds.), *Theories of Theories of Mind*, pp. 184–99. Cambridge: Cambridge University Press.

Astington, J., and Jenkins, J. (1995). Theory of mind development and social understanding. *Cognition and Emotion*, 9, 151–65.

Atran, S. (1989). Basic conceptual domains. *Mind and Language*, 4, 5–16.

(1990). *Cognitive Foundations of Natural History: Towards an Anthropology of Science*. Cambridge: Cambridge University Press.

(1998). Folk biology and the anthropology of science: cognitive universals and cultural particulars. *Behavioral and Brain Sciences*, 21, 547–609.

Bahn, P. (1991). Pleistocene images outside Europe. *Proceedings of the Prehistoric Society*, 57(1), 99–102.

Bailey, A., Palferman, S., Heavey, L., and Le Couteur, A. (1998). Autism: the phenotype in relatives. *Journal of Autism and Developmental Disorders*, 28(5), 381–404.

Barkow, J., Cosmides, L., and Tooby, J. (eds.), (1992). *The Adapted Mind: Evolutionary Psychology and the Generation of Culture.* New York: Oxford University Press.

Baron-Cohen, S. (1994). How to build a baby that can read minds: cognitive mechanisms in mindreading. *Cahiers de Psychologie Cognitive/Current Psychology of Cognition*, 13(5), 513–52.

(1995). *Mindblindness.* Cambridge, MA: MIT Press.

Baron-Cohen, S., Leslie, A., and Frith, U. (1985). Does the autistic child have a theory of mind? *Cognition*, 21(1), 37–46.

(1986). Mechanical, behavioral and intentional understanding of picture stories in autistic children. *British Journal of Developmental Psychology*, 4, 113–25.

Baron-Cohen, S., and Swettenham, J. (1996). The relationship between SAM and ToMM: two hypotheses. In P. Carruthers and P. Smith (eds.), *Theories of Theories of Mind*, pp. 158–68. Cambridge: Cambridge University Press.

Barrett, J. (1998). Cognitive constraints on Hindu concepts of the divine. *Journal for the Scientific Study of Religion*, 37, 608–19.

Barrett, J., and Keil, F. (1996). Conceptualizing a non-natural entity: anthropomorphism in God concepts. *Cognitive Psychology*, 31, 219–47.

Bartlett, F. (1932). *Remembering: A Study in Experimental and Social Psychology.* Cambridge: Cambridge University Press.

Bednarik, R. (1995). Concept mediated marking in the Lower Palaeolithic. *Current Anthropology*, 36, 605–34.

Bellugi, U., Klima, E., and Wang, P. (1997). Cognitive and neural development: clues from genetically based syndromes. In D. Magnusson, T. Greitz, T. Hokfelt, N. Lars-Goran, L. Terenius, and B. Winblad (eds.), *The Lifespan Development of Individuals: Behavioral, Neurobiological, and Psychosocial Perspectives: A Synthesis* pp. 223–43. New York: Cambridge University Press.

Bennett, J. (1976). *Linguistic Behaviour.* Cambridge: Cambridge University Press.

Bickerton, D. (1990). *Language and Species.* Chicago: The University of Chicago Press.

(1995). *Language and Human Behavior.* Seattle: University of Washington Press (London: UCL Press, 1996.).

Blair, R. (1995). A cognitive developmental approach to morality: investigating the psychopath. *Cognition*, 57(1), 1–29.

Blair, R., and Morton, J. (1995). Putting cognition into sociopathy. *Behavioral and Brain Sciences*, 18, 548.

Bloch, M. (1998). *How We Think They Think: Anthropological Approaches to Cognition, Memory and Literacy.* Boulder, CO: Westview Press.

Block, N. (1995). A confusion about a function of consciousness. *Behavioral and Brain Sciences*, 18, 227–47.

Bloom, P. (1997). Intentionality and word learning. *Trends in Cognitive Sciences*, 1, 9–12.

Bock, G., and Cardew, G. (1997). *Characterizing Human Psychological Adaptations.* Chichester: John Wiley and Sons.

Borgerhoff Mulder, M. (1991). Human behavioural ecology. In J. Krebs and N. Davies (eds.), *Behavioural Ecology. An Evolutionary Approach*, pp. 69–98. Oxford: Blackwell.

Bornstein, M., and Stiles-Davis, J. (1984). Discrimination and memory for symmetry in young children. *Developmental Psychology*, 20, 637–49.

Botterill, G., and Carruthers, P. (1999). *The Philosophy of Psychology*. Cambridge: Cambridge University Press.

Boyd, R., and Richerson, P. (1985). *Culture and the Evolutionary Process*. Chicago: University of Chicago Press.

Boyer, P. (1994a). Cognitive constraints on cultural representations: natural ontologies and religious ideas. In L. Hirschfeld and S. Gelman (eds.), *Mapping the Mind: Domain-Specificity in Culture and Cognition*, pp. 391–411. New York: Cambridge University Press.

(1994b). *The Naturalness of Religious Ideas: A Cognitive Theory of Religion*. Berkeley/Los Angeles: University of California Press.

(1996). What makes anthropomorphism natural: intuitive ontology and cultural representations. *Journal of the Royal Anthropological Institute (n.s.)*, 2, 1–15.

(1998). Cognitive tracks of cultural inheritance: how evolved intuitive ontology governs cultural transmission. *American Anthropologist*, 100, 876–89.

(1999). Cultural inheritance tracks and cognitive predispositions: the example of religious concepts. In H. Whitehouse (ed.), *Mind, Evolution and Cultural Transmission*. Cambridge: Cambridge University Press.

Boyer, P., and Ramble, C. (in preparation). Cognitive templates for religious concepts: cross-cultural evidence for recall of counterintuitive representations.

Boysen, S., Berntson, G., and Prentice, J. (1987). Simian scribbles: a reappraisal of drawing in the chimpanzee (*Pan troglodytes*). *Journal of Comparative Psychology*, 101, 82–9.

Bretherton, I., and Beeghly, M. (1982). Talking about internal states: the acquisition of a theory of mind. *Developmental Psychology*, 18(6), 906–21.

Brown, D. (1991). *Human Universals*. New York: McGraw-Hill.

Brown, J. R., Donelan-McCall, N. and Dunn, J. (1996). Why talk about mental states? The significance of children's conversations with friends, siblings, and mothers. *Child Development*, 67(3), 836–49.

Butterworth, B. (1999). *The Mathematical Brain*. London: Macmillan.

Byrne, R. (1996a). Relating brain size to intelligence in primates. In P. Mellars and K. Gibson (eds.), *Modelling the Early Human Mind*, pp. 49–56. Cambridge: McDonald Institute Monographs.

(1996b). *The Thinking Ape*. Oxford: Oxford University Press.

Byrne, R., and Whiten, A. (eds.), (1988). *Machiavellian Intelligence: Social Expertise and the Evolution of Intellect in Monkeys, Apes and Humans*. Oxford: Oxford University Press.

(1997). *Machiavellian Intelligence II: Extensions and Evaluations*. Cambridge: Cambridge University Press.

Cachel, S., and Harris, J. (1995). Ranging patterns, land-use and subsistence in *Homo erectus* from the perspective of evolutionary biology. In J. Bower and S. Sartono (eds.), *Evolution and Ecology of Homo erectus*, pp. 51–66. Leiden: Pithecanthropus Centennial Foundation.

Call, J., and Tomasello, M. (1999). A nonverbal theory of mind test. The performance of children and apes. *Child Development*, 70, 381–95.

Caramazza, A., and Shelton, J. (1998). Domain-specific knowledge systems in the brain: the animate-inanimate distinction. *Journal of Cognitive Neuroscience*, 10, 1–34.

Carey, S., and Spelke, E. (1994). Domain-specific knowledge and conceptual change. In L. Hirschfeld and S. Gelman (eds.), *Mapping the Mind: Domain-Specificity in Cognition and Culture,* pp. 169–200. New York: Cambridge University Press.

Carruthers, P. (1996a). Autism as mindblindness. In P. Carruthers and P. Smith (eds.), *Theories of Theories of Mind,* pp. 257–73. Cambridge: Cambridge University Press.

(1996b). *Language, Thought and Consciousness.* Cambridge: Cambridge University Press.

(1996c). Simulation and self-knowledge: a defence of theory-theory. In P. Carruthers and P. K. Smith (eds.), *Theories of Theories of Mind,* pp. 22–38. Cambridge: Cambridge University Press.

(1998a). Conscious thinking: language or elimination? *Mind and Language,* 13, 323–42.

(1998b). Thinking in language? Evolution and a modularist possibility. In P. Carruthers and J. Boucher (eds.), *Language and Thought,* pp. 94–119. Cambridge: Cambridge University Press.

(2000). *Phenomenal Consciousness: A Naturalistic Theory.* Cambridge: Cambridge University Press.

Carruthers, P., and Boucher, J. (eds.), (1998). *Language and Thought.* Cambridge: Cambridge University Press.

Carruthers, P., and Smith, P. (eds.), (1996). *Theories of Theories of Mind.* Cambridge: Cambridge University Press.

Carston, R. (1998). *Pragmatics and the Explicit-Implicit Distinction.* PhD, University College, London.

Cavalli-Sforza, L., and Feldman, M. (1981). *Cultural Transmission and Evolution: A Quantitative Approach.* Princeton: Princeton University Press.

Chalmers, D. (1996). *The Conscious Mind.* Oxford: Oxford University Press.

Changeux, J.-P. (1985). *Neuronal Man: The Biology of Mind.* Princeton, NJ: Princeton University Press.

Chase, P., and Dibble, H. (1987). Middle Palaeolithic symbolism: a review of current evidence and interpretations. *Journal of Anthropological Archaeology,* 6, 263–93.

Cheney, D., and Seyfarth, R. (1990). *How Monkeys See the World.* Chicago: Chicago University Press.

Cheng, P., and Holyoak, K. (1985). Pragmatic reasoning schemas. *Cognitive Psychology,* 17, 391–416.

(1989). On the natural selection of reasoning theories. *Cognition,* 33, 285–313.

Cheng, P., Holyoak, K., Nisbett, R., and Oliver, L. (1986). Pragmatic versus syntactic approaches to training deductive reasoning. *Cognitive Psychology,* 18, 293–328.

Cherniak, C. (1986). *Minimal Rationality.* Cambridge, MA: MIT Press.

Chomsky, N. (1959). Review of *Verbal Behavior* by B. F. Skinner. *Language,* 35, 26–58.

(1980). *Rules and Representations.* New York: Columbia University Press.

(1988). *Language and Problems of Knowledge.* Cambridge, MA: MIT Press.

Chumbley, J. (1986). The role of typicality, instance dominance, and category dominance in verifying category membership. *Journal of Experimental Psychology: Learning, Memory and Cognition,* 12, 257–67.

Churchland, P., and Sejnowski, T. (1992). *The Computational Brain*. Cambridge, MA: MIT Press.

Clark, A. (1989). *Microcognition*. Cambridge, MA: MIT Press.

(1996). *Being There: Putting Brain, Body and World Together Again*. Cambridge, MA: MIT Press.

Clark, A., and Chalmers, D. (1998). The extended mind. *Analysis*, 58(1), 7–19.

Clark, G. (1977). *World Prehistory*. Cambridge: Cambridge University Press.

(1992). A comment on Mithen's ecological interpretation of Palaeolithic art. *Proceedings of the Prehistoric Society*, 58, 107–9.

Clarkin, J., Widiger, T., Frances, A., Hurt, S., and Gilmore, M. (1983). Prototypic typology and the borderline personality disorder. *Journal of Abnormal Psychology*, 92(3), 263–275.

Cohen, L. (1981). Can human irrationality be experimentally demonstrated? *Behavioral and Brain Sciences*, 4, 317–370.

Corballis, M., and Lea, S. (eds.), (1999). *The Descent of Mind: Psychological Perspectives on Hominid Evolution*. Oxford: Oxford University Press.

Cosmides, L. (1989). The logic of social exchange: has natural selection shaped how humans reason? Studies with the Wason selection task. *Cognition*, 31(3), 187–276.

Cosmides, L., and Tooby, J. (1987). From evolution to behavior: evolutionary psychology as the missing link. In J. Dupré (ed.), *The Latest on the Best: Essays on Evolution and Optimality*, pp. 277–306. Cambridge, MA: MIT Press.

(1992). Cognitive adaptations for social exchange. In J. Barkow, L. Cosmides, and J. Tooby (eds.), *The Adapted Mind: Evolutionary Psychology and the Generation of Culture*, pp. 163–228. Oxford: Oxford University Press.

(1994). Origins of domain specificity: the evolution of functional organization. In L. Hirschfeld and S. Gelman (eds.), *Mapping the Mind: Domain-Specificity in Cognition and Culture*, pp. 85–116. New York: Cambridge University Press.

Crawford, C., and Krebs, D. L. (1998). *Handbook of Evolutionary Psychology: Ideas, Issues and Applications*. Mahwah, NJ: Lawrence Erlbaum Associates.

Crick, F., and Koch, C. (1990). Towards a neurobiological theory of consciousness. *Seminars in the Neurosciences*, 2, 263–75.

Crump, T. (1990). *The Anthropology of Numbers*. Cambridge: Cambridge University Press.

Cummins, D. (1996). Evidence for the innateness of deontic reasoning. *Mind and Language*, 11, 160–190.

Cutting, A., and Dunn, J. (1999). Theory of mind, emotion understanding, language and family background: individual differences and inter-relations. *Child Development*, 70(4), 853–65.

Davies, M., and Stone, T. (eds.), (1995a). *Folk Psychology*. Oxford: Blackwell.

(1995b). *Mental Simulation: Evaluations and Applications*. Oxford: Blackwell.

Dawkins, R. (1976). *The Selfish Gene*. Oxford: Oxford University Press.

(1982). *The Extended Phenotype*. Oxford: Oxford University Press.

Dawkins, R., and Krebs, J. R. (1978). Animal signals: information or manipulation? In J. Krebs and N. Davies (eds.), *Behavioural Ecology*, pp. 282–309. Oxford: Blackwell Scientific Publications.

de Villiers, J., and Pyers, J. (1997). *On reading minds and predicting action*. Paper presented at the Society for Research in Child Development, Washington, DC.

de Waal, F. (1996). *Good Natured*. Cambridge, MA: Harvard University Press.

Deacon, T. (1997). *The Symbolic Species: The Co-evolution of Language and the Human Brain*. London: Penguin Books.

Dehaene, S., and Cohen, L. (1995). Towards an anatomical and functional model of number processing. *Mathematical Cognition*, 1, 83–120.

Dennett, D. (1978). Towards a cognitive theory of consciousness. In D. Dennett (ed.), *Brainstorms*, pp. 149–73. Hassocks: Harvester Press.

(1983). Intentional systems in cognitive ethology: the 'panglossian paradigm' defended. *Behavioural and Brain Sciences*, 6, 343–90.

(1987). *The Intentional Stance*. Cambridge, MA: MIT Press.

(1991a). *Consciousness Explained*. London: Penguin Books.

(1991b). Real patterns. *The Journal of Philosophy*, 89, 27–51.

(1995). *Darwin's Dangerous Idea: Evolution and the Meanings of Life*. New York: Simon and Schuster.

(1997). 'Darwinian Fundamentalism': an exchange. *New York Review of Books*, 14 August.

(1998). Reflections on language and mind. In P. Carruthers and J. Boucher (eds.), *Language and Thought*, pp. 284–94. Cambridge: Cambridge University Press.

D'Errico, F. (1991). Microscopic and statistical criteria for the identification of pre-historic systems of notation. *Rock Art Research*, 8, 83–93.

D'Errico, F., and Cacho, C. (1994). Notation versus decoration in the Upper Palaeolithic: a case study from Tossal de la Roca, Alicante, Spain. *Journal of Archaeological Science*, 21, 185–200.

Dickinson, A., and Balleine, B. (1999). Causal cognition and goal-directed action. In C. Heyes and L. Huber (eds.), *The Evolution of Cognition*. Cambridge, MA: MIT Press.

Donald, M. (1991). *Origins of the Modern Mind: Three Stages in the Evolution of Culture and Cognition*. Cambridge, MA: Harvard University Press.

Dretske, F. (1993). Conscious experience. *Mind*, 102, 263–83.

(1995). *Naturalizing the Mind*. Cambridge, MA: MIT Press.

Dunbar, R. (1980). Determinants and consequences of dominance among female gelada baboons. *Behavioral Ecology and Sociobiology*, 7, 253–65.

(1988). *Primate Social Systems*. London: Chapman and Hall.

(1992). Neocortex size as a constraint on group size in primates. *Journal of Human Evolution*, 20, 469–93.

(1993). Co-evolution of neocortical size, group size and language in humans. *Behavioural and Brain Sciences*, 16(4), 681–735.

(1996). *Grooming, Gossip, and the Evolution of Language*. Cambridge, MA: Harvard University Press.

(1998). The social brain hypothesis. *Evolutionary Anthropology*, 6, 178–90.

(1999). Culture, honesty and the freerider problem. In C. Power, C. Knight and R. Dunbar (eds.), *The Evolution of Culture*, pp. 194–213. Edinburgh: Edinburgh University Press.

Dunbar, R., and Bever, J. (1998). Neocortex size predicts group size in carnivores and some insectivores. *Ethology*, 104, 695–708.

Dunn, J. (1995). Children as psychologists: the later correlates of individual differences in understanding of emotions and other minds. *Cognition and Emotion*, 9(2–3), 187–201.

Dunn, J., Brown, J., and Beardsall, L. (1991). Family talk about feeling states and children's later understanding of others' emotions. *Developmental Psychology*, 27(3), 448–55.

Dunn, J., and Cutting, A. (1999). Understanding others, and individual differences in friendship interactions in young children. *Social Development*, 8(2), 201–19.

Dunn, J., and McGuire, S. (1994). Young children's nonshared experiences: a summary of studies in Cambridge and Colorado. In E. Hetherington, D. Reiss and R. Plomin (eds.), *Separate Social Worlds of Siblings: The Impact of Nonshared Environment on Development*, pp. 111–28. Hillsdale, NJ: Lawrence Erlbaum Associates.

Dunn, J., and Plomin, R. (1990). *Separate Lives: Why Siblings are so Different* (1st edn). New York: Basic Books.

(1991). Why are siblings so different? The significance of differences in sibling experiences within the family. *Family Process*, 30(3), 271–83.

Durham, W. (1991). *Coevolution: Genes, Culture, and Human Diversity*. Stanford: Stanford University Press.

(1992). Applications of evolutionary culture theory. *Annual Review of Anthropology*, 21, 331–55.

Eley, T. (1997). General genes: a new theme in developmental psychopathology. *Current Directions in Psychological Science*, 6, 90–5.

Eley, T., and Stevenson, J. (1999). Using genetic analyses to clarify the distinction between depressive and anxious symptoms in childhood and adolescence. *Journal of Abnormal Child Psychology*, 27, 105–14.

Elman, J., Bates, E., Johnson, M., Karmiloff-Smith, A., Parisi, D., and Plunkett, K. (1996). *Rethinking Innateness: A Connectionist Perspective on Development*. Cambridge, MA: MIT Press.

Enquist, M., and Leimar, O. (1993). The evolution of cooperation in mobile organisms. *Animal Behaviour*, 45, 747–57.

Evans, J., and Over, D. (1996). *Rationality and Reasoning*. Hove: Psychology Press.

Falk, D. (1985). Hadar AL 162–28 endocast as evidence that brain enlargement preceded cortical reorganization in hominid evolution. *Nature*, 313, 45–7.

(1989). Ape-like endocast of 'ape-man' Taung. *American Journal of Physical Anthropology*, 80, 335–39.

Farah, M. (1990). *Visual Agnosia*. Cambridge, MA: MIT Press.

Flynn, J. (1987). Massive IQ gains in 14 nations: what IQ tests really measure. *Psychological Bulletin*, 101, 171–91.

Fodor, J. (1968). The appeal to tacit knowledge in psychological explanation. *Journal of Philosophy*, 65, 627–40.

(1983). *The Modularity of Mind: An Essay on Faculty Psychology*. Cambridge, MA: MIT Press.

(1987). *Psychosemantics*. Cambridge, MA: MIT Press.

(1996). Deconstructing Dennett's Darwin. *Mind and Language*, 11, 246–62.

(1998). The trouble with psychological Darwinism. *London Review of Books*, 20(2).

Folstein, S., and Rutter, M. (1977). Infantile autism: a genetic study of 21 twin pairs. *Journal of Child Psychology and Psychiatry*, 18, 297–321.

Fombonne, E., Siddons, F., Archard, S., Frith, U., and Happé, F. (1994). Adaptive behaviour and theory of mind in autism. *European Child and Adolescent Psychiatry*, 3, 176–86.

Fonagy, P., Redfern, S., and Charman, A. (1997). The relationship between belief-desire reasoning and projective measure of attachment security. *British Journal of Developmental Psychology*, 15, 51–61.

Frank, R. (1988). *Passions Within Reason*. New York: W. W. Norton.

Friedlander, M., Martin, K., and Wassenhove-McCarthy, D. (1991). Effects of monocular visual deprivation on geniculo-cortical innervation of area 18 in cat. *The Journal of Neuroscience*, 11, 3268–88.

Frith, U. (1989). *Autism: Explaining the Enigma*. Oxford: Blackwell.

Frith, U., and Happé, F. (1998). Why specific developmental disorders are not specific: on-line and developmental effects in autism and dyslexia. *Developmental Science*, 1(2), 267–72.

Frith, U., Happé, F., and Siddons, F. (1994). Autism and theory of mind in everyday life. *Social Development*, 3, 108–24.

Frost, D. (1982). Anomalous visual connections to somatosensory and auditory systems following brain lesions in early life. *Brain Research*, 255(4), 627–35.

 (1990). Sensory processing by novel, experimentally induced cross-modal circuits. *Annals of the New York Academy of Sciences*, 682, 70–82.

Gallistel, C., and Gelman, R. (1992). Preverbal and verbal counting and computation. *Cognition*, 44, 79–106.

Gangestad, S. (1997). Evolutionary psychology and genetic variation: non-adaptive, fitness-related, and adaptive. In G. Bock and G. Cardew (eds.), *Characterizing Human Psychological Adaptations. Ciba Foundation Symposium #208*, pp. 212–30. New York: John Wiley and Sons.

Garfield, J. (ed.), (1987). *Modularity in Knowledge Representation and Natural-Language Understanding*. Cambridge, MA: MIT Press.

Gatewood, J. (1985). Actions speak louder than words. In J. Dougherty (ed.), *Directions in Cognitive Anthropology*, pp. 199–220. Urbana: University of Illinois Press.

Gell, A. (1998). *Art and Agency: An Anthropological Theory*. Oxford: Oxford University Press.

Gelman, R. (1990). First principles organize attention and learning about relevant data: number and the animate-inanimate distinction as examples. *Cognitive Science*, 14, 79–106.

Gelman, S., Gottfried, G., and Coley, J. (1994). Essentialist beliefs in children: the acquisition of concepts and theories. In L. Hirschfeld and S. Gelman (eds.), *Mapping the Mind: Domain-Specificity in Cognition and Culture*, pp. 341–65. Cambridge: Cambridge University Press.

Gennaro, R. (1996). *Consciousness and Self-Consciousness*. Amsterdam: John Benjamins Publishing.

Gentner, D. (1989). The mechanisms of analogical learning. In S. Vosniadou and A. Ortony (eds.), *Similarity and Analogical Reasoning*, pp. 199–241. Cambridge: Cambridge University Press.

Gerard, A., and Mandler, J. (1983). Ontological knowledge and sentence anomaly. *Journal of Verbal Learning and Verbal Behaviour*, 22, 105–20.

Gergely, G., Nadasdy, Z., Csibra, G., and Biro, S. (1995). Taking the intentional stance at 12 months of age. *Cognition*, 56(2), 165–93.

Gigerenzer, G. (1994). Why the distinction between single-event probabilities and frequencies is important for psychology (and vice versa). In G. Wright and P. Ayton (eds.), *Subjective Probability*, pp. 129–62. New York: John Wiley.

(1996). On narrow norms and vague heuristics: a reply to Kahneman and Tversky (1996). *Psychological Review*, 103, 592–96.

Gigerenzer, G., and Hug, K. (1992). Domain-specific reasoning: social contracts, cheating, and perspective change. *Cognition*, 43(2), 127–71.

Gilbert, S. (1994). *Developmental Biology*. Sunderland, MA: Sinauer Associates.

Godfrey-Smith, P. (1991). Signal, decision, action. *Journal of Philosophy*, 88(12), 709–22.

Goldin-Meadow, S., and Mylander, C. (1990). Beyond the input given. *Language*, 66, 323–55.

Goldman, A. (1993). The psychology of folk psychology. *Behavioural and Brain Sciences*, 16, 15–28.

Goldsmith, H. (1991). A zygosity questionnaire for young twins: a research note. *Behaviour Genetics*, 21(3), 257–69.

Gómez, J.-C. (1998). Some thoughts about the evolution of LADS, with special reference to TOM and SAM. In P. Carruthers and J. Boucher (eds.), *Language and Thought*, pp. 94–119. Cambridge: Cambridge University Press.

Goodwin, D., and Guze, S. (1995). *Psychiatric Diagnosis* (5th edn). New York: Oxford University Press.

Goody, E. (1997). Social intelligence and language: another Rubicon? In A. Whiten and R. Byrne (eds.), *Machiavellian Intelligence II*, pp. 365–96. Cambridge: Cambridge University Press.

Goody, J. (1977). *The Domestication of the Savage Mind*. Cambridge: Cambridge University Press.

Gopnik, A., and Meltzoff, A. (1997). *Words, Thoughts and Theories*. Cambridge, MA: MIT Press.

Gopnik, M. (1990a). Dysphasia in an extended family. *Nature*, 344, 715.

(1990b). Feature blindness: a case study. *Language Acquisition*, 1, 139–64.

Gopnik, M., and Crago, M. (1991). Familial aggregation of a developmental language disorder. *Cognition*, 39, 1–50.

Gottlib, I. (1992). Interpersonal and cognitive aspects of depression. *Current Directions in Psychological Science*, 1, 149–54.

Gould, S. (1989). *Wonderful Life: The Burgess Shale and the Nature of History*. New York: Norton.

(1997). Darwinian fundamentalism. *New York Review of Books*, 44(10), 34–7.

Gould, S., and Lewontin, R. (1979). The spandrels of San Marco and the Panglossian paradigm. *Proceedings of the Royal Society*, B205, 581–98.

Grandin, T., and Scariano, M. (1986). *Emergence Labeled Autistic*. Tunbridge Wells: D. J. Costello.

Grice, P. (1957). Meaning. *Philosophical Review*, 66, 377–88.

(1969). Utterer's meaning and intention. *Philosophical Review*, 78, 147–77.

(1989). *Studies in the Way of Words*. Cambridge, MA: Harvard University Press.

Griffiths, P. (1997). *What Emotions Really Are*. Chicago: University of Chicago Press.

Hacking, I. (1975). *The Emergence of Probability*. Cambridge: Cambridge University Press.

Hagen, E. (1998). *The functions of postpartum depression and the implications for general depression*. Paper presented at the Tenth Annual Meeting of the Human Behavior and Evolution Society, Davis, CA, 8–12 July 1998.

(Undated MS). The functions of postpartum depression.

Happé, F. (1994). *Autism: An Introduction to Psychological Theory*. London: University College London Press.

(1995). The role of age and verbal ability in the theory of mind task performance of subjects with autism. *Child Development*, 66, 843–55.

Harrold, F. (1992). Paleolithic archaeology, ancient behavior, and the transition to modern *Homo*. In G. Bräuer and F. Smith (eds.), *Continuity or Replacement: Controversies in Homo sapiens Evolution*, pp. 219–30. Rotterdam: Balkema.

Hauser, M. (1996). *The Evolution of Communication*. Cambridge, MA: MIT Press, Bradford Books.

Heelas, P., and Lock, A. (1981). *Indigenous Psychologies: The Anthropology of the Self*. New York: Academic Press.

Hempel, C. (1965). Fundamentals of taxonomy. In C. Hempel (ed.), *Aspects of Scientific Explanation*, pp. 137–54. New York: The Free Press.

Hetherington, E., Reiss, D., and Plomin, R. (1994). *Separate Social Worlds of Siblings: The Impact of Nonshared Environment on Development*. Hillsdale, NJ: Lawrence Erlbaum Associates.

Heyes, C., and Dickinson, A. (1990). The intentionality of animal action. *Mind and Language*, 5, 87–104.

Hill, C. (1991). *Sensations: A Defence of Type Materialism*. Cambridge: Cambridge University Press.

Hirschfeld, L. (1989). Rethinking the acquisition of kinship terms. *International Journal of Behavioral Development*, 12, 541–68.

(1996). *Race in the Making: Cognition, Culture and the Child's Construction of Human Kinds*. Cambridge, MA: MIT Press.

Hirschfeld, L., and Gelman, S. (eds.), (1994). *Mapping the Mind: Domain-Specificity in Cognition and Culture*. New York: Cambridge University Press.

Hodder, I. (1993). Social cognition. *Cambridge Archaeological Journal*, 3, 253–57.

Holloway, R. (1983a). Cerebral brain endocast patterns of the AL 162–28 Hadar *A. afarensis* hominid. *Nature*, 303, 420–22.

(1983b). Human paleontological evidence relevant to language behavior. *Human Neurobiology*, 2, 105–14.

Holyoak, K., and Thagard, P. (1995). *Mental Leaps: Analogy in Creative Thought*. Cambridge, MA: MIT Press.

Hopkins, J. (1999a). Patterns of interpretation: speech, action, and dream. In L. Marcus (ed.), *Sigmund Freud's The Interpretation of Dreams*. Manchester: Manchester University Press.

(1999b). Psychoanalysis, metaphor, and the concept of mind. In M. Levine (ed.), *The Analytic Freud*. London: Routledge.

(1999c). Wittgenstein, Davidson, and Radical Interpretation. In F. Hahn (ed.), *The Library of Living Philosophers: Donald Davidson*. Carbondale: University of Illinois Press.

Horgan, T., and Tienson, J. (1996). *Connectionism and the Philosophy of Psychology*. Cambridge, MA: MIT Press.

Howell, F., Cole, G., Kleindienst, M., Szabo, B., and Oakley, K. (1972). Uranium series dating of bone from the Isimila prehistoric site, Tanzania. *Nature*, 237, 51–2.

Hublin, J.-J., Spoor, F., Braun, M., Zonneveld, F., and Condemi, S. (1996). A late Neanderthal associated with Upper Palaeolithic artefacts. *Nature*, 381, 224–6.

Hughes, C., and Cutting, A. (in press). Nature, nurture and individual differences in early understanding of mind. *Psychological Science*.

Hughes, C., and Dunn, J. (1997). 'Pretend you didn't know': preschoolers' talk about mental states in pretend play. *Cognitive Development*, 12, 477–99.

(1998). Understanding mind and emotion: longitudinal associations with mental-state talk between young friends. *Developmental Psychology*, 34(5), 1026–37.

Hughes, C., Soares-Boucaud, I., Hochmann, J., and Frith, U. (1997). Social behaviour in pervasive developmental disorders: effects of informant, group and 'theory-of-mind'. *European Child and Adolescent Psychiatry*, 6, 191–98.

Hull, D. (1986). On human nature. *Proceedings of the Philosophy of Science Association*, 2, 3–13. Reprinted in Hull, D. (ed.) (1989), *The Metaphysics of Evolution*, pp. 11–24. Albany: SUNY Press.

Humphrey, N. (1976). The social function of intellect. In P. Bateson and R. Hinde (eds.), *Growing Points in Ethology*, pp. 303–17. Cambridge: Cambridge University Press.

(1986). *The Inner Eye*. London: Faber and Faber.

Hurford, J., Studdert-Kennedy, M., and Knight, C. (eds.), (1998). *Evolution of Language*. Cambridge: Cambridge University Press.

Irons, W. (1979). Natural selection, adaptation and human social behaviour. In N. Chagnon and W. Irons (eds.), *Evolutionary Biology and Human Social Behaviour: An Anthropological Perspective*, pp. 4–39. North Scituate: Duxbury.

Isaac, G. (1977). *Olorgesailie*. Chicago: The University of Chicago Press.

Jackendoff, R. (1992). Is there a faculty of social cognition? In R. Jackendoff (ed.), *Languages of the Mind*, pp. 69–81. Cambridge, MA: MIT Press.

Jackson, F. (1982). Epiphenomenal qualia. *Philosophical Quarterly*, 32, 127–36.

(1986). What Mary didn't know. *Journal of Philosophy*, 83, 291–95.

Jenkins, J., and Astington, J. (1996). Cognitive factors and family structure associated with theory of mind development in young children. *Developmental Psychology*, 32(1), 70–8.

Joffe, T., and Dunbar, R. (1997). Visual and socio-cognitive information processing in primate brain evolution. *Proceedings of the Royal Society of London*, B264, 1303–7.

Johnson, A., and Earle, T. (1987). *The Evolution of Human Societies: From Foraging Group to Agrarian State*. Stanford: Stanford University Press.

Jolicoeur, P., Gluck, M., and Kosslyn, S. (1984). Pictures and names: making the connection. *Cognitive Psychology*, 16, 243–75.

Jones, P. (1981). Experimental implement manufacture and use: a case study from Olduvai Gorge, Tanzania. In J. Young, E. Jope, and K. Oakley (eds.), *Emergence of Man*, pp. 189–95. London: Royal Society and British Academy.

Kahneman, D., Slovic, P., and Tversky, A. (1982). *Judgement Under Uncertainty: Heuristics and Biases*. Cambridge: Cambridge University Press.

Kahneman, D., and Tversky, A. (1972). Subjective probability: a judgment of representativeness. *Cognitive Psychology*, 3, 340–54.

(1973). On the psychology of prediction. *Psychological Review*, 80, 237–51.

Kanner, L. (1943). Autistic disturbances of affective contact. *Nervous Children*, 2, 217–50.

Karim, W. (1981). *Ma'Betisek Concepts of Living Things*. London: The Athlone Press.

Karmiloff-Smith, A. (1992). *Beyond Modularity: A Developmental Perspective on Cognitive Science.* Cambridge, MA: MIT Press.

—— (1998). Is atypical development necessarily a window on the normal mind/brain? The case of Williams syndrome. *Developmental Science,* 1(2), 273–77.

Karmiloff-Smith, A., Klima, E., Bellugi, U., Grant, J., and Baron-Cohen, S. (1995). Is there a social module? Language, face processing, and theory of mind in individuals with Williams syndrome. *Journal of Cognitive Neuroscience,* 7(2), 196–208.

Keil, F. (1994). The birth and nurturance of concepts by domains: the origins of concepts of living things. In L. Hirschfeld and S. Gelman (eds.), *Mapping the Mind: Domain-Specificity in Cognition and Culture,* pp. 234–54. New York: Cambridge University Press.

Keller, C., and Keller, J. (1996). *Cognition and Tool Use: The Blacksmith at Work.* Cambridge: Cambridge University Press.

Kessler, R., McGonagle, K., Zhao, S., Nelson, C., Hughes, M., Eshleman, S., Wittchen, H.-U., and Kendler, K. (1994). Lifetime and 12-month prevalence of DSM-III-R psychiatric disorders in the United States. *Archives of General Psychiatry,* 51, 8–19.

Killackey, H., Chiaia, N., Bennett-Clarke, C., Eck, M., and Rhoades, R. (1994). Peripheral influences on the size and organization of somatotopic representations in the fetal rat cortex. *Journal of Neuroscience,* 14, 1496–1506.

Kinderman, P., Dunbar, R., and Bentall, R. (1998). Theory of mind deficits and causal attribution. *British Journal of Psychology,* 89, 191–204.

Kirk, R. (1994). *Raw Feeling.* Oxford: Oxford University Press.

Kitcher, P. (1985). *Vaulting Ambition.* Cambridge, MA: MIT Press.

Klein, R. (1995). Anatomy, behaviour and modern human origins. *Journal of World Prehistory,* 9, 167–98.

Knapp, C., Murphy, D., and Stich, S. (1998). Adaptionism and evolutionary design: prospects and problems for a theory of social cognition. Paper delivered to a workshop of the Hang Seng Centre for Cognitive Studies, University of Sheffield, April 1998.

Kosslyn, S. (1994). *Image and Brain: The Resolution of the Imagery Debate.* Cambridge, MA: MIT Press.

Kosslyn, S., Alpert, N., and Thompson, W. (1995). Identifying objects at different levels of hierarchy: a Positron Emission Tomography study. *Human Brain Mapping,* 3, 1–26.

Kovecses, Z. (1990). *Emotion Concepts.* New York: Springer Verlag.

Kozulin, A. (1986). *Vygotsky in Context. Translator's preface to Thought and Language by Lev Vygotsky.* Cambridge, MA: MIT Press.

Krebs, J., and Dawkins, R. (1984). Animal signals: mind-reading and manipulation. In J. Krebs and N. Davies (eds.), *Behavioural Ecology,* pp. 380–402. Sunderland, MA: Sinauer Associates.

Kurbat, M. (1997). Can the recognition of living things really be impaired? *Neuropsychologia,* 35, 813–27.

Lakoff, G. (1993). The contemporary theory of metaphor. In A. Ortony (ed.), *Metaphor and Thought,* pp. 202–51. Cambridge: Cambridge University Press.

Leakey, M. (1971). *Olduvai Gorge,* vol. 3. Cambridge: Cambridge University Press.

Leibniz, G. (1973). Monadology. In G. Parkinson (ed.), *Leibniz, Philosophical Writings*. London: Everyman Classics Edition.

Lennenberg, E. (1967). *Biological Foundations of Language*. New York: John Wiley.

Leslie, A. (1987). Pretense and representation: the origins of 'theory of mind'. *Psychological Review*, 94(4), 412–26.

——(1991). The theory of mind impairment in autism: evidence for a modular mechanism of development? In A. Whiten (ed.), *Natural Theories of Mind*, pp. 63–78. Oxford: Blackwell.

——(1994). ToMM, ToBY, and agency: core architecture and domain specificity. In L. Hirschfeld and S. Gelman (eds.), *Mapping the Mind: Domain-Specificity in Cognition and Culture*, pp. 119–48. New York: Cambridge University Press.

Leslie, A., and Frith, U. (1988). Autistic children's understanding of seeing, knowing, and believing. *British Journal of Developmental Psychology*, 6, 315–24.

Leslie, A., and Thaiss, L. (1992). Domain specificity in conceptual development: neuropsychological evidence from autism. *Cognition*, 43(3), 225–51.

Lesna, I., and Sabelis, M. (1999). Diet-dependent female choice for males with 'good genes' in a soil predatory mite. *Nature*, 401, 581–84.

Lewin, R. (1999). *Human Evolution* (4th edn). Oxford: Blackwell Science.

Lewis, C., Freeman, N., Hagestadt, C., and Douglas, H. (1994). Narrative access and production in preschoolers' false belief reasoning. *Cognitive Development*, 9(4), 397–424.

Lewis, C., Freeman, N., Kyriakidou, C., Maridaki-Kassotaki, K., and Berridge, D. (1996). Social influences on false belief access: specific sibling influences or general apprenticeship? *Child Development*, 67, 2930–47.

Lewis, D. (1990). What experience teaches. In W. Lycan (ed.), *Mind and Cognition*, pp. 499–519. Oxford: Blackwell.

Lindly, J., and Clark, G. (1990). Symbolism and modern human origins. *Current Anthropology*, 31, 233–61.

Linn, M., and Petersen, A. (1986). A meta-analysis of gender differences in spatial ability: implications for mathematics and science achievement. In J. Hyde and M. Linn (eds.), *The Psychology of Gender*, pp. 67–101. Baltimore: Johns Hopkins University Press.

Lloyd, G. (1991). *Methods and Problems in Greek Science: Selected papers*. Cambridge: Cambridge University Press.

Loar, B. (1990). Phenomenal states. *Philosophical Perspectives*, 4, 81–108.

Luce, R., and Raiffa, H. (1957). *Games and Decisions*. New York: Wiley.

Lumsden, C. J., and Wilson, E. O. (1981). *Genes, Mind and Culture*. Cambridge, MA: Harvard University Press.

Lycan, W. (1996). *Consciousness and Experience*. Cambridge, MA: MIT Press.

MacKie, E. (1997). Maeshowe and the winter solstice: ceremonial aspects of the Orkney Grooved Ware culture. *Antiquity*, 71, 338–59.

Marino, L. (1996). What can dolphins tell us about primate evolution? *Evolutionary Anthropology*, 5, 81–6.

Marks, I., and Nesse, R. (1994). Fear and fitness: an evolutionary analysis of anxiety disorders. *Ethology and Sociobiology*, 15(5–6), 247–61.

Marr, D. (1982a). Representation and recognition of the movement of shapes.

Proceedings of the Royal Society London, B, Biological Sciences, 214, 501–24.

(1982b). *Vision*. San Francisco: W. H. Freeman.

Marshack, A. (1972). *The Roots of Civilization*. London: Weidenfeld and Nicolson.

(1991). The Tai Plaque and calendrical notation in the Upper Palaeolithic. *Cambridge Archaeological Journal*, 1, 25–61.

(1997). The Berekhat Ram figurine: a late Acheulian carving from the Middle East. *Antiquity*, 71, 327–37.

Martin, N., Boomsma, D., and Machin, G. (1997). A twin-pronged attack on a complex trait. *Nature Genetics*, 17, 387–92.

Marzke, M. (1996). Evolution of the hand and bipedality. In A. Lock and C. Peters (eds.), *Handbook of Human Symbolic Evolution*, pp. 126–54. Oxford: Oxford University Press.

Maynard Smith, J. (1982). *Evolution and the Theory of Games*. Cambridge: Cambridge University Press.

Mayr, E. (1976). Cause and effect in biology. In E. Mayr (ed.), *Evolution and the Diversity of Life: Selected Essays*, pp. 359–71. Cambridge, MA: Harvard University Press.

(1982). *The Growth of Biological Thought*. Cambridge, MA: Harvard University Press.

McCarthy, L., and Gerring, J. (1994). Revising psychiatry's charter document DSM-IV. *Written Communication*, 11, 147–92.

McGinn, C. (1991). *The Problem of Consciousness*. Oxford: Blackwell.

McGuire, M., Fawzy, F., Spar, J., Weigel, R., and Troisi, A. (1994). Altruism and mental disorders. *Ethology and Sociobiology*, 15(5–6), 299–321.

McGuire, M., and Troisi, A. (1998). *Darwinian Psychiatry*. New York: Oxford University Press.

Mealey, L. (1995). The sociobiology of sociopathy: an integrated evolutionary model. *Behavioral and Brain Sciences*, 18, 523–99.

Medin, D., and Atran, S. (eds.). (1999). *Folkbiology*. Cambridge: MIT Press.

Meins, E. (1997). *Security of Attachment and the Social Development of Cognition*. Hove: Psychology Press.

Mellars, P. (1996). *The Neanderthal Legacy*. Princeton, NJ: Princeton University Press.

Mellars, P., and Gibson, K. (1996). *Modelling the Early Human Mind*. Cambridge: McDonald Institute Monographs.

Meltzoff, A. (1995). Understanding the intentions of others: re-enactment of intended acts by 18-month-old children. *Developmental Psychology*, 31, 838–50.

Miller, G. (1998). How mate choice shaped human nature: a review of sexual selection and human evolution. In C. Crawford and D. Krebs (eds.), *Handbook of Evolutionary Psychology: Ideas, Issues and Applications*, pp. 87–129. Hillsdale, NJ: Lawrence Erlbaum Associates.

Miller, N. (1959). Liberalization of basic S–R concepts. In S. Koch (ed.), *Psychology: A Study of a Science*, vol. 2. New York: McGraw Hill.

Millikan, R. (1984). *Language, Thought, and Other Biological Categories*. Cambridge, MA: MIT Press.

(1989). Biosemantics. *Journal of Philosophy*, 86, 281–97.

(1993). *White Queen Psychology and Other Essays for Alice.* Cambridge, MA: MIT Press.

(1998a). A common structure for concepts of individuals, stuffs, and real kinds: more mama, more milk, more mouse. *Behavioral and Brain Sciences,* 9(1), 55–100.

(1998b). Language conventions made simple. *The Journal of Philosophy,* XCV(4), 161–80.

Milton, K. (1988). Foraging behaviour and the evolution of primate intelligence. In R. Byrne and A. Whiten (eds.), *Machiavellian Intelligence,* pp. 285–306. Oxford: Clarendon Press.

Mineka, S., Davidson, M., Cook, M., and Keir, R. (1984). Observational conditioning of snake fear in rhesus monkeys. *Journal of Abnormal Psychology,* 93(4), 355–72.

Mineka, S., Keir, R., and Price, V. (1980). Fear of snakes in wild and laboratory-reared rhesus monkeys. *Animal Learning and Behavior,* 8, 653–63.

Mineka, S., and Tomarken, A. (1989). The role of cognitive biases in the origins and maintenance of fear and anxiety disorders. In L. Nilsson and T. Archer (eds.), *Aversion, Avoidance and Anxiety: Perspectives on Aversely Motivated Behavior,* pp. 195–221. Hillsdale, NJ: Lawrence Erlbaum Associates.

Mithen, S. (1993). Individuals, groups and the Palaeolithic record: a reply to Clark. *Proceedings of the Prehistoric Society,* 59, 393–98.

(1996a). Early Palaeolithic 'concept mediated' marks, mental modularity and the origins of art. *Current Anthropology,* 37, 666–70.

(1996b). *The Prehistory of the Mind.* London: Thames and Hudson.

(1999a). Palaeoanthropological perspectives on the theory of mind. In S. Baron-Cohen, H. Flusberg, and D. Cohen (eds.), *Understanding Other Minds: Perspectives from Autism and Cognitive Neuroscience,* pp. 494–508. Oxford: Oxford University Press.

(1999b). Symbolism and the supernatural. In R. Dunbar, C. Knight, and C. Power (eds.), *The Evolution of Culture,* pp. 147–69. Edinburgh: Edinburgh University Press.

Moore, C. (1996). Evolution and the modularity of mindreading. *Cognitive Development,* 11, 605–21.

Morris, D. (1962). *The Biology of Art.* London: Methuen.

Morton, J., and Johnson, M. (1991). CONSPEC and CONLERN: a two-process theory of infant face-recognition. *Psychological Review,* 98, 164–81.

Moss, H., Tyler, L., and Jennings, F. (1997). When leopards lose their spots: knowledge of visual properties in category-specific deficits for living things. *Cognitive Neuropsychology,* 14, 901–50.

Muller, W. (1997). *Developmental Biology.* New York: Springer.

Myerson, R. (1991). *Game Theory: Analysis of Conflict.* Cambridge, MA: Harvard University Press.

Nagel, T. (1974). What is it like to be a bat? *Philosophical Review,* 82, 435–56.

(1986). *The View from Nowhere.* Oxford: Oxford University Press.

Neale, M., and Cardon, L. (1992). *Methodology for Genetic Studies of Twins and Families.* Dordrecht: Kluwer Academic Publications.

Neander, K. (1991). Functions as selected effects: the conceptual analyst's defense. *Philosophy of Science,* 58, 168–84.

Nesse, R., and Williams, G. (1994). *Why We Get Sick*. New York: Times Books.

Nichols, S., Stich, S., Leslie, A., and Klein, D. (1996). Varieties of off-line simulation. In P. Carruthers and P. Smith (eds.), *Theories of Theories of Mind*, pp. 39–74. Cambridge: Cambridge University Press.

Noble, W., and Davidson, I. (1996). *Human Evolution, Language, and Mind: A Psychological and Archaeological Inquiry*. Cambridge: Cambridge University Press.

O'Brien, M. (ed.), (1996). *Evolutionary Archaeology: Theory and Application*. Salt Lake City: University of Utah Press.

O'Connell, S. (1995). *Theory of Mind in Chimpanzees*. PhD thesis, University of Liverpool.

Office of Population Censuses and Surveys. (1991). *Standard Occupational Classification*. London: HMSO.

O'Leary, D. (1993). Do cortical areas emerge from a protocortex? In M. Johnson (ed.), *Brain Development and Cognition: A Reader*, pp. 323–37. Oxford: Basil Blackwell.

O'Leary, D., and Stanfield, B. (1989). Occipital cortical neurons with transient pyramidal tract axons extend and maintain colaterals to subcortical but not intracortical targets. *Journal of Neuroscience*, 9(7), 2230–46.

Pallas, S., and Sur, M. (1993). Visual projections induced into the auditory pathway of ferrets: II. Corticocortical connections of primary auditory cortex. *Journal of Comparative Neurology*, 337(2), 317–33.

Papineau, D. (1987). *Reality and Representation*. Oxford: Blackwell.

(1993). *Philosophical Naturalism*. Oxford: Blackwell.

(1998). Teleosemantics and indeterminacy. *Australasian Journal of Philosophy*, 76(1), 1–14.

(1999). Normativity and judgement. *Proceedings of the Aristotelian Society*, 73, 17–43.

Pascual-Leone, A., and Torres, F. (1993). Plasticity of the sensorimotor cortex representation of the reading finger in Braille readers. *Brain*, 116, 39–52.

Pawlowski, B., Lowen, C., and Dunbar, R. (1998). Neocortex size, social skills and mating success in primates. *Behaviour*, 135, 357–68.

Peacocke, C. (1983). *Sense and Content: Experience, Thought, and their Relations*. Oxford: Clarendon Press.

Perner, J., Leekham, S., and Wimmer, H. (1987). Three-year olds' difficulty with false belief: the case for a conceptual deficit. *British Journal of Developmental Psychology*, 5, 125–37.

Perner, J., Ruffman, T., and Leekham, S. (1994). Theory of mind is contagious: you catch it from your sibs. *Child Development*, 65, 1228–38.

Perner, J., and Wimmer, D. (1985). 'John thinks that Mary thinks that . . .' Attribution of second-order beliefs by 5 and 10 year-old children. *Journal of Experimental Child Psychology*, 39, 437–71.

Peterson, C. C., and Siegal, M. (1997). Domain specificity and everyday biological, physical and psychological thinking in normal, autistic, and deaf children. In H. M. Wellman and K. Inagaki (eds.), *The Emergence of Core Domains of Thought: Children's Reasoning about Physical, Psychological and Biological Phenomena*, pp. 55–70. San Francisco: Jossey-Bass Inc.

Petrill, S. (1997). Molarity versus modularity of cognitive functioning? A behavioural genetic perspective. *Current Directions in Psychological Science*, 6, 96–9.

Phillips, D. (1993). Twin studies in medical research: can they tell us whether diseases are genetically determined? *Lancet*, 341, 1008–9.

Piaget, J., and Inhelder, B. (1967). *The Child's Conception of Space* (F. Langlon and J. Lunzer, trans.). New York: Norton.

Pinker, S. (1994). *The Language Instinct*. London: Penguin Books.

——— (1997a). Evolutionary psychology: an exchange. *New York Review of Books*, 9 October.

——— (1997b). *How the Mind Works*. London: Penguin Books.

Pinker, S., and Bloom, P. (1990). Natural language and natural selection. *Behavioral and Brain Sciences*, 13(4), 707–84.

Plomin, R. (1995). Genetics and children's experiences in the family. *Journal of Child Psychology and Psychiatry*, 36, 33–68.

Plomin, R., and Daniels, D. (1987). Why are children in the same family so different from one another? *Behavioral and Brain Sciences*, 10, 1–60.

Plomin, R., and DeFries, J. (1985). *Origins of Individual Differences in Infancy*. Orlando: Academic Press, Inc.

Plomin, R., DeFries, J., McClearn, G., and Rutter, M. (1997). *Behavioral Genetics*. New York: W. H. Freeman and Co.

Plomin, R., Fulker, D., Corley, R., and DeFries, J. C. (1997). Nature, nurture and cognitive development from 1 to 16 years: a parent-offspring adoption study. *Psychological Science*, 8, 442–47.

Plomin, R., Owen, M. J., and McGuffin, P. (1994). The genetic basis of complex human behaviours. *Science*, 264, 1733–9.

Plomin, R., Rende, R., and Rutter, M. (1991). Quantitative genetics and developmental psychopathology. In D. Cicchetti and S. Toth (eds.), *Rochester Symposium on Developmental Psychopathology: Internalising and Externalising Expressions of Dysfunction*, vol. 2, pp. 155–202. Hillsdale, NJ: Lawrence Erlbaum Associates.

Poland, J., Von Eckardt, B., and Spaulding, W. (1994). Problems with the DSM approach to classifying psychopathology. In G. Graham and G. Stephens (eds.), *Philosophical Psychopathology*, pp. 235–60. Cambridge, MA: MIT Press.

Polich, J. (1985). Semantic categorization and event-related potentials. *Brain and Language*, 26, 304–21.

Povinelli, D., and Nelson, K. (1990). Inferences about guessing and knowing in chimpanzees. *Journal of Comparative Psychology*, 104, 203–10.

Povinelli, D., Parks, K., and Novak, M. (1991). Do rhesus monkeys (*Macaca mulatta*) attribute knowledge and ignorance to others? *Journal of Comparative Psychology*, 105, 318–25.

Premack, D. (1990). The infant's theory of self-propelled objects. *Cognition*, 36, 1–16.

Price, J., Sloman, L., Gardner, R., Gilbert, P., and Rohde, P. (1994). The social competition hypothesis of depression. *British Journal of Psychiatry*, 164, 309–15.

Pustejovsky, J. (1996). *The Generative Lexicon*. Cambridge, MA: MIT Press.

Pylyshyn, Z. (1984). *Computation and Cognition*. Cambridge, MA: MIT Press.

Pyszczynski, T., and Greenberg, J. (1987). Self-regulatory perseveration and the depressive self-focussing style: a self-awareness theory of reactive depression. *Psychological Bulletin*, 102(1), 122–38.

Quartz, S., and Sejnowski, T. (1994). Beyond modularity: neural evidence for constructivist principles in development. *Behavioral and Brain Sciences*, 17, 725–6.

Quine, W. (1951). Two Dogmas of Empiricism. *Philosophical Review*, 60. Reprinted with additions in his *From a Logical Point of View*, pp. 20–46, Cambridge, MA: Harvard University Press, 1953.

Regard, M., and Landis, T. (1997). 'Gourmand Syndrome': eating passion associated with right anterior lesions. *Neurology*, 48(5), 1185–90.

Reith, E., and Dominin, D. (1997). The development of children's ability to attend to the visual projection of objects. *British Journal of Developmental Psychology*, 15, 177–96.

Renfrew, C. (1982). *Towards an Archaeology of Mind*. Cambridge: Cambridge University Press.

Renfrew, C. (ed.), (1990). *The Prehistory of Orkney*. Edinburgh: Edinburgh University Press.

Renfrew, C., and Scarre, C. (1998). *Cognition and Material Culture: The Archaeology of Symbolic Storage*. Cambridge: McDonald Institute Monographs.

Renfrew, C., and Zubrow, E. (eds.), (1994). *The Ancient Mind: Elements of Cognitive Archaeology*. Cambridge: Cambridge University Press.

Reznick, J. S., Corley, R., and Robinson, J. (1997). A longitudinal twin study of intelligence in the second year. *Monographs of the Society for Research in Child Development*, 62(1), 1–154.

Robson Brown, K. (1993). An alternative approach to cognition in the Lower Palaeolithic: the modular view. *Cambridge Archaeological Journal*, 3, 231–45.

Roe, D. (1970). *Prehistory: An Introduction*. Berkeley: University of California Press.

Roe, P. (1980). Art and residence among the Shipibo Indians of Peru: a study in microacculturation. *American Anthropologist*, 82, 42–71.

Rohles, F., and Devine, J. (1967). Further studies of the middleness concept with the chimpanzee. *Animal Behavior*, 15, 107–12.

Rosenthal, D. (1986). Two concepts of consciousness. *Philosophical Studies*, 49, 329–59.

(1993). Thinking that one thinks. In M. Davies and G. Humphreys (eds.), *Consciousness*, pp. 197–223. Oxford: Blackwell.

Ruff, C., Trinkaus, E., and Holliday, T. (1997). Body mass and encephalization in Pleistocene *Homo*. *Nature*, 387, 173–7.

Ruffman, T., Perner, J., Naito, M., Parkin, L., and Clements, W. (1998). Older but not younger siblings facilitate false belief understanding. *Developmental Psychology*, 34(1), 161–74.

Russell, J. (1996). *Agency: Its Role in Mental Development*. Hove: Lawrence Erlbaum Associates.

Sacks, O. (1989). *Seeing Voices*. London: Picador.

(1995). *An Anthropologist on Mars: Seven Paradoxical Tales*. New York: Knopf.

Samuels, R. (1998a). Evolutionary psychology and the massive modularity hypothesis. *British Journal for the Philosophy of Science*, 49, 575–602.

(1998b). What brains won't tell us about the mind: a critique of the neurobiological argument against representational nativism. *Mind and Language*, 13(4), 548–70.

Samuels, R., Stich, S., and Bishop, M. (forthcoming). Ending the rationality wars: how to make disputes about human rationality disappear.

Samuels, R., Stich, S., and Tremoulet, P. (1999). Rethinking rationality: from bleak implications to Darwinian modules. In E. LePore and Z. Pylyshyn (eds.), *What is Cognitive Science?*, pp. 74–120. Oxford: Basil Blackwell.

Sartori, G., Coltheart, M., Miozzo, M., and Job, R. (1994). Category specificity and informational specificity in neuropsychological impairment of semantic memory. In C. Umilta and M. Moscovitch (eds.), *Attention and Performance XV: Conscious and Non-Conscious Information Processing*, pp. 537–50. Cambridge, MA: MIT Press.

Schaller, S. (1991). *A Man Without Words*. New York: Summit Books.

Schepartz, L. (1993). Language and modern human origins. *Yearbook of Physical Anthropology*, 36, 91–126.

Schiffer, S. (1972). *Meaning*. Oxford: Clarendon Press.

Schiller, P. (1951). Figural preferences in the drawings of a chimpanzee. *Journal of Comparative and Physiological Psychology*, 44, 101–10.

Schlaggar, B., and O'Leary, D. (1991). Potential of visual cortex to develop an array of functional units unique to somatosensory cortex. *Science*, 252, 1556–60.

Schlaug, G., Jancke, L., Huang, Y., and Steinmetz, H. (1995). Increased corpus callosum size in musicians. *Neuropsychologia*, 33, 1047–55.

Scholl, B. J. (1997). Neural constraints on cognitive modularity? *Behavioral and Brain Sciences*, 20(4), 575–6.

Searle, J. (1983). *Intentionality*. Cambridge: Cambridge University Press.

Segal, G. (1996). The modularity of theory of mind. In P. Carruthers and P. Smith (eds.), *Theories of Theories of Mind*, pp. 141–57. Cambridge: Cambridge University Press.

Severi, B. (1993). Talking about souls. In P. Boyer (ed.), *Cognitive Aspects of Religious Symbolism*. Cambridge: Cambridge University Press.

Shallice, T. (1987). Impairments of semantic processing: multiple dissociations. In R. Job, G. Sartori, and M. Coltheart (eds.), *The Cognitive Neuropsychology of Language*, pp. 111–27. London: Lawrence Erlbaum Associates.

Siegal, M. (1996). Conversation and cognition: perceptual and cognitive development. In R. Gelman (ed.), *Handbook of Perception and Cognition*, pp. 243–82. San Diego: Academic Press.

Skinner, B. (1957). *Verbal Behavior*. New York: Appleton Century Crofts.

Skuse, D., James, R., Bishop, D., Coppins, B., Dalton, P., Aamodt-Leeper, G., Bacarese-Hamilton, M., Creswell, C., McGurk, R., and Jacobs, P. (1997). Evidence from Turner's syndrome of an imprinted X-linked locus affecting cognitive function. *Nature*, 387, 705–8.

Skyrms, B. (1996). *Evolution of the Social Contract*. Cambridge: Cambridge University Press.

Slomkowski, C., and Dunn, J. (1996). Young children's understanding of other people's beliefs and feelings and their connected communication with friends. *Developmental Psychology*, 32(3), 442–7.

Smith, D. (1973). Systematic study of chimpanzee drawing. *Journal of Comparative and Physiological Psychology*, 82, 406–14.

Smith, N., and Tsimpli, I.-M. (1995). *The Mind of a Savant: Language-learning and Modularity*. Oxford: Blackwell.

Smuts, B., Cheney, D., Seyfarth, R., Wrangham, R., and Struhsaker, T. (eds.), (1987). *Primate Societies*. Chicago: University of Chicago Press.

Sober, E. (1984). *The Nature of Selection*. Cambridge, MA: MIT Press.

   (1993). *Philosophy of Biology*. Oxford: Oxford University Press.

Sodian, B., and Frith, U. (1992). Deception and sabotage in autistic, retarded and normal children. *Journal of Child Psychology and Psychiatry*, 33, 591–605.

Spelke, E. (1994). Initial knowledge: six suggestions. *Cognition*, 50(1–3), 431–45.

Spemann, H. (1938). *Embryonic Development and Induction*. New Haven, CT: Yale University Press.

Sperber, D. (1990a). The epidemiology of beliefs. In C. Fraser (ed.), *Psychological Studies of Widespread Beliefs*, pp. 25–44. Oxford: Oxford University Press.

   (1990b). The evolution of the language faculty: A paradox and its solution. *Behavioral and Brain Sciences*, 13(4), 756–8.

   (1994a). The modularity of thought and the epidemiology of representations. In L. Hirschfeld and S. Gelman (eds.), *Mapping the Mind: Domain-Specificity in Cognition and Culture*, pp. 39–67. New York: Cambridge University Press.

   (1994b). Understanding verbal understanding. In J. Khalfa (ed.), *What is Intelligence?*, pp. 179–98. Cambridge: Cambridge University Press.

   (1996). *Explaining Culture: A Naturalistic Approach*. Oxford: Blackwell.

Sperber, D. (forthcoming). Metarepresentations in an evolutionary perspective. In D. Sperber (ed.), *Metarepresentations*. Oxford: Oxford University Press.

Sperber, D., Premack, D., and Premack, A. (eds.), (1995). *Causal Cognition*. Oxford: Oxford University Press.

Sperber, D., and Wilson, D. (1995). *Relevance: Communication and Cognition* (2nd edn). Oxford: Basil Blackwell. (First edition 1986).

   (1996). Spontaneous deduction and mutual knowledge. *Behavioral and Brain Sciences*, 110(4), 179–84.

   (1998). The mapping between the mental and the public lexicon. In P. Carruthers and J. Boucher (eds.), *Language and Thought*, pp. 184–200. Cambridge: Cambridge University Press.

Stainton, R. J. (1994). Using non-sentences: an application of Relevance Theory. *Pragmatics and Cognition*, 2(2), 269–84.

Stanfield, B., and O'Leary, D. (1985). Fetal occipital cortical neurones transplanted to the rostral cortex can extend and maintain a pyramidal tract axon. *Nature*, 313, 135–7.

Steffan, H., Baron, G., and Frahm, H. (1981). New and revised data on volumes of brain structures in insectivores and primates. *Folia Primatologica*, 35, 1–29.

Stein, E. (1996). *Without Good Reason*. Oxford: Clarendon Press.

Sterelny, K. (1995). Understanding life: recent work in philosophy of biology. *British Journal for the Philosophy of Science*, 46, 155–84.

Stevens, A., and Price, J. (1996). *Evolutionary Psychiatry: A New Beginning*. London: Routledge.

Stich, S. (1983). *From Folk Psychology to Cognitive Science*. Cambridge, MA: MIT Press.

(1990a). *The Fragmentation of Reason.* Cambridge, MA: MIT Press.

(1990b). Rationality. In D. Osherson and E. Smith (eds.), *Thinking: An Invitation to Cognitive Science,* vol. 3, pp. 173–96. Cambridge, MA: MIT Press.

Stich, S., and Nisbett, R. (1980). Justification and the psychology of human reasoning. *Philosophy of Science,* 47, 188–202.

Stich, S., and Ravenscroft, I. (1996). What is folk psychology? In S. Stich, *Deconstructing the Mind,* pp. 115–35. New York: Oxford University Press.

Stone, T., and Young, A. (1997). Delusions and brain injury: the philosophy and psychology of belief. *Mind and Language,* 12(3–4), 327–64.

Strawson, P. (1964). Intention and convention in speech acts. *Philosophical Review,* 73, 439–60.

Stringer, C., and Gamble, C. (1993). *In Search of the Neanderthals.* London: Thames and Hudson.

Sugden, R. (1986). *The Economics of Rights, Co-operation, and Welfare.* Oxford: Blackwell.

Taylor, M., and Carlson, S. (1997). The relation between individual differences in fantasy and theory of mind. *Child Development,* 68, 436–55.

Thorndike, R., Hagen, E., and Sattler, J. (1986). *Stanford-Binet Intelligence Scales.* Chicago: Riverside Publishing Co.

Tobias, P. (1987). The brain of *Homo habilis*: a new level of organisation in cerebral evolution. *Journal of Human Evolution,* 16, 741–61.

Tomasello, M., and Call, J. (1997). *Primate Cognition.* New York: Academic Press.

Tomasello, M., Kruger, A., and Ratner, H. (1993). Cultural learning. *Behavioral and Brain Sciences,* 16, 495–552.

Tononi, G., and Edelman, G. (1998). Consciousness and complexity. *Science,* 282, 1846–51.

Tooby, J., and Cosmides, L. (1990a). On the universality of human nature and the uniqueness of the individual: the role of genetics and adaptation. *Journal of Personality,* 58, 17–67.

(1990b). The past explains the present: emotional adaptations and the structure of ancestral environments. *Ethology and Sociobiology,* 11, 375–424.

(1992). The psychological foundations of culture. In J. Barkow, L. Cosmides, and J. Tooby (eds.), *The Adapted Mind: Evolutionary Psychology and the Generation of Culture,* pp. 19–136. New York: Oxford University Press.

(1995). Foreword to *Mindblindness* by Simon Baron-Cohen, pp. xi–xviii. Cambridge, MA: MIT Press.

Toth, N., Schick, K., Savage-Rumbaugh, E., Sevcik, R., and Savage-Rumbaugh, D. (1993). Pan the tool-maker: investigations into the stone tool-making and tool-using capabilities of a bonobo (*Pan paniscus*). *Journal of Archaeological Science,* 20, 81–91.

Trivers, R. (1971). The evolution of reciprocal altruism. *Quarterly Review of Biology,* 46, 35–57.

Tschudin, A. (1998). *Relative Neocortex Size and its Correlates in Dolphins.* PhD thesis, University of Natal.

Tye, M. (1995). *Ten Problems of Consciousness.* Cambridge, MA: MIT Press.

Uttal, D. (1996). Angles and distances: children's and adults' reconstruction and scaling of spatial configurations. *Child Development,* 67, 2763–9.

Van Esterik, P. (1979). Symmetry and symbolism in Ban Chiang painted pottery. *Journal of Anthropological Research*, 35, 495–508.

Van Schaik, C. (1982). Why are diurnal primates living in groups? *Behaviour*, 87, 120–44.

Vandenberg, S. (1972). Assortative mating, or who marries whom? *Behavior Genetics*, 2, 127–57.

Varley, R. (1998). Aphasic language, aphasic thought: an investigation of propositional thinking in an a-propositional aphasic. In P. Carruthers and J. Boucher (eds.), *Language and Thought,* pp. 128–45. Cambridge: Cambridge University Press.

Wakefield, J. C. (1997). Diagnosing DSM IV – Part I: DSM IV and the concept of disorder. *Behaviour Research and Therapy*, 35, 633–49.

Walker, A., and Leakey, R. (eds.), (1993). *The Nariokotome Homo erectus Skeleton.* Cambridge, MA: Harvard University Press.

Walker, S. (1985). *Atimodemo. Semantic Conceptual Development among the Yoruba.* PhD thesis, Cornell University.

(1992). Developmental changes in the representation of word-meaning: cross-cultural findings. *British Journal of Developmental Psychology*, 10, 285–99.

Warrington, E., and Shallice, T. (1984). Category-specific semantic impairments. *Brain*, 107, 829–53.

Wasser, S., and Barash, D. (1983). Reproductive suppression among female mammals: implications for biomedicine and sexual selection theory. *Quarterly Review of Biology*, 58, 513–38.

Watson, P., and Andrews, P. (1998). An evolutionary theory of major depression. Paper presented at the Tenth Annual Meeting of the Human Behavior and Evolution Society, Davis, CA, 8–12 July 1998.

Watts, I. (1999). The origins of symbolic culture. In R. Dunbar, C. Knight, and C. Power (eds.), *The Evolution of Culture,* pp. 113–46. Edinburgh: Edinburgh University Press.

Wellman, H. (1990). *The Child's Theory of Mind.* Cambridge, MA: MIT Press.

(1993). Early understanding of mind: the normal case. In S. Baron-Cohen, H. Tager-Flusberg, and D. Cohen (eds.), *Understanding Other Minds: Perspectives from Autism,* pp. 10–39. Oxford: Oxford University Press.

Wellman, H., and Gelman, S. (1992). Cognitive development: foundational theories of core domains. *Annual Review of Psychology*, 43, 337–75.

Whiten, A. (1993). Evolving a theory of mind: the nature of non-verbal mentalism in other primates. In S. Baron-Cohen, H. Tager-Flusberg, and D. Cohen (eds.), *Understanding Other Minds: Perspectives from Autism* (pp. 367–96). Oxford: Oxford University Press.

(1996). When does smart behaviour-reading become mind-reading? In P. Carruthers and P. Smith (eds.), *Theories of Theories of Mind,* pp. 277–92. Cambridge: Cambridge University Press.

Whiten, A. (ed.), (1991). *Natural Theories of Mind.* Oxford: Oxford University Press.

Williams, G. (1997). *The Pony Fish's Glow.* New York: Basic Books.

Wilson, D., and Sperber, D. (forthcoming). Truthfulness and relevance.

Wilson, D. S. (1994). Adaptive genetic variation and human evolutionary psychology. *Ethology and Sociobiology*, 15(4), 219–35.

Wilson, E. (1975). *Sociobiology: The New Synthesis.* Cambridge, MA: Harvard University Press.

(1978). *On Human Nature.* Cambridge, MA: Harvard University Press.

Wimmer, H., and Perner, J. (1983). Beliefs about beliefs: representation and constraining function of the wrong beliefs in young children's understanding of deception. *Cognition,* 13, 103–28.

Wood, B., and Collard, M. (1999). The genus *Homo. Science,* 284, 65–71.

Woolfolk, R., Novalany, J., Gara, M., Allen, L., and Polino, M. (1995). Self-complexity, self-evaluation, and depression: an examination of form and content within the self-schema. *Journal of Personality and Social Psychology,* 68(6), 1108–20.

Wrangham, R. (1980). An ecological model of female-bonded primate groups. *Behaviour,* 75, 262–300.

Wright, R. (1972). Imitative learning of a flaked tool technology: the case of an orang-utan. *Mankind, 8,* 296–306.

Wynn, K. (1992a). Addition and subtraction by human infants. *Nature,* 358, 749–50.

(1992b). Evidence against empiricist accounts of the origins of numerical knowledge. *Mind and Language,* 7, 315–32.

Wynn, T. (1979). The intelligence of later Acheulean hominids. *Man,* 14, 371–91.

(1989). *The Evolution of Spatial Competence.* Urbana: University of Illinois Press.

(1991). Tools, grammar, and the archaeology of cognition. *Cambridge Archaeological Journal,* 1, 191–206.

Wynn, T., and McGrew, W. (1989). An ape's view of the Oldowan. *Man,* 24, 283–98.

Wynn, T., and Tierson, F. (1990). Regional comparison of the shapes of later Acheulean handaxes. *American Anthropologist,* 92, 73–84.

Wynn, T., Tierson, F., and Palmer, C. (1996). Evolution of sex differences in spatial cognition. *Yearbook of Physical Anthropology,* 39, 11–42.

Yellen, J., Brooks, A., Cornelissen, E., Mehlman, M., and Stewart, K. (1995). A Middle Stone Age worked bone industry from Katanda, Upper Simliki Valley, Zaire. *Science,* 268, 553–6.

Youngblade, L., and Dunn, J. (1995). Individual differences in young children's pretend play with mother and sibling: links to relationships and understanding of other people's feelings and beliefs. *Child Development,* 66(5), 1472–92.

Author index

Subject index